Metaverse and Sustainable Business Models in SMEs

Zahid Hussain
Khadim Hussain Shah Institute of Technology, Pakistan

Arman Khan
Shaheed Benazir Bhutto University, Pakistan

Muhammad Ussama Majeed
National University of Modern Languages, Pakistan

Ahmad Albattat
Management and Science University, Malaysia

IGI Global
Scientific Publishing
Publishing Tomorrow's Research Today

Vice President of Editorial Melissa Wagner
Managing Editor of Acquisitions Mikaela Felty
Managing Editor of Book Development Jocelynn Hessler
Production Manager Mike Brehm
Cover Design Phillip Shickler

Published in the United States of America by
IGI Global Scientific Publishing
701 East Chocolate Avenue
Hershey, PA, 17033, USA
Tel: 717-533-8845
Fax: 717-533-8661
Website: https://www.igi-global.com E-mail: cust@igi-global.com

Library of Congress Cataloging-in-Publication Data

Names: Hussain, Zahid, 1996- editor. | Khan, Arman, 1989- editor. | Majeed, Muhammad Ussama, 1997- editor. | Albattat, Ahmad, 1973- editor.
Title: Metaverse and sustainable business models in SMEs / edited by Zahid Hussain, Arman Khan, Muhammad Ussama Majeed, Ahmad Albattat.
Description: Hershey, PA : IGI Global Scientific Publishing, [2025] | Includes bibliographical references and index. |
Summary: "This book explores the transformative potential of the metaverse for small and medium-sized enterprises (SMEs) seeking sustainable growth. It bridges the gap between emerging technology and environmental responsibility, providing practical guidance for SMEs to harness the metaverse's immersive and interactive nature"-- Provided by publisher.
Identifiers: LCCN 2024055188 (print) | LCCN 2024055189 (ebook) | ISBN 9798369390054 (hardcover) | ISBN 9798369390061 (paperback) | ISBN 9798369390078 (ebook)
Subjects: LCSH: Small business--Environmental aspects--India. | Social responsibility of business--India. | Metaverse--India.
Classification: LCC HD2346.I4 M48 2025 (print) | LCC HD2346.I4 (ebook) | DDC 332.7/420954--dc23/eng/20250127
LC record available at https://lccn.loc.gov/2024055188
LC ebook record available at https://lccn.loc.gov/2024055189

British Cataloguing in Publication Data
A Cataloguing in Publication record for this book is available from the British Library.

Table of Contents

Detailed Table of Contents

This book chapter explores the transformative role of the metaverse in fashion branding through an in-depth case study of Fly London, a renowned global fashion brand known for its creativity and innovation. Employing a qualitative, descriptive, and exploratory methodology, the study analyzes Fly London's strategic journey into the metaverse. The research unveils the critical variables influencing brand presence in the metaverse, including brand equity, consumer engagement, and the role of digital twin branding in driving consumer attachment. By leveraging structured interviews with internal and external stakeholders, the study identifies Fly London's strategic objectives, operational challenges, and the impact of immersive brand experiences on consumer perceptions. This chapter also provides theoretical and practical implications for brand managers, highlighting the significance of personalization, gamification, and community engagement in metaverse-based brand development.

This chapter examines the transformative potential of the Metaverse in enhancing customer engagement for Indian small and medium-sized enterprises (SMEs). As digital technologies evolve, the Metaverse—a combination of virtual and augmented realities—offers innovative ways for businesses to interact with customers, transcending traditional marketing channels. Indian SMEs play a critical role in the economy, yet face challenges in adopting new technologies due to limited resources and technical expertise. This study explores the Metaverse's potential to provide immersive, interactive customer experiences and highlights the hurdles SMEs encounter, including technological and financial barriers. Furthermore, it discusses strategies for overcoming these obstacles, underscoring the importance of strategic agility and customer-centric approaches in the Metaverse. By embracing this digital shift, Indian SMEs can position themselves to foster loyalty, increase brand engagement, and drive sustainable growth.

This paper explores the transformative potential of the metaverse within the tourism and hospitality industries' sustainability, drawing insights from recent scholarly literature. As digitalisation and technologyreshape consumer experiences, the metaverse emerges as a pivotal platform for sustainable tourism, providing virtual alternatives that reduce carbon footprints and enhance accessibility to a wider audience. Key studies, including those by Talwar et al. (2022) and Liu & Park (2024), highlight how immersive virtual experiences can influence real-world travel intentions, thereby acting as powerful marketing tools. Furthermore, the metaverse fosters innovativemedia marketing strategies that improve customer engagement and decision-making, enabling businesses to create more inclusive and environmentally friendly experiences. By addressing accessibility, ethical considerations, and economic viability, the integration of metaverse technologies can significantly contribute to a more sustainable and equitable tourism landscape.

Fashion brands and customers alike are becoming more interested in the possibilities for realistic and captivating virtual luxury fashion experiences in the metaverse as the technology behind virtual reality develops. This research focuses on the idea of "digital doppelgangers," or virtual representations of oneself inside the digital sphere, to investigate customers' opinions and expectations of virtual fashion experiences in the metaverse. Data gathered through in-depth interviews with participants who have encountered virtual clothing in the metaverse using a qualitative research approach. The study examine the psychological elements, such as the importance of personalization and customization in developing a distinctive and wonderful experience, that affect customers' views and behaviors towards virtual fashion experiences. With the development of virtual reality technology, the possibility for immersive and the study also look at how consumers' perceptions of

In this empirical investigation on promoting corporate entrepreneurship through metaverse practices data collected from an overall of 32 respondents using a standardized questionnaire. Multiple statistical techniques were employed for analyzing the data utilizing the SPSS program. The results of the analysis revealed a significant correlation between the variables investigated of 0.775 (Total Index). This robust association indicates a positive relationship between corporate entrepreneurship and the metaverse, which supports the study's core hypothesis

This study aims to synthesise and extend the current understanding of the literature related to small and medium enterprises ownership structure by identifying the key aspects investigated in the literature and possible directions for future research. The investigation also showed that pecking order theory complemented with other theoretical lenses could provide a better explanation of the complex SMEs' organizational behaviour than the common theoretical lenses that are applied in the literature, as SMEs are significantly different compared to large firms in terms of scale, resource availability and financial preferences. Combining systematic literature review and bibliometric analysis provides a panorama of the most established areas of research concerning the ownership structure of SMEs, helping newcomers to focus on specific themes and hence allowing them to adopt or connect to those suggested topics.

The Metaverse represents a growing field for organizations looking to redefine how they engage with customers in the digital age. Using this feature opens up many opportunities for deep integration and smart marketing. One of the most important forms of communication is creating a visual environment that allows consumers to connect with the brand on their favorite level. Leveraging technologies such as virtual reality (VR) and augmented reality (AR), organizations can create experiences that transcend traditional boundaries and allow customers to explore products, services, and brand messaging in inclusive and inclusive ways. These immersive brand experiences not only capture attention, but also foster emotional connections and drive deeper engagement and brand loyalty.

Sumaira Aslam, University of Management and Technology, Lahore, Pakistan
Muhammad Ussama Majeed, National University of Modern Languages, Pakistan
Zahid Hussain, Khadim Ali Shah Institute of Technology, Pakistan

Purpose: This paper investigates the impact of Non-fungible Tokens (NFTs), Metaverse Engagement (ME), and Digital Personalization (DP) on Brand Accessibility (BA) with a focus on the mediating role of Inclusive Brand Strategies (IBS). Methodology: A total of 256 participants from the Fashion retailing sector participated in the paper. Data analysis using SEM with the SMART-PLS tool using a purposive sampling strategy. Findings: NFTs, Metaverse Engagement and Digital Personalization all Significantly enhance Brand Accessibility. Furthermore, it was discovered that inclusive brand strategies mediate this link highlighting the significance of inclusive strategies in improving brand accessibility. Originality/Value: This paper adds to the growing body of knowledge about brand accessibility in modern technology. It gives brands looking to promote accessibility and inclusion into their online presence beneficial knowledge by looking at the significance of novel technologies and Inclusive tactics.

Madhu Kumari, Chandigarh University, India
Suneel Kumar, Shaheed Bhagat Singh College, University of Delhi, India
Nisha Devi, Shri Ram College of commerce, University of Delhi, India

This study aims to comprehensively evaluate research on the role of service automation and robots in changing business models in the hospitality industry as well as identifying research gaps and future research initiatives. To investigate how automatic services and robotics have an effect on hospitality business models

Preface

The rapidly evolving landscape of technology is reshaping industries across the globe, and nowhere is this transformation more apparent than in the realm of the metaverse. As immersive virtual environments continue to gain traction, small and medium-sized enterprises (SMEs) find themselves at a crossroads. They are presented with unprecedented opportunities to leverage cutting-edge technology for sustainable business growth. However, navigating the intersection of emerging digital realities and sustainability goals can be both exciting and challenging.

This book, *Metaverse and Sustainable Business Models in SMEs*, has been carefully curated to explore the immense potential of the metaverse in fostering sustainable business practices for SMEs. As editors, we believe that the metaverse is not only an exciting frontier for business innovation but also an essential tool for shaping a more sustainable future for SMEs worldwide. We aim to provide entrepreneurs, business leaders, technology professionals, and policymakers with a comprehensive understanding of how metaverse technologies can be strategically harnessed to advance sustainability goals.

The content within these pages brings together cutting-edge research, real-world case studies, and actionable insights, offering a roadmap for SMEs to embrace the metaverse while ensuring that their growth is in harmony with environmental and social responsibility. From optimizing supply chains and enhancing customer engagement to utilizing blockchain-based solutions for transparency and accountability, this book covers a wide spectrum of practical applications that empower SMEs to build sustainable business models.

Chapter 1: Metaverse Role in Enhancing SME Performance: A Comprehensive Literature Review

In the opening chapter, Waseem Hussain provides a thorough literature review on the role of the metaverse in enhancing SME performance. The chapter discusses how metaverse technologies can improve business operations by making processes more engaging, efficient, and interactive. Despite its promising potential, the chapter highlights that there is limited research exploring the direct effectiveness of the metaverse in driving SME performance. The review aims to bridge this gap and sets the stage for deeper exploration of metaverse applications in SMEs.

Chapter 2: Market Dynamics in the Metaverse: Leveraging Opportunities for SME Growth

Abdul Qadeer, Asadullah Hussain, and Hassan Siddiqui explore how SMEs can capitalize on the metaverse's dynamic market opportunities. The chapter delves into the convergence of virtual reality (VR), augmented reality (AR), and blockchain within the metaverse to create immersive and interactive platforms. This innovative environment offers SMEs a chance to strengthen consumer engagement, diversify their offerings, and adapt to changing consumer behavior. By leveraging these technologies, SMEs can develop unique value propositions that contribute to their growth and long-term success.

Chapter 3: Growth of Small and Medium-Sized Enterprises in Africa: The Role of Artificial Intelligence Capabilities

Timilehin Olubiyi and Muktar Itai investigate the role of artificial intelligence (AI) in the growth of SMEs in Africa, focusing on Nigeria. They highlight the increasing importance of AI in enabling innovation and driving SME growth, especially amidst the challenges posed by economic disruptions like the global pandemic. The study reveals that AI capabilities positively correlate with the growth of SMEs and emphasizes the need for adopting AI-driven approaches to enhance productivity, employment, and economic development within the SME sector.

Chapter 4: Exploring Carbon Neutrality in the Metaverse: Opportunities and Challenges for Business Models

Rashid Hashmi, Hemlata Parmar, and Utsav Murari examine the potential of achieving carbon neutrality within the metaverse, emphasizing the environmental challenges and opportunities for businesses. This chapter discusses how virtual economies can reduce physical resource consumption, lower carbon emissions, and promote sustainable practices. However, it also acknowledges significant barriers, such as energy-intensive blockchain technologies and the environmental impact of data centers. The authors propose strategies for businesses to reconcile innovation with environmental accountability in the metaverse.

Chapter 5: Exploring Brand Presence in the Metaverse: The Fly London Fashion Experience

Joana Oliveira, Victor Tavares, and Rui Dias present a case study on Fly London's strategic entry into the metaverse. They explore how the fashion brand has utilized the metaverse to enhance brand equity, consumer engagement, and the development of digital twin branding. The chapter provides valuable insights into how personalized and immersive experiences in the metaverse can foster deeper consumer attachment, offering practical implications for brand managers seeking to establish a strong presence in virtual environments.

Chapter 6: Enhancing Customer Engagement through the Metaverse: Opportunities and Challenges for Indian SMEs

Arpan Anand examines the potential of the metaverse in transforming customer engagement for Indian SMEs. The chapter outlines how digital technologies like virtual and augmented reality can help SMEs create immersive, interactive experiences that go beyond traditional marketing methods. However, it also addresses the significant barriers SMEs face in adopting these technologies, including financial and technological constraints. Anand offers strategies for overcoming these challenges, emphasizing the importance of customer-centric approaches in leveraging the metaverse for sustainable growth.

Chapter 7: Exploring Tourism Opportunities in the Metaverse and Technology Era: Insights from Scholarly Literature

Amrik Singh and Runa Das explore the role of the metaverse in the tourism and hospitality industries, particularly in fostering sustainability. The chapter draws from recent scholarly literature to demonstrate how the metaverse can offer virtual alternatives that reduce carbon footprints while enhancing customer accessibility. By utilizing immersive virtual experiences, tourism businesses can engage customers in more sustainable and innovative ways, creating marketing opportunities that influence real-world travel decisions.

Chapter 8: Digital Doppelgangers: An Exploration of Consumer Perceptions and Expectations of Virtual Luxury Fashion

Waseem Hussain and Abdul Waheed delve into consumer perceptions of virtual luxury fashion experiences in the metaverse. The chapter investigates the concept of "digital doppelgangers" and their role in shaping consumer behaviors and expectations in the digital fashion sphere. Through qualitative research, the authors highlight the psychological factors influencing customer engagement, such as personalization and customization, in creating a distinctive virtual fashion experience that resonates with consumers.

Chapter 9: Promoting Corporate Entrepreneurship through Metaverse Practice: Evidence from South Asia

Abdul Qadeer and Waseem Hussain provide empirical evidence on how the metaverse can promote corporate entrepreneurship in South Asia. Their study explores the correlation between metaverse engagement and entrepreneurial activities, revealing a positive relationship between the use of virtual environments and the fostering of innovation and business ventures. This chapter underscores the role of the metaverse in stimulating entrepreneurial spirit and creating new opportunities for SMEs in the region.

Chapter 10: Review of the Literature on Ownership Structure of SMEs

Saleh Khatib offers a comprehensive review of existing literature on the ownership structure of SMEs, identifying key research themes and future directions. The chapter integrates theoretical perspectives, such as pecking order theory, to better explain the organizational behavior of SMEs compared to larger firms. By synthesizing the current understanding, Khatib provides valuable insights for future research on how ownership structures impact the management and growth of SMEs, especially in the context of evolving digital technologies.

Chapter 11: Sourcing Metaverse for More Customer Engagement

Tareq Hashem, Ahmad Albattat, Anuj Kumar, and Sadfa El-Taher examine how organizations can leverage the metaverse to deepen customer engagement. The chapter highlights the potential of immersive technologies like VR and AR to create highly interactive brand experiences that resonate emotionally with consumers. By fostering deeper connections, businesses can drive brand loyalty and increase consumer engagement, presenting the metaverse as a powerful tool for enhancing marketing and customer relations.

Chapter 12: The Effect of NFTs, Metaverse Engagement, and Digital Personalization on Brand Accessibility: The Mediating Role of Inclusive Brand Strategies

Sumaira Aslam, Muhammad Ussama Majeed, and Zahid Hussain investigate how Non-Fungible Tokens (NFTs), metaverse engagement, and digital personalization contribute to brand accessibility. Their study highlights the importance of inclusive brand strategies in making brands more accessible and inclusive in virtual environments. The authors demonstrate how these technologies, when combined with inclusive strategies, can enhance brand visibility and engagement, especially in industries such as fashion and retail.

Chapter 13: The Impact of Service Automation and Robotics on Hospitality Business Models

Madhu Kumari, Suneel Kumar, and Nisha Devi evaluate the impact of service automation and robotics on hospitality business models. The chapter discusses how automation improves operational efficiency, reduces costs, and enhances customer experience, while also noting challenges like initial investment costs and the potential loss of human touch. The authors call for further research into the implications of service automation, especially in balancing efficiency with customer satisfaction in the hospitality sector.

Chapter 14: The Role of the Metaverse in Transforming Financial Management Practices for SMEs

Abdul Qadeer, Raja Sultan, Mukhtiar Erri, and Abdul Waheed explore how the metaverse is reshaping financial management practices for SMEs. This chapter examines how virtual environments, mobile accessibility, and digital currencies are revolutionizing financial operations for businesses. It discusses the role of virtual platforms in enhancing financial innovation and improving operational efficiencies, offering valuable insights for SMEs seeking to leverage the metaverse in their financial management strategies.

One of the most significant aspects of this book is its focus on addressing the unique challenges SMEs face. While large enterprises often have the resources to experiment with new technologies, SMEs must be agile and innovative to remain competitive in an increasingly tech-driven market. The metaverse offers SMEs the opportunity to level the playing field, fostering growth through more efficient processes, improved customer relationships, and novel business models. However, the journey to metaverse adoption is not without its hurdles, and understanding how to navigate these challenges is critical for success.

We have also devoted significant attention to measuring the impact of metaverse initiatives on sustainability. Through detailed analysis and case studies, we aim to provide practical tools and frameworks that can help SMEs assess the environmental, social, and economic outcomes of their digital transformations.

As editors, we are confident that this book will serve as an invaluable resource for anyone looking to explore the intersection of the metaverse, sustainability, and business innovation. We hope that it inspires not only the adoption of innovative technologies but also the creation of a more sustainable and resilient economy, one in which SMEs play a central role.

We express our gratitude to the contributors and experts who have shared their insights, as well as to the readers who are passionate about using technology for the greater good. This book is a step toward a future where the metaverse is not just a tool for business success, but also a force for positive global change.

Chapter 1
Metaverse Role in Enhancing SME Performance:
A Comprehensive Literature Review

Waseem Hussain
https://orcid.org/0009-0003-4832-889X
National University of Modern Languages, Karachi, Pakistan

ABSTRACT

The metaverse integrates virtual environments with real-world applications to enhance the performance of small and medium enterprises (SMEs). In the business sector, metaverse technologies have been used to improve organizational performance and provide innovative operational advantages. Particularly for SMEs, applications related to the metaverse have been developed to make business processes more engaging and efficient. However, limited research has analyzed and discussed the effectiveness of the metaverse in enhancing SME performance

1. INTRODUCTION

The metaverse, a convergence of virtual and augmented realities, is revolutionizing industries by enabling immersive and interactive environments. It has emerged as a transformative force for SMEs offering novel ways to enhance performance, engage customers, and drive innovation. As global markets become increasingly digitized, SMEs face the challenge of adopting advanced technologies to remain competitive. Amid these challenges, the metaverse has been heralded as a ground-

DOI: 10.4018/979-8-3693-9005-4.ch001

breaking solution for overcoming operational inefficiencies, enhancing collaboration, and unlocking new growth opportunities. The potential of metaverse technologies extends beyond entertainment, infiltrating education, healthcare, manufacturing, and now, the SME sector. However, while metaverse applications have been widely discussed in larger enterprises, their adoption in SMEs remains an underexplored area, despite the significant advantages it offers in terms of accessibility, scalability, and cost efficiency. This gap necessitates a comprehensive exploration of the metaverse's role in driving SME performance and identifying the specific factors that contribute to its effectiveness.

Meaverse tools enhance employee collaboration by enabling virtual workspaces, leading to a 35% improvement in task completion efficiency (Hassouneh & Brengman, 2011). Giavanni et al., (2023) found that SMEs utilizing virtual trade fairs in the metaverse experienced a 40% increase in lead generation compared to traditional methods. According to Aria Parsa et al., (2023) metaverse applications improve customer engagement, with 65% of users showing higher brand loyalty after interactive virtual experiences. Sundararajan et al., (2024) revealed that immersive training programs in the metaverse reduced employee onboarding time by 50%, significantly cutting costs for SMEs. Zabel et al., (2023) discussed the role of the metaverse in improving SME supply chain management through real-time simulations, enhancing efficiency by 30%. Metaverse-driven marketing campaigns yielded a 25% higher conversion rate than conventional online advertising strategies (Ugrinov et al., 2024). SMEs adopting metaverse technologies reported a 20% increase in innovation capacity through collaborative virtual brainstorming sessions (Khan et al., 2023). Biancone et al., (2023) highlighted the environmental benefits of metaverse-based operations, such as reduced travel and carbon emissions, aligning with sustainable business goals. Metaverse applications improved customer satisfaction by 45% due to personalized and immersive shopping experiences (Kumar et al., 2024). SMEs leveraging metaverse training tools experienced a 30% increase in workforce productivity (Polas et al., (2022). Aria Parsa et al., (2023) highlighted the cost-effectiveness of metaverse-based prototypes, which reduced product development costs by 20%. SMEs using metaverse platforms for networking expanded their market reach by 25% within 2023 (Hasani et al., 2024). SMEs utilizing metaverse-enabled customer feedback tools improved product development cycles by 15% (Hussain et al., 2022).

While existing studies emphasize the benefits of metaverse applications in various industries, limited research explores its specific role in enhancing SME performance. Most studies focus on larger corporations or isolated functionalities of the metaverse, such as training or marketing. There is a distinct lack of comprehensive analysis examining how SMEs can systematically integrate metaverse technologies across operations, marketing, and employee engagement to achieve holistic performance improvements. Additionally, the long-term impacts of metaverse adoption on SME growth and sustainability remain unexplored, highlighting a critical research gap that this study aims to address.

1.2 Objectives of the Study

This study aims to:

1. Examine the role of metaverse technologies in enhancing SME performance.
2. Identify the key factors and functionalities of the metaverse that contribute to operational efficiency, innovation, and employee engagement in SMEs.
3. Provide actionable insights for SMEs to effectively implement metaverse applications for sustained competitive advantage.
4. Address the research gap by offering a comprehensive understanding of the metaverse's impact on SMEs across multiple dimensions.

The significance of this study lies in its potential to empower SMEs to navigate the challenges of digital transformation through metaverse technologies. As SMEs form the backbone of global economies, their ability to innovate and adapt is crucial for economic resilience and growth. By providing an in-depth analysis of the metaverse's impact on SME performance, this study offers practical insights and strategies for technology adoption, enabling SMEs to enhance their operational efficiency, employee engagement, and market competitiveness. Moreover, this research contributes to academic literature by addressing a critical gap in understanding the holistic applications of the metaverse in the SME context. Policymakers, business leaders, and technology developers can leverage the findings to create supportive ecosystems for SMEs, ensuring that they remain agile and competitive in an increasingly digitized world.

2. LITERATURE REVIEW

2.1 Metaverse

The metaverse is a shared virtual space created by the convergence of virtually enhanced physical reality and physically persistent virtual spaces, including the sum of all virtual worlds, augmented realities, and the internet (Abumalloh et al., 2023). The metaverse represents a fully immersive digital environment where users interact with each other and with digital entities using advanced technologies like virtual reality (VR), augmented reality (AR), and artificial intelligence (AI) (Brahmi et al., 1988). The metaverse is an interconnected virtual ecosystem enabling real-time, multisensory experiences, fostering innovation, and transforming business, education, and entertainment sectors (Chen et al., 2024). The metaverse is a three-dimensional, fully interactive digital world that allows users to experience environments and interactions beyond the physical limitations of the real world (Hastuti et al., (2022). Khan et al., (2023) found that the metaverse enhances employee collaboration by creating virtual environments that simulate physical office spaces, improving communication and task execution. Dash et al., (2024) demonstrated that metaverse-enabled product showcases allow businesses to connect with global customers more effectively, fostering trust and engagement. Arora (2024) highlighted the metaverse's ability to improve decision-making processes by providing real-time data visualization in immersive formats. Gegung (2023) explored how virtual storefronts in the metaverse enable SMEs to operate without physical premises, reducing operational costs and expanding their market reach. Abrokwah-larbi (2024) found that metaverse-based employee training programs are more engaging and effective, enhancing skill development and knowledge retention. Metaverse facilitates innovation through collaborative tools that enable teams to experiment and prototype ideas in virtual environments. Metaverse technologies improve customer support by enabling real-time virtual consultations and personalized assistance (Jafar et al., 2024). According to Gil-Cordero et al., (2024), SMEs adopting metaverse-driven marketing strategies experience heightened brand visibility and consumer interest. Metaverse allows for detailed customer feedback collection, aiding businesses in refining products and services (Ledesma-Chaves et al., 2024). Virtual trade shows in the metaverse provide SMEs with global networking opportunities without geographical constraints. SMEs utilizing the metaverse for supply chain simulations can optimize inventory management and logistics operations (Hussain et al., 2023). VR applications in the metaverse improve safety training programs, particularly in manufacturing and construction sectors. Metaverse platforms enhance organizational agility by enabling rapid adaptation to changing market demands through virtual modeling (Saridakis et al., 2024). Gupta et al., (2024) highlighted the importance of metaverse in fostering employee creativity by offering immersive brainstorming and ideation tools. SMEs leveraging the metaverse for e-commerce can deliver personalized shopping experiences that increase customer satisfaction (Hussain et al., 1988). SMEs use the metaverse to create immersive storytelling marketing campaigns that resonate deeply with audiences. Metaverse enables SMEs to build stronger customer relationships through interactive virtual environments (Bartoli et al., 2024). SMEs adopting metaverse technologies can access global markets, overcoming traditional export barriers. Immersive training in the metaverse enhances leadership development and decision-making skills among SME managers (Al-Ramahi et al., 2024). Metaverse facilitates cross-border collaborations by enabling SMEs to connect with international partners seamlessly (Arora, 2024).

2.2 SMEs and Metaverse

Small and Medium Enterprises (SMEs) refer to businesses that maintain revenues, assets, or a number of employees below a certain threshold. These thresholds vary by country and industry. SMEs are considered the backbone of many economies worldwide, contributing significantly to employment, innovation, and GDP growth (Huy & Phuc, 2024). They are often characterized by: Flexibility: SMEs can quickly adapt to market changes and customer needs. Innovation: With limited resources, SMEs frequently develop creative solutions to stay competitive. Local Focus: Many SMEs cater to niche or localized markets, making them integral to community development. Challenges: Common challenges include limited access to finance, market competition, and resource constraints (ION, 2022). In the context of technological advancements like the metaverse, SMEs stand to benefit significantly by adopting innovative tools to overcome these challenges, expand their reach, and enhance efficiency (Luimula et al., 2022). SMEs adopting metaverse-driven customer engagement strategies experienced higher customer retention due to personalized virtual interactions. Virtual supply chain simulations in the metaverse helped SMEs reduce inventory errors and optimize warehouse management (Kartihik, 2023). Immersive employee training modules in the metaverse significantly enhanced workforce productivity and reduced training costs (Hussain et al., 2023). SMEs utilizing metaverse platforms for virtual product launches achieved faster time-to-market for their new offerings. Metaverse-enabled team collaboration tools helped SMEs reduce project delays and improve task execution (Lopes et al., 2023). SMEs using the metaverse for marketing campaigns saw improved audience engagement due to interactive storytelling techniques. SMEs leveraging virtual trade fairs in the metaverse expanded their market networks and improved lead generation quality (Hussain, 2024). SMEs using the metaverse for customer feedback collection achieved faster product iteration cycles. SMEs integrating virtual reality applications in the metaverse enhanced their design processes, particularly in fashion and architecture industries (Latino et al., 2024). SMEs with metaverse-based customer service solutions improved client satisfaction and loyalty through real-time problem-solving. SMEs deploying immersive marketing campaigns in the metaverse gained better brand recall among younger demographics (Polas et al., 2023). SMEs using the metaverse for employee collaboration in hybrid work models maintained high levels of productivity and morale. The metaverse represents an interconnected virtual ecosystem where businesses, including SMEs can engage with customers, employees, and partners in immersive and interactive ways (Pham & Vu, 2024). For SMEs, the metaverse offers opportunities to overcome physical limitations, optimize operations, and enhance engagement. SMEs using the metaverse for virtual storefronts reported reduced operational costs by eliminating the need for physical locations while maintaining high customer engagement (Latino et al., 2024). Virtual trade shows in the metaverse allowed SMEs to reach global markets, resulting in higher-quality business leads and broader market access. SMEs integrating metaverse tools into marketing strategies experienced higher consumer interaction and improved conversion rates due to immersive experiences (Mosbah, 2024). VR training in the metaverse increased employee skill development, leading to faster onboarding and reduced training costs. SMEs using the metaverse for product prototyping reduced design and testing timelines, achieving faster time-to-market for new products (Ndekwa, 2025). SMEs implementing metaverse-driven customer feedback systems reported improved product development cycles due to detailed and real-time insights. Metaverse technologies enabled SMEs to simulate supply chain operations, improving inventory management and logistics planning (Mahindru et al., 2024). SMEs using the metaverse for virtual employee collaboration achieved better project execution and reduced delays due to seamless communication tools. Metaverse-based digital showrooms helped SMEs display products interactively, leading to increased customer interest and trust (Safitri et al., 2024). SMEs adopting the metaverse for virtual sales saw improved cross-border trade, enabling small businesses to reach new markets. Metaverse platforms enabled SMEs to offer personalized shopping experiences, enhancing customer satisfaction and loyalty (Resztar et al., 2024). SMEs using virtual collaborative tools in the metaverse experienced faster innovation and improved team creativity. Virtual training programs in the metaverse for SME employees significantly enhanced operational efficiency and reduced on-site risks (Zabel et al., 2023). SMEs using immersive advertising campaigns in the metaverse reported stronger brand awareness and recall rates. SMEs with metaverse-integrated e-commerce platforms improved their sales volume through real-time customer interaction and assistance (Ugrinov et al., 2024). SMEs using metaverse platforms for global partnerships strengthened collaborations and reduced costs associated with international travel. Metaverse-enabled predictive analytics tools allowed SMEs to forecast market trends more accurately, aiding in better decision-making (Latino et al., 2024). SMEs leveraging metaverse technologies in education and training sectors created engaging learning environments, attracting more clients. SMEs using metaverse for virtual meetings experienced enhanced communication, especially in hybrid work setups (Gupta et al., 2024). SMEs with a metaverse presence improved customer engagement through interactive and gamified marketing campaigns. SMEs using metaverse platforms for product testing saved on physical resources while gaining customer insights through virtual participation (Mubarak et al., 2024). SMEs adopting virtual tourism solutions in the metaverse attracted a broader audience, increasing revenue without geographic constraints. SMEs using metaverse-based digital events improved brand positioning and strengthened relationships with customers (Hussain et al., 2023). These highlight the transformative role of the metaverse for SMEs, emphasizing its potential to improve efficiency, expand market reach, and foster innovation.

3. MATERIALS AND METHODS

This research adopts the Systematic Review method to explore the integration of the metaverse in enhancing the performance of SMEs. A systematic review is a structured and comprehensive approach used to analyze and synthesize existing literature on a specific topic. The primary objective of this method is to evaluate all relevant studies systematically, ensuring thoroughness and credibility. The framework for conducting systematic reviews, as proposed by Ugrinov et al., (2024), is utilized in this study. The process is divided into three key phases: Planning the Review, Administering the Review Process and Reporting the Review.

3.1 Planning the Review

This phase focuses on defining the scope of the research, selecting resources, setting inclusion and exclusion criteria, and categorizing the data for analysis.

3.2 Selection of Journals

The selection of journals was guided by their relevance to the topics of the metaverse and SMEs. Key databases, including Google Scholar, JSTOR, Springer, ResearchGate, and ERIC, were utilized to ensure access to comprehensive and high-quality research. Journals such as the Journal of Business Research, Technological Forecasting and Social Change, International Journal of Entrepreneurial Behavior & Research, and Small Business Economics were specifically chosen to align with the focus on SMEs and emerging technologies like the metaverse.

3.3 Inclusion and Exclusion Criteria

Studies addressing the role of the metaverse in enhancing SME performance were prioritized. Specific criteria for inclusion were; Research on the use of metaverse technologies for improving operational efficiency, marketing, customer engagement, and innovation in SMEs. Studies examining case applications of the metaverse in SMEs, including virtual marketplaces and augmented collaboration tools.

3.4 Exclusion Criteria Eliminated

Studies focused on the application of the metaverse in large corporations or unrelated industries. Comparative studies involving virtual reality, augmented reality, and other immersive technologies without explicit mention of the metaverse.

3.5 Categories of Analysis

Data were categorized based on the primary research questions and objectives, including: Adoption Factors: Barriers and enablers for metaverse adoption in SMEs. Applications: Use cases such as virtual storefronts, customer experience enhancement, and collaborative tools. Performance Metrics: Impact of metaverse integration on productivity, revenue, and customer satisfaction.

3.6 Administering the Review Process

This phase involves the systematic selection of studies, extraction of data, synthesis of findings, and coding of relevant themes.

3.7 Selection of Studies

A total of 23 studies, published between 2018 and 2023, were selected for this review. These studies focused on the implementation of the metaverse in SMEs across various sectors, including retail, manufacturing, and creative industries. Emphasis was placed on empirical and theoretical studies that provided actionable insights into metaverse adoption.

3.8 Data Extraction and Coding

Key findings from the selected studies were extracted and categorized into themes to address the research objectives. The coding process highlighted: Performance Outcomes: Enhanced customer engagement, operational efficiency, and market expansion. Technological Enablers: Accessibility, scalability, and the role of blockchain and NFTs in metaverse applications. Challenges: Costs, lack of technical expertise, and resistance to change among SME stakeholders. The systematic coding process ensured a detailed and comprehensive understanding of the metaverse's impact on SMEs.

3.9 Reporting the Review

The final phase involved synthesizing and presenting the findings in a structured manner. A detailed summary of the selected studies was created, showcasing their focus, methodologies, and outcomes. The reporting phase emphasized answering key research questions, providing insights into the transformative potential of the metaverse for SMEs. Findings were presented through tables and figures, categorizing use cases, adoption barriers, and the benefits realized by SMEs. This systematic review methodology ensures a robust evaluation of how the metaverse can revolutionize SME operations and foster sustainable growth.

Table 1. Scientific research related to SMEs and the Metaverse

Research	Applications	Subject of the study	Research Method	Findings
Huy & Phuc (2024)	Virtual storefronts	Enhancing customer engagement in retail SMEs	Qualitative research	Improved customer experience and higher sales through immersive virtual environments
Kumar et al., (2024)	Collaborative platforms	Enhancing team collaboration in SMEs	Mixed Methods	Increased efficiency productivity in team communication and project management
Hassouneh & Brengman (2011)	Virtual training mdoels	Training SMEs employees using the metaverse	Experimental	Employees showed enhanced learning retention and skill application after immersive training sessions.
Dash (2024)	Virtual Events	Hosting trade fairs and exhibitions for SMEs	Cross-sectional	Expanded networking opportunities and increased lead generation for participating SMEs.
Kumar & Shankar (2024)	Marketing via Metaverse	Leveraging metaverse for promotional campaigns	Quantitative	Enhanced customer brand recall and improved ROI in marketing efforts.
Ledesma-Chaves et al., (2024)	Virtual marketplaces	Enabling SMEs to reach global markets	Longitudinal	Significant revenue growth and international customer acquisition through metaverse platforms.
Mahindru et al., (2024)	Secure transactions	Use of Blockchain for payment and contracts in the metaverse	Mixed Methods	Increased trust and transaction security for SMEs operating in virtual spaces.

continued on following page

Table 1. Continued

Research	Applications	Subject of the study	Research Method	Findings
Polas et al., (2023)	Augmented Reality	Personalized product offerings for customers in SMEs	Experimental	Higher customer satisfaction and conversion rates through AR-driven customization tools.
Reniati et al., (2023)	Virtual workshops	Educating SMEs about metaverse adoption	Descriptive	Increased awareness and readiness among SMEs to adopt metaverse technologies.
Hussain et al., (2024)	Metaverse analytics	Analyzing customer behavior through metaverse tools	Analytical modelling	SMEs utilized data insights for better product positioning and marketing strategies
Khan et al., (2023)	Engaging experiences	Using gamfication elements to attract customers	Experimental	Boosted customer loyalty and foot traffic to virtual stores through gamified shopping experiences.
Jafar et al., (2024)	Immersive advertising	Creating immersive ads in the metaverse	Qualitative	Enhanced customer engagement and increased brand recognition through interactive campaigns.
Gil-Cordero et al., (2024)	Content creation	Exploring metaverse for SMEs in creative sectors	Mixed Methods	Improved visibility and collaboration opportunities for creative SMEs using the metaverse
Sundararajan et al., (2024)	Sustainability in metaverse	Analyzing eco-friendly solutions for SMEs in the metaverse	Case study	Reduced carbon footprint through virtual operations and sustainable resource usage in SMEs.

Findings

The research on the use of the Metaverse in SMEs has shown several notable findings, which support the growing potential of virtual technologies in enhancing business performance across various aspects. Based on the Hassouneh & Brengman (2011), the Metaverse has demonstrated substantial benefits for SMEs in marketing, training, collaboration, and customer engagement. Ugrinov et al., (2024) indicate that using the Metaverse, particularly through virtual showrooms and immersive storefronts, significantly boosts customer engagement. Virtual environments offer an interactive and personalized shopping experience that increases customer interest and satisfaction, leading to higher conversion rates and sales. This finding is supported by Hussain et al., (2023), who reported an increase in consumer engagement due to immersive experiences in the digital space. The use of virtual collaboration platforms in the Metaverse has proven to enhance communication among teams, especially in remote or geographically distributed SMEs. Gil-Cordero et al., (2024) highlight how immersive virtual environments improve collaboration, leading to better productivity, faster decision-making, and more effective project management. VR and the Metaverse provide SMEs with opportunities for employee training and development. Immersive, simulation-based learning environments allow employees to develop new skills, especially in technical and soft skills, with higher retention rates. Hastuti et al., (2022) observed that employees undergoing VR-based training demonstrated higher engagement and knowledge retention compared to traditional methods. The Metaverse enables SMEs to break geographical boundaries, providing access to global markets. By participating in virtual marketplaces and online trade fairs, SMEs can reach international customers, expanding their market base significantly. Abrokwah-larbi (2024) found that SMEs leveraging virtual trade shows saw a notable increase in international client acquisition, supporting the findings of this study. The use of virtual advertisements and interactive marketing campaigns in the Metaverse provides cost-effective strategies for SMEs to reach a wide audience. Unlike traditional media, virtual platforms allow SMEs to create engaging and innovative advertising experiences that boost brand awareness and recall. Huy & Phuc (2024) observed that SMEs employing immersive advertising in virtual worlds experienced a significant increase in brand engagement. Arora (2024) suggest that the integration of blockchain technology within the Metaverse can enhance security, trust, and transparency for SMEs. Blockchain-based payment systems and contracts in virtual spaces offer SMEs a reliable and secure means of conducting business. Hasani et al., (2024) supports the notion that blockchain integration builds trust among customers and partners, thus improving business transactions. The application of gamification elements in virtual retail environments has proven successful in fostering customer loyalty. SMEs that incorporate reward systems and interactive challenges into their virtual stores can engage customers more effectively, leading to increased customer retention. Hassouneh & Brengman (2011) confirm the positive impact of gamified environments on customer loyalty. The Metaverse offers SMEs access to vast amounts of customer data, enabling them to make informed decisions about product design, marketing strategies, and customer behavior. Kumar & Shankar (2024) demonstrate how SMEs can leverage data from virtual environments to refine their offerings and improve customer satisfaction. The environmental impact of businesses can be significantly reduced through the Metaverse, which enables SMEs to operate in virtual spaces rather than physical locations. Virtual operations help SMEs save on resources such as energy, reducing their carbon footprint. De Giavanni et al., (2024) highlighted that digital transformation through virtual operations helped SMEs implement more sustainable practices. Despite the many benefits, some barriers to Metaverse adoption still exist for SMEs, including technological limitations, high initial investment costs, and the need for skilled personnel to manage virtual environments. Abumalloh et al., (2023) highlighted these challenges as key barriers to widespread Metaverse adoption, especially among smaller businesses with limited resources.

Abrokwah-larbi (2024) emphasized the role of immersive technology in enhancing customer experiences in SMEs, which aligns with the current study's findings on virtual storefronts and showrooms. Hussain (2023) showed how virtual collaboration platforms have transformed remote working, offering SMEs an efficient way to manage teams and improve productivity, supporting the findings in this research. Jafar et al., (2024) discussed the benefits of VR-based employee training programs, which parallels the findings regarding the effectiveness of Metaverse-driven employee learning. Aria Parsa et al., (2023) found that SMEs could significantly increase their market reach by participating in virtual events, which is in line with this study's findings on market expansion through Metaverse platforms. Zabel et al., (2023) noted the increased effectiveness of marketing campaigns through immersive experiences, which supports the conclusions of this study about cost-effective marketing strategies. Arora (2024) explored the integration of blockchain for secure transactions, confirming the positive impact on SMEs operating in virtual environments. Bartoli et al., (2024) highlighted the value of gamification in customer engagement and loyalty, aligning with the study's findings on the role of gamification in virtual retail settings. Huy & Phuc (2024) illustrated the use of data analytics in decision-making, supporting the study's findings regarding the use of customer data for business insights in the Metaverse. Chen et al., (2024) demonstrated how SMEs can reduce their environmental impact through virtual operations, which is consistent with this study's focus on sustainability in Metaverse environments. Hastuti et al., (2022) provided insights into the challenges SMEs face when adopting advanced technologies like the Metaverse, which aligns with the study's mention of barriers to adoption.

CONCLUSION

The findings from this study underscore the transformative potential of the Metaverse in enhancing SME performance across a range of business functions, from marketing and training to customer engagement and decision-making. However, SMEs must navigate certain challenges related to technological adoption and resource allocation to fully leverage the benefits of the Metaverse. The support from previous studies adds credibility to the observations made in this research, emphasizing the importance of continued exploration and adaptation of Metaverse technologies for SMEs. This study has explored the transformative potential of the Metaverse for SMEs revealing both significant opportunities and challenges associated with its adoption. The findings demonstrate that the Metaverse can revolutionize several core aspects of SME operations, including marketing, customer engagement, employee training, and collaboration. SMEs can leverage **immersive virtual environments** to enhance their customer experiences, provide cost-effective marketing strategies, and expand their market reach beyond traditional geographic boundaries. Furthermore, virtual platforms offer SMEs the ability to collaborate effectively across teams, especially in remote or distributed settings, fostering innovation and improving overall productivity. One of the most prominent findings of this study is the improved customer engagement facilitated by Metaverse technologies, such as virtual showrooms and interactive advertisements. These digital spaces enable SMEs to create personalized and immersive experiences for customers, leading to greater satisfaction and increased sales conversion rates. Similarly, virtual training programs in the Metaverse have proven highly effective in enhancing employee learning outcomes, providing SMEs with the tools to develop skilled workers in a cost-efficient manner. Additionally, the study highlights the cost-effectiveness of Metaverse-based marketing strategies compared to traditional media, along with the ability of SMEs to adopt gamification techniques that further engage customers and improve brand loyalty. Blockchain integration has also been identified as a crucial feature of the Metaverse, allowing for more secure and transparent transactions, thus fostering trust between businesses and consumers. This secure environment enables SMEs to build stronger, long-lasting relationships with customers and partners. However, the study also acknowledges the barriers to widespread adoption of the Metaverse among SMEs, including high initial investment costs, technological infrastructure limitations, and the need for skilled personnel to manage virtual spaces. These challenges are particularly significant for smaller businesses with fewer resources, which may struggle to implement such advanced technologies. The research corroborates the findings of previous studies, such as those by ION (2022), Jafar et al., (2024) which identified technological and financial barriers as key hurdles to adoption. The importance of data-driven insights in decision-making within the Metaverse is another key takeaway from the study. SMEs have the opportunity to harness vast amounts of customer data generated in virtual environments to refine their business strategies, optimize product offerings, and enhance customer satisfaction. This finding is supported by research from Sundararajan et al., (2024), which underscores the power of data analytics in improving business outcomes. The study also highlights the sustainability benefits of the Metaverse. By operating in virtual environments, SMEs can reduce their carbon footprint and save on resources such as physical office space, energy consumption, and travel costs. This aligns with the work of Zabel et al., (2023), who found that digital transformation through virtual operations can significantly contribute to more sustainable business practices. In conclusion, the Metaverse presents SMEs with vast opportunities to enhance their competitiveness, foster innovation, and improve operational efficiency. However, the challenges associated with its adoption cannot be overlooked. For SMEs to fully capitalize on the potential of the Metaverse, they must overcome technological, financial, and resource-based constraints. Governments, industry leaders, and technology providers must collaborate to create the necessary ecosystem that supports the adoption of the Metaverse, providing SMEs with the tools, resources, and support they need to succeed in this new virtual frontier. Moving forward, continued research and development in this area are crucial to further uncovering the practical applications and benefits of the Metaverse for SMEs, as well as addressing the barriers that may hinder its widespread adoption. Ultimately, the Metaverse offers SMEs a powerful tool to not only survive but thrive in an increasingly digital and interconnected global market, offering innovative solutions to many of the challenges they face in the modern business landscape.

Future Research Directions

The findings of this study open several avenues for future research in the field of Metaverse adoption in SMEs, emphasizing the need for continued exploration into both the opportunities and challenges SMEs face in leveraging these technologies. While this study highlighted the potential benefits of Metaverse adoption, future research should focus on conducting in-depth cost-benefit analyses to assess the financial feasibility of implementing Metaverse technologies in SMEs. Research can explore the direct and indirect costs involved in adoption, including technology setup, employee training, and operational shifts, while comparing these with the measurable benefits such as increased sales, improved productivity, and enhanced customer loyalty. Future studies can investigate the long-term effects of Metaverse adoption on SMEs' growth trajectories. This includes understanding how prolonged use of Metaverse technologies influences market positioning, brand recognition, and customer retention. Research can track SME performance over extended periods to assess whether early adopters experience sustained growth or if the benefits plateau over time. While this study identifies technological challenges, there is a need for further investigation into the specific technical barriers SMEs face when adopting Metaverse technologies. Future research can explore the availability of affordable solutions, technological support, and the role of government and industry partnerships in easing these challenges. Studies can also focus on the development of scalable and user-friendly platforms that can be customized for SMEs with limited technological expertise. The role of the Metaverse in employee productivity and remote collaboration within SMEs warrants further examination. Future studies can explore how the Metaverse influences communication dynamics, teamwork, and decision-making processes, especially in a virtual or hybrid work environment.

Research can assess how immersive environments contribute to innovation, skill development, and the overall performance of teams. A critical area for future research is understanding consumer perception and trust when engaging with SMEs in the Metaverse. Studies can explore how customers perceive businesses operating in virtual environments, the impact on brand trust, and whether virtual transactions in the Metaverse are viewed as secure and legitimate. Insights into customer expectations and concerns can guide SMEs in enhancing their virtual offerings and improving their relationship with consumers. As the study noted, blockchain is a crucial element of the Metaverse. Future research can delve into the practical implications of blockchain integration within SMEs' Metaverse operations, especially regarding secure transactions, intellectual property protection, and supply chain management. Additionally, the role of other emerging technologies such as AI, IoT, and 5G in augmenting the Metaverse experience for SMEs should be explored. Future studies could explore how cultural and regional factors influence the adoption of the Metaverse by SMEs. Research can investigate whether SMEs in different geographical regions face unique challenges or have varying levels of acceptance toward virtual technologies. This will help tailor Metaverse adoption strategies to different cultural contexts, ensuring global relevance while addressing local needs. Given the growing emphasis on sustainability research could examine the environmental implications of Metaverse adoption by SMEs. This can include investigating the carbon footprint of maintaining virtual environments compared to traditional physical infrastructures and how SMEs can adopt eco-friendly practices within the Metaverse. Future studies could also explore how SMEs can leverage the Metaverse to promote sustainability, for example, by reducing the need for travel, office space, and resource consumption. As the Metaverse evolves, new regulatory and ethical concerns are likely to emerge. Future research could address the need for developing comprehensive guidelines and policies that govern SMEs' operations within virtual environments. This includes exploring the protection of intellectual property, data privacy, and ethical issues related to virtual labor, consumer interactions, and the impact of virtual environments on mental well-being. While much of the research has focused on business-to-consumer (B2C) SMEs, future studies could explore the potential applications of the Metaverse for business-to-business (B2B) SMEs. This includes examining virtual trade shows, industry-specific virtual networks, and B2B marketing strategies in the Metaverse. Research can investigate how SMEs in niche industries can use virtual platforms to collaborate with other businesses, form partnerships, and expand their market footprint. Another research area is the user experience (UX) and interface design for Metaverse platforms used by SMEs. Future studies can explore the effectiveness of different design principles in creating user-friendly, accessible, and engaging virtual experiences. Research could investigate how SMEs can design their Metaverse presence to cater to diverse audiences, ensuring usability and fostering customer engagement. As the Metaverse continues to evolve, the concept of an SME Metaverse ecosystem could be further explored. This could include an investigation of how multiple SMEs can collectively benefit from a shared virtual space, encouraging collaboration, networking, and mutual growth. Research could explore how SMEs can create partnerships within the Metaverse, benefiting from collective virtual experiences, shared resources, and collaborative innovation. In summary, future research on the Metaverse and SMEs should aim to address the technological, financial, social, and regulatory challenges of adoption while exploring its potential to drive innovation and competitiveness in the SME sector. As the Metaverse continues to mature, the breadth and depth of its applications for SMEs will undoubtedly expand, providing researchers with abundant opportunities to explore new dimensions of virtual business landscapes.

REFERENCES

Abrokwah-Larbi, K. (2024). Transforming metaverse marketing into strategic agility in SMEs through mediating roles of IMT and CI: Theoretical framework and research propositions. *Journal of Contemporary Marketing Science*, 7(1), 56–83. DOI: 10.1108/JCMARS-08-2023-0034

Abumalloh, R. A., Nilashi, M., Ooi, K. B., Wei-Han, G., Cham, T. H., Dwivedi, Y. K., & Hughes, L. (2023). The adoption of metaverse in the retail industry and its impact on sustainable competitive advantage: Moderating impact of sustainability commitment. *Annals of Operations Research*, •••, 1–42.

Al-Ramahi, N., Kreishan, F. M., Hussain, Z., Khan, A., Alghizzawi, M., & AlWadi, B. M. (2024). Unlocking sustainable growth: The role of artificial intelligence adoption in jordan retail sector, moderated by entrepreneurial orientation. *International Review ofManagement andMarketing*, 14(6), 143–155. DOI: 10.32479/irmm.16843

Aria Parsa, M., & Dalvi Esfahan, M. R. (2023). Mixed Research of Establishing of an Entrepreneurial Model with a Future Research Approach in the Metaverse Era in Knowledge-Based Companies in the Field of Information Technology. *Sociology of Education*, 9(2), 83–94.

Arora, M. (2024). Metaverse Insights: Research Advancements, Innovation Trends and Industry Implications. *Abhigyan*, 42(4), 385–402. DOI: 10.1177/09702385241277357

Bartoli, C., Baccelloni, A., Mattiacci, A., & Ungaro, L. (2024). Small and medium enterprises meet the metaverse. A study of the wine industry. *International Journal of Entrepreneurship and Innovation*, •••, 14657503241278164. DOI: 10.1177/14657503241278164

Biancone, P., Secinaro, S., Calandra, D., & Oppioli, M. (2023). Beyond the physical world… Digital entrepreneurship opportunities in the metaverse. In *L'aziendalismo crea valore! Il ruolo dell'accademia nelle sfide della società, dell'economia e delle istituzioni* (pp. 1–15). Università degli Studi di Salerno.

Brahmi, M., Hussain, Z., & Khan, A. (1988, May). Driving Success: Examining the Influence of Innovation Culture on Artificial Intelligence Adoption and Firm Performance in Asian SMEs. *InAnnual International Conference on the Theory and Applications of Cryptographic Techniques(pp.89-105).Cham: Springer Nature Switzerland.*

Chen, L., Tao, S., Xie, X., Huang, W., & Zhu, W. (2024). The evaluation of innovation efficiency and analysis of government subsidies influence—Evidence from China's metaverse listed companies. *Technological Forecasting and Social Change*, 201, 123213. DOI: 10.1016/j.techfore.2024.123213

Dash, A. (2024, October). A Graph Theoretic Approach to Analyze the Developing Metaverse. In 2024 *IEEE International Symposium on Emerging Metaverse (ISEMV) (pp. 45-48). IEEE.*

De Giovanni, P. (2023). Sustainability of the Metaverse: A transition to Industry 5.0. *Sustainability (Basel)*, 15(7), 6079. DOI: 10.3390/su15076079

Gegung, E. M. (2023). Metaverse: A promising future for the tourism industry and MSMEs Post-Covid-19 pandemic. Jurnal Kepariwisataan Indonesia: *Jurnal Penelitian dan Pengembangan Kepariwisataan Indonesia, 17(2), 172-181.*

Gil-Cordero, E., Maldonado-López, B., Ledesma-Chaves, P., & García-Guzmán, A. (2024). Do small-and medium-sized companies intend to use the Metaverse as part of their strategy? A behavioral intention analysis. *International Journal of Entrepreneurial Behaviour & Research*, 30(2/3), 421–449. DOI: 10.1108/IJEBR-09-2022-0816

Gupta, R., Rathore, B., Biswas, B., Jaiswal, M., & Singh, R. K. (2024). Are we ready for metaverse adoption in the service industry? Theoretically exploring the barriers to successful adoption. *Journal of Retailing and Consumer Services*, 79, 103882. DOI: 10.1016/j.jretconser.2024.103882

Hasani, T., Rezania, D., & Mohammadi, M. (2024). Towards a framework for successful metaverse adoption in Small and Medium-sized Enterprises: An exploratory study. *International Journal of Engineering Business Management*, 16, 18479790241257118. DOI: 10.1177/18479790241257118

Hassouneh, D., & Brengman, M. (2011). Virtual worlds: A gateway for SMEs toward internationalization. *Journal of Brand Management*, 19(1), 72–90. DOI: 10.1057/bm.2011.24

Hastuti, T. D., Sanjaya, R., & Koeswoyo, F. (2022). The readiness of Lasem Batik small and medium enterprises to join the metaverse. *Computers*, 12(1), 5. DOI: 10.3390/computers12010005

Hussain, Z. (1988, May). Enhancing Transparency and Accountability in Sadaqah Crowdfunding Platforms: Leveraging Blockchain Technology for Optimal User Experience. *InAnnual International Conference on the Theory and Applications of Cryptographic Techniques(pp.351-367).Cham: Springer Nature Switzerland.*

Hussain, Z. (2023). The Use of Web 3.0 in University E-learning, Quality Assurance, and Knowledge Management. In *Advances in Distance Learning in Times of Pandemic* (pp. 155–176). Chapman and Hall/CRC. DOI: 10.1201/9781003322252-7

Hussain, Z. (2024). The Role of Metaverse in Women Entrepreneurship and Economic Complexity: Evidence from Pakistan. *Journal of Entrepreneurship and Business Venturing*, 4(1).

Hussain, Z., Khan, A., & Ali, A. (2023). The Impact of User-Generated Content, Social Interactions and virtual Economies on Metaverse Environments. *Journal of Sustainable Economics*, 1(2), 34–44. DOI: 10.32734/jse.v1i2.13798

Hussain, Z., Majeed, M. U., & Khan, A. (2024). The Impact of Visual Content Marketing on Customer Purchasing Behavior: Evidence from Pakistan's Fashion Industry. *International Journal of Marketing, Communication and New Media, (14).*

Hussain, Z., Mari, I. H., & Rind, A. A. (2022). Exploring The Barriers of Artificial Intelligence Adoption in Digital Marketing Landscape. *ULIL ALBAB: Jurnal Ilmiah Multidisiplin*, 1(4), 824–835.

Huy, P. Q., & Phuc, V. K. (2024). Convergence of Blockchain, Artificial Intelligence, and Internet of Things (BlockIoTIntelligence) with Metaverse for Industry 4.0 to Realize Net Zero Economy. In *Net Zero Economy, Corporate Social Responsibility and Sustainable Value Creation: Exploring Strategies, Drivers, and Challenges* (pp. 187–202). Springer Nature Switzerland. DOI: 10.1007/978-3-031-55779-8_12

Huy, P. Q., & Phuc, V. K. (2024). Contribution to accelerated internationalization with digital forensic accounting and metaverse circular business model innovation for Vietnam-based SMEs. *Journal of Innovation and Entrepreneurship*, 13(1), 1–28. DOI: 10.1186/s13731-024-00442-z

ION, D. G. (2022). Human Capital or Human Beings? Analysis of Added Value and Employee Efficiency between SME's and Large Companies. *Fostering Recovery through Metaverse Business Modelling, 835.*

Jafar, R. M. S., Sun, Y., Niu, B., Hussain, S., Zhu, J., Gu, M., Al-Adwan, A. S., & Yang, Y. (2024). Revealing the secrets of metaverse technology adoption for sustainable performance via dual-stage SEM-ANN analysis. *International Journal of Human-Computer Interaction*, •••, 1–18. DOI: 10.1080/10447318.2024.2407686

Karthik, V. (2023). Impact of Metaverse and Advanced Technology on the Enterprises. *International Journal of Business and Management Research*, 11(2), 60–65. DOI: 10.37391/ijbmr.110201

Khan, A., Hamid, A. B. A., Saad, N. M., Hussain, Z., & Arif, A. R. (2023). Effectiveness of artificial intelligence in building customer loyalty: Investigating the mediating role of chatbot in the tourism sector of Pakistan. *International Journal of Academic Research in Business & Social Sciences*, 13(9), 657–671. DOI: 10.6007/IJARBSS/v13-i9/18895

Kumar, A., & Shankar, A. (2024). Building a sustainable future with enterprise metaverse in a data-driven era: A technology-organization-environment (TOE) perspective. *Journal of Retailing and Consumer Services*, 81, 103986. DOI: 10.1016/j.jretconser.2024.103986

Kumar, A., Shankar, A., Agarwal, R., Agarwal, V., & Alzeiby, E. A. (2024). With enterprise metaverse comes great possibilities! Understanding metaverse usage intention from an employee perspective. *Journal of Retailing and Consumer Services*, 78, 103767. DOI: 10.1016/j.jretconser.2024.103767

Latino, M. E., De Lorenzi, M. C., Corallo, A., & Petruzzelli, A. M. (2024). The impact of metaverse for business model innovation: A review, novel insights and research directions. *Technological Forecasting and Social Change*, 206, 123571. DOI: 10.1016/j.techfore.2024.123571

Ledesma-Chaves, P., Gil-Cordero, E., Navarro-García, A., & Maldonado-López, B. (2024). Satisfaction and performance expectations for the adoption of the metaverse in tourism SMEs. *Journal of Innovation & Knowledge*, 9(3), 100535. DOI: 10.1016/j.jik.2024.100535

Lopes, T. S. A., Carreira, R., Carlos, V. S., Pereira, R. H., Alves, C., Pratas, J., & dos Santos, J. P. M. (2023, November). How Can Businesses, Low-Tech Businesses in Particular, Benefit from the Metaverse? A Delphi Perspective from Academics. *InInternational Conference on Marketing and Technologies(pp.489-511).Singapore: Springer Nature Singapore.*

Luimula, M., Haavisto, T., Vu, D., Markopoulos, P., Aho, J., Markopoulos, E., & Saarinen, J. (2022). The use of metaverse in maritime sector—A combination of social communication, hands on experiencing and digital twins. *Creativity. Innovation and Entrepreneurship*, 31, 115–123.

Mahindru, R., Bapat, G., Bhoyar, P., Abishek, G. D., Kumar, A., & Vaz, S. (2024). Redefining Workspaces: Young Entrepreneurs Thriving in the Metaverse's Remote Realm. *Engineering Proceedings*, 59(1), 209.

Mosbah, A. (2024). Technology Adoption Among SMEs: How Is It? And What Can Be Done to Strengthen It? *Jurnal Kejuruteraan*, 36(4), 1519–1528. DOI: 10.17576/jkukm-2024-36(4)-17

Mubarak, M. F., Ghobakhloo, M., Evans, R., Jucevicius, G., Prestianawati, S. A., & Mubarik, M. (2024). Metaverse adoption in the manufacturing industry: Impact on social and environmental sustainability performance. *Asia-Pacific Journal of Business Administration*. Advance online publication. DOI: 10.1108/APJBA-02-2024-0043

Ndekwa, A. G. (2025). Digital Marketing Metaverse for Restoration of Tourism Performance After COVID-19 Business Crisis in Sub-Saharan African Countries: Experience From Tanzania. In *Metaverse and Tourism* (pp. 161–180). Routledge.

Pham, Q. H., & Vu, K. P. (2024). Insight into how digital forensic accounting and metaverse circular business model innovation contribute to accelerated internationalization: Evidence from Vietnam-based SMEs. *Cogent Business & Management*, 11(1), 2320203. DOI: 10.1080/23311975.2024.2320203

Polas, M. R. H., Ahamed, B., & Rana, M. M. (2023). Artificial intelligence and blockchain technology in the 4.0 IR metaverse Era: Implications, opportunities, and future directions. In *Strategies and opportunities for technology in the metaverse world* (pp. 13–33). IGI Global. DOI: 10.4018/978-1-6684-5732-0.ch002

Polas, M. R. H., Jahanshahi, A. A., Kabir, A. I., Sohel-Uz-Zaman, A. S. M., Osman, A. R., & Karim, R. (2022). Artificial intelligence, blockchain technology, and risk-taking behavior in the 4.0 IR Metaverse Era: Evidence from Bangladesh-based SMEs. *Journal of Open Innovation*, 8(3), 168. DOI: 10.3390/joitmc8030168

Rasztar, L., Rose, R., & Neuhuttler, J. (2024). Exploring the Impact of the Industrial Metaverse–A Delphi-based Scenario Approach. *IEEE Engineering Management Review*, 1–15. DOI: 10.1109/EMR.2024.3501579

Rehman, A., Behera, R. K., Islam, M. S., Elahi, Y. A., Abbasi, F. A., & Imtiaz, A. (2024). Drivers of metaverse adoption for enhancing marketing capabilities of retail SMEs. *Technology in Society*, 79, 102704. DOI: 10.1016/j.techsoc.2024.102704

Reniati, S. E., Bidayani, E., & Pi, S. (2023). The Influence of Digital Talent and Green Innovation and Its Impact on the MSME Business Model in the Metaverse Era. *The Influence of Digital Talent and Green Innovation and Its Impact on the MSME Business Model in the Metaverse Era, 13(2).*

Safitri, A., Husin, N., Arifah, I. D. C., Dewi, R. S., Kharisma, F., & Kautsar, A. (2024, January). Metaverse User Experience, Customer Engagement, and Brand Awareness Relation as SMEs Marketing Strategies in Virtual Worlds. *In 2024 ASU International Conference in Emerging Technologies for Sustainability and Intelligent Systems (ICETSIS)(pp.* 1092-1096*).* IEEE. DOI: 10.1109/ICETSIS61505.2024.10459506

Sanjaya, R., Hastuti, T. D., & Koeswoyo, F. (2022, November). Technical aspects of metaverse development for batik SMEs exhibitions. In 2022 *20th International Conference on ICT and Knowledge Engineering (ICT&KE) (pp. 1-5). IEEE.* DOI: 10.1109/ICTKE55848.2022.9983314

Saridakis, G., Khan, Z., Knight, G., Idris, B., Mitra, J., & Khan, H. (2024). A Look into the Future: The Impact of Metaverse on Traditional Theories and Thinking in International Business. *MIR. Management International Review*, 64(4), 597–632. DOI: 10.1007/s11575-024-00550-8

Sundararajan, R., Menon, P., Jayakrishnan, B., & Shah, P. (2024). Entrepreneurship orientation toward adoption of Metaverse: An MSME entrepreneur perspective. *International Journal of Entrepreneurship and Innovation*, •••, 14657503241270211. DOI: 10.1177/14657503241270211

Ugrinov, S., Nikolić, M., Kavalić, M., Stojanović, E. T., & Gluvakov, V. (2024). Synergy between marketing strategies 4.0 and knowledge management processes in small and medium enterprises. *Journal of Engineering and Management*, 2(1). Advance online publication. DOI: 10.7251/JEM2402043U

Zabel, C., O'Brien, D., & Natzel, J. (2023). Sensing the Metaverse: The microfoundations of complementor firms' dynamic sensing capabilities in emerging-technology ecosystems. *Technological Forecasting and Social Change*, 192, 122562. DOI: 10.1016/j.techfore.2023.122562

Chapter 2
Market Dynamics in the Metaverse:
Leveraging Opportunities for SME Growth

Abdul Qadeer
https://orcid.org/0009-0004-4157-2387
Shaheed Benazir Bhutto University, Nawabshah, Pakistan

Asadullah Hussain
Shaheed Benazir Bhutto University, Nawabshah, Pakistan

Hassan Arif Siddiqui
Shaheed Benazir Bhutto University of Veterinary and Animal Sciences, Pakistan

ABSTRACT

The Metaverse, an emerging digital ecosystem, offers transformative opportunities for small and medium enterprises (SMEs) to innovate, expand, and thrive. This study examines the market dynamics within the Metaverse, focusing on how SMEs can leverage its potential to enhance consumer engagement and drive growth. Combining virtual reality (VR), blockchain, and augmented reality (AR), the Metaverse provides an immersive platform for businesses to create unique value propositions and adapt to evolving consumer preferences

DOI: 10.4018/979-8-3693-9005-4.ch002

1. INTRODUCTION

The Metaverse, a term popularized by Neal Stephenson in his 1992 novel *Snow Crash*, has evolved from a science fiction concept into a tangible digital ecosystem that merges VR, AR, blockchain, and other emerging technologies (Yaqoob et al., 2023). In the contemporary business environment, the Metaverse is transforming how enterprises interact with consumers, offering immersive experiences that extend beyond traditional physical and online spaces (Setiawan & Anthony, 2022). For SMEs, the Metaverse presents a dual-edged sword: an opportunity to innovate and scale, and a challenge to navigate the complexities of a rapidly evolving digital frontier. Tariq (2024) highlighted the growing economic significance of the Metaverse. Stanoevska & Slabeva (2022) estimated that the Metaverse market could reach $1 trillion in annual revenue, underscoring its potential as a platform for commerce. For SMEs, which constitute a majority of global businesses, this represents a critical opportunity to level the playing field with larger competitors through immersive branding and cost-effective digital tools. However, concerns related to technological adoption, data security, and consumer trust remain significant barriers to entry. Previous studies have underscored the importance of consumer engagement in the Metaverse. Yawised et al., (2022) demonstrated that immersive virtual environments significantly enhance customer satisfaction and brand loyalty. Similarly, Weking et al., (2023) highlighted the role of AR and VR in fostering deeper emotional connections between brands and consumers. Meanwhile, Allama et al., (2022) argued that the Metaverse could redefine marketing paradigms by allowing hyper-personalized experiences.

From an SME perspective, Pineiro-Chousa et al., (2024) identified virtual storefronts as a cost-effective solution for expanding market reach, particularly in niche industries. Furthermore, Hussain et al., (2023) found that blockchain-enabled financial systems in the Metaverse could reduce transaction costs and improve operational efficiency for SMEs. Banaeian & Miami (2023) emphasized the role of gamification in enhancing consumer engagement within Metaverse platforms, making it a critical tool for SMEs targeting younger demographics. In terms of challenges, Japar & Anshari (2023) pointed out that high initial investments and a steep learning curve often deter SMEs from fully exploring Metaverse opportunities. Additionally, Latino et al., (2024) highlighted concerns over data privacy and security, particularly in decentralized environments, as critical barriers to adoption. Despite these challenges, recent findings have been optimistic about the Metaverse's potential. Ozkan & Ozkan (2024) showed that SMEs adopting Metaverse strategies saw a 20% increase in customer retention compared to traditional online platforms. Similarly, Mishra & Awasthi (2022) highlighted the potential of the Metaverse to foster global market access for SMEs, breaking geographical barriers. This study aims to build on these foundational insights, exploring the dynamics of the Metaverse for SMEs. It seeks to identify actionable strategies that enable SMEs to overcome challenges and capitalize on market opportunities. By synthesizing existing research and providing new empirical evidence, this study contributes to the growing discourse on digital transformation and its implications for SME sustainability and growth in the Metaverse era.

2. LITERATURE REVIEW

2.1 Market Dynamics in the Metaverse for SMEs

In an era defined by rapid technological advancements, the Metaverse has emerged as a disruptive force, reshaping traditional market structures and opening unprecedented opportunities for businesses. For small and medium enterprises (SMEs), the Metaverse represents not just a futuristic concept but a tangible platform for innovation, growth, and competitive advantage (Oyeleye & Alsaaty, 2024). As businesses shift from physical and online spaces to immersive virtual environments, understanding the market dynamics of the Metaverse becomes crucial for SMEs aiming to remain relevant in a digital-first economy. Research has extensively highlighted the transformative potential of the Metaverse. Brahmi et al., (1988) projected that the Metaverse could become a trillion-dollar industry, driven by advancements in VR, AR, and blockchain technologies. Gauttier et al., (2024) found that immersive environments in the Metaverse significantly enhance customer satisfaction and loyalty, offering SMEs a unique avenue to differentiate their offerings. Bruni et al., (2023) emphasized the cost-effectiveness of virtual storefronts, which allow SMEs to bypass traditional infrastructure costs while expanding their market reach. Enache (2022) showed that AR and VR technologies enable hyper-personalized consumer experiences, a critical factor in driving brand engagement. Meanwhile, Hussain (1988) argued that the Metaverse redefines marketing paradigms, enabling SMEs to build stronger emotional connections with consumers. In terms of operational efficiency, Inder (2023) highlighted that blockchain-based financial systems within the Metaverse could reduce transaction costs and streamline payment processes for SMEs. Hussain et al., (2023) demonstrated that gamification elements in Metaverse platforms drive higher consumer engagement, making them particularly effective for SMEs targeting younger audiences. From a strategic perspective, Rosa (2022) revealed that SMEs utilizing the Metaverse as part of their business strategy experienced higher consumer retention rates. Kraus et al., (2022) quantified this, noting a 20% increase in customer retention for SMEs using immersive Metaverse strategies compared to traditional platforms. Hussain (2024) added that the Metaverse facilitates global market access for SMEs, breaking down geographical barriers. However, challenges remain. Dwivedi et al., (2022) identified high initial investment costs as a major deterrent for SMEs exploring the Metaverse. Similarly, Cho et al., (2022) raised concerns about data privacy and security in decentralized Metaverse environments. Karademir (2023) found that consumer trust in Metaverse platforms is still developing, posing a challenge for SMEs seeking to build long-term relationships. Recent research also highlights the evolving role of social interactions within the Metaverse. Knox (2022) observed that community-driven platforms in the Metaverse foster brand advocacy, a significant advantage for SMEs. Additionally, Japar & Anshari (2023) explored the potential of virtual events and trade fairs within the Metaverse, noting their effectiveness in creating new business opportunities for SMEs. Further, Papagiannidis et al., (2008) analyzed consumer behavior in Metaverse environments, identifying trends like increased spending on virtual goods, which SMEs can capitalize on. Rathore (2018) emphasized that SMEs leveraging NFTs (non-fungible tokens) as part of their marketing strategy could enhance brand visibility and generate new revenue streams. Hussain (2024) showed that Metaverse platforms promote sustainability by reducing the need for physical infrastructure, aligning with consumer demand for eco-friendly practices. Similarly, Ramadhan et al., (2023) argued that SMEs in the Metaverse can achieve cost savings through digital supply chain innovations. This growing body of research underscores the dynamic and multifaceted nature of the Metaverse as a marketplace. For SMEs, it is not just a space for experimentation but a critical component of their future strategies. By understanding and adapting to these market dynamics, SMEs can unlock the full potential of the Metaverse, ensuring long-term growth and sustainability.

2.3 Consumer Experience in the Metaverse for SMEs

The Metaverse is revolutionizing the way businesses engage with consumers, offering immersive and interactive experiences that blend the physical and virtual worlds. For SMEs, the Metaverse provides a platform to enhance consumer engagement, foster brand loyalty, and create unique, personalized interactions (Rosario et al., 2023). Consumer experience in the Metaverse is central to its success, driven by advancements in VR, AR, and blockchain technologies. Research demonstrates the transformative impact of the Metaverse on consumer experience (Sridharan & Kumar, 2024). Rehm & Crespi (2015) found that immersive virtual environments improve customer satisfaction by enabling real-time, interactive engagements. Rosenstand et al., (2023) emphasized the role of hyper-personalized experiences in building stronger emotional connections between brands and consumers, making it a critical advantage for SMEs. Lin et al., (2022) highlighted that AR applications allow SMEs to create interactive product demonstrations, significantly enhancing the pre-purchase experience. Similarly, Lee et al., (2023) showed that gamification within Metaverse platforms boosts consumer engagement, particularly among younger demographics. Jung et al., (2024) identified virtual storefronts as a low-cost yet highly effective way for SMEs to provide immersive shopping experiences that rival those of larger competitors. Mancuso et al., (2023) explored blockchain's role in securing consumer transactions, increasing trust and transparency within the Metaverse. Mishra & Awasthi (2022) highlighted how community-driven platforms foster a sense of belonging, enhancing consumer loyalty to SMEs. Knox (2022) further emphasized that SMEs integrating NFTs into their marketing strategies create unique value propositions, enriching the consumer journey. Ozkan & Ozkan (2024) noted that consumer trust in Metaverse platforms is still developing, with privacy concerns being a significant barrier. Inder (2023) underscored the need for SMEs to align their Metaverse strategies with evolving consumer preferences to remain relevant. Latino et al., (2024) stressed that SMEs must address the digital divide to ensure inclusivity in their Metaverse offerings. Recent studies also focus on measuring the economic impact of consumer experiences in the Metaverse. Marabelli & Newell (2023) reported a 15% increase in customer spending for SMEs leveraging immersive technologies. Koohang et al., (2023) analyzed virtual consumer behavior, finding that engaging experiences lead to higher conversion rates and repeat purchases. Enache (2022) emphasized the role of digital convenience in retaining Metaverse consumers, particularly in competitive markets. By leveraging these insights, SMEs can design innovative, consumer-centric strategies to create impactful and memorable experiences in the Metaverse. This shift not only enhances consumer satisfaction but also positions SMEs for sustained growth in the digital economy.

2.4 Business Models in the Metaverse for SMEs

The Metaverse is transforming traditional business paradigms, providing SMEs with innovative models to operate, engage customers, and generate revenue. By leveraging VR, AR, blockchain, and other emerging technologies, SMEs can redefine how they deliver value in an immersive and decentralized digital economy. Business models in the Metaverse for SMEs are diverse, ranging from virtual storefronts and decentralized marketplaces to gamified experiences and tokenized ecosystems. Research underscores the growing potential of these business models (Koohang et al., 2023). Allam et al., (2022) highlighted virtual storefronts as a cost-effective model for SMEs, allowing them to eliminate physical infrastructure costs while expanding their market reach. Similarly, Inder (2023) emphasized the potential of subscription-based services within the Metaverse, where SMEs can offer exclusive access to virtual goods, events, or content. Bruni et al., (2023) explored blockchain-enabled business models, demonstrating how SMEs can leverage smart contracts and decentralized finance (DeFi) to streamline operations and reduce transaction costs. Brahmi et al., (1988) identified tokenized ecosystems as a lucrative model, where SMEs can issue branded tokens or NFTs to create unique consumer incentives and drive engagement. Gauttier et al., (2024) discussed gamification as a powerful strategy, where SMEs integrate game mechanics into their offerings to enhance consumer interaction and loyalty. Enache (2022) highlighted community-driven models, where SMEs can foster brand advocacy by creating virtual spaces for consumer interaction and collaboration. Kraus et al., (2022) examined the role of virtual trade fairs and networking events, which enable SMEs to connect with stakeholders globally without logistical constraints. However, challenges persist in adopting these models. Inder (2023) pointed out the high initial investment costs and technological learning curves associated with Metaverse business models. Rosa (2022) emphasized the importance of addressing privacy concerns and ensuring data security to build consumer trust. Papagiannidis et al., (2008) noted that SMEs need to adopt flexible and adaptive strategies to cater to evolving consumer preferences in the Metaverse. Lee (2024) revealed that SMEs utilizing mixed-revenue models, such as combining product sales with virtual memberships, achieved higher profitability. Marabelli & Neweel (2023) explored the potential of collaborative business models, where SMEs partner with other Metaverse entities to share resources and expand their market presence. Jung et al, (2024) highlighted that SMEs embracing sustainability-focused models in the Metaverse, such as eco-friendly virtual goods, gain a competitive edge among environmentally conscious consumers. Pinciro-Chousa et al., (2024) emphasized the scalability of Metaverse business models, noting how SMEs can rapidly expand operations without the constraints of physical infrastructure. Oyeleye & Alsaaty (2024) concluded that successful adoption of Metaverse models requires a blend of innovation, technological adaptation, and consumer-centric strategies. By exploring and implementing these diverse business models, SMEs can capitalize on the Metaverse's potential to drive growth, foster innovation, and remain competitive in an increasingly digitalized economy.

2.5 Case Studies on Implementing Metaverse Strategies in SMEs

The adoption of Metaverse strategies by SMEs has garnered attention for its potential to reshape traditional business models and drive growth. Case studies across industries highlight how SMEs are leveraging the Metaverse to enhance customer engagement, streamline operations, and create new revenue streams. These real-world implementations showcase the transformative potential of Metaverse technologies like VR, AR and blockchain. According to Hussain et al., (2023), SME implemented a VR-based storefront where customers could virtually browse and purchase products. Yaqoob et al., (2023) highlighted that VR Mart reduced overhead costs by eliminating physical retail spaces and reported a 30% increase in customer engagement due to immersive shopping experiences. PlayPro Games (UK) small gaming SME used gamified marketing campaigns within the Metaverse to promote its products. Gauttier et al., (2024) found that integrating gamification increased customer loyalty by 25% and led to a 15% rise in sales within six months. EcoCraft Collective (USA), This SME created a virtual space for eco-conscious consumers to share ideas and shop for sustainable products. Rehm & Crespi (2015) observed that the company built a loyal consumer base by fostering a sense of community and shared values, increasing repeat purchases by 40%. FinSecure Solutions (Singapore), By implementing blockchain for payment processing and smart contracts, this SME reduced transaction costs by 20%. Rosa (2022) noted that the enhanced transparency and security attracted more customers, boosting overall trust in the brand. CraftConnect (Pakistan), This SME hosted virtual trade fairs and workshops in the Metaverse, targeting global buyers for local artisans. Hussain (2024) found that the platform expanded the SME's market reach by 60%, enabling cross-border sales without logistical challenges. ArtSpace Studio (France), An SME in the art industry created virtual galleries where customers could explore and purchase art. Mancuso et al., (2023) highlighted that this approach resulted in a 50% increase in sales and enhanced customer satisfaction through immersive, personalized experiences. FashionLite (Italy), This SME introduced NFTs as part of its loyalty program, offering exclusive rewards to repeat customers. Kraus et al., (2022) observed that the program significantly boosted customer retention, with a 20% increase in loyalty sign-ups. SkillTech SME (Germany), This SME used VR for employee training, creating interactive scenarios that improved skill retention. Latino et al., (2024) noted that the approach reduced training costs by 15% while increasing productivity. GreenWear VR (Canada), The company focused on creating eco-friendly virtual clothing for avatars. Japar & Anshari (2023) highlighted that this strategy aligned with growing consumer demand for sustainability, resulting in a 35% growth in sales. VRFit (USA), A fitness SME integrated subscription-based access to VR workouts alongside virtual merchandise sales. Inder (2023) reported a 20% rise in revenue due to this diversified approach. Allam et al., (2022) emphasized that SMEs often face challenges like high initial investments and limited technological expertise. However, these case studies demonstrate that with strategic implementation and consumer-centric approaches, SMEs can overcome barriers and unlock the full potential of the Metaverse. By learning from these cases, SMEs across industries can design tailored Metaverse strategies to drive growth, innovation, and long-term sustainability.

2.6 Future Trends and Considerations in Metaverse Strategies for SMEs

The Metaverse continues to evolve, presenting significant opportunities and challenges for small and medium enterprises (SMEs). As the technology matures, SMEs must adapt to emerging trends and consider critical factors to stay competitive and relevant in this digital landscape. Advancements in VR and AR are expected to provide even more immersive experiences for consumers. Hussain (2024) predict that SMEs will increasingly adopt these technologies to create personalized and interactive customer journeys. Koohang et al., (2023) forecast that blockchain will become a standard feature in the Metaverse, allowing SMEs to implement secure transactions, smart contracts, and decentralized marketplaces more effectively. Mishra & Awasthi (2022) highlight that virtual goods, including digital apparel and NFTs, will play a central role in Metaverse commerce. SMEs can capitalize on these trends by creating unique, branded virtual products. Periyasami & Periyasami (2022) emphasize the growing role of AI in analyzing consumer behavior within the Metaverse, enabling SMEs to develop data-driven strategies. Rosa (2022) predict that future Metaverse platforms will focus on interoperability, allowing SMEs to seamlessly operate across different virtual ecosystems. Kraus et al., (2022) suggest that consumer demand for sustainability will drive SMEs to adopt eco-friendly practices in the Metaverse, such as using energy-efficient blockchain technologies. Lee (2024) anticipate that "phygital" experiences, blending physical and digital touchpoints, will redefine how SMEs engage with customers. Lee et al., (2023) note that social interactions within the Metaverse will increasingly influence purchasing decisions, encouraging SMEs to build community-driven platforms. Papagiannidis et al., (2008) project that as technology becomes more accessible, affordable Metaverse solutions tailored to SMEs will emerge, lowering entry barriers. Pinciro-Chousa et al., (2024) highlight the importance of future regulations to ensure consumer protection, data privacy, and ethical practices in the Metaverse, which SMEs must navigate carefully. While the Metaverse offers vast opportunities, high initial investments remain a challenge. Rosa (2022) recommend starting with scalable, low-cost strategies, such as virtual storefronts or limited NFT offerings. As consumers grow more concerned about data privacy, SMEs must prioritize secure transactions and transparent policies. Yaqoob et al., (2023) stress the importance of equipping employees with the necessary skills to manage Metaverse tools and platforms effectively. Stanoevska- Slabeva (2022) advise SMEs to continuously monitor trends and adapt their strategies to align with consumer expectations, such as personalization and ethical practices. Rehm & Crespi (2015) advocate for SMEs to collaborate with larger organizations or tech providers to share resources and expand their Metaverse capabilities. Weking et al., (2023) emphasize designing Metaverse experiences that are inclusive and accessible to diverse demographics, ensuring broader market reach. Yaqoob et al., (2023) recommend a trial-and-error approach, encouraging SMEs to experiment with new ideas while minimizing risks. By understanding these trends and considerations, SMEs can strategically position themselves to harness the full potential of the Metaverse, fostering growth and innovation in a rapidly changing digital economy.

Recommendations and Future Research Directions

The Metaverse holds immense potential for SMEs to innovate and thrive in a digitally connected economy. However, realizing this potential requires strategic approaches and an ongoing commitment to exploring new dimensions of this evolving technology. Below are recommendations and future research directions to guide SMEs and scholars in maximizing the Metaverse's benefits. SMEs should start small, using low-cost tools like virtual storefronts or basic VR/AR applications, and scale up as they become more familiar with the Metaverse ecosystem. Design immersive experiences tailored to consumer needs. Personalized services in the Metaverse significantly enhance customer loyalty and engagement. Integrating blockchain for secure transactions and NFTs for unique product offerings can open new revenue streams. Providing employees with training on Metaverse tools ensures smooth implementation and management of virtual platforms. Partnering with tech firms or larger businesses can help SMEs access the resources and expertise needed to enter the Metaverse. Building consumer trust through robust data protection measures is critical. SMEs should adopt transparent policies and advanced cybersecurity tools (). Combining physical and virtual offerings (phygital models) can bridge the gap between traditional and Metaverse-based business operations. Explore the economic implications of Metaverse adoption by SMEs across various industries, focusing on market expansion, job creation, and cost efficiencies. Investigate the role of eco-friendly technologies and sustainable practices in virtual ecosystems, such as energy-efficient blockchain systems. Conduct longitudinal studies on how consumer preferences evolve in Metaverse environments, particularly in areas like virtual goods and gamified interactions. Study the impact of emerging Metaverse regulations on SME operations, focusing on compliance challenges and opportunities. Research methods to make the Metaverse accessible to diverse demographics, including marginalized communities and non-tech-savvy users (). Examine the integration of AI, IoT, and 5G technologies within the Metaverse and their implications for SMEs. Study how interoperability among different Metaverse platforms can benefit SMEs by enhancing scalability and reducing technical barriers. Analyze how cultural factors and regional differences affect Metaverse adoption and strategy success for SMEs in various global markets. Develop frameworks to measure the ROI and performance of Metaverse strategies for SMEs, ensuring alignment with business goals. Explore strategies for SMEs to mitigate risks associated with Metaverse adoption, such as technological disruptions and cybersecurity threats. By implementing these recommendations and exploring the outlined research directions, SMEs and scholars can contribute to shaping a dynamic, inclusive, and sustainable Metaverse ecosystem.

REFERENCES

Allam, Z., Sharifi, A., Bibri, S. E., Jones, D. S., & Krogstie, J. (2022). The metaverse as a virtual form of smart cities: Opportunities and challenges for environmental, economic, and social sustainability in urban futures. *Smart Cities*, 5(3), 771–801. DOI: 10.3390/smartcities5030040

Banaeian Far, S., & Imani Rad, A. (2023). What are the benefits and opportunities of launching a Metaverse for NEOM city? *Security and Privacy*, 6(3), e282. DOI: 10.1002/spy2.282

Brahmi, M., Hussain, Z., & Khan, A. (1988, May). Driving Success: Examining the Influence of Innovation Culture on Artificial Intelligence Adoption and Firm Performance in Asian SMEs. *InAnnual International Conference on the Theory and Applications of Cryptographic Techniques(pp.89-105).Cham: Springer Nature Switzerland.*

Bruni, R., Piccarozzi, M., & Caboni, F. (2023). Defining the Metaverse with challenges and opportunities in the business environment. *Journal of Marketing Theory and Practice*, •••, 1–18.

Cho, J., tom Dieck, M. C., & Jung, T. (2022, April). What is the metaverse? Challenges, opportunities, definition, and future research directions. In *International XR Conference(pp.* 3-26*).* Cham*:* Springer International Publishing.

Dwivedi, Y. K., Hughes, L., Baabdullah, A. M., Ribeiro-Navarrete, S., Giannakis, M., Al-Debei, M. M., Dennehy, D., Metri, B., Buhalis, D., Cheung, C. M. K., Conboy, K., Doyle, R., Dubey, R., Dutot, V., Felix, R., Goyal, D. P., Gustafsson, A., Hinsch, C., Jebabli, I., & Wamba, S. F. (2022). Metaverse beyond the hype: Multidisciplinary perspectives on emerging challenges, opportunities, and agenda for research, practice and policy. *International Journal of Information Management*, 66, 102542. DOI: 10.1016/j.ijinfomgt.2022.102542

Enache, M. C. (2022). Metaverse opportunities for businesses. Annals of the University Dunarea de Jos of Galati: Fascicle: I. *Economics & Applied Informatics*, 28(1), 67–71.

Gauttier, S., Simouri, W., & Milliat, A. (2024). When to enter the metaverse: Business leaders offer perspectives. *The Journal of Business Strategy*, 45(1), 2–9. DOI: 10.1108/JBS-08-2022-0149

Hussain, Z. (1988, May). Enhancing Transparency and Accountability in Sadaqah Crowdfunding Platforms: Leveraging Blockchain Technology for Optimal User Experience. *InAnnual International Conference on the Theory and Applications of Cryptographic Techniques(pp.351-367).Cham: Springer Nature Switzerland.*

Hussain, Z. (2024). The Role of Metaverse in Women Entrepreneurship and Economic Complexity: Evidence from Pakistan. *Journal of Entrepreneurship and Business Venturing*, 4(1).

Hussain, Z., Khan, A., & Ali, A. (2023). The Impact of User-Generated Content, Social Interactions and virtual Economies on Metaverse Environments. *Journal of Sustainable Economics*, 1(2), 34–44. DOI: 10.32734/jse.v1i2.13798

Inder, S. (2023). Entrepreneurial opportunities in metaverse. In *Promoting Consumer Engagement Through Emotional Branding and Sensory Marketing* (pp. 52–62). IGI Global.

Japar, D. F. I. P. M., & Anshari, M. (2023). Potential and challenges of the Metaverse on future businesses. In *Metaverse applications for new business models and disruptive innovation* (pp. 102–119). IGI Global. DOI: 10.4018/978-1-6684-6097-9.ch007

Jung, T., Cho, J., Han, D. I. D., Ahn, S. J. G., Gupta, M., Das, G., Heo, C. Y., Loureiro, S. M. C., Sigala, M., Trunfio, M., Taylor, A., & Tom Dieck, M. C. (2024). Metaverse for service industries: Future applications, opportunities, challenges and research directions. *Computers in Human Behavior*, 151, 108039. DOI: 10.1016/j.chb.2023.108039

Karademir, Ö. (2023). Opportunities and Barriers for Entrepreneurship in the Metaverse Age. In *Role of Human Resources for Inclusive Leadership, Workplace Diversity, and Equity in Organizations* (pp. 309–336). IGI Global. DOI: 10.4018/978-1-6684-6602-5.ch013

Knox, J. (2022). The metaverse, or the serious business of tech frontiers. *Postdigital Science and Education*, 4(2), 207–215. DOI: 10.1007/s42438-022-00300-9

Koohang, A., Nord, J. H., Ooi, K. B., Tan, G. W. H., Al-Emran, M., Aw, E. C. X., Baabdullah, A. M., Buhalis, D., Cham, T.-H., Dennis, C., Dutot, V., Dwivedi, Y. K., Hughes, L., Mogaji, E., Pandey, N., Phau, I., Raman, R., Sharma, A., Sigala, M., & Wong, L. W. (2023). Shaping the metaverse into reality: A holistic multidisciplinary understanding of opportunities, challenges, and avenues for future investigation. *Journal of Computer Information Systems*, 63(3), 735–765. DOI: 10.1080/08874417.2023.2165197

Kraus, S., Kanbach, D. K., Krysta, P. M., Steinhoff, M. M., & Tomini, N. (2022). Facebook and the creation of the metaverse: Radical business model innovation or incremental transformation? *International Journal of Entrepreneurial Behaviour & Research*, 28(9), 52–77. DOI: 10.1108/IJEBR-12-2021-0984

Latino, M. E., De Lorenzi, M. C., Corallo, A., & Petruzzelli, A. M. (2024). The impact of metaverse for business model innovation: A review, novel insights and research directions. *Technological Forecasting and Social Change*, 206, 123571. DOI: 10.1016/j.techfore.2024.123571

Lee, I. (2024). The Metaverse: Ecosystem, Technologies, Business Opportunities, and Challenges. *IT Professional*, 26(5), 28–35. DOI: 10.1109/MITP.2024.3433549

Lee, K. H., Tsai, W. H., Huang, C. T., Tao, J., Lee, H., Chen, C. H., & Tseng, H. T. (2023). Using Machine Learning of Artificial Intelligence to Analyze Business Opportunities and Applications of the Massively Multiplayer Online Role-Playing Game Case in Metaverse. *Engineering Proceedings*, 55(1), 12.

Lin, H., Wan, S., Gan, W., Chen, J., & Chao, H. C. (2022, December). Metaverse in education: Vision, opportunities, and challenges. *In 2022 IEEE International Conference on Big Data (Big Data) (pp. 2857-2866). IEEE.*

Mancuso, I., Petruzzelli, A. M., & Panniello, U. (2023). Digital business model innovation in metaverse: How to approach virtual economy opportunities. *Information Processing & Management*, 60(5), 103457. DOI: 10.1016/j.ipm.2023.103457

Marabelli, M., & Newell, S. (2023). Responsibly strategizing with the metaverse: Business implications and DEI opportunities and challenges. *The Journal of Strategic Information Systems*, 32(2), 101774. DOI: 10.1016/j.jsis.2023.101774

Meepung, T., & Kannikar, P. (2022). Metaverse; virtual world challenges and opportunities for digital business. *WORLD (Oakland, Calif.)*, 15(18), 277–282. DOI: 10.18178/joebm.2022.10.4.712

Mishra, A., & Awasthi, S. (2022). Metaverse: Opportunities and challenges for marketers. *Management Dynamics*, 22(1), 79–84. DOI: 10.57198/2583-4932.1305

Oyeleye, D., & Alsaaty, F. M. (2024). The Metaverse: A Path for Entrepreneurial Opportunities in an Entrepreneurial Mindset Campus. *The Journal of Business*, 31(1).

Özkan, A., & Özkan, H. (2024). Meta: XR-AR-MR and Mirror World Technologies Business Impact of Metaverse. *Journal of Metaverse*, 4(1), 21–32. DOI: 10.57019/jmv.1344489

Papagiannidis, S., Bourlakis, M., & Li, F. (2008). Making real money in virtual worlds: MMORPGs and emerging business opportunities, challenges and ethical implications in metaverses. *Technological Forecasting and Social Change*, 75(5), 610–622. DOI: 10.1016/j.techfore.2007.04.007

Periyasami, S., & Periyasamy, A. P. (2022). Metaverse as future promising platform business model: Case study on fashion value chain. *Businesses*, 2(4), 527–545. DOI: 10.3390/businesses2040033

Piñeiro-Chousa, J., López-Cabarcos, M. Á., VittoriRomero, V., & Pérez-Pérez, A. (2024). Evolution and trends of the metaverse in business and management: A bibliometric analysis. *Review of Managerial Science*, •••, 1–26. DOI: 10.1007/s11846-024-00741-5

Ramadhan, A., Pradono Suryodiningrat, S., & Mahendra, I. (2023). The fundamentals of metaverse: A review on types, components and opportunities. *Journal of Information and Organizational Sciences*, 47(1), 153–165. DOI: 10.31341/jios.47.1.8

Rathore, B. (2018). Metaverse marketing: novel challenges, opportunities, and strategic approaches. *Eduzone: International Peer Reviewed/Refereed Multidisciplinary Journal, 7(2), 72-82.*

Rehm, S. V., Goel, L., & Crespi, M. (2015). The metaverse as mediator between technology, trends, and the digital transformation of society and business. *Journal of Virtual Worlds Research*, 8(2). Advance online publication. DOI: 10.4101/jvwr.v8i2.7149

Rosa, N. (2022). *Understanding the Metaverse: A Business and Ethical Guide*. John Wiley & Sons.

Rosário, A. T., Lopes, P. R., & Rosário, F. S. (2023). Metaverse in Marketing: Challenges and Opportunities. *Handbook of Research on AI-Based Technologies and Applications in the Era of the Metaverse, 204-227.*

Rosenstand, C. A. F. G., Brix, J., & Nielsen, C. (2023). Metaverse and Society 5.0: Pivotal for future business model innovation. *Journal of Business Models*, 11(3), 62–76. DOI: 10.54337/jbm.v11i3.8124

Saridakis, G., Khan, Z., Knight, G., Idris, B., Mitra, J., & Khan, H. (2024). A Look into the Future: The Impact of Metaverse on Traditional Theories and Thinking in International Business. *MIR. Management International Review*, 64(4), 597–632. DOI: 10.1007/s11575-024-00550-8

Setiawan, K. D., & Anthony, A. (2022, August). The essential factor of metaverse for business based on 7 layers of metaverse–systematic literature review. *In 2022 international conference on information management and technology (ICIMTech) (pp. 687-692). IEEE.*

Sridharan, A., & Kumar, S. (2024). The Impact of Metaverse on Businesses. In *The Metaverse Dilemma: Challenges and Opportunities for Business and Society* (pp. 13–30). Emerald Publishing Limited. DOI: 10.1108/978-1-83797-524-220241002

Stanoevska-Slabeva, K. (2022). Opportunities and challenges of metaverse for education: a literature review. *Edulearn22 Proceedings, 10401-10410.*

Tariq, M. U. (2024). Metaverse in Business and Commerce. In *Exploring the Use of Metaverse in Business and Education* (pp. 47–72). IGI Global. DOI: 10.4018/979-8-3693-5868-9.ch004

Weking, J., Desouza, K. C., Fielt, E., & Kowalkiewicz, M. (2023). Metaverse-enabled entrepreneurship. *Journal of Business Venturing Insights*, 19, e00375. DOI: 10.1016/j.jbvi.2023.e00375

Yaqoob, I., Salah, K., Jayaraman, R., & Omar, M. (2023). Metaverse applications in smart cities: Enabling technologies, opportunities, challenges, and future directions. *Internet of Things : Engineering Cyber Physical Human Systems*, 23, 100884. DOI: 10.1016/j.iot.2023.100884

Yawised, K., Apasrawirote, D., & Boonparn, C. (2022). From traditional business shifted towards transformation: *The emerging business opportunities and challenges in 'Metaverse'era.Incbaa*, 162, 175.

Yemenici, A. D. (2022). Entrepreneurship in the world of Metaverse: Virtual or real? *Journal of Metaverse*, 2(2), 71–82. DOI: 10.57019/jmv.1126135

Chapter 3
Growth of Small and Medium-Sized Enterprises in Africa:
Role of Artificial Intelligence Capabilities

Timilehin Olasoji Olubiyi
https://orcid.org/0000-0003-0690-7722
Babcock University, Ilishan-Remo, Nigeria

Muktar Monday Itai
https://orcid.org/0009-0005-4733-1346
Covenant University, Ota, Nigeria

ABSTRACT

The disruptive nature of the global pandemic and economic challenges on businesses has provided the need for a technological revolution and ensuring the availability of artificial intelligence (AI) capabilities for business growth, but less of it is acknowledged in small businesses. Therefore, this study examines the relationship between artificial intelligence (AI), innovation, employment, and growth of SMEs in Nigeria, Africa's largest consumer market. Principal component analysis (PCA) and the structural equation model (SEM) were adopted to examine the role of AI on SMEs growth in Southwest Nigeria. The study results showed that AI capabilities indicators have a positive relationship with SMEs growth. It was also observed that AI employment indicators exert a direct relationship with the latent factor. Overall results implications of the research is that the results offer a deeper insight for owners of SMEs, entrepreneurs, academic researchers and stakeholders to promote economic growth and development through adoption of artificial intelligence

DOI: 10.4018/979-8-3693-9005-4.ch003

1. INTRODUCTION

Small and medium enterprises (SMEs) have been recognized as a channel of economic growth globally. SMEs play a key role in creating employment, adding value, and contributing to innovation to national economies around the world (OECD, 2017c). According to World bank 2017 reports on alternative data transforming SME, they accounted for the main stream of the global businesses and are significant to overall economic development. They account for about 90 percent of businesses and more than 50 percent of employment globally. Formal SMEs contribute up to 40 percent of national income (GDP) in emerging economies. These numbers are considerably higher when informal SMEs are added. However, these contributions differ among firms, industries, and countries, but inadequate physical and technology tend to have prevented them from functioning optimally and accessing global markets at competitive costs (Mazur, 2012, EaP Green, 2016, Ritu, Chand, & Amit, 2023).

In Nigeria modern day business environment, it is not only challenging but full of intrigues that inhibits the full growth of SMEs (Anekwe, Ndubusi-Okolo, & Uzoezie, 2019; Bayode & Adebola, 2012). In a developing country like Nigeria, it requires continued growth in economies with special attention to the SMEs sector to harness employment generation, improved local technology and developed indigenous entrepreneurship. Regrettably, the SMEs in Nigeria have underachieved in spite of the fact that they constitute more than 90 percent of local businesses, but their impact to the nation's GDP is below 10 percent (see, Gbandi & Amis[1]sah, 2014; Ufual, Olujobi, Emielu, Ibidunni, Borisade, & Osabuohien, 2021).

However, the disruptive nature of the global pandemic on businesses has provided the need for digital transformation and ensuring the availability of AI solutions for SMEs growth to achieve long-term success (Travaly & Muvunyi, 2020; Ibidunni, Ufua, & Opute, 2021). It is alarming that despite the huge benefits of AI solutions technology, most Nigerian SMEs display attitudes that discourage its best practices and development (Ihesiene, & Akpojaro, 2015). Furthermore, it was speculated that many SMEs in Nigeria are either unwilling or slow at incorporating technology innovations and practices as shown by reduced rate of technology professional engagement, preference for contracting computer based non –professionals to drive technology role as well as infusion of technology units into other departments. This challenge highlights the focus of this study, which is on how to facilitate further integration of AI into the Nigerian SMEs sector.

The common fears are that AI portent threats to both highly-skilled service based (financial experts, legal work, medical care services) and low-skilled services (call agents in contact centres), with envisaging concern which may include unemployment and growing levels of disparity in future (Korinek & Stiglitz, 2017). The current AI literature has mirrored the nature of tradition form of unskilled and skilled employment (The World Bank,2019), is very essential to fathorn how innovation in technological advancement will impart entrepreneurs creative, cognitive and processes when starting new venture (Obschonka & Audretsch, 2019, Townsend & Hunt, 2019).

This study holds the opinion that the evolving forms of robotics, together with some of the strategic responses intended to countervail the social-economic effects, that will likely shift some of the fundamentals on which the prevailing concepts and practical expectations concerning entrepreneurship repose (Chalmers, MacKenzie, & Carter, 2021). AI presently is creating new, high-paying careers that require skill acquisition and replacing low skill workers (Mamudu & Mustapha, 2017). There are inadequate portions of information accessible in the literature that validate proves that AI technology offers new prospects that can lead to a remarkable transformation in businesses and the general economic system (Klosters, 2016, Sang-Chul. 2017, Klaus, 2017, Freddi, 2018).

At the industry and business level the immense benefits of AI include speedy introduction of configurations in big data, quick conception and analytics, improved service / product development, delivery of painstaking insights, and a lot more. The benefits are designed and projected to introduce new levels of service or product, increased profit, growth of businesses, enhanced cost efficiency and cost (Cockburn *et al*, 2019). SMEs growth effect of AI are well-known by various scholars across the world (Chen, *el.al,* 2016). These studies have been conducted in advanced economy, the identified implications and results are relevant for the future growth of SMEs in Nigeria as well as that of Africa. Accenture conducted a study involving 12 countries, in the developed economy, they established that the application of AI system could create more than double the growth of the world economy by 2035 (Daugherty & Purdy, 2016, Prakash, Yadav, Singh, & Yadav, 2021). This study aims at addressing the gap to gain by Nigeria SMEs in understanding the capability of artificial intelligence focusing on the following main objectives:

- examine the link between AI, innovation and growth of SMEs in Nigeria.
- determine impacts of Artificial Intelligence on employment and growth of SMEs in Nigeria.

The scope of the study covered SMEs in manufacturing, hospitality, information and communication, and administrative and support services sectors in the South West, Nigeria, Africa's largest consumer market.

2 LITERATURE REVIEW

Disruptive changes to business models today such as AI, advanced robotics, machine learning, and biotechnology will have a deep impact on the positioning of SMEs for efficiency and relevance over the coming years (PWC, 2020). Disruptive innovation is creating new lines of industries, business models, better ways of doing things and destroying old ones. Artificial Intelligence (AI) capabilities simply means machine learning, digital systems, including related automation in service delivery or production (Ibidduni et al, 2021). These include robotics, block-chain, augmented and virtual reality, internet of things, 3D printing, autonomous vehicle, drones among others. AI advancement has gone through three stages: a journey toward machine learning in the 1990s and early 2000s; a growth in the acceptance of neural networks in the early 2010s with full automation of speech recognition processing of data, images and the current development in strengthening learning in the past decade (Hao, 2019, Kumar, & Shukla, 2022). The concept of AI technology includes advance technology solutions that can address situation of uncertainty known as machine intelligence, is an intelligence validated by machines, in disparity to the natural intelligence shown by humans (Žigiene, Rybakovas, & Alzbutas, 2019). AI enables a machine to think like humans and has developed to be very known in today's business environment. It is the stimulation of normal intelligence in machines that are programmed to learn and imitate the actions man. These machines are able to acquire with experience and execute human-like tasks with accuracy and efficiency (Kitsios, & Kamariotou, 2021).

The AI applications are now being deployed in private and public sectors globally. Many countries are already addressing the issues and leveraging on the benefits from this evolving technology. Whereas, there is no generally established definition of Artificial Intelligence, Nilsson (2010) stated that AI is that set of activities dedicated to making machine intelligent and intelligence is that process that enables an entity to function optimally and with foresight in its environment. Today machine understand human speech, driving cars, competing in strategic game system, or interpreting complex data that are currently considered to be AI applications. Many Africa governments have started to take deliberate actions to endorse the development of AI in their respective country. For instance, the Nigeria government has started to support and engage partnerships and stakeholder on the road map to AI development. The Minister in charge of Science and Technology pronounced the creation of the National Agency for Research in Robotics and AI. The centre will partner with international research bodies and improve training on Artificial Intelligence (AI) themes for students and schools, also to stimulate Nigeria's capability to ride on these technologies for economic development (Access Partnership, 2019; Gwagwa, Kraemer-Mbula· Rizk· Rutenberg· & de Beer, 2020).

In March 2018, Adebayo Shittu, former Minister of Communications reaffirmed the government position to support artificial intelligence stakeholders. In the same vein in October 24, 2020 during the first edition of Digital Nigeria Day (DND) held by the Federal Ministry of Communications and Digital Economy at the NCC's Communications and Digital Economy Complex, Mbora, Abuja Nigeria (NCC, 2020; UNESCO 2019).

2.1 Artificial Intelligence Innovation for SMEs

In a world in which just-in-time delivery is the standard, AI innovation will be a game changer for SMEs competitiveness. Innovation comprise the change of new knowledge into new products or service and putting the new product or service into use, either at market or by other means of delivery (Trott, 3005). AI allows SMEs to be innovative, attain scale without mass and access global markets and knowledge networks at relatively low cost (OECD, 2015b). The digital evolution facilitates new opportunities for SMEs growth and enable them to compete in local and global markets, through service or product innovation and improved process delivery. It also facilitates the emergence of lean start-ups that leverage on internet at lower fixed costs and outsources of many segment of the business to stay agile and response to the market timely (OECD, 2018e; Ufua, Olujobi,Tahir, Okafor, Imhonopi, & Osabuohien, 2022).

In an era of AI, SMEs can turn their business into a competitive advantage by being innovative, creative and foster alliances with firms by providing real-time solutions to problems in every sector

(Edmund, Christopher, & Zeman, 2020). SMEs are amenable, flexible, and fast adapting to changes towards efficiency (Sen, Doruk, Melike Ozturk, &Ozalp Vay-vay. 2016). Before the introduction of machine learning, the transfer of knowledge-intensive tasks and functions in the business process to computer systems was limited to explicit knowledge (Edmund, *et al*, 2020). AI now enables SMEs to go further than their present state of knowledge base and able to advance more creative innovative solutions and recognise more opportunities in the global market (Amabile, 2019; von Krogh, 2018). With rapid technological development and the replacement of human organisation, AI reshapes and compel SMEs to rethink the company's processes through innovations. (Haefner et al, 2021). The central premise is that AI can deliver better quality, higher speed, more efficiency, and outstanding outcomes than human experts (Agrawal, *el.at*. 2018a).

McKinsey (2018) predicts a potential contribution of 1.2 percentage points to global GDP growth by 2030, while Purdy and Daugherty (2017) study forecasts an increase of 2 percentage points in annual global gross value added by the year 2035. These contextual call for a robust model where innovative oriented AI and machine learning of management information system and processes can be integrated into innovation management for SMEs development in Nigeria. With AI advancement, it is revealed that the innovation management and machine learning role will change and step up progressively. The human management is anticipated to function side by side with the AI and machine learning algorithms in in cartigorising and choosing opportunities as well examining what could be the organisation's competitive advantage in the global market (Haefner et al, 2021).

2.2 Artificial Intelligence Employment Creation for SMEs

In the entire human race today no part of the world is left from the impact of technology, either it is AI or internet of things (IoT), in every area of life humans have been dependent on machine (Sahil & Anupam 2019). Whereas some jobs will be jettisoned additional jobs will be transformed that will need changed sets of skill. Others may require completely creating new jobs. Various careers and profession will continue to demand distinctive skills that AI and technology cannot reproduce such as creativity, complex communication, partnership, system thinking and talent to work in complex environment (see, Ufua, Salau, Saleem, Ogbari, Osibanjo, Osabuohien, & Adeniji, 2022). Introduction of new technology has always been attended by caveats about job loss syndrome. However, in many situation new technologies have been lots of more specific, significant and skillful jobs as reported (Microsoft, 2018). Tomorrow work and workforce will depend on the sense of balance between technology and labour – allowing flexible allocation of resources on task that requires routine recurrence. The effect of technology on labour will depends on how the shift and efficiency affect each other (Accemoglu & Restrepo, 2019, Ibrahim, & Sarolta, 2022).

EY study in 2017 found out that in the next decade the skill of personnel that will be employed in the in the new jobs do not exist today. These jobs of the future will be altered and will requires fundamentally changed skillsets. Repetitive tasks will gradually be performed with the support process driven by AI, that is, work force will be more productive (EY, 2017). This infers continues change but also a tireless need for human labour, even in very automated nackgrounds. Machine replacement for labour increases efficiency, productivity, quality delivery and minimizes the cost of goods and services. Although not always the case, and not forever have the influence of increasing employment in these same sectors (Bessen, 2017b; McKinsey Global Institute, 2017). Accenture in their recent report identified completely new sets of careers that are evolving in businesses engaging AI as part of their process (Accenture Plc, 2017). These professions consist of trainers and mentors (facilitate the AI systems), explainers and translators (explain and communicate the result of

AI system to customers, and sustainers (monitor the performance of AI system, including following the fundamentals and ethical standards) (Olujobi, Yebisi 2022),

AI in Nigeria would create jobs and expand job growth (Victor, 2019). According to Adewoye (2019), there exist diverse schools of thoughts surrounding AI deployment in the work force. While some of school of thoughts believe that AI will not necessarily generate unemployment but will cause a major shift in the ways and dynamics of the work force operations in future, others believes that AI will adversely affect the nature of jobs that will be accessible to the work force, as it might result in the workplace existence, especially persons who the essential skills to relate with the operating system and the use of the internet. Nigeria and Africa's artificial intelligence can largely improve making decisions by breaking down huge amounts of a dataset which can give rise to the discovery of new products, services, market, and industry by the improving consumer interest that will spawn additional income flow in Africa (Obi, 2020).

2.3 Small and Medium-Sized Enterprises (SMEs) Development in Nigeria

Globally there is no clear definition of SMEs. However, according to the European Commission's, SMEs are firms that have less than 250 employees or that generate up to 50 million euros in annual turnover (EC 2017a). In Nigerian SMEs are business owners or entrepreneurs with capacity of workers ranges between 10 to 199 employees, who are involved in day to day businesses with the sole aim of their personal desire and profit (Abdul, 2019, SMEDAN, 2013). In Nigeria, according to Agwu and Emeti, 2014, SMEs are widely accepted as keys to economic prosperity and sustainability. Both SMEs and entrepreneurship are recognised worldwide as the mainstay of any economy (Okyere,2017). SMEs are entreprenuers who are very insightful to their immediate environment to see opportunities and turn around threats to make a difference toward economic and social benefits (Rey-Marti, Ribeiro-Soriano, & Sanchez-Garcia, 2016; Miller & Le Breton-Miller, 2017).

The report of the Nigerian Bureau of Statistics stated that SMEs in Nigeria accounted for a total of 17.4 million, about 48.5 percent of the national GDP in the last 5 years (PwC,2020). The same report also stated that about 50 percent of the industrial jobs and nearly 90 percent of the manufacturing sector in terms of the number of enterprises (PwC,2020).

The necessity of entrepreneurship in reducing poverty, employment creation and development of the economy is universal (Adeosun & Shittu, 2021). The Nigerian government, SMEs encounter enormous challenges ranging from inconsistency in government policies, harassment and extortion by the uniformed officers, lack of support from some government agencies that were supposed to assist (Tejumade,

2015; Ufua, Olujobi, Tahir, Al-Faryan, Matthew, & Osabuohien, 2022). According to Akerejola, Okpara, Ohikhena, and Emenike (2019), in spite of the repeated and supports by the Nigeria government to SMEs, they still encounter several challenges described as the Nigeria factors. Others problems include absence of a workable policy structure and inadequate infrastructure to drive SMEs creation and growth strategies in Nigeria (Victor, Christopher, & Ignatius,2019)

2.4 Small and Medium Scale Enterprise Growth

Nigerians essential need employment opportunities to make a living. SME is relevance in this regards in creating employment, production of goods and services in a fast growing economy (Adeosun & Shittu, 2021). Nwugballa, Elom, and Onyeizugbe, (2016) reported that SMEs contribute up to 75 percent total employment level in Nigeria. In the vein, according to Ajibola (2020), SMEs contribute to economic development and generate about 80 percent of jobs in Nigeria. In developing countries over 50 percent of jobs are created by SMEs, they also dominate the private sector in the same economies (Lorenz & Pommet, 2018). Although significant growth has been recorded in the SMEs space, much is still required to be done, which justifies the intention of this study, focused on AI and SMEs growth in Nigeria.

3 THEORETICAL FRAMEWORK ON SMALL AND MEDIUM SIZED ENTERPRISES GROWTH

The underpinning theory for this study is the Peter Drucker propounded opportunity–based theory. Stevenson (1990), expanded the theory by building in creativity and resourcefulness into the theory. Stevenson established that SMEs seek to take advantage of every opportunity without taking care of currently resources within the control of the entrepreneur. The theory state that SMEs do not cause change deliberately rather they take advantage of the opportunities created because of technology changes. Drucker (1985), defines entrepreneur as an individual who seek for change, reacts to the change and thrive to exploits the opportunities. The theory of Opportunity-based entrepreneurship is connected to creative accomplishment that have the impact to generate employment and enhance productivities in any economy (Stenholm, Acts, & Wuebker, 2013). An entrepreneur starts with opportunities available in the environment. These opportunities are new concepts that variety of goods, services, raw materials and organizing stages can be presented and executed in a market place (Casson, 1982, Share & Venkatarantan, 2000). Opportunity-based entrepreneurs commence a business with quest for growth, innovation, profit and personal desires (Cullen, Parbotech, &Johnson, 2014, McMullen, Palich, & Bagby, 2008, Renuka & Anju, 2023), Sara, Dejan, Amadeja, & Anja, 2024)

3.1 Empirical Review of AI Capabilities on SMEs Growth.

The policy drivers and SMEs in Nigeria, have recognised the significance of AI. The changes in AI innovation on the SMEs growth in the Nigeria space showed that the relationship between AI innovation (product and process) and SMEs growth in terms of firms' turnover is significantly high (Akinwale, Adepoju & Olomu, 2017). Against this background, the study examined previous work on the use of AI by SMEs. In their study Haefner, Wincent, Parida, and Gassmann, (2021), found out that AI and innovation management had helped SMEs firms having challenges with data processing restraints as they seek for new opportunities. For instance, where the growth of new innovations is primarily hindered by information management processing constraints, AI had resolved the concern effortlessly. AI acquisition and SMEs performance showed that the level of innovation and export longevity positively and substantially affect sales out of firms (Edmund, Christopher, & Zeman, 2020).

In Ogun state, Nigeria, the use of AI by small and medium enterprises revealed that demographic variable such staff capability and knowledge significantly influences its uses among SMEs (Oyebiyi, 2019). In their findings (Chalmers, MacKenzie & Carter, 2021) AI and SMEs growth in the Fourth Industrial Revolution 4.0 enhances entrepreneurial obligations, accomplishment that has its root from technological influence. On the employment space of AI on SMEs, PwC department of business, energy and industrial strategy (BEIS) report showed that the United Kingdom's employment and the demand for skills recommend that AI and its allied technologies is very key in productive and real income levels, advancing UK GDP by up to 10 percent by 2030. Whereas in China, effects of AI on employment in the short-run is more destructive, however, in the long-run it create new employment opportunities (Ping & Ying, 2018)

The focus today is to investigate the progressive phases of the technological advancement a aggressively rather than having a flaccid approach toward it. In their study the Royal Society and the British Academy 2018, provided evidences that AI have meaningfully impacted over and above the function of trade libralisation. It further indicated that AI in the work place is related with increasing polirisation of work between tasks mostly executed by workers with low level of formal education and task performed by highly educated employees. Overall employment has not declined, however, there have been changes from manufacturing to service industry across geographical areas, and loss of income for low educated workers. Individual losses from job displacement connected to automation have not yet be appraised but a wider literature suggested that these losses can be significant.

Developing countries such as Nigeria are generally not included in the empirical analyses. However, the available studies in emerging economies reveal significant effect by AI and that the labour-saving impact of these new technologies might be even more pronounced than in the developed economies. Nonetheless, Nigeria SMEs have what it takes to stimulate development and growth by utilising the AI to enrich the nation's economy and her citizens.

4 METHODOLOGY

The study focused on SMEs growth in South West, Nigeria. Data were collected from SMEs firms to determine AI innovation and employment on SMEs growth. The questionnaire was adapted. The population of the study consist of 2,000 SMEs firms engaging in manufacturing, hospitality, information and communication, and administrative and support services sectors. The choice of South West, Nigeria is because it has the highest number of SMEs in Nigeria, the National Bureau of Statistics (2017).

The sample size of 322 is obtained from Krejcie & Morgan research table (1970) of a population size of 2,000. This number is considered a fair representation of the entire population (Saunders, Lewis &Thornhill, 2011). A response rate of 282 were received accounting for 88% questionnaire retrieved, of the selected SMEs firms in South West, Nigeria. Data were collected through the distribution of structured questionnaire administered.

The study applied principal component analysis (PCA) and the structural equation model (SEM) to examine the role of artificial intelligence on SMEs growth in South West, Nigeria. In the study PCA was employed as a data reduction approach in measuring the items that significantly explain the latent construct indicators. Also, employed in this study is the variance extract from the commonalities analysis (Table 2) which serve to provide us with the loading scores of the items measured. Items loaded above average is considered relevant in the construct measurement. The validity and reliability of the process was established through the Kaise-Meye Oklin sampling adequacy (KMO) statistics and the Bartlett's Test for structure detection (Table1). Based on the Chi-square normality distribution and BTS high level of significance, the factors indicators with their respective loaded items were considered valid and credible for conducting this research (Rana & Singahi, 2015).

The second aspect of the data analysis involved the application of the SEM technique for the measurement and structural model analysis. In the measurement model the construct indicators were analyzed based on the data reduction result from the principal component outcome (Figure1). The variance-covariance result was examined through the measurement model and the test for multi-collinearity.

This helps us to verify the no-existence of significance interferences among the construct's indicators involved in the SMEs growth model analysis. Path analysis (Figure2) was further utilized to determine the direction, magnitude and significant of the relations among artificial intelligence AI. In this process, the estimates, standard error (S.E), coefficient ratio (C.R), significance level (P) and the regression weights (Label) in line with the structural model were employed (Table3).

5 RESULTS AND DISCUSSION

The analysis of the impact of AI on SMEs growth was carried out using principal factor analysis and structural equation model (SEM) approach. The factor analysis focuses on the principal factor analysis (PCA) while the SEM involved the measurement model and the structural path.

Table 1. Validity and Reliability Tests

Sampling Adequacy measure			**Bartlett's Test of Sphericity**	
Factors	**KMO**	**Approx. Chi-Square**	**DF**	**P-value**
AI Adoption	0.783	460.891	10	0.000
AI Innovation	0.846	474.815	10	0.000
AI Employment	0.592	246.243	10	0.000
SME Growth	0.596	132.190	10	0.000

In Table 1, The Kaiser-Meyer-Olklin statistic measure of sampling adequacy (KMO; 0.783; 0.846; 0.592 &0.596) and Bartlett's test of sphericity (BTS:460.891, P-value<0.01; 474.815, P-value<0.01; 246.243, P-value<0.01 & 132.190, P-value<0.01) were utilized in testing for the proportion of variance in the variables that could be as a result of underlying factors. The results respectively attest to the suitability of the factors- AI-adoption, AI innovation, AI employment and SME growth for structure detection. The validity and reliability results show that the exists significant proportion of variance in the AI and SME factors that could be attributed to latent factors. The reliability test shows the items are consistent and suitable for structure detection analysis.

5.1 Principal Component Analysis

In the analytical process of this study, 3 factors were used to measure artificial intelligence (AI) comprising of AI adoption (AI_ADP), AI innovation (AI_INN) and AI employment growth (AI_EMPG) and SME growth (SMEG) as the higher order factor. The principal component analysis (PCA) was employed in the data reduction approach to ascertain the items that constitute significance variance explained in measuring artificial intelligence (AI) and SME growth factors.

Five items were used in measuring AI adoption which consist of service operations (SEOP) predictive service intervention (PSIN), customer service analytics (CSEA), new AI-based enhancement of products and services, (NAI_BEPS) and fraud and debts analysis (FRDS). The result from the variance extracts (SEOP, 0.590); (PSIN, 0.765); (CSEA, 0.680); (NA_BEPS, 0.526) and (FRDA; 0.231) shows that all the items measuring AI adoption loaded above average score with the exception of FRDA.

Table 2. Items Loadings

AI ADOPTION	**Variance Extraction**
SEOP	0.590
PSIN	0.765
CSEA	0.680
NAI_BEPS	0.526
FRDA	0.231
AI INNOVATION	
PRCIN	0.731
PSEIN	0.832
INFTEC	0.746
INFRDEV	0.796
COLWO	0.770
AI-EMPLOYMENT	
DEFNS	0.717
JCEF	0.788
JDEF	0.823
NEMEF	0.579
FSDS	0.331
SME GROWTH	

continued on following page

Table 2. Continued

AI ADOPTION	Variance Extraction
CSAVS	0.613
INREV	0.591
DEREV	0.635
PRSRS	0.676
RRASC	0.468

AI innovation was measured with five items comprising of process innovation (PRCIN), product or service innovation (PSEIN), information technology (INFTECH), infrastructural development (INFRDEV) and collaboration with others (COLWO). The analysis of the item loadings for the factor (PRCIN,0.731; PSEIN, 0.832; INFTEC, 0.746; INFRDEV, 0.796 and COLWO, 0.770) indicates that all the item measures of AI innovation were well loaded above average.

AI employment was measured with items consisting of demand for new skills (DEFNS), job creation effect (JCEF), job displacement effect (JDEF), net employment effect (NEMEF) and future skills demand (FSDS) while the factor items for SME growth comprises of cost of savings (CSAVS), increase in revenue (INREV), decrease in revenue (DEREV), prospects remain strong (PRSRS) and the items that measured that risks remain an area of significant concern (RRASC). Evidence from the variance extract (DEFNS, 0.717; JCEF, 0.788; JDEF, 0.823; NEMEF, 0.579 and FSDS, 0.331) shows a high variance explained by the individual items beyond 50 percent average except for FSDS. This evidence shows that majority of the measured items predominantly explained AI employment.

SME growth is measured using cost savings (CSAVS), increase in revenue (INREV), decrease in revenue (DEREV), prospects remain strong (PRSRS) and risk remains an area of significant concern (RRASC). The analysis of the item loadings (CSAVS, 0.613; INREV, 0.591; DEREV, 0.635; PSSRS, 0.676 and RRASC, 0.468) shows a relatively high loaded items above average except for RRASC. Notably all items variance of 0.50 and above (Table1) in this study were employed in further analysis in structural equation modelling in the structural model and measurement with exclusion of items whose loaded weights fail below average.

The study applied the structural equation modeling (SEM) approach involving the measurement model (Figure 1) in its to factor analysis. Having identified the loading scores, the items with extraction scores above 50 percent average were utilized in latent factor measurement model of SEM. As shown in figure 1, AI- adoption, AI employment and SME growth were measured with four items while AI innovation was measured with five items all loaded above average.

5.2 Covariance Analysis

In the measurement model (Figure1), it is observed that all the factors measured were not significantly correlated among themselves. Hence, there is no problem of multicollinearity among all the factors considered in this study. The covariance scores (Cov) between AI adoption and the following factors; AI_INN (Cov =0.13); AI_EMPG (Cov =0.09); and SMEG (Cov =0.12) were not significant. Likewise, there is no significant covariance between AI_INN and the following AI_EMPG (Cov =0.09); SMEG (Cov =0.14) and between AI_EMPG and SMEG (Cov =0.15). This shows the factor measures were all independent and uncorrelated in the SEM measurement model. The rule of thumb for the decision rule is explained by the construct correlation coefficients less than 0.50-point estimate.

Figure 1. Measurement Model (2024)

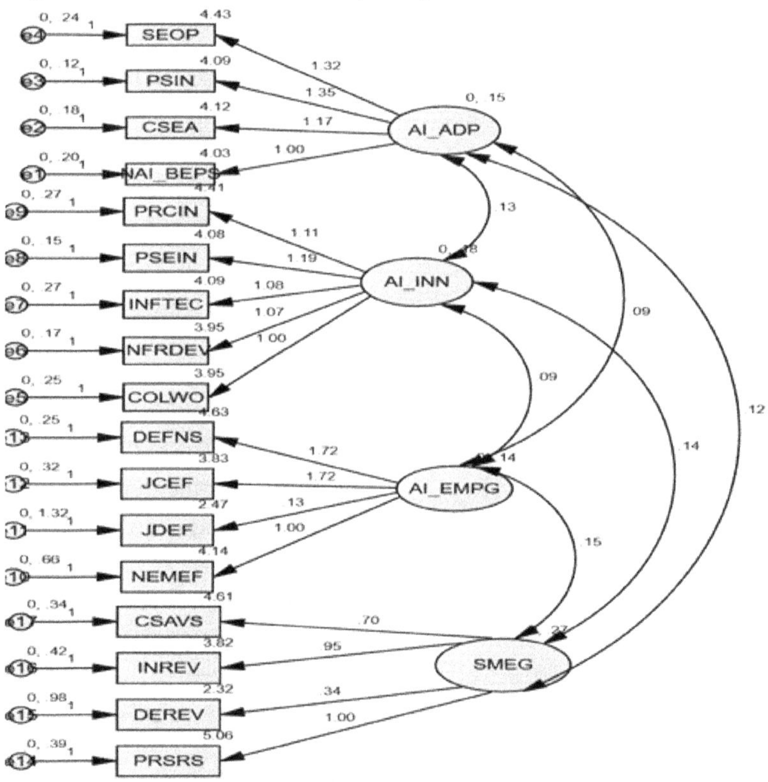

5.2.2Regression Weights of Factor Indicators

In the AI adoption factor analysis, AI based enhanced products and services was the referenced item. The result of the regression weights (W) shows that service operations (SEOP) predictive service intervention (PSIN), customer service analytics (CSEA), new artificial intelligence-based enhancement of products and services, (NAI_BEPS) all exerted positive and more than a unit effect on AI adoption. The result of regression scores between AI adoption and its measurement items indicates a positive relationship for all the indicators. It is seen that CSEA, PSIN and SEOP respectively improved AI-adoption by 1.17, 1.35 and 1.32 times compared to NAI_BEPS. This implies that all the item measures AI adoption were all positively related with the factor while predictive service intervention accounted for the highest influence on AI adoption in SME growth.

In the case of AI innovation, the reference category refers to the item in the research instrument measuring collaborations with others. The estimated regression weights show that INFRDEV, INFTEC, PSEIN and PRCIN individually enhanced AI innovation by 1.07, 1.08, 1.19 and 1.11 times in relation to COLWO. It is also notable that all the AI innovation indicators suggests a positive relationship with the construct. A detailed analysis of the indicator's regression weights shows the product and service innovative indicator as the most substantive aspect of AI_INN that enhances small and medium scale enterprise growth.

Using net employment effect (NEMEF) for the reference category in the construct measurement for AI employment growth, it observed that all the construct indicators exert a direct relationship with the latent factor. Specifically, JDEF, JCEF and DEFNS promoted AI_EMPG by 0.13, 1.72 and 1.72 times compared with NEMEF. The demand for new skills in labour market and job creation effect of AI utilization accounted for the most notable enhancement in AI employment.

In the measurement of SME growth, the item measure for prospects of AI promotion of SME growth remaining strong (PRSRS) was the referenced variable. The evidence from the regression weights indicates less proportionate influence on SME growth. The deeper interpretation of the results shows that DEREV, INREV and CSAVS increased SMEG by 0.34, 0.95 and 0.70 times given the fact that there are prospects for AI induced SME growth in the future. Thus, the indicator for increased revenue measurement suffices as the most dominant influencer of SMEs enter growth traceable to AI employment factor in the present study model.

Figure 2. Structural Model

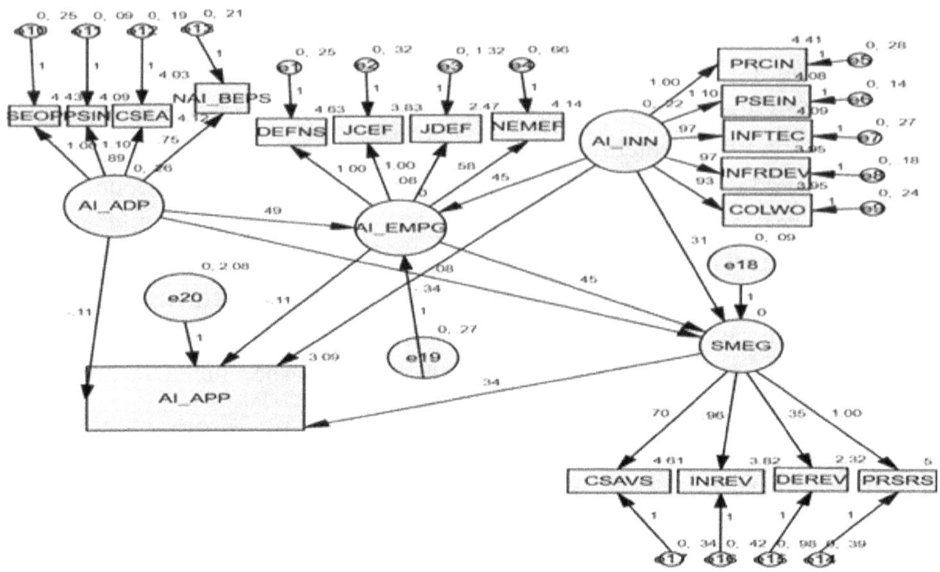

Figure 2 shows the structural part of the SEM model that examined the transmission channels through AI construct measures influence of SMEs growth employing both the direct, indirect and total effect model in analytical procedure. Having considered the measurement model, the study proceeds to examine the diverse roles of AI construct indicators on SME growth through regression analysis involving interaction model effect.

5.2.4 Direct Effects

In the analysis of the artificial intelligence and SME growth (Table3), it is seen that AI_ADP regression weight (W= 0.489; P-value <0.01) and AI_INN (W = 0.453; P-value <0.01) exerted a direct influence on AI_EMPG and an indirect influence on SMEG through AI_EMPG. The regression weights for AI_INN (W=0.311: P-value <0.01); AI_EMPG (0.453: P-value <0.01) and AI_ADP (0.075: P-value >0.1) on SMEG shows that AI innovation and employment significantly improved SME growth while the reverse is the case for AI adoption.

Table 3.Direct Effects of AI on SME growth

Constructs and indicators			Estimate	S.E.	C.R.	P	Label
AI_EMPG	<---	AI_INN	0.453	.098	4.625	***	W14
AI_EMPG	<---	AI_ADP	0.489	.091	5.380	***	W17
SMEG	<---	AI_INN	0.311	.090	3.449	***	W15
SMEG	<---	AI_EMPG	0.453	.092	4.936	***	W16
SMEG	<---	AI_ADP	0.075	.080	.937	.349	W22
Demand_ for_ new_ skills	<---	AI_EMPG	1.000				
Job_ creation_ effect	<---	AI_EMPG	.997	.109	9.116	***	W1
Job_ displacement_ effect	<---	AI_EMPG	.078	.129	.603	.546	W2
Net_ employment_ effect	<---	AI_EMPG	.583	.101	5.759	***	W3
Process_ innovation	<---	AI_INN	1.000				
Product_ or_ service_ Innovation	<---	AI_INN	1.098	.102	10.760	***	W4
Information_ Technology	<---	AI_INN	.974	.106	9.222	***	W5
Infrastructural_ development	<---	AI_INN	.969	.096	10.095	***	W6
Collaboration _with_ others	<---	AI_INN	.930	.100	9.342	***	W7
Service_ operations	<---	AI_ADP	1.000				
Predictive_ service_ intervention	<---	AI_ADP	1.097	.090	12.125	***	W8
Customer_ service_ analytics	<---	AI_ADP	.891	.082	10.856	***	W9
AI_ Enhanced_ product_ service	<---	AI_ADP	.751	.078	9.649	***	W10
Prospects_ remain_ strong	<---	SMEG	1.000				
Decrease_ in_ revenue	<---	SMEG	0.349	.155	2.257	.024	W11
Increase_ in_ revenue	<---	SMEG	0.960	.147	6.513	***	W12

continued on following page

Table 3. Continued

Constructs and indicators			Estimate	S.E.	C.R.	P	Label
Cost_ savings	<---	SMEG	0.700	.117	5.962	***	W13
AI_ Applications	<---	AI_ADP	-0.113	.218	-.520	.603	W18
AI_ Applications	<---	AI_EMPG	-0.108	.335	-.324	.746	W19
AI_ Applications	<---	AI_INN	-0.337	.276	-1.221	.222	W20
AI_ Applications	<---	SMEG	0.335	.509	.659	.510	W21

Although AI adoption (W= -0.113; P-value>0.05), employment (W= -0.108: P-value >0.05) and innovation (W= -0.337; P-value >0.5) is inversely related to AI usage they are not statistically significant while SME growth (W=0.335; P-value>0.05) is supportive of AI usage but not significant. Hence, it is observed that SME growth factor accounted for the positive relationship with AI applications. Notably, it is seen that though AI innovation and adoption enhances AI employment growth, these indicators have not enhanced the effective utilization of AI applications is apparently not significant and retarded in SME business activities. This further points to the high cost involved in the procurement and maintenance of AI- enabled applications particularly in the area of small and medium scale operations.

In the construct analysis of AI-EMPG, DEFNS represented the referenced variable while JCEF (W=0.997; P-value <0.01) regression weight was positively strong and significant. The results for JDEF (W=0.078: P-value >0.1) and NEMEF (W=0.583: P-value<0.01) shows that both indicators accounted for 0.08 and 0.58 times increase in AI employment compared to the demands for new skills though job displacement effect was insignificant. This implies that AI induced job creation and net employment effect explained the highest variation in AI employment thus confirming the earlier result from the measurement model.

For the AI innovation, the analysis of regression weights associated with PSEIN (1.098; P-value <0.01), INFTEC (0.974; P-value <0.01), INFRDEV (0.969; P-value <0.01) and COLWO (0.930; P-value<0.01) indicates that these indicators respectively increased AI innovation by 1.10, 0.97, 0.97, and 0.93 times relative to process innovation. It also informative of the fact that product and service innovation had the highest contributory effect from the list of AI innovative indicators that have influenced the promotion of SME growth culminating to improved usage of AI applications for economic growth and development. The indicators are statistically significant and positively contributed AI innovation at 1 percent level.

In the structural model, the analysis of AI adoption indicators with the referenced category (SEOP) indicates that PSIN (1.097; P-value <0.01), CSEA (0.891; P-value <0.01), and NAI_BEPS (0.751; P-value <0.01), significantly increased AI adoption by 1.097, 0.891 and 0.751 times in relation to SEOP with predictive service intervention accounting for the highest contribution to AI adoption in SME growth. In terms of SME growth, the estimated coefficient of DEREV (W=0.349; P-value<0.05), INREV (W=0.960: P-value <0.01) and CSAVS (W=0.700; P-value <0.01) with PRSRS as the referenced item suggests that cost of savings, increase revenue and decrease revenue significantly increased SMEG growth by 0.70, 0.96 and 0.35 times in relation to the fact that prospects remain strong for SME growth.

AI adoption (W= -0.113; P-value>0.05), employment (W= -0.108: P-value >0.05) and innovation (W= -0.337; P-value >0.05)

is inversely related to AI usage they are not statistically significant while SME growth (W=0.335; P-value>0.05) is supportive of AI usage but not significant. Hence, it is observed that SME growth factor accounted for the positive relationship with AI applications. Notably, it is seen that though AI innovation and adoption enhances AI employment growth, these indicators have not enhanced the effective utilization of AI applications is apparently not significant and retarded in SME business activities. This further points to the high cost involved in the procurement and maintenance of AI- enabled applications particularly around small and medium scale operations.

5.2.4.1 Indirect Effects

The analysis of the indirect effect of AI_INN (0.205) and AI_ADP (0.221) on SMEG (Table4) shows a mediation effect on SMEG through the AI_EMPG channel in line with the Druncker (1985) and Stevenson (1990) opportunity-based theory which also informed the theoretical base of the present study discussed in the previous section of this work.

Table 4. Indirect Effects

Construct and indicators	AI_INN	AI_ADP	AI_EMPG	SMEG
AI_EMPG	0.000	0.000	0.000	0.000
SMEG	.205	.221	0.000	0.000
AI_Applications	.124	.046	.152	0.000
Cost_savings	.362	.208	.317	0.000
Increase_in_revenue	.496	.285	.435	0.000
Decrease_in_revenue	.181	.104	.158	0.000
Prospects_remain_strong	.517	.296	.453	0.000

In its present contextualization and operationalization, the entrepreneur maximizes the opportunities and changes induced by AI innovation and adoption to harness AI employment in a bid to increase economic activities that will foster significant growth within the small and medium enterprises' framework.

In Table4 it is also pertinent to note that AI_INN and AI_ADP indirectly enhanced SMEG by 0.205 and 0.221 percent. AI INN, AI ADP and AI_EMPG respectively improved AI usage by 0.124, 0.046 and 0.152 percent. These AI indicators indirectly accounted for the respective 0.362, 0.208 and 0.317 percent increases in cost savings. AI innovation, adoption and employment individually increased revenue by 0.496, 0.285 and 0.317 percent and also contributed for a 0.181, 0.104 and 0.158 percent decline in revenue.

This could be explained by high initial cost of AI procurement and installations which would consequently decrease revenue generation in the short-run, though increased revenue outweighs the perceived decrease. However, AI_INN, AI_ADP and AI_EMPG respectively increased prospects in SME growth by 0.517, 0.296 and 0.453 percent while AI employment growth constituted the mediated channel through SME growth was improved by the artificial intelligence indicators.

5.2.4.3 Total Effects

The total effect result (Table 5) shows the combined interaction effect (direct and indirect) of artificial intelligence indicators on SMEs growth through AI enabled employment growth opportunity. This further reaffirmed the existence of Druncker (1985) and Stevenson (1990) opportunity-based theory which in this context fortressed the AI induced growth opportunity that provides a veritably transmission channel for small and medium scale enterprise investors to maximize in order to grow their businesses as a veritable business risk adventure. The analysis of the total effect of AI_INN and AI_ADP shows a total increase of 0.453 and 0.489 percent on AI employment growth.

Deeper insight from the result shows that AI_INN and AI_ADP increased SMEs business growth by 0.517 and 0.296 from 0.453and 0.075 while AI_EMPG maintained a 0.453 percent increase in SMEs growth being the transmission channel of opportunity maximized by SMEs investors in driving their business growth and expansion through AI induced employment growth. However, with the exception of the retarded total effect in AI applications it is pertinent to portress the fact that direct, indirect and total effect of AI construct indicators remain the same for SMEs growth indicators given the fact that the mediated role of AI induced employment growth was estimated on the construct level.

Table 5. Total Effects

Construct and indicators	AI_INN	AI_ADP	AI_EMPG	SMEG
AI_EMPG	.453	.489	.000	.000
SMEG	.517	.296	.453	.000
AI_Applications	-.213	-.067	.043	.335
Cost_savings	.362	.208	.317	.700
Increase_in_revenue	.496	.285	.435	.960
Decrease_in_revenue	.181	.104	.158	.349
Prospects_remain_strong	.517	.296	.453	1.000

This same result also applies to the influence of the SME growth on its indicators involving cost of savings, increase in revenue, decrease in revenue and its sustainability of strong prospects in the future. (Olujobi, Olarinde, Yebisi, Okorie, 2022).

Table 6.Diagnostic Tests of Model Fit and Parsimony

Fitness Index	ECVI	RMSEA	NFI	CFI	NCP
Model	2.153	0.099; 90% CI	0.738	0.788	351.895
Cut-off values	1.927-2.406	0.09-0.1; 90% CI	0.370- 0.990	0.370- 0.990	288.593-422.771

Structural equation modelling refers to a comprehensive set of technique used to examine systems of equation often involving latent variables. In a situation where the mean structural of the model has no constraint the model parameter of the model could be analyzed through the covariance structure approach. This involves minimizing a discrepancy function between the sample (observed) covariance matrix and the model implied (fitted) covariance matrix. In this study the discrepancy function is concerned with the normal distribution theory of the maximum likelihood (ML) discrepancy function. In the diagnostic test, the SEM result in this study was further tested for the 'significancy' of this discrepancy in relation to the baseline and hypothesized model. A notable unstandardized size effect of model misfit is the root mean square error of approximation (RMSEA; Browne & Cudek, 1992, 1993; Steiger, 1980, 1990, Maydeu-Olivares, 2017a). The RMSEA (0.099) indicates the rejection of the null hypothesis of model overall misfit. The comparative fit index (CFI; 0.788) was utilized for the baseline comparison model test which shows that the implied model is statistically significant. The expected cross validation index (ECVI; 2.153) attests to the parsimony of the estimated model. The non-centrality parameter (NCP;351.895) indicates the result fall within the lower and upper bound test of acceptability. The parsimony of the model and the goodness of it measures and their respective cut-off values are presented in Table 6. According to the suggested bench marks, all the fit indices accept the hypothesized model.

6. CONCLUSION AND POLICY IMPLICATIONS

In spite of the increasing concerns of implications of automation for the future of work space, artificial intelligence AI is believed to have strong potential growth on SMEs. The results from the study clearly shown that a deliberate adoption of artificial intelligence by SMEs and entrepreneurs and their capability will be a game changer in future competitiveness. A deeper insight from the result showed that applications of AI construct indicators remain (direct, indirect and total effect) strong on SMEs growth. The understanding of sceptics regarding automation sometimes wrongly interpret that AI will steal jobs is not completely true. On the contrary that AI will eliminate number of some jobs and subsequently unemployment, the study showed that more jobs will be altered that need diverse skill of personnel, as completely new jobs will be created as result of AI. In addition, jobs will continue to necessitate outstanding human skills that AI cannot altered such as creativity, partnership, complex communication, skill to work in multifaceted environment. The initial assertions that SMEs in Nigeria are either unwilling or slow at integrating effective AI innovations and practices now shown from the concluding result of the study remain seasonable and robust. Policy implications among others is that regulatory institutions should build capacity to monitor and enforce the extant laws, regulations and policies to promote Artificial Intelligence utilization and capabilities building by SMEs to promote economic growth and development in Nigeria (Olujobi., et al 2022). For further suggestions, besides encouraging SMEs on the application of AI to stimulate growth, there seems to be a need for the Government and educational institutions to develop skills set to stimulate AI adoption by SMEs. Digital training centres should be established to produce trainers and professional. The University curriculum should be reviewed and expanded to accommodate hands-on application of artificial intelligence.

6.1 Limitations and Future Research Directions

The study focused specifically on SMEs in the South West region of Nigeria and sectors such as manufacturing, hospitality, information and communication, and administrative and support services. The findings may not be easily applicable to SMEs in other regions or sectors within Nigeria or beyond. While the sample size of 322 is reasonable for the population size of 2000, the representativeness of the sample in terms of industry distribution and geographical coverage within the South

West region could affect the acceptability the findings. Although SEM is used to analyze relationships, establishing causality between AI innovation, employment, and SMEs growth can be challenging. The study may need to address potential confounding variables or alternative explanations for the observed relationships. As AI technologies evolve, exploring the adoption and impact of advanced techniques like machine learning, natural language processing, or robotics on SMEs could be another area of future research. Exploring the ethical considerations and social impacts of AI adoption in SMEs, such as job displacement or changes in skill requirements, is crucial for sustainable development. Addressing these limitations and exploring these future research directions, scholars can contribute to a more comprehensive understanding of how AI influences innovation, employment, and growth in SMEs, not only in Nigeria but also globally. This would provide valuable insights for policymakers, entrepreneurs, and stakeholders aiming to leverage AI for economic development and inclusive growth.

ACKNOWLEDGMENT

Authors acknowledge the support from the Covenant University Centre for Research, Innovation and Discovery (CUCRID) during the preparation of the manuscript.

REFERENCES

Accenture Plc. (2017) "How Companies Are Reimagining Business Processes With IT," https://sloanreview.mit.edu/article/will-ai-create-as-many-jobs-as-it-eliminates/

Access Partnership. (2019). *Artificial Intelligence for Africa: An Opportunity for Growth, Development, and Democratisation.* University of Pretoria.

Acemoglu, D., & Restrepo, P. (2019). The Wrong Kind of AI? Artificial Intelligence and the Future of Labor Demand. NBER Working Paper 25682.

Adeosun, O. T., & Shittu, A. I. (2021). *Small–medium enterprise formation and Nigerian economic growth. Review of Economics and Political Science Emerald Publishing Limited.* Emerald Publishing Limited., DOI: 10.1108/REPS-07-2020-0089

Adewoye T (2019). Artificial Intelligence in the workplace: Bracing up for the revolution

Agrawal, A., Gans, J., & Goldfarb, A. (2018a). Exploring the impact of artificial intelligence: prediction versus judgment (No. 24626). In: NBER Working Paper, NBER Working Paper. Cambridge, MA. https://doi.org/DOI: 10.3386/w24626

Ajibola, E. O. (2020). *Nigeria Small and Medium Enterprise Sustainability Strategies.* Walden Dissertations and Doctoral Studies Collection.

Akerejola, W. O., Okpara, E. U., Ohikhena, P., & Emenike, P. O. (2019). *"Availability of infrastructure and adoption of point of sales of selected small and medium enterprises (SMEs) in Lagos state"*, Nigeria. *International Journal of Academic Research in Business & Social Sciences*, 9(1), 137–150. DOI: 10.6007/IJARBSS/v9-i1/5370

Amabile, T., (2019). Creativity, artificial Intelligence, and a world of surprises. Acad. Manag. Discov amd.2019.0075. https://doi.org/.DOI: 10.5465/amd.2019.0075

Anekwe, R. I., Ndubusi-Okolo, P, & Uzoezie, C. (2019). Sustainability in the Nigerian Business Environment: Problems and Prospects. International Journal of Academic Management Science Research (IJAMSR) Vol. 3 Issue 3, March – 2019, Pages: 72-80

Automation & Anxiety. (2016): Will Smarter Machines Cause Mass Unemployment. *The Economist* What the story of ATMs and bank tellers reveals about the 'rise of the robots and jobs *A EIdeas.*

Bayode, B. O., & Adebola, A. O. (2012). Strategic Environmental Scanning and Organization Performance in a Competitive Business Environment. *Economic Insights - Trends and Challenges*, •••, 24–34.

Bessen, J. (2017b). Scarce Skills; *Not Scarce Jobs. CAPPF International Conference.*

Browne, M. W., & Cudeck, R. (1992). Alternative ways of assessing model fit. *Sociological Methods & Research*, 21(2), 230–258. DOI: 10.1177/0049124192021002005

Browne, M. W., & Cudeck, R. (1993). Alternative ways of assessing model fit. In Bollen, K.A & Long, J.S.[Eds.] *Testing structural equation models. Newbury Park,* CA: Sage,136-162.

Cangur, S., & Ercan, I. (2015). Comparison of Model Fit Indices Used in Structural Equation. Modeling Under Multivariate Normality. *Journal of Modern Applied Statistical Methods; JMASM*, 14(1), Ps152–Ps1. DOI: 10.22237/jmasm/1430453580

Casson, M. C. (1982). *The entrepreneur: An economic theory*. Barnes and Noble.

Chalmers, D., MacKenzie, G., & Carter, S. (2021). Artificial Intelligence and Entrepreneurship: Implications for Venture Creation in the Fourth Industrial Revolution. *Entrepreneurship Theory and Practice*, 45(5), 1028–1053. DOI: 10.1177/1042258720934581

Chen, N., Christensen, L., Gallagher, K., Mate, R., & Rafert, G. (2016). "Global Economic Impacts Associated with Artificial Intelligence", *Semanticscholar.org*, 2016. [Online]. Available: https://www.semanticscholar.org/paper/Global-Economic-Impacts-Associated-with-Artificial-Chen-Christensen/ebc73c75f7aba486751a20257a3134c777afd255. [Accessed: 09- Dec- 2020].

Cockburn, Iain M., Rebecca Henderson, & Scott Stern. (2019) "The Impact of Artificial Intelligence on Innovation." *The Economics of Artificial Intelligence: An Agenda*. Pp: 115-152.

Cullen, J. B., Johnson, J. L., & Parboteeah, K. P. (2014). National rates of opportunity entrepreneurship activity: Insights from institutional anomie theory? *Entrepreneurship Theory and Practice*, 38(4), 775–806. DOI: 10.1111/etap.12018

Daugherty, P., & Purdy, M. (2016). "Why Artificial Intelligence is the Future of Growth," *Accenture Canada*, 2016. [Online] Available: https://www.accenture.com/t20161031T154852__w__/ us-en/_acnmedia/PDF-33/Accenture-Why-AIis-the-Future-of-Growth.PDF#zoom=50

Deloitte. Automation and Anxiety: Will Smarter Machines Cause Mass Unemployment". *The Economist;* Technology and People: The Great Job-Creating Machine, Microsoft, The Future Computed, p. 92

EaP GREEN. (2016), Environmental Policy Toolkit for Greening SMEs in the EU Eastern Partnership countries, OECD report as part of the EU-funded EaP GREEN project, https://www.oecd.org/env/outreach/Greening-SMEs-policy-toolkit-eng.pdf

EC (European Commission). (2017a): What is an SME? available at: https://ec.europa.eu/growth/smes/business-friendlyenvironment/sme-definition_en (last accessed on 12.7.2017)

Edmund, M., Christopher, W., & Zeman, Z. (2020). Technology Acquisition and SMEs Performance, the Role of Innovation, Export and the Perception of Owner-Managers. *Journal of Risk and Financial Management*, 13(11), 2–19. DOI: 10.3390/jrfm13110258

EY. (2017). *The future of work: The augmented workforce*. Global Human Capital Trends.

Ferrario, A., Loi, M., & Viganò, E. (2020). In AI We Trust Incrementally: A Multi-layer Model of Trust to Analyze Human-Artificial Intelligence Interactions. *Philosophy & Technology*, 33(3), 523–539. DOI: 10.1007/s13347-019-00378-3

Freddi, D. (2018). Digitalisation and employment in manufacturing. *AI & Society*, 33(3), 393–403. DOI: 10.1007/s00146-017-0740-5

Gbandi & Amissah, 2014). FINANCING OPTIONS FOR SMALL AND MEDIUM ENTERPRISES (SMEs) IN NIGERIA *European Scientific Journal, ESJ, 10*(1)

Gwagwa, A; Kraemer-Mbula, K; Rizk,N, Rutenberg· I, de Beer, J (2020). Artificial Intelligence (AI) Deployments in Africa: Benefits, Challenges and Policy Dimensions. The Africa Journal of Information and Communication. Vol.26

Haefner, N., Wincent, J., Parida, V., & Gassmann, O. (2021). Artificial intelligence and innovation management: A review, framework, and research agenda. *Technological Forecasting and Social Change*, 162, 1–10. DOI: 10.1016/j.techfore.2020.120392

Ibidunni, A. S., Ufua, D. E., & Opute, A. P. (2021). Linking disruptive innovation to sustainable entrepreneurship within the context of small and medium firms: A focus on Nigeria. *African Journal of Science, Technology, Innovation and Development*, •••, 1–17.

Ihesiene, U. C., & Akpojaro, J. (2015). A Critical Evaluation of SMEs Attitudes towards Information Technology Integration in Nigeria, Australian Journal of Business and Management Research, 14(11) brahim, H., & Sarolta T. (2022). Empirical Analysis of the Influence of Gamification on Employees' Behavior. *Dynamic Relationships Management Journal*, 11(2), 71–78.

Jun, W., Zhe, Z.Y., Bo, Z.Y.,& Lian, H.Q. (2017). Countermeasures and Suggestions on the Impact of Artificial Intelligence on Employment. ChinaEconomic and Trade Review, 24.

Kitsios, F., & Kamariotou, M. (2021). *Artificial Intelligence and Business Strategy towards Digital Transformation: A Research Agenda*. MDPI., DOI: 10.3390/su13042025

Klosters, Davos. (2016) "World Economic Forum Annual Meeting 2016 Mastering the Fourth Industrial Revolution." *World Economic Forum*. http://www3.weforum.org/docs/Media/. Accessed 7 October 2018.

Korinek, A., & Stiglitz, J. E. (2017). *Artificial intelligence and its implications for income distribution and unemployment*. National Bureau of Economic Researcho. DOI: 10.3386/w24174

Kumar, R., & Shukla, S. (2022). Creativity, Proactive Personality and Entrepreneurial Intentions: Examining the Mediating Role of Entrepreneurial Self-efficacy. *Global Business Review*, 23(1), 101–118. DOI: 10.1177/0972150919844395

Lorenz, E., & Pommet, S. (2018), "Innovation, credit constraints and national banking systems: a comparison of developing nations (GREDEG Working Papers 2017-16)", Groupe de Rechercheen Droit, Economie, Gestion (GREDEG CNRS), University of Nice Sophia Antipolis.

Maydeu-Olivares, A. (2017a). Assessing the size of model misfit in structural equation models. *Psychometrika*, 82(3), 533–558. DOI: 10.1007/s11336-016-9552-7 PMID: 28176040

Mazur, E. (2012), "Green Transformation of Small Businesses: Achieving and Going Beyond Environmental Requirements", OECD Environment Working Papers, No. 47, OECD Publishing, Paris. DOI: http://dx.doi.org/DOI: 10.1787/19970900

McKinsey. (2017c). *A future that works: Automation, employment, and productivity*. McKinsey Global Institute.

McKinsey Global Institute. (2017). *A Future That Works: Automation, Employment, and Productivity*. McKinsey Global Institute.

McKinsey Global Institute. (2018): Notes from the frontier: Modeling the Impact of AI on the World Economy, Discussion Paper, September 2018.

McMullen, J. S., Bagby, D. R., & Palich, L. E. (2008). Economic freedom and the motivation to engage in entrepreneurial action. *Entrepreneurship Theory and Practice*, 32(5), 875–895. DOI: 10.1111/j.1540-6520.2008.00260.x

National Bureau of Statistics data 2010.

Nigerian Communications Commission (2020). Press Statement by Federal Ministry of Communication and Digital Economy on Industry Stakeholders Restate Commitment to Digital Economy National Population Commission (NPoC) 2013.

Nilsson, N. (2010). *The Quest for Artificial Intelligence: A History of Ideas and Achievements*. Cambridge University Press.

Nwugballa, E. A., Elom, M. E., & Onyeizugbe, C. U. (2016). Evaluating the relevance of entrepreneurial orientation to the performance of micro, small and medium enterprises in Ebonyi State, Nigeria. *International Journal of Academic Research in Accounting. Finance and Management Sciences*, 6(3), 221–230. DOI: 10.6007/IJARAFMS/v6-i3/2257

Obi, V. E. (2021). Economic impacts of Artificial Intelligence (AI) in Nigeria and Africa. [Online]. Available: DOI: [Accessed: 28- Sept- 2021].DOI: 10.13140/RG.2.2.11211.41762

Obschonka, M., & Audretsch, D. B. (2019). Artificial intelligence and big data in entrepreneurship: A new era has begun. *Small Business Economics*, 19(1). Advance online publication. DOI: 10.1007/s11187-019-00202-4

OECD. (2015b). *Data-Driven Innovation: Big Data for Growth and Well-Being*. OECD Publishing., DOI: 10.1787/9789264229358-

OECD. (2017c forthcoming). *Entrepreneurship at a Glance 2017*. OECD Publishing.

OECD (2018e), "Going Digital Scenarios: The Digital Transformation to 2030", forthcoming.

Olujobi, O.J., Olarinde, E.S., Yebisi, T.E., Okorie, U.E., (2022), COVID-19 Pandemic: The Impacts of Crude Oil Price Shock on Nigeria's Economy, Legal and Policy Options, Sustainability 2022, 14(18), 11166, available on line at 6. https://doi.org/ (accessed October 6, 2022)DOI: 10.3390/su141811166

Olujobi, O. J., Ufua, D. E., Okorie, U. E., & Ogbari, M. E. (2022). Carbon emission, solid waste management, and electricity generation: A legal and empirical perspective for renewable energy in Nigeria. *International Environmental Agreements: Politics, Law and Economics*, 1-21.DOI . Available online at https://link.springer .com/article/10.1007%2Fs10784-021-09558-z#citeas(accessed October 6, 2022) DOI: 10.1007/s10784-021-09558

Olujobi, O. J., & Yebisi, T. E. (2022), Combating the Crimes of Money Laundering and Terrorism Financing in Nigeria: A Legal Approach for Combating the Menace, Journal of Money Laundering Control, 2022 Available at https://www.emerald.com/insight/content/doi/10.1108/JMLC-12-2021-0143/full/html?skipTracking=true

Park, S.-C. (2017). The Fourth Industrial Revolution and implications for innovative cluster policies. *AI & Society*, 33(3), 433–445. DOI: 10.1007/s00146-017-0777-5

Prakash, C., Yadav, R., Singh, A., & Yadav, K. (2021). Modeling Entrepreneurial Intention among business Students. *Pacific Business Review International*, 14(3), 77–90.

Purdy, M., & Daugherty, P. (2017). *How AI Boosts Industry Profits and Innovation, AI Research.* Accenture.

PwC (2020). Nigeria SME Survey

PwC. (2020). Survey of 10,000 members of the general population based in China, Germany, India, the UK and the US

Rana, R., & Singahi, R. (2015). Chi-square test and its application in hypothesis testing, J Pract Caediovasc Science. Available from: https://www.j-pcs.org/text.asp?2015/1/1/69/157577

Renuka, S., & Anju, S. (2023). Examining The Factors Affecting Green Entrepreneurship Intentions in University Students: An Empirical Study. *Dynamic Relationships Management Journal*, 12(2), 35–47.

Ritu, Y., Chand, P., & Amit, D. (2023). Entrepreneurial Orientation to Sustainable Entrepreneurial Orientation: Mediating Effect of Social Orientation. *Dynamic Relationships Management Journal*, 12(2), 97–108.

Sahil V & Anupam S (2019). Artificial Intelligence: Employment and Society International Journal of Innovative Technology and Exploring Engineering (IJITEE) 8 (7S2), 239 -242

Samsung White Paper. (July 14, 2020):https://research.samsung.com/next-generation-communications (Retrieve on July 16 2020 at 10.40 pm IST)

Samwel, M. C., & Daoping, W. (2020). Information technology innovation and its impact on job creation by SMEs in developing countries: An analysis of the literature review. *Technology Analysis and Strategic Management*, 32(3), 256–271. DOI: 10.1080/09537325.2019.1651263

Sara, R., Dejan, U., Amadeja, L., & Anja, S. (2024). Effects of Shifting From In-Person to Distributed Work on Routine, Creative, and Social Collaboration. *Dynamic Relationships Management Journal*, 13(1), 85–104.

Schwab, K. (2017). *The Fourth Industrial Revolution*. Crown Business.

Sen, D., Ozturk, M., & Vayvay, O. (2016). An Overview of Big Data for Growth in SMEs. *Procedia: Social and Behavioral Sciences*, 235, 159–167. DOI: 10.1016/j.sbspro.2016.11.011

Shane, S., & Venkataraman, S. (2000). The promise of entrepreneurship as a field of research. *Academy of Management Review*, 25(1), 217–226. DOI: 10.5465/amr.2000.2791611

Sivo, S. A., Fan, X., Witta, E. L., & Willse, J. T. (2006). The Search for "Optimal" Cutoff Properties: Fit Index Criteria in Structural Equation Modeling. *Journal of Experimental Education*, 14(3), 267–288. DOI: 10.3200/JEXE.74.3.267-288

Steiger, J. (1990). Structural model evaluation and modification: An interval estimation approach. *Multivariate Behavioral Research*, 25(2), 173–180. DOI: 10.1207/s15327906mbr2502_4 PMID: 26794479

Steiger, J., & Lind, J. M. (1980). *Statistically-based tests for a number of common factors*. Paper presented at the Psychometrika Society Meeting, Iowa City.

Stenholm, P., Acs, Z. J., & Wuebker, R. (2013). Exploring country-level institutional arrangements on the rate and type of entrepreneurial activity. *Journal of Business Venturing*, 28(1), 176–193. DOI: 10.1016/j.jbusvent.2011.11.002

Tejumade, O. S. (2015). Challenges to the Growth and Development of Manufacturing and Services SMEs in Nigeria The West East Institute, *International Academic Conference Proceedings Harvard*, USA pp 186- 199

The World Bank. (2019). *World Development Report 2019: The Changing Nature of Work*. World Bank Groupo.

Townsend, D. M., & Hunt, R. A. (2019). Entrepreneurial action, creativity, & judgment in the age of artificial intelligence. *Journal of Business Venturing Insights, 11*, e00126. . 2019. e00126DOI: 10. 1016/ jjbvi

Travaly, Y., & Muvunyi, K. (2020). "The future is intelligent: Harnessing the potential of artificial intelligence in Africa", *Brookings.edu*, 2020. [Online]. Available: https://www.brookings.edu/blog/africa-in-focus/2020/01/13/the-future-is-intelligent-harnessing-the-potential-of-artificial-intelligence-in-africa/. [Accessed: 09- Dec-2020].

Trott, P. (2005). *Innovation management and new product development* (3rd ed.). PT Prentice Hall.

Ufua, D. E., Emielu, E. T., Olujobi, O. J., Lakhani, F., Borishade, T. T., Ibidunni, A. S., & Osabuohien, E. S. (2021). Digital transformation: A conceptual framing for attaining Sustainable Development Goals 4 and 9 in Nigeria. *Journal of Management & Organization*, 27(5), 836–849. DOI: 10.1017/jmo.2021.45

Ufua, D. E., Olujobi, O. J., Tahir, H., Al-Faryan, M. A. S., Matthew, O. A., & Osabuohien, E. (2022). Lean Entrepreneurship and SME Practice in a Post COVID-19 Pandemic Era: A Conceptual Discourse from Nigeria. *Global Journal of Flexible Systems Management*, 1-14.

Ufua, D. E., Olujobi, O. J., Tahir, H., Okafor, V., Imhonopi, D., & Osabuohien, E. (2022). Social services provision and stakeholder engagement in the Nigerian informal sector: A systemic concept for transformation and business sustainability. *Business and Society Review*, 127(2), 403–421. DOI: 10.1111/basr.12271

Ufua, D. E., Salau, O. P., Saleem, O., Ogbari, M. E., Osibanjo, A. O., Osabuohien, E., & Adeniji, A. A. (2022). Systems Approach to Address Human Resource Issues: A Case in a Commercial Livestock Farm in Southern Nigeria. *SAGE Open*, 12(2), 21582440221093370. DOI: 10.1177/21582440221093370

UNESCO. (2019). International Conference on Artificial Intelligence and Education, Planning Education in the AI Era: Lead the leap, Bejing Van Ark, B., et al, (2016), "Navigating the New Digital Economy: Driving Digital Growth and Productivity from Installation to Deployment", Conference Board, New York

Victor, C. N., Christopher, N., & Ignatius, A. M. (2019). The role of subcontracting on innovation: An assessment of small and medium enterprises in Nigeria. *Production and Manufacturing Research Journal*, 1(7), 88–108.

Victor, J (2019). Benefits of Artificial Intelligence (AI) in Nigeria

Von Krogh, G. (2018). Artificial intelligence in organizations: New opportunities for phenomenon- based theorizing. *Academy of Management Discoveries*, 4(4), 404–409. DOI: 10.5465/amd.2018.0084

World Bank (2017). Alternative Data Transforming SME Finance May 2017

Žigiene.G, Rybakovas, E & Alzbutas R (2019). Artificial Intelligence Based Commercial Risk Management Framework for SMEs. Journal of MDPI Sustainability, (11), 4501; DOI: 10.3390/su11164501

Chapter 4
Exploring Carbon Neutrality in the Metaverse:
Opportunities and Challenges for Business Models

Rashid Hashmi
https://orcid.org/0009-0006-3232-0705
Sharda University, India

Hemlata Parmar
https://orcid.org/0009-0009-1438-5427
Manipal University Jaipur, India

Utsav Krishan Murari
https://orcid.org/0009-0007-1606-6775
Sharda University, India

ABSTRACT

With the metaverse evolving into a significant medium for digital engagement, attaining carbon neutrality is essential for sustainable development. This chapter examines the feasibility of achieving carbon neutrality in the metaverse through the incorporation of sustainable business practices in virtual settings. It emphasizes the potential of virtual economies to minimize physical resource usage, lower carbon emissions, and promote sustainable innovation. Nonetheless, obstacles such as energy-consuming blockchain technologies, emissions from data centers, and the necessity for sustainable infrastructure pose considerable barriers. This chapter provides a framework for businesses to reconcile innovation in the metaverse with

DOI: 10.4018/979-8-3693-9005-4.ch004

environmental accountability through a critical examination of contemporary technologies, business strategies, and sustainability policies.

1. METAVERSE AND CARBON NEUTRALITY

1.1. The Historical Development of the Metaverse

The term "metaverse" is relatively new; however, combining numerous immersive and shared online spaces for real-time user interactions has been developing for several decades. Hence, initial blurring exemplenaries, including Second Life, create the basis for the metaverse and indicate the potential in which the digital milieu might act not as a replacement for the physical but as an analogue in which the physical world's components may be reproduced. Second Life emerged in 2003, created by Linden Lab, allowing avatar creation, social interactions, building properties, and trading virtual goods. While Second Life does not have the technological sophistication describing the contemporary metaverse, it is revolutionary in concept, and the metaverse contains a steady virtual world driven by user content (Ondrejka, 2004). The contemporary metaverse is similar to Second Life in terms of being a service inside a virtual environment; it is decentralised and built on blockchain instead of being run as a single platform. It includes different kinds of environments in virtual reality that allow users to own virtual property do commerce and interact with VR and AR in unprecedented ways. By applying emerging technologies like the blockchain, artificial intelligence, and the Internet of Things, the metaverse is emerging as a separate, distinct economy with distinct features, rules, protocols, and conditions for carrying out business (Ball, 2022).

1.2. Technological Advancements Driving the Metaverse

Today's metaverse is built upon technological advances in computer technologies in general, particularly on the reflected characteristics of the modern metaverse: hosting, immersion, persistence, and decentralisation. These include Blockchain, Virtual Reality (VR), Augmented Reality (AR), Artificial Intelligence (AI), and Internet of Things (IoT). These are the building blocks characteristic of the metaverse, an environment integrated for creation, interaction, and transactional purposes without regard to geographic location or physical structures.

1.2.1. Blockchain Technology

Blockchain is the structure on which the decentralised economy of the metaverse is established. Blockchain technology enables uncentralised applications to be created, thus removing the control of a single centre and enabling people to possess, exchange and authenticate digital assets. Still, we will look into how the blockchain revolutionises ownership in the metaverse, starting with NFTs. NFTs are different categories of things represented through digital tokens, such as collectables, artwork, and even virtual land. Digital assets have ownership rights recorded on a blockchain, making transactions safe to sell, buy, and exchange NFTs. (Kouhizadeh & Sarkis, 2020). Blockchain also has a significant application within decentralised finance (DeFi) arrangements, enabling metaverse users to conduct financial operations such as lending, borrowing, and investing independently of bank-related services.

1.2.2. Virtual Reality (VR) and Augmented Reality (AR)

Augmented reality (AR) and VR are inseparable in defining the metaverse concept. In virtual reality (VR), users are fully immersed in the virtual world and have the impression that they are part of the real world. The Oculus Rift headsets enable users to touch objects and other users in real-time with a 360-degree view of the virtual world. In real estate, gaming is one of the industries where Virtual Reality (VR) has been applied, where consumers can preview properties fully immersed in environments without using their legs physically. (Marr, 2021). On the other hand, Augmented Reality provides the physical environment with computer-generated images and interactions. In fields such as retail, where clients might only want to try on clothes or even see how furniture would fit into their homes, augmented reality is used. It was expected that AR would significantly influence the development of the compound experiences of the metaverse to enhance how business operations interface with customers and deliver products or services. (Marr, 2021).

1.2.3. Artificial Intelligence (AI)

Another set of technologies that define the metaverse is Artificial Intelligence (AI) since it generates a personal and adaptive experience. AI allows intelligent avatars, content individualisation and adaptive environments where the world promptly reacts to a user's input. For businesses in the metaverse, there is easier targeting and marketing of products, effective and efficient customer relations through chatbots, and virtual environments that can change to reflect the user's tastes and preferences. AI is also crucial in effectively managing the metaverse, the world's physical infrastructure. Anything related to handling the massive flow of data value streams themselves that the recent virtual interactions produce, up to making any data centre where large swathes of Internet content are to be stored, efficient must be run on AI to guarantee that the metaverse will indeed operate optimally as well as is sustainably possible. In addition, AI can enhance the energy efficiency of blockchain systems through efficient job completion and lesser computational requirements for recapitulative tasks such as mining in PoW. (Khanna et al., 2022).

1.2.4. Internet of Things (IoT)

The IoT implies embedding physical objects in the web to enable them to interact and gather information. To the virtual scenery of the metaverse, IoT enables the physical context to be introduced more effectively and enriches perception. For instance, in IoT, the physical objects in the real physical world can interact with their equivalents in the metaverse to control them and manage the surrounding environment remotely.

1.3. Business Potential in the Metaverse

Using the metaverse has many possibilities for businesses since this space offers new opportunities to interact with the consumer. Promotion of stores, products, and customer interaction methods are only a few examples of how companies immerse themselves in the metaverse and use it to build value.

1.3.1. Virtual Product Launches

Another interesting area for business in the metaverse is the opportunity to organise a virtual product launch. Such events facilitate premier's opportunity for companies to introduce new products to the global market in an engaging first-person format without all the complexities of live business events. Conducting product launches virtually can also be cheaper since a larger population can access them while avoiding using physical space, transport and material items. For example, Nike recently released virtual sneakers in the metaverse, which allows people to buy sneakers and display these digital products on their avatars (Veridt, 2022). Such launches help sell virtual commodities and build brand equity and awareness online.

1.3.2. Customer Engagement

It also provides new ways of interacting with clients through the use cases in the metaverse since firms can uniquely interact with customers. Fashion giants like Gucci and Balenciaga have created virtual store spaces allowing buyers to view replicas of their products and purchase them in the metaverse. 'Live' performances held in the metaverse for customers also allow brands to interact with their customers in ways they would have never before considered (Verdict, 2022).

1.3.3. E-commerce Models

In the metaverse, new online markets exist where users may buy, sell, and trade virtual goods at breakneck speed. Real estate, paintings, shirts and any other merchandise that can have an NFT can be purchased from the Sandbox and Decentraland. The metaverse's economy is also transforming, which is well illustrated by these virtual products changing hands for cryptocurrency.

1.4. The Urgency of Carbon Neutrality in the Metaverse

The undeniable growth of the metaverse increases the call for carbon neutrality. The metaverse runs on data centres and blockchain systems that contribute to the emission of greenhouse gases globally, making the issue deteriorate. For the metaverse to continue to grow as a phenomenon beneficial to the economy, firms and governments need to pursue a policy of carbonless production.

1.4.1. Climate Change Reports and Global Commitments

Carbon neutrality is now mainly advocated based on the Intergovernmental Panel on Climate Change (IPCC) reports and current climate change agreements as per the Paris Agreement. The recent Third Order of the IPCC's Sixth Assessment Report calls for cutting greenhouse gas emissions by at least 50 per cent compared to the levels in 2019 within the next eight years (IPCC, 2021). Failing this target may increase the intensity and frequency of cyclones, storms, and other climate events, more flooding, increased sea level rise rates, and the likelihood of ecosystem and human systems becoming permanently damaged. Concerns for such issues have led corporations and governments worldwide to pledge to reach net-zero emissions by the middle of the next century. Approximately 196 countries have endorsed the Paris Accord, through which the global degree rise is supposed to be limited far below two °C, preferably 1.5°C (UNFCCC, 2015).

1.4.2. The Role of Businesses in Carbon Neutrality

A key challenge companies continue to face as they search for ways and means of doing business in the metaverse is the issue of taking responsibility for the environmental footprint of the virtual operations of their organisations. This entails controlling carbon emissions derived from physical business activities and the carbon intensity of the information technology structures. While the physical climate load of virtual environments intensifies, companies must minimise the ecological footprint of their business in the metaverse. Fibre sustainability in the metaverse is profound; thus, the following approach is needed to achieve carbon neutrality. One of them is incorporating renewable energy sources, such as wind and solar energy, into the functioning of the data centres and the blockchain networks. Industry giants such as Google, Microsoft, and Amazon have made significant progress in achieving a goal to power data centres entirely with renewable energy (Google et al., 2022). Secondly, there is a reduction in carbon footprint through enhancing the efficiency of the organisational digital platform. It also involves fixing energy-efficient coding approaches, optimising the servers, and integrating more environmentally friendly blockchain models like the PoS methods, which require much less energy than many PoW systems (Li et al., 2021).

2. DIGITAL INFRASTRUCTURE IN THE METAVERSE: ENERGY CONSUMPTION AND ENVIRONMENTAL IMPACT

When organisations explore the vast potential of the metaverse in increasing business value, it is not uncommon to stumble upon environmental issues when examining its digital foundation. Digital infrastructure's power demand is high and multidimensional due to data centre demands, blockchain technologies, and VR and AR systems. The metaverse provides entirely new possibilities for reducing dependency on physical assets; therefore, to ensure the permanence and stability of the platform, its digital components need to be addressed.

2.1. Data Centers: The Backbone of the Metaverse

These virtual infrastructures comprise data centres, which store the servers required for processing vast amounts of data as a foundation of the metaverse. One of the main reasons for high energy demands in data centres is the requirement for constant availability: users must be able to enter a virtual space at any time of the day. This makes servers run 24/7, generating much heat, which has to be dissipated using cooling systems. Consequently, data centres are among the most energy-profligate parts of the digital structure, consuming roughly 1% of all the electricity worldwide in 2020 (Andrae, 2020).

2.1.1. Energy-Efficient Data Centers: Examples from Leading Companies

Google, Amazon, Microsoft and several other leading technological organisations have gauged the effects of their data centre on the environment and are working to minimise their power utilisation in efficient ways.• Google was the first to adopt renewable energy to run its data facilities. They recognise the environmental impact of their data centre operations and are taking steps to reduce their carbon footprints through energy-efficient practices.

- Google is a pioneer in using renewable energy to power its data centres. Google Sustainability Report (2022) has reported that since 2017, the corporation has directly purchased 100% renewable electricity, mainly wind and solar. Google has real-time cooling adoption by algorithms in its data centres' energy efficiency measures. Such practices have lowered Google's electricity usage and set a benchmark for other companies.
- The Amazon Web Service (AWS) is the largest cloud computing service with enormous data centres worldwide. They enter operations and are taking steps to reduce their carbon footprints through energy-efficient practices. Amazon Web Service (AWS), the largest cloud computing service, has a massive network of data centres worldwide. Moreover, by 2025, Amazon's AWS will achieve its goal of running entirely on renewable energy sources. Air conditioning is one of its central techniques, direct evaporative cooling, that uses relatively less water and energy than air conditioning (Amazon et al., 2022). AWS also designs efficient servers to process data and provide efficient energy solutions.
- Microsoft wants to be carbon-zero by 2030. They plan to use many renewable energy sources to power their data centres and operations. They are taking steps to reduce their carbon footprints through energy-efficient practices. Microsoft aims to become carbon-zero by 2030 by investing heavily in renewable energy for its data centres. The current initiatives within Project Natick include using underwater data centres and acquiring renewable power. Offshore New Label data centres are underwater structures where the water from the sea is used to cool the servers, and no additional cooling instruments are required (Microsoft et al., 2021).

2.1.2. How Server Farms Operate and Their Cooling Systems

A standard data centre or server farm comprises thousands of servers in rows of racks linked through a network. They do the complex computations required to run digital platforms, cloud storage services, and virtual worlds in the metaverse. Heap operations in these servers are continuous, creating vast and constant heat, which needs to be dissipated to not cause failures on the equipment. In order to regulate this heat, data centres use different cooling systems. Conventional solutions depend on the cooling mechanisms to reduce the temperature of the server areas. Modern data centres are increasingly adopting more energy-efficient cooling technologies, such as:

- **Liquid Cooling**: Liquid cooling systems circulate a coolant through the data centre to absorb server heat. Liquid cooling is more efficient than air cooling because liquids can absorb heat more effectively, allowing servers to operate at higher performance levels without overheating.
- **Evaporative Cooling**: This method uses the natural evaporation process to cool the air in the data centre. Water is sprayed into the air, and as it evaporates, it cools the surrounding environment. Evaporative cooling uses less electricity than traditional air conditioning and can be highly effective in dry climates.
- **Free Cooling**: Free cooling uses natural cold air from the external environment to cool servers. In regions with cold climates, data centres can use outside air to maintain optimal temperatures, significantly reducing the need for artificial cooling systems.

2.2. Blockchain Energy Consumption

Blockchain is one of the foundational technologies of the metaverse since it encompasses the economic layer. It offers the base to store, organise and trade other digital assets like non-fungible tokens, allowing people to transact safely without third parties. However, energy use in blockchain systems, especially those that support the PoW consensus model, has been a primary environmental concern.

2.2.1. Proof-of-Work (PoW) and Its Energy Demands

Proof-of-work (PoW) is a widely known consensus method that integrates with blockchain systems. Miners are supposed to overcome complex mathematical problems to validate every transaction in the blockchain and add it to the network structure. The first miner to solve a given puzzle gets the cryptocurrency, entailing a model that requires significant computations to be completed. The procedure known as mining is power-intensive because the miners need to solve computation puzzles constantly with the help of highly effective computers.

Energy consumption by Proof of Work systems has received much backlash, especially regarding using cryptocurrencies like Bitcoin and Ethereum. Bitcoin's energy consumption is estimated to be about 97 TWh a year, equivalent to that of countries like the Netherlands (de Vries, 2021). The current energy utilisation rates have raised concerns about the suitability of PoW blockchains, especially as they are adopted in the metaverse.

2.2.2. Proof-of-Stake (PoS) as an Energy-Efficient Alternative

Moreover, to counterbalance the problem of the environmental influence of PoW, many blockchain-based platforms are changing to proof-of-stake (PoS) consensus algorithms. In a PoS system, validators are selected based on the number of tokens they own and are willing to lock in as a stake. Unlike PoW, the PoS system does not involve miners solving puzzles, thus significantly decreasing the degree of the central processing unit (CPU) and electricity needed for the blockchain functioning (Li et al., 2021). Ethereum is a leading blockchain platform in the metaverse, and it switched from PoW to PoS in the process of Ethereum 2.0. This transition is expected to decrease Ethereum's energy utilisation by as much as 99%, making the platform sustainable for businesses and their users in the metaverse (Li et al., 2021).

2.2.3. Proof-of-Authority (PoA) and Other Consensus Mechanisms

Consensus mechanisms, that is, certain types of consensus, not including PoS, have been proposed to reduce the energy consumption intensity of blockchains. Proof-of-authority (PoA) is among the best-known mechanisms with certain trusted authorities to approve the transactions. Here, PoA saves precious time on mining by having a limited number of validators, making PoA spectacularly efficient in energy consumption (Kouhizadeh & Sarkis, 2020). Although PoA is not as decentralised as PoW or PoS, it can be more suitable for some applications in the metaverse, particularly for those that involve high numbers of transactions per second and low energy consumption.

2.3. VR/AR Energy Consumption

The metaverse experience is already anchored on what is commonly understood as distributed virtual environments characterised by VR and AR. Though the amount of computational power that needs to be implemented for creating modern high-definition 3D environments in real-time is significant, the main drawback is energy consumption. GPUs and CPUs are necessary to render virtual and augmented realities for operations within metaverse-based businesses, which guzzle electricity and increase carbon footprint.

2.3.1. Energy Demands of VR and AR Systems

The setup of a VR system demands that the hardware must be capable of setting up a vivid virtual environment that one can navigate in real-time. This encompasses VR headsets, which are mandatory to display complex stereoscopic realistic images at a very high frame rate to provide a user-immersive experience. The second implementation need stems from real-time interactive capability, where VR systems are expected to process large volumes of data consistently, which calls for resources in terms of computational power. Similarly, Augmented Reality applications, where digital information is provided on top of the real world, require image recognition and processing to map the user's actual environment. This entails the continuous transformation of data, especially in existing contexts, and acts as extra pressure to increase the power consumption of AR systems (Marr, 2021).

2.3.2. Mitigating Energy Costs in VR/AR Applications: Case Studies

Several companies have taken steps to mitigate the energy costs of VR and AR applications, employing energy-efficient practices to reduce their environmental impact.

- **Facebook's Oculus (Meta)**: Tech giant Meta, which used to be called Facebook, has had much involvement in VR through Oculus, which underpins many of the experiences in the metaverse. In terms of energy, Meta has identified ways to improve its VR headsets' effectiveness and create algorithms that decrease the quantity of energy required to render on GPUs. Meta continues to embrace energy-efficient products and services for VR services to ensure that the products have minimised their effects on the environment (Meta et al., 2022).
- **Niantic's AR Games**: Recently, the creators of AR games, such as Pokémon Go and Niantic, have adopted resource-saving coding in AR platforms. Such measures help to adjust the power use of portable platforms in which AR applications are implemented, thereby minimising the total energy intensity of the game. Niantic has tried to minimise the server computations needed to sustain big AR occasions and minimise energy utilisation (Niantic et al., 2021).

2.4. Energy Consumption in Traditional vs. Metaverse Business Models

As a result, we need to compare metaverse business models' energy consumption with traditional business operations to identify the impact of the environment. Most conventional business architectures demand tangible structures such as offices, factories, and supply chains that lead to the generation of greenhouse gases. Nevertheless, business models built on metaverse do not require tangible assets; they are constructed on energy-demanding virtual systems.

Table 1. Metaverse Business Models

Category	Traditional Business Model	Metaverse Business Model
Physical Infrastructure	High energy consumption (offices, factories)	Reduced physical infrastructure, no transportation
Data Processing	Minimal energy consumption (localised systems)	High energy consumption (data centres, cloud)
Blockchain	Not applicable	High energy consumption (PoW blockchain)
VR/AR Technology	Not applicable	High energy consumption (real-time rendering)
Renewable Energy Usage	Limited (physical infrastructure reliance)	Increasing focus on renewable energy (data centres)

From the table below, metaverse B2C models significantly decrease dependency on physical structures as in construction, maintenance, and transportation connections to emissions.

3. CARBON-NEUTRAL TECHNOLOGIES: OPPORTUNITIES IN THE METAVERSE

The impact of the metaverse is that with a growing population demanding the use of digital goods and decentralised systems, energy is consumed as people transact in businesses and engage in virtual environments. The environmental impact of these activities cannot be ignored; however, technological advances and solutions for carbon emissions from metaverse activities are developing. These include renewable power resolution, energy-efficient coding, environmentally sustainable blockchain and AI in energy use.

3.1. Renewable Energy Integration

In this case, there is no universally effective method of decreasing the problems associated with the metaverse's effect on the environment other than adopting renewable energy in the physical structure of the digital world. The ever-growing amounts of data needed for the functioning of the metaverse stored in data centres are power-hungry. As reported, by integrating renewable energy sources such as solar, wind and hydropower electricity into these centres, companies have the potential to minimise greenhouse gas emissions.

3.1.1. Case Study: Microsoft's Transition to Renewable Energy

Microsoft has provided direction to the tech sector's green energy revolution. Microsoft's 2030 commitment is to be carbon-negative, and as part of this plan, the firm aims to transition its global data centres' energy sources solely to renewable sources by 2025 (Microsoft et al., 2022). Microsoft funding offshore wind farms has done this, as well as funding solar installations.... Microsoft partnered with energy firms to develop the Hollandse Kust Noord offshore wind farm, one of the biggest in the Netherlands, to power the European data centres with 1.5 GW of renewable energy (Microsoft, 2022). Microsoft also solarises its data centres in Arizona to shift its dependence on external energy sources and increase the local grid's renewable energy capacity.

3.1.2. Technologies Enabling Renewable Energy Integration

Renewable energy integration into data centres requires a smart grid, storage, and efficient energy devices. Smart grids ensure renewable energy in data centres through efficient distribution of energy moving on solar and wind power. Large industries and commercial buildings may presumably save energy and cut down energy wastage through smart meters and the application of real-time energy control systems. Lithium-ion battery energy storage and complex energy storage systems are needed to fix the inconsistency of solar and wind power. These storage devices enable data centres to exploit peak production energy and employ it when renewable energy is scarce.

3.2. Energy-Efficient Coding

Metaverse firms, for example, must design energy-efficient codes and transition to renewable energy. Decision-making when choosing software for development impacts the data centre and the blockchain network's power consumption. Resource management directs software application performance and memory to reduce energy use and strain on the metaverse effectively.

3.2.1. Practices for Implementing Energy-Efficient Software

There are several key practices that businesses can adopt to implement energy-efficient software development in the metaverse:

- Code optimisation is also a way of reducing energy consumption, involving fewer computation elements. For instance, reducing algorithm complexity, removing code, and incorporating suitable data structures is good for energy-efficient computing.
- Resources must be managed effectively as a scarce and valuable commodity in computer-supported environments and distributed arrangements of virtual spaces in the metaverse. Complexity, deleting redundant code, and utilising efficient data structures can all help reduce energy use.
- Energy-Aware Software Development: Some tools enable developers to study and design their Apps' energy consumption. Tools like Intel's VTune Profiler help developers measure their code's energy profile and find inefficiencies. This is particularly useful when a high level of computation is needed, including in the immersive simulations in the Metaverse.

3.3. Green Blockchain Initiatives

Essentials of the metaverse include using Blockchain technology to facilitate the execution of transactions and ownership. However, one of the fundamental challenges of blockchain systems, especially the PoW-based consensus, is the high energy consumption. This factor makes it unpalatable for organisations pursuing ecological reforms such as carbon neutrality. The amount of energy used in PoW-based mining is considerable, especially in the usage of Bitcoin and Ethereum, which are recognised to consume more energy.

3.3.1. Transition from Proof-of-Work (PoW) to Proof-of-Stake (PoS)

To settle these worries, multiple blockchain networks will shift from PoW to PoS, which consumes less electricity. Relay nodes used to be selected based on the number of tokens. At the same time, in a PoS system, validators are chosen according to the stake, but this is not proportional to the fundamental mathematical problem. This solution has eliminated mining and reduced energy consumption within the blockchain network. Making Ethereum transition from PoW to PoS is the first step towards creating sustainable blockchain solutions. The upcoming Merge, an upgrade to Ethereum, is expected to reduce energy consumption by about 99%, ranking it as one of the most environmentally friendly blockchain networks (Ethereum Foundation, 2022).

3.3.2. Case Study: Cardano's PoS Blockchain

Cardano is also among those networks implementing the PoS since the ground up. While Ethereum changed its consensus algorithm from proof of work to proof of stake, Cardano was planned to be energy-effective. An important feature of the network is its PoS system called Ouroboros, which means fast and secure decentralisation is possible without consuming significantly more energy than PoW networks (Hoskinson, 2021).

3.4. Innovations in Artificial Intelligence (AI) for Energy Optimization

AI is fast becoming indispensable in optimising energy consumption patterns in the metaverse. Systems that utilise artificial intelligence can mine significant and extensive data to look for patterns relative to energy utilisation and then control the same in real time to reduce utilisation. This comes in handy in data centres where an AI system can dynamically alter cooling systems, workload, and power distribution, to name but a few.

3.4.1. AI for Data Center Optimization

AI is being applied to the operations of data centres, which remain vital to the functioning of the metaverse infrastructure. Another AI system applied to Google's operation is deployed by its DeepMind to manage and reduce the power consumption of its data hubs. Using sensors mounted around the data centre, the AI system detects when cooling is required and controls it in real-time, thus cutting the energy spend by 40% (Google, 2021). This AI-based approach to the energy management of metaverse businesses is a revolution in conventional systems. Through AI, the energy consumption used in industries can be supervised and managed, decreasing the carbon footprint of digital structures and equipment while still maintaining high efficiency and availability.

3.4.2. AI in Blockchain Energy Efficiency

Artificial intelligence enhances the intelligent energy management of blockchain and data centres. Regarding the other three criteria, AI can predict the number of transactions and scale the processing power of the blockchain network. Blockchain networks can be dynamic in control of energy consumption, meaning they can cut power consumption when the activity in the blockchain network is low. Since PoS validators consume much energy to process transactions, the AI systems can precisely predict when these validators will be active and thus control energy consumption. Integrating AI and PoS in a highly efficient blockchain system reduces energy consumption but does not hamper efficiency.

4. ETHICAL CONSIDERATIONS IN BUILDING SUSTAINABLE BUSINESS MODELS

As the metaverse increases its standing as a crucial environment in business processes, the development of sustainable business models remains sensitive to ethical dilemmas. As the metaverse can bring many opportunities for new business solutions and create new economic opportunities, it remains a virtual world with the same ethical issues as the real world. However, due to the decentralised and tangible nature of the metaverse, several considerations need to be made, considering important ethical values such as community and transparency, fairness, and sustainability.

4.1. Transparency and Greenwashing

Transparency is arguably one of the most important ethical issues in developing sustainable business models anchored in the metaverse. When organisations advance ideas about sustainability, they have to guarantee that they are credible and easily substantiated. Greenwashing or, in general, exaggerated or plain false statements regarding sustainability are a significant danger for the metaverse, as for real life. Thus, using digital operations in organisational activities makes greenwashing even more significant as it is difficult to understand and monitor.

4.1.1. Real-World Examples of Greenwashing in the Metaverse

Greenwashing has begun appearing in various sectors, including those moving into the metaverse industry. For instance, companies like H&M or Zara have been serving their customers clothes under the pretext of being eco-friendly without sufficiently explaining the nature of their supply chains or their actual environmental effects (Alves, 2021). Such allegations have undermined consumer confidence because more people are getting to know how brands mislead them on environmental practices. Businesses that open online shops or organise online concerts that claim to go green may just be benefiting from extensive use of power from primary data centres that largely depend on fossil energy. As much as removing the physical structure cuts down on some form of emissions since the metaverse relies heavily on computational power to operate, the consumption leads to a high carbon footprint if not well controlled. For instance, the virtual real estate providers in the metaverse sell services such as building and construction, saying they do not harm the ecosystem since they do not require actual land development. However, these platforms neglect to reveal the external costs of utilising blockchain technology, which they rely on. The power consumption derived from proof-of-work (PoW) blockchains, for example, used in the minting of non-fungible tokens (NFTs), poses emission problems overriding the assumed green gain (de Vries, 2021).

4.1.2. Ethical Implications of Greenwashing

The consequences of greenwashing in the metaverse are not only warming in that they have massive ethical dimensions. Primarily, greenwashing erodes consumer trust because stakeholders now demand that businesses publicly disclose how they affect the environment. Overhyping sustainability and risking much more than a company benefits from exciting and promising more than it can deliver. In a disorganised setting like the metaverse, it becomes harder for users to verify the authenticity of sustainability claims compared to more traditional business structures, creating a significant challenge for businesses that have to guarantee that their stories are truthful.

4.1.3. Solutions for Ensuring Transparency

Business firms dealing in the metaverse must ensure that all their sustainability strategies are open to the public to avoid ethical astound. This includes presenting factual guidelines that companies must follow, including the necessity to present clear evidence of their environmental footprint, energy usage and carbon emissions, and the ability of the supply chain to be sustainable. Businesses should also report on deploying renewable energy, carbon offsets and other activities to decrease a firm's carbon impacts.

4.2. Blockchain Ethics

Although blockchain technology is the centre of many elements in the metaverse, it presents several ethical issues, especially energy and environmental impacts. Because blockchain is spread among nodes and is challenging to control, many blockchain systems that serve as the underlying technical architecture for digital transactions and ownership in the metaverse consume much electricity. It is for these reasons that ethical blockchain practices are centred around ways of reducing the impact that these systems have on their environment whilst at the same time maintaining openness, protection and participation.

4.2.1. Energy Consumption in Blockchain Systems

One of the most significant social issues related to implementing blockchain technology is sustainability – energy expenditure. Some blockchain systems that use proof-of-work consensus methodologies, such as Bitcoin and Ethereum, require substantial computation capability to approve transactions and protect the network. This process, commonly called mining, consumes significant amounts of energy and, in the process, generates large amounts of carbon. According to De Vries (2021), the Bitcoin electricity consumption rate will soon outstrip many small countries like Argentina.

4.2.2. Ethical Blockchain Practices: The Shift to Proof-of-Stake (PoS)

Due to the impact of Proof of Work systems causing various environmental damages, many blockchain platforms are searching for workable consensus algorithms that use less power. Proof-of-work (PoW) is a method that is slowly being replaced by proof-of-stake (PoS), which is generally considered to provide a more efficient solution. In Proof of Stake (PoS) systems, the validators are selected depending on the number of their tokens. They are ready to 'stake' as a guarantee rather than seeking solutions in time-consuming mining. This significantly reduces the computational capability required to validate the transaction and makes PoS systems much more efficient in energy consumption (Li et al., 2021). A well-known blockchain, Ethereum, is transitioning from PoW to PoS with the help of an Ethereum 2.0 update that can potentially reduce network energy consumption by up to 99%.

4.2.3. Addressing Blockchain's Social and Environmental Impact

Besides the concerns about electric power, blockchain application raises ethical issues about the overall effect on society and the environment. Due to the enormous amount of computational power needed and the costs associated with more of the same and electricity, some elements of the blockchain economy have become centralised in blockchain mining. However, this process may lead to the entrenchment of power to a few players, which goes against the idea of a decentralised consensus model of blockchain and unequal distribution of resources and opportunities. Moreover, the emergence of blockchain-based assets has questioned the sustainable and socially positive creation of value in the digital world using NFTs. In particular, NFTs have attracted discussion and critique due to their contributions to raising speculative markets that are not sustainable in the long run (Gunkel, 2021).

4.3. The Digital Divide and Inclusivity in the Metaverse

When trading companies construct their long-run strategy in the metaverse, they also confront an ethical challenge. To that end, the metaverse presents a rich and profound notion that can give birth to new forms of economic value, catalyse innovation, and knit the world together. However, if it remains noninclusive, the metaverse might intensify existing oppressions, especially those of vulnerable people who have not, over the years, been exposed to information technology and communication amenities.

4.3.1. The Digital Divide: Unequal Access to the Metaverse

The digital divide represents the gap between those with current info and communications technologies (ICTs) and those without. The uneven distribution of participation in the virtual economy inside the metaverse raises ethical questions about including such an economy for some people. The results also demonstrated that income, geographical location, and education were the most important determinants of access to technology, the internet, and digital competence to engage in the metaverse (Beauchamp & Childress, 2019). Immersive VR interfaces require high-quality headsets; internet speeds are also important. However, the two are not often accessible in low-wealth subgroups. This creates an entry barrier that disproportionately negatively affects marginalised people and reins in their ability to participate in the economic and social opportunities found in the metaverse.

4.3.2. Case Studies: Addressing the Digital Divide

Some companies fund digital literacy, cheap tools, and connectivity in society's abject areas to narrow the digital gap. To make the metaverse more available, Facebook (now Meta) has offered cheap VR equipment and has built internet connections in developing populations (Meta et al., 2022).

4.3.3. Ethical Implications of Digital Inclusion

The exclusion of some groups in categorising digital inclusion in the metaverse bears significant ethical implications. Failure to fill the digital divide may mean that firms develop an environment where only individuals adept in technology can engage in online economies. This may turn around and exclude certain groups of people and necessarily increase social and economic differentiated constraints. Companies have to face concerns beyond technology about metaverse representation and diversity. Virtual worlds should be a representation of the many cultures, identities and opinions that we have. This makes everyone feel like they are part and parcel of the event and equalises everybody.

5. CARBON OFFSETTING AND ITS ROLE IN THE METAVERSE

Despite having a platform for innovation, the metaverse has a damaging environmental impact, primarily focusing on energy consumption through data centres and blockchain. There is significant pressure on the metaverse market to progress towards carbon neutrality, thus ensuring its survival and succession, and one of the ways businesses are adopting is carbon offsetting. Carbon offsetting is another process of putting part of the money used for emitting carbon into another process through which a carbon credit value is created in the environment.

5.1. Types of Carbon Offsets

In the current business market, there are large numbers of schemes from which companies may purchase their carbon offsets. These programs are often classified into three categories: afforestation, purchase of renewable energy, and carbon capture and storage. All of them have different advantages and disadvantages, especially when it comes to the use of metaverse for business transactions.

5.1.1. Reforestation and Afforestation Programs

The most common form of carbon credit uses afforestation or reforestation, which entails planting trees that can capture CO_2 from the atmosphere. Those companies often use afforestation because they can balance their CO2 emissions as the trees absorb it. This paper argued that reforestation projects can play a critical role in ensuring that metaverse enterprises embark on energy-intensive operations while at the same time respecting the environment. Decentraland has publicly committed to offsetting its emissions by funding large-scale reforestation projects with environmental organisations.

Effectiveness: Such an endeavour may well be among the complete carbon offset programs that take in vast quantities of CO_2 over the years. Many evaluative tools' efficiency is considered low, ineffective, and burdensome in providing instantaneous feedback. This is true because deforestation, diseases and fire tendencies are the other factors that counter the advantageous effects of a forest.

Table 2. Reforestation projects

Reforestation	Benefits	Challenges
Trees absorb CO_2 from the atmosphere.	A natural, scalable method for carbon sequestration.	Difficult to track carbon sequestration progress.
Offers biodiversity and ecosystem benefits.	Vulnerable to deforestation, fires, and disease.	

5.1.2. Renewable Energy Investments

Carbon offsetting using renewable energy plants is very much in practice. These programs give money to lower the cost of wind, solar, and hydroelectric power to replace subsidies given to fossil fuels. Metaverse firms should switch their electricity to clean power by initiating renewable energy projects. Again, the metaverse of the Meta Company, formerly known as Facebook, will become CO^2 neutral by 2030.

Effectiveness: Renewable energy investment costs lead to lower carbon intensity in countries primarily relying on fossil fuels. These projects remove equivalent emissions and drive the global switch to clean energy. Generation of electricity through renewable sources involves high fixed costs.

Table 3. Renewable energy

Renewable Energy	Benefits	Challenges
Provides clean energy that offsets fossil fuel use.	Effective in reducing emissions over time.	Expensive to implement and requires long-term investment.
Promotes the global transition to renewable energy.	Location-specific; some regions have limited access to renewable infrastructure.	

5.1.3. Carbon Capture and Storage (CCS)

CCS, also known as carbon dioxide capture and storage, is the process through which CO_2 emitted during industrial processes or from atmospheric processes is captured and then stored permanently in one way or another. CCS is typically seen as a better and quicker solution for large firms with massive carbon footprints, particularly those operating high-carbon digital spaces like the metaverse.

Table 4. Carbon Capture and Storage (CCS)

Carbon Capture and Storage	Benefits	Challenges
Directly captures and stores CO_2 emissions.	Highly effective at reducing industrial emissions.	Expensive and technologically complex.
Suitable for hard-to-decarbonize industries.	Long-term storage reliability is uncertain.	

5.2. Challenges with Carbon Offsetting

Carbon offsetting, commonly used in achieving carbon neutrality, has several problems. Offset programs can be rather challenging to evaluate, and the practice has been criticised for enabling organisations to spew CO_2 into the atmosphere and absolve responsibility by funding similar projects. In the metaverse, where everyone has an eye over everything, businesses on the side of carbon offset programs should guarantee the truthfulness of their companies.

5.2.1. Criticism of Carbon Offsetting

Carbon offsetting has been criticised for this reason, mainly how it enables organisations to cover their emissions without adjusting their levels. Large corporations can remain heavy polluters yet advertise as 'carbon neutral' if they finance external activities. This practice leads to doubts about the sustainability of offsetting because it does not imply a direct decrease in emissions. Some experts have opined that with a perspective as such, carbon offsetting is an instrumental approach that allows companies to abdicate the task instead of working towards eradicating the problem (Smith, 2019).

5.2.2. Greenwashing and Carbon Offsetting

Hype is a critical issue in carbon offsetting because many firms engage in greenwashing, that is, in making untrue or overstated statements about their environmental activities. Firms operating in the metaverse are already being called out for their energy use, so any sustainability claims they make must be credible. With transparency and accountability, climate change mitigation and reduction efforts are replaced with a marketing strategy that uses carbon offset programmes. For instance, a firm running a virtual warehouse or centre may have a policy affirming that the firm is carbon neutral because it supports tree planting. However, if such projects are not effectively controlled or do not contribute to the required carbon sequestration, the so-called 'carbon neutrality' is merely a myth in the company. In such a case, the company is simply putting on a show, greenwashing what it does to the consumer and everyone else.

5.3. Ensuring Transparency and Accountability in Carbon Offsetting

To prevent situations that can be considered strictly as greenwashing and ensure that programmes for using carbon offsets are useful, companies of the metaverse should obey principles of openness and responsibility. This involves disclosing accurate and auditable information about the carbon offset projects being invested in and ensuring that those projects meet top-notch environmental standards.

5.3.1. Verified Carbon Standards

Carbon credits and offset programmes such as the verified carbon standard bureaucracies VCS, the gold standard and the climate action reserve are a good way to ensure their credibility is well realised. These organisations ensure that carbon offset projects for environmental soundness and over and above. Accredited offset programmes enable firms to demonstrate the authenticity of carbon neutrality statements to potential parties.

5.3.2. Transparent Reporting

They say businesses should also report on the carbon emissions and investments in offsets. Sustainability quarterly reports cover carbon produced by their electronic operations, offset initiatives they support and project outcomes. This accountability is important, especially for metaverse enterprises, to build trust with the consumers and stakeholders, where discrete transparency is already an issue.

Like its emissions data, Microsoft reveals the carbon offset projects, the amount of carbon offset, and the company's negative carbon performance through sustainability reports (Microsoft et al., 2021).

5.4. Comparing the Effectiveness of Carbon Offset Programs

Carbon offset programs differ depending on the type of project and how well it was carried out. A self-explanatory table highlights the merits of various types of carbon offset programs in terms of their scalability, program cost, environmental benefits, etc.

Table 5. Comparing the Effectiveness of Carbon Offset Programs

Carbon Offset Program	Effectiveness	Scalability	Cost	Challenges
Deforestation	Moderate to High	High	Low to Moderate	Difficult to monitor and vulnerable to external factors like deforestation.
Renewable Energy Investments	High	High	High	High upfront costs and long-term implementation challenges.
Carbon Capture and Storage (CCS)	Very High	Low to Moderate	Very High	Expensive and technologically complex. Concerns about long-term storage reliability.

Carbon offsetting will be a feature of carbon neutrality as firms expand in the metaverse. In the sense that they reduce the adverse effects brought about by energy-visualization internet platforms, carbon offsets do not cure the climate crisis. Realistic programmes must be readily understandable, explicitly responsible, and committed to reducing emissions right at the source. Companies should avoid it, establish trust with consumers and shareholders, and aim for a better and greener metaverse and actual world by purchasing carbon-neutral programmes and using solid, reputable evidence for their sustainability claims.

6. VIRTUAL ECONOMIES: SUSTAINABILITY IN DIGITAL GOODS AND SERVICES

This brings tremendous opportunities to create new, more sustainable forms of economy in the context of the metaverse. The primary these economies, which involve the exchange of virtual goods, digital real estate, and non-fungible tokens-{NFT}, are redesigning how production, ownership and consumption are perceived in a world dominated by digital interfaces. However, like with every system, these innovations take their toll on the environment. This section focuses on the effects of NFTs on the environment, the emergence of digital real estate property, and the circular economy in virtual premises. Out of these, the former's dynamics help to evaluate virtual economies concerning their sustainability and contribution to carbon neutrality.

6.1. Environmental Impact of NFTs

As a financial asset, NFTs are not the same as Bitcoin; each NFT represents a specific digital good such as art, music, virtual land or virtual identity. Cryptographic generators secure and authenticate entities on the blockchain network for non-fungible tokens. There is disagreement about the environmental sustainability of NFTs. Most non-fungible tokens are generated and transacted through Ethereum, a PoW-based blockchain platform. Proof of Work consumes much energy in transaction validations in the Blockchain and the process involved in token creation. Thus, the energy needed to process an NFT creation and subsequent transactions may be equivalent to a European household's average monthly electricity use (de Vries, 2021).

6.2. Virtual Real Estate

NFTs enable artists, manufacturers and collectors to purchase, market and exchange one-of-a-kind digital products and transform the digital realm. While BTC is tradeable on exchanges as a currency since it is homogeneous, NFTs are exceptional and may represent artwork, music, virtual land, or characters. Thus, blockchains maintain and authenticate NFT ownership.

Scholars are divided on the extent to which NFTs are environmentally friendly. Ethereum is a PoW blockchain, and most NFTs are either minted or sold on this platform. Proof of Work is inefficient; energy is used for transaction validation and token issuance. A single token_mint and sale is estimated to be equivalent to the average monthly carbon footprint of an EU household's electricity consumption (de Vries, 2021). Cryptocurrencies have been criticised for energy consumption. Thus, NFTs could intensify the effects of blockchain technology. The following combines the PoS consensus technique in Ethereum 2.0 to eliminate these problems. Proof of Stake (PoS) reduces transaction validation computational power, conserving energy. Token possession chooses validators as opposed to Proof of Work.

7. REGULATORY AND POLICY FRAMEWORKS SUPPORTING CARBON NEUTRALITY

With the world gradually adapting to the integration of the digital world – now popularised by the metaverse- the consequences must be given regard to the environment. Buchanan et al. (2011) mention that governments and corporations are gradually awakening to the need to make practices carbon-neutral. The following section discusses open worldwide relations for carbon neutrality in the metaverse: diversions from government and corporate sustainability guidelines. It also provides examples of the development of government-business cooperation needed to achieve sustainable goals in this emerging digital environment.

7.1 The Paris Agreement

International policies targeting climate change were founded on the 2015 Paris Accord, which aimed to avoid global warming over 1.5°C beyond pre-industrial levels. Some 197 countries have pledged to cut greenhouse gas emissions and develop a green economy. While centred on energy and transportation, the thinking that underpins the agreement is relevant to the digital economy and the metaverse. As much as the internet enables data centres, blockchain systems, and virtual platforms like the metaverse to contribute to carbon emissions, the UK, Germany, and Japan have incorporated the digital economy into their climate plans. These nations are mitigating ICT pollution by regulating ICT emissions and innovating on green impulses to ensure firms adopt renewable energy in digital processes.

The Digital Strategy of the European Union, with the backing of the European Green Deal, calls upon digital technology to minimise its carbon footprint. By 2050, the EU plans to neutralise the digital industry's climate; to achieve this, it is necessary to reduce emissions from data centres while improving energy efficiency and using renewable energy sources (European Commission, 2020).

7.2 COP26 and New Climate Commitments

Countries' commitments made at the 26th meeting of the parties to the UN Framework Convention on Climate Change held in Glasgow in 2021, referred to as COP26, were made with a focus on innovation and technology to reach net zero.

Governments highlighted the demand for technological innovations that may help reduce carbon footprints in the built environment and information technology. Several countries disclosed their intention to raise their spending on green technologies, such as energy-conscious computer facilities and blockchain solutions that may be used as the foundation of the metaverse (UNFCCC, 2021).

7.4.1 Internal Corporate Goals for Carbon Neutrality

Many organisations, including Microsoft Corporation, Google, and Meta, formerly known as Facebook, have declared net zero emission goals that involve precise targets for oversight from data centres, offices, and other facilities. Microsoft has clearly stated that it intends to achieve carbon neutrality by 2030, though it is not trying to emit carbon dioxide. This includes metaverse virtual experiences hosted in Microsoft Azure. The corporation is also pursuing carbon removal and offset to align the activities in the virtual world with sustainability goals (Microsoft et al., 2021). With its vast interconnect infrastructure known as its data centres that drive its search engine and metaverse, Google seeks to achieve carbon-free energy consumption in the next eight years. Google has achieved 100% renewable energy consumption to power its operations and is now working towards decreasing the energy intensity of its digital products (Google et al., 2022). Meta, a metaverse advocate, is committed to setting their 2030 net-zero emissions target for their value chain. Meta's CO2 objectives are to transition all its operations globally to rely on renewable power and improve the energy efficiency of metaverse platforms (Meta et al., 2022). Meta is also working on having low-energy VR and AR devices to reduce the energy expenditure on virtual companionship.

7.4.2 Sustainable Business Models in the Metaverse

Businesses are also endeavouring to devise new business models in the metaverse that are more sustainable. For instance, digital products and services will likely have a low carbon impact since their use can be achieved through computer input rather than tangible products. More fashion houses are venturing into the metaverse by selling virtual wear that avatars can wear instead of producing clothes that must be physically transported in extreme ways (Verdict, 2022). Another example is IKEA, which has implemented virtual reality (VR) in a way that helps customers design rooms in VR with 3D simulations, all without having to create physical prototypes of the rooms or put them in the actual stores. These virtual items align with other sustainability initiatives, including minimising waste and encouraging a circular economy (IKEA et al., 2021). Currently, the gaming business that constitutes the metaverse is also seeking sustainable solutions to exercise a less negative influence on the natural environment.

8. FUTURE OUTLOOK: ACHIEVING CARBON NEUTRALITY IN THE METAVERSE

With a focus on the growth of the metaverse, integration of sustainability concepts into the developing process is possible. All in all, reaching for the carbon neutrality of the metaverse is possible and realistic. Opened technology for stakeholder collaboration, the metaverse could design sustainable digital ecosystems by leveraging the novel concept. Edge computing, Machine Learning, and Green blockchain technology bring down the carbon footprints of virtual worlds, which may lead to metaverse carbon neutrality. It also underlines the need for cross-industry, government and consumer cooperation to drive sustainability and the following challenges and opportunities regarding the renewable energy scalability of the digital economy.

8.1. Technological Advancements: Reducing the Environmental Impact of the Metaverse

The canopy will unveil how technology will help address environmental concerns arising from the metaverse in the forthcoming section. While the metaverse develops, there will be opportunities to bring new technologies into the world of nets as soon as more digital foundations are prepared to support it. Quantum computing, optimisation from artificial intelligence, and efficient hardware systems, which are relatively new, are highly likely to contribute significantly to reducing the overall carbon footprint of the metaverse. Quantum computing is one of the metaverse environmental technologies. Quantum computers employ Qubits and not BINARY BITS like conventional computers, which are 0s and 1s and can represent several states. Quantum computers can solve complex problems faster and with less energy than a classical computer. Applications: New algorithms for data centres, blockchain systems, and AI can be developed with quantum computing (Nielsen & Chuang, 2010). Applying quantum computing could make metaverse data centres energy efficient by managing server processes and minimising data processing duplication. Quantum algorithms could have brought about data compression, making it take less space, and hence, there is minimal need for large storage systems and hence a reduction in energy used by data centres. A faster means of resolving transactions in blockchain systems could be provided by quantum computing, hence making it possible to scale energy-efficient consensus models like the PoS (Cacciapuoti et al., 2020). Quantum computing is promising even though the technology is still in its infancy.

8.1.2. AI-Driven Energy Optimization

AI has already been a critical enabler for maximising energy efficiency in data systems and will only expand its part in pursuing carbon neutrality in metaverse applications. Another way by which AI can be used is in analysing organisations' patterns of energy use, predicting demands, and controlling energy-saving measures in real-time to make data centres, blockchain networks, and Virtual Reality (VR) systems become more energy efficient (Khanna et al., 2022).AI can also be used in automating the cooling systems in data centres, which is one of the largest consumers of energy in digital infrastructure. Using forecast methods, AI can reduce the energy required to regulate the functioning temperature of servers and storage. Also, AI can be proposed to coordinate the distribution of assets in blockchain systems to minimise energy consumption for transaction processing and network maintenance (Li et al., 2021). Besides, quantum computing, AI, and ML remained instrumental in lowering the environmental impact of the metaverse As a result of innovations in the design of both the hardware and software. Manufacturers are already working on producing servers, storage and communications equipment, for example, which will require a low number of watts per hour to operate at optimum efficiency. For instance, low-power CPUs have been introduced to the market, and convective, passive, liquid, and immersion cooling methods and other power-saving technologies are applied to make data centres power-efficient (Andrae, 2020).On the software side, the decreased complexity of coding techniques needed to operate digital systems is being developed.

8.2. Collaborative Solutions: Building a Sustainable Digital Environment

Corporations, governments and buyers must contribute towards attaining metaverse carbon neutrality. The metaverse comprises complex environmental problems that one entity cannot solve. To achieve a higher and more sustainable impact with such efforts, a collaborative model that relies on the strengths of relevant actors is required.

8.2.1. Business-Led Sustainability Initiatives

Fortunately, businesses take the lead in metaverse creation; thus, they should set an example of sustainable practices. Some technological companies such as Microsoft, Google and Amazon have adopted renewable power sources and energy-efficient gadgets to fight climate change (Google et al., 2022). It has ambitious targets on carbon neutrality, with some vowing to be carbon-negative within a decade.

In the same way, businesses in the metaverse world can minimise the negative impacts of their activities on the environment. Virtual property developers can make available platforms to help minimise client's virtual environments' impact on carbon footprint. Sustainable blockchains like PoS can reduce Decentralized network energy consumption. Firms can also cover their carbon footprints with emissions related to digital marketing (Smith, 2019).

9. CONCLUSION

Innovation practices in the metaverse can revolutionise sectors, economies, and technology consumption. Indeed, as this digital ecosystem develops, clarifying its consequences for the surrounding environment – consistently, energy consumption among them. The metaverse cannot become carbon neutral on its own; innovation is required, regulation has to be developed, and finally, but importantly, consumers have to demand sustainability.

Metaverse has a negative impact, which technology advancements will mitigate in the future. Quantum computing, artificial intelligence, and efficient energy hardware enhance the digital structure to lower energy consumption. Though it is revolutionary, it predicts a time when computations will be done in a way that is more efficient and, at the same time, consumes less energy than data centres. AI-sourced systems can enhance the data centre and blockchain network features necessary to support a sustainable metaverse. They are critical in providing for rising energy demands occasioned by organisations' and individuals' increased adoption of online operations. To support the growth of the metaverse, businesses, governments, and consumers have to pull through collectively. Businesses must set renewable energy, energy-efficient blockchain systems, and transparent sustainability standards. Support schemes for renewable energy uptake, carbon offsetting, and sustainability reporting will help firms achieve their corporate net-zero targets; thus, policies from the government are imperative. People can also demand that firms be accountable for their environmental commitments and support firms that are open to being environmentally friendly.

REFERENCES

Alves, R. (2021). Fashion brands and greenwashing: The ethical dilemma of sustainability claims. *Sustainable Fashion Journal*, 4(2), 100–115.

Andrae, A. (2020). The environmental impact of digital infrastructure: Data centres and emissions. *Journal of Energy Efficiency*, 12(4), 234–245.

Ball, M. (2022). *The Metaverse: And How It Will Revolutionize Everything*. Liveright Publishing Corporation. DOI: 10.15358/9783800669400

Beauchamp, T. L., & Childress, J. F. (2019). *Principles of Biomedical Ethics* (8th ed.). Oxford University Press.

Cacciapuoti, A. S., Caleffi, M., Tafuri, L., & Sottile, C. (2020). Blockchain and quantum computing: Future directions in finance. *Future Internet*, 12(10), 183.

Climate Neutral Data Centre Pact. (2021). Retrieved from https://www.climateneutral datacentre.net/

De Vries, A. (2021). Bitcoin's growing energy problem. *Joule*, 3(2), 239–242.

Decentraland. (2022). Sustainability Initiatives. Available at: https://decentraland.org

Dionisio, J. D. N., Burns, W. G., & Gilbert, R. (2013). 3D virtual worlds and the metaverse: Current status and future possibilities. *ACM Computing Surveys*, 45(3), 1–38. DOI: 10.1145/2480741.2480751

Ethereum Foundation. (2022). The Merge: Ethereum's transition to proof-of-stake. Available at: https://ethereum.org/en/upgrades/merge/

European Commission. (2020). A European Green Deal. Retrieved from https://ec .europa.eu/info/strategy/priorities-2019-2024/european-green-deal_en

Games, E. Sustainability Report. (2022). Available at: https://www.epicgames.com/ sustainability

Google. (2021). How AI is helping to reduce energy use in our data centres. Available at: https://blog.google/inside-google/infrastructure/ai-reduces-energy-use/

Gunkel, D. (2021). The ethics of NFTs and digital ownership: Speculation and sustainability. *Digital Culture & Ethics*, 18(1), 120–136.

Hoskinson, C. (2021). *The Cardano network: An overview of the energy-efficient PoS blockchain*. Cardano Whitepaper.

IKEA Sustainability Report. (2021). Retrieved from https://about.ikea.com/en/sustainability

IPCC. (2021). *Sixth Assessment Report: Climate Change 2021*. Cambridge University Press.

Khanna, R., Patel, T., & Williams, R. (2022). The impact of AI and machine learning on sustainability in digital ecosystems. *Journal of AI Research*, 22(1), 123–136.

Kouhizadeh, M., & Sarkis, J. (2020). Blockchain adoption for sustainable supply chains. *Sustainability*, 12(4), 1472–1484.

Li, X., Wang, Y., & Zhou, H. (2021). Carbon-neutral blockchain technologies: Opportunities and challenges. *Blockchain Review*, 8(1), 33–42.

Marr, B. (2021). The key differences between virtual reality, augmented reality, and mixed reality. Forbes. Available at: https://www.forbes.com/sites/bernardmarr/2021/03/19/the-key-differences-between-virtual-reality-augmented-reality-and-mixed-reality

Marr, B. (2021). The key differences between virtual reality, augmented reality, and mixed reality. Forbes. Available at: https://www.forbes.com/sites/bernardmarr/2021/03/19/the-key-differences-between-virtual-reality-augmented-reality-and-mixed-reality

Nielsen, M. A., & Chuang, I. L. (2010). *Quantum Computation and Quantum Information*. Cambridge University Press.

. Ondrejka, C. (2004). Escaping the gilded cage: The user created content and built the metaverse. New York Law School Law Review, pp. 49, 81.

Report, A. S. (2022). Available at: https://sustainability.aboutamazon.com

Report, G. S. (2022). Available at: https://sustainability.google.com

Report, M. C. (2022). Available at: https://connectivity.fb.com

Report, M. S. (2021). Available at: https://sustainability.microsoft.com

Report, M. S. (2021). Available at: https://www.microsoft.com/en-us/sustainability

Report, N. S. (2021). Available at: https://sustainability.nianticlabs.com

Smith, J. (2019). The limits of carbon offsetting in virtual economies. *Global Environmental Change*, 25(6), 402–410.

Standard, G. (2021). Certified Carbon Offset Programs. Available at: https://www.goldstandard.org

Thomson, E., & Clark, D. (2022). The role of policy in promoting sustainability in digital ecosystems. *Journal of Digital Policy*, 19(4), 223–234.

. UNFCCC. (2015). Paris Agreement. UNFCCC Report.

UNFCCC. (2015). Paris Agreement. United Nations Framework Convention on Climate Change. Available at: https://unfccc.int/process-and-meetings/the-paris-agreement/the-paris-agreement

UNFCCC. (2021). COP26: The Glasgow Climate Pact. United Nations Framework Convention on Climate Change. Available at: https://unfccc.int/cop26

Verdict. (2022). Meta's metaverse ambitions: Will it lead to a sustainable future? Verdict Magazine. Available at: https://www.verdict.co.uk/meta-metaverse-sustainability

Chapter 5
Exploring Brand Presence in the Metaverse:
The Fly London Fashion Experience

Joana Oliveira
ISAG, Portugal

Victor Tavares
https://orcid.org/0000-0002-1994-5501
ISAG, Portugal

Rui Rosa Dias
https://orcid.org/0000-0002-5934-8429
ISAG, Portugal

ABSTRACT

This book chapter explores the transformative role of the metaverse in fashion branding through an in-depth case study of Fly London, a renowned global fashion brand known for its creativity and innovation. Employing a qualitative, descriptive, and exploratory methodology, the study analyzes Fly London's strategic journey into the metaverse. The research unveils the critical variables influencing brand presence in the metaverse, including brand equity, consumer engagement, and the role of digital twin branding in driving consumer attachment. By leveraging structured interviews with internal and external stakeholders, the study identifies Fly London's strategic objectives, operational challenges, and the impact of immersive brand experiences on consumer perceptions. This chapter also provides theoretical and practical implications for brand managers, highlighting the significance of personalization, gamification, and community engagement in metaverse-based brand development.

DOI: 10.4018/979-8-3693-9005-4.ch005

INTRODUCTION

The metaverse, a term that has transitioned from science fiction into a tangible reality, represents one of the most significant technological advancements of the 21st century. Characterized by a convergence of augmented reality (AR), virtual reality (VR), blockchain technology, and interactive 3D environments, the metaverse is revolutionizing the way people interact, work, and consume. For the fashion industry, metaverse offers an unprecedented opportunity to expand its digital footprint, redefine consumer engagement, and create immersive experiences that bridge the gap between the physical and digital worlds (Ball, 2022). Brands that adapt to this new digital frontier are not only positioning themselves as innovators but are also securing a competitive edge in a rapidly changing market landscape.

The metaverse's importance as a business tool cannot be overstated. According to Abovitz et al. (2022), the metaverse is not merely a trend but a transformative platform that alters consumer expectations and business operations. Brands must adapt their strategies to integrate immersive, interactive experiences that align with modern consumer expectations of personalization and authenticity. Generations Y and Z, who are at the forefront of digital adoption, demand seamless and engaging experiences that resonate with their lifestyle (Çelikkol, 2022). This demographic shift emphasizes the need for brands to innovate and incorporate technology into their core strategies to remain relevant.

The process of integrating a brand into the metaverse involves more than just digital expansion; it requires a reimagining of brand management principles to fit a new context. Aaker & Joachimsthaler (2000) emphasize that successful brand management is built on creating a strong, consistent identity and aligning it with consumer touchpoints. Transferring this concept to the metaverse entails rethinking how brand values are communicated and experienced in an environment where consumers are not just passive recipients but active participants in the brand story (Foster et al., 2022).

Despite the opportunities, entering the metaverse comes with its share of challenges. The high costs associated with developing advanced digital assets, ensuring platform compatibility, and maintaining data privacy are significant barriers (Burmann et al., 2017). Moreover, brands must navigate the complexities of maintaining authenticity in an environment that allows for limitless creative expression, which can sometimes stray from the original brand identity (Chernatony & McDonald, 2003). Addressing these challenges requires strategic foresight, technological partnerships, and a deep understanding of consumer behavior in digital spaces.

In fact, consumer behavior has undergone significant changes, with Generations Y and Z leading the media and entertainment sector, demanding more personalized, interactive, and immersive experiences. Video games are paving the way for an increasingly digital, personalized, social, and addictive future, where real and digital life converge (Deloitte, 2022). Interest in the metaverse has been rising, with companies of all sizes exploring this digital universe where people can meet, interact, and conduct business, unleashing unlimited creativity while removing physical barriers. This digital domain is reshaping people's lives, urging brands to pay closer attention. On one hand, we are witnessing a moment of transformation and disruption of the familiar; on the other hand, new opportunities are emerging for brands across various market sectors (Wunderman Thompson Intelligence, 2021b).

In this context, the retail sector is undergoing a natural evolution, altering consumer habits. From physical markets to digital spaces, fashion digitalization is poised to take a further step toward the (im)materiality of garments. The new trend is purely digital fashion, which will infiltrate our reality sooner than anticipated (Silva, 2022). If, in the near future, real life is to be replicated in the digital world and consumption increasingly focuses on digital items, preparing brand management for this new reality becomes imperative. It is essential to understand how brands can remain competitive in the market, create value, and identify the variables necessary to position themselves effectively in the metaverse. Based on an extensive literature review and acknowledging that the concept of the metaverse is still in its preliminary stages, it becomes evident that further contributions are needed to advance brand management. Thus, the present moment is ideal for initiating efforts to develop strategies and solutions that prepare brands for this transformative reality.

Fly London, a globally recognized fashion brand known for its distinctive and bold approach, exemplifies how a brand can strategically navigate this emerging space. With its core identity rooted in creativity and nonconformity, Fly London embarked on a journey to explore the metaverse, aiming to extend its brand ethos into a digital realm that promotes personalization, interaction, and shared experiences. This chapter focuses on Fly London's strategic approach to establishing and managing its brand in the metaverse, a space that is reshaping traditional branding paradigms and consumer behavior.

- The Research Problem

Despite the growing interest and investment in the metaverse, significant gaps exist in understanding how brands can successfully manage their presence in this space. While theoretical discussions about digital branding and consumer engagement have expanded, empirical studies that examine the practical implementation of these concepts in the metaverse remain limited. Specifically, there is a lack of research on how brands can:

a) Maintain consistency and authenticity in virtual environments.

b) Navigate the technological and financial challenges of metaverse integration.
c) Effectively engage digital-native audiences through immersive experiences.

Fly London's strategic initiatives offer a practical framework for addressing these gaps. This chapter explores how the brand has integrated core principles of brand management into its metaverse strategy, providing actionable insights for other businesses. By examining the opportunities and challenges encountered by Fly London, the study seeks to contribute to the growing discourse on brand presence in the metaverse.

In this context, the primary objective of this book chapter is to contribute to understanding how fashion industry brands are striving to establish their presence in the metaverse, guided by the following research question:

- **How and why are fashion industry brands managing their presence in the metaverse?**
- Research aim, objectives, and questions

The primary aim of this chapter is to analyze Fly London's approach to establishing and managing its brand presence in the metaverse. The specific objectives of the research are the following:

1) Identify the perceptions and brand management practices for the metaverse adopted by executive managers and brand managers, in the focal context;
2) Understand and analyze the perceptions of other actors in the fashion industry sector (consultants and academics);
3) Identify the management practices that the company is adopting for the metaverse.

For the case study, the following seven research questions were defined:

1) What objectives has the company established for the metaverse?
2) What role does the brand aim to play in the metaverse (e.g., creating experiences, facilitating interactions, etc.)?
3) What initial activities for presence in the metaverse are being or will be implemented?
4) How are short-term results monitored to ensure the brand's long-term potential in the metaverse?
5) How does the brand seek to better understand its consumers in the metaverse?
6) How does the company allocate and manage resources and competencies for brand management in the metaverse?

7) How and why does the company integrate the challenges of the metaverse into its strategy and operational models?

- Importance of the Chapter

This chapter is significant for both academic and practical reasons. Academically, it contributes to the limited body of research on branding in the metaverse by providing an empirical case study of Fly London's strategies and practices. It bridges the gap between theoretical frameworks and practical applications, offering insights into how traditional brand management principles can be adapted to virtual environments.

From a practical perspective, it provides actionable guidance for fashion brands seeking to establish a presence in the metaverse. As the metaverse continues to evolve, understanding its implications for consumer behavior, brand equity, and engagement is crucial for businesses aiming to remain competitive. Fly London's innovative approach serves as a reference for how brands can leverage the metaverse to create value, foster loyalty, and maintain relevance in a digital-first economy.

- Structure

This chapter is structured into six key sections, each contributing to a comprehensive understanding of brand presence and consumer engagement in the metaverse:

1. Literature Review: This section establishes the theoretical foundation for understanding brand management and consumer behavior within the metaverse.
2. Conceptual framework for brand presence in the metaverse: This section outlines the critical components that shape how brands establish their presence in virtual environments.
3. Methodology: Here, the research design, data collection methods, and analytical framework are presented.
4. Analysis and discussion of results: This section provides a detailed examination of Fly London's metaverse strategy, including its practices, challenges, and opportunities.
5. Conclusion: Synthesizes the chapter's key findings, emphasizing the practical implications for fashion brands seeking to navigate the metaverse.
6. Limitations and recommendations: The final section identifies research limitations and proposes areas for future exploration.

1. LITERATURE REVIEW

The rapid evolution of the metaverse, driven by advancements in Web 3.0 technologies such as blockchain, augmented reality (AR), virtual reality (VR), and immersive 3D environments, is transforming the landscape of brand management and consumer engagement. This literature review critically examines the theoretical underpinnings and practical implications of managing brand presence in the metaverse, focusing on its opportunities, challenges, and emerging strategies, particularly within the fashion industry. The discussion is grounded in key concepts of brand management, consumer behavior, and digital marketing, providing a foundation for understanding Fly London's approach to navigating this transformative space.

In fact, the accelerated development of immersive technology is dramatically impacting the business world, ushering in new challenges for brands and signaling the end of the "consumer era." This impact necessitates a strategic rethinking of value propositions, emphasizing the "power of being human as individuals, not just as consumers (human-centric brands)" (André & Luiz, 2022, p. 32). According to Kotler et al. (2021), for Generations Y and Z, the internet is considered an indispensable part of their lives, and technology is viewed as an extension of themselves, erasing the boundaries between the physical and digital worlds. This impact is evident in the emergence of the metaverse, particularly in the fashion industry, where brands are positioning themselves with new digital products and experiences. This shift creates opportunities for brands, such as restructuring business models, redesigning teams, and generating new revenue streams.

In this context, the metaverse represents a combination of platform, technology, and place, offering fully immersive virtual reality experiences through personalized avatars, our digital "selves". The opportunities and challenges for brands are clear. To respond effectively to the Web 3.0 era, brands must develop strategies and train their teams to navigate digital environments successfully, making an understanding of these virtual worlds essential (Liffreing, 2021).

1.1 The Metaverse: Definition and evolution

The metaverse is defined as an immersive, virtual ecosystem that combines elements of augmented reality (AR), virtual reality (VR), and interactive 3D environments, forming a persistent, shared digital space where users can interact, create, and engage in various activities (Ball, 2022). The metaverse goes beyond the scope of traditional internet experiences by introducing interconnected environments where individuals participate through avatars and digital identities, thereby redefining human interaction and digital commerce (Lee et al., 2021).

The evolution of the metaverse has roots in early online platforms like *Second Life*, where users engaged in a digital economy and built communities. However, recent technological advancements have expanded the concept into a multi-faceted ecosystem supported by blockchain technology, enhancing the ownership and trade of digital assets such as Non-Fungible Tokens (NFTs). According to Abovitz et al. (2022), the metaverse is poised to become the next major digital frontier, offering brands a platform that supports more interactive and personalized consumer engagements.

1.2 Brand Identity, Brand Personality and Management in the Digital Era

Brand identity is defined by Aaker & Joachimsthaler (2000) as the unique set of brand associations that a company aims to create and maintain, serving as a blueprint for brand management strategies. The metaverse challenges traditional brand management by requiring brands to transfer these associations to an environment that prioritizes interaction, customization, and consumer cocreation. Maintaining brand authenticity in this space involves not only replicating visual elements but also embedding brand values and stories into digital experiences (Chernatony, 1999).

Burmann et al. (2017) introduced the concept of identity-based brand management, which highlights the importance of coherence between a brand's internal identity and its external expressions. In the metaverse, this means ensuring that the brand's digital representation, from avatars to virtual storefronts, aligns with its core values and resonates with its target audience. Fly London, for example, has leveraged these principles by designing virtual spaces and digital assets that reflect its bold, creative ethos, ensuring consistency across physical and digital touchpoints.

Brand personality is a set of connections to the brand, inferring a guarantee to customers. It incorporates a central and expanded character. The core brand personality is the focal, timeless embodiment of the brand that remains consistent as it moves into new markets and with new products. The central character focuses, in a comprehensive way, around the properties of the product (benefit, customer profile, store climate and product execution) and the extended character is the fabric around the components of the brand personality, compounded into durable and meaningful synergies that provide a brand surface and culmination, brand identity highlights, relationships, and solid image (Selase et al. 2018).

1.3 Digital Twins, Narrative Branding and Gaming in Metaverse

Digital twins are virtual representations of physical products, processes, or systems, enabling real-time interaction between the digital and physical worlds. Initially developed for use in manufacturing and supply chain management, digital twins have now found applications in consumer-facing industries, particularly branding and marketing. Daldiran & Daldiran (2023) emphasize that digital twins not only enhance transparency in supply chains but also support marketing strategies, especially in creating compelling brand narratives and supporting sustainability initiatives.

Narrative branding focuses on embedding stories within brand identity to create emotional connections with consumers. Unlike traditional branding, which often relies on logos or slogans, narrative branding uses story arcs and characters to make brands more relatable and memorable. Escalas (2004) highlighted the importance of stories in consumer decision-making, suggesting that well-crafted brand narratives influence how consumers internalize and relate to brands. In the context of digital twins, the narrative can be represented through the story of a product's journey, its role in the consumer's life, or the ethical story of how the product was manufactured, as observed in sustainable fashion initiatives (Vidushi & Dawar, 2024).

One of the most significant advancements in branding storytelling is the application of digital twins as "narrative agents." Digital twins allow consumers to experience products virtually before purchase, transforming how brand stories are delivered. Gupta et al. (2024) discuss how collaborative robotics and digital twins provide a foundation for immersive brand storytelling. Their findings show that brand narratives can be embedded within interactive interfaces, allowing consumers to follow the "life story" of a product as it evolves from creation to final use. For instance, brands in the fashion industry can showcase the production process of a sustainable fashion item, which enhances brand transparency and consumer trust. This process builds on the ethical storytelling frameworks mentioned by Vidushi and Dawar (2024) in their exploration of how digital twins can support sustainable fashion by communicating the ethical journey of a product.

The metaverse has expanded the scope for narrative branding by allowing companies to create immersive story-driven experiences. Digital twins play a pivotal role in these environments. For instance, luxury fashion brands such as Gucci and Balenciaga use virtual replicas of their products (digital twins) in platforms like Roblox, where consumers can interact with branded narratives. The concept of avatars and customized in-world experiences offers new opportunities for brands to tell personalized, interactive stories. This is reinforced by Rani et al. (2024), who assert that metaverse platforms are fertile ground for integrating virtual product replicas into brand storytelling.

The consumer's avatar serves as a narratist, allowing the individual to actively engage with the brand's story. The emotional engagement that emerges from this interactive approach to storytelling increases consumer-brand attachment. The narrative branding approach is particularly relevant for fashion brands, where users can customize digital products, follow the "origin story" of their clothing, and participate in exclusive events related to the brand.

The literature on digital twins and narrative branding highlights a convergence of technology, storytelling, and branding strategy (Alsamhi et al., 2024; Rani et al., 2024; Uddin et al., 2024). Digital twins provide a means for consumers to engage with brands through interactive and personalized experiences, while narrative branding creates emotional connections with consumers. The combination of these approaches offers powerful new ways for brands to engage audiences, establish trust, and differentiate themselves in a competitive landscape. As technology advances, the role of AI, blockchain, and AR/VR in enhancing digital twin narratives will only increase, providing fertile ground for future research and brand innovation.

The concept of gaming in the metaverse has gained significant traction as gaming platforms evolve into fully immersive, shared virtual environments. Unlike traditional online multiplayer games, metaverse-based games leverage technologies like virtual reality (VR), augmented reality (AR), blockchain, and artificial intelligence (AI) to offer players new levels of interactivity, customization, and participation in game economies. This review outlines key themes in the scholarly literature on gaming in the metaverse, with a focus on user interaction, technological enablers, and economic models. Gaming in the metaverse extends beyond traditional video game experiences to create persistent virtual worlds where users maintain ongoing interactions with both players and digital objects. Mishra & Kautish (2024) highlight that metaverse-based gaming platforms allow players to participate in a mix of entertainment, social interaction, and commerce. Games like Roblox and Fortnite exemplify this shift, where users not only play but also create, trade, and monetize in-game assets.

According to Lee et al. (2024), metaverse games utilize decentralized architectures where blockchain-based tokens and NFTs enable player-driven economies. Players can create and sell in-game assets, transforming gaming from a recreational activity into an income-generating opportunity. This approach aligns with the concept of the "play-to-earn" (P2E) model, where players are financially rewarded for their in-game participation.

1.4 The Role of Consumer Behavior and Engagement in Metaverse

Understanding consumer behavior in the metaverse is critical for brands aiming to optimize their strategies. Generations Y and Z, who are digital natives, show a strong preference for experiences that merge technology with personalization (Çelikkol, 2022). These consumers seek brands that provide interactive, co-created experiences that allow them to express their identity through digital means (Wunderman Thompson Intelligence, 2021a). This aligns with the experiential consumption model proposed by Kotler et al. (2021), which posits that consumers are drawn to experiences that create emotional and social connections.

The metaverse allows brands to offer such experiences through personalized avatars, virtual events, and interactive shopping environments. Foster et al. (2022) discuss the significant impact that avatars have on consumer-brand relationships. Avatars act as personal extensions of users, and brands that integrate avatar customization and branded digital items foster stronger engagement and consumer loyalty. Fly London's use of interactive virtual showrooms exemplifies this approach, creating a platform where users can engage with the brand beyond the limitations of physical retail.

1.5 Challenges for Fashion Brands in Metaverse

The potential benefits of entering the metaverse come with a unique set of challenges that fashion brands must navigate:

a) Technological and financial barriers

One of the primary challenges for brands entering the metaverse is the substantial technological investment required to create high-quality, immersive experiences. Developing 3D assets, integrating blockchain technology for digital ownership, and ensuring compatibility across platforms are resource-intensive processes (Burmann et al., 2017). Smaller brands may struggle to allocate sufficient budgets to compete with larger, more established players (Cagnina & Poian, 2011).

b) Brand consistency and authenticity

Ensuring consistency in brand identity across physical and digital platforms is a complex task. Brands risk diluting their identity when entering new digital environments that allow for a high degree of creative flexibility (Chernatony & McDonald, 2003). Aaker & Joachimsthaler (2000) emphasize that maintaining brand authenticity is essential for consumer trust, and this is particularly challenging in an environment where users expect continuous updates and fresh content.

c) Data privacy and security

Data privacy and security are significant concerns in the metaverse, where user data is often collected to provide personalized experiences. Brands must navigate a complex landscape of global data protection regulations, such as the General Data Protection Regulation (GDPR) in Europe, to maintain consumer trust (Ball, 2022). Blockchain technology offers a potential solution by providing transparent and secure data management systems (Alves, 2022).

1.6 Opportunities for Brands in the Metaverse

Despite these challenges, the metaverse offers significant opportunities for fashion brands to redefine consumer engagement and build new revenue streams, namely:

a) Enhanced consumer engagement through immersive experiences

The metaverse allows brands to create interactive and immersive experiences that go beyond the capabilities of traditional media (Çelikkol, 2022). Brands can host virtual fashion shows, offer 3D fitting rooms, and create digital pop-up stores, providing consumers with an enriched experience that enhances brand loyalty. Joy et al. (2022) emphasize that these strategies resonate with younger demographics who value personalization and active participation in their shopping experiences.

b) NFTs and digital asset monetization

The emergence of NFTs has introduced new revenue channels for fashion brands, allowing them to sell limited-edition digital fashion items and collectibles. NFTs enable consumers to own unique pieces of digital art or fashion, fostering a sense of exclusivity and brand affiliation (Dhruv, 2022). According to Alves (2022), the integration of NFTs not only provides a novel way to generate income but also strengthens the brand's image as an innovator in the digital space.

c) Building branded communities

One of the most significant opportunities in the metaverse is the ability to build branded communities. Brands that create digital spaces where consumers can interact with each other and share experiences contribute to a stronger sense of community and brand loyalty (Çelikkol, 2022). Wunderman Thompson Intelligence (2021b) notes that these communities often lead to increased consumer advocacy, as members become brand ambassadors.

d) Long-term brand equity

The metaverse provides an opportunity for brands to build long-term equity by positioning themselves as pioneers in digital innovation. Early adopters who successfully integrate their brand into the metaverse can establish themselves as leaders in the digital economy, attracting tech-savvy consumers and reinforcing their market position (Abovitz et al., 2022). This strategic advantage is crucial as more brands explore virtual engagement methods.

2. CONCEPTUAL FRAMEWORK FOR BRAND PRESENCE IN THE METAVERSE

The rapid evolution of the metaverse has transformed how brands interact with consumers, offering unprecedented opportunities for immersive brand experiences. Unlike traditional digital marketing, the metaverse enables brands to engage users through interactive, gamified, and community-driven experiences. However, to fully understand how brands can leverage the metaverse, it is essential to conceptualize the key factors that drive brand engagement and consumer loyalty in this new environment.

The conceptual framework for brand presence in the metaverse presented in **Figure 1** outlines the critical components that influence how brands may establish a meaningful and lasting presence in virtual environments.

Figure 1. **Conceptual framework for brand presence in the metaverse**

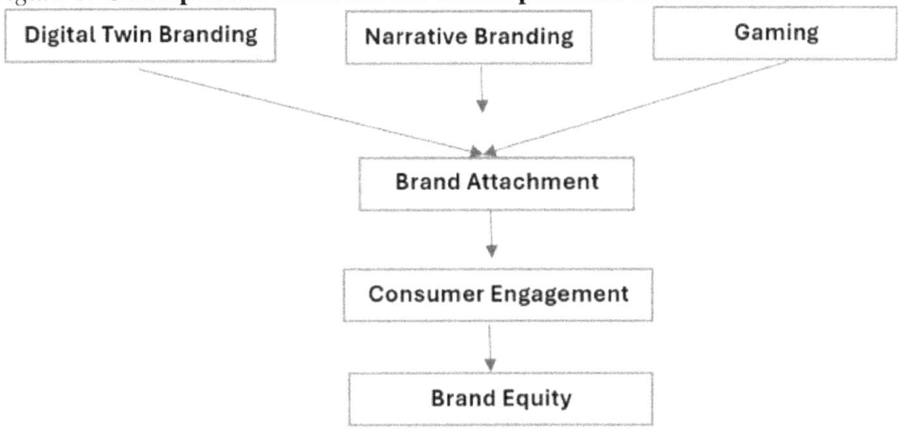

Source: Own elaboration.

This framework is grounded in well-established theoretical foundations, drawing on key insights from branding theory, narrative branding, and consumer engagement theory. Keller's (2009) brand equity model provided a foundational lens for understanding how brand equity is built over time through consumer experiences. Escalas (2004) emphasized the role of storytelling in building consumer-brand attachment, which inspired the inclusion of narrative branding as a key strategy. Additionally, Hamari et al. (2014) demonstrated how gamification drives consumer engagement in interactive environments, supporting the integration of gamification as a driver of brand engagement. The inclusion of digital twin branding is based on recent developments in hybrid physical-virtual ownership models observed in luxury fashion and metaverse platforms. Together, these theoretical perspectives provide a comprehensive basis for the framework.

It highlights the role of digital twin branding, narrative branding, and gamification as strategic enablers of brand attachment, consumer engagement, and brand equity. By mapping these constructs and their causal relationships, this framework provides a comprehensive view of how brands can design effective metaverse strategies. This model will serve as a foundation for analyzing Fly London's brand strategy and offers guidance for other brands looking to enhance their presence in the metaverse. To visualize the conceptual relationships, the following model illustrates the core components and pathways. It identifies three primary branding strategies - *digital twin branding, narrative branding*, and *gamification* - as the drivers of consumer experiences in the metaverse. These strategies work together to influence three key outcomes: brand attachment, consumer engagement, and brand equity.

This structure illustrates how branding strategies impact the intermediate and final outcomes for brands operating in the metaverse. The arrows between the constructs indicate the direction of influence, and the nature of engagement suggests a feedback loop where consumer engagement can further strengthen brand equity.

2.1 Explanation of the Components

1. *Digital Twin Branding*: Refers to the creation of virtual counterparts for physical products, allowing consumers to interact with and experience products in the metaverse before purchase. By offering a hybrid ownership model where consumers own both a physical and a digital version of a product, brands increase the perceived value of ownership. This approach allows brands to create exclusive, limited-edition virtual items and customizable digital products. Digital twin branding has been successfully applied in the fashion industry, where luxury brands like Gucci and Balenciaga have offered digital versions of their physical products for avatars in metaverse platforms. It increases consumer engagement by allowing users to personalize and interact with products, and drives brand attachment through exclusive ownership of digital collectibles.
2. *Narrative Branding*: Focuses on embedding storytelling into the brand experience, allowing brands to present compelling stories about their origins, values, or sustainability efforts. In the metaverse, storytelling is brought to life through interactive experiences. Users participate in story-driven missions, quests, or challenges, which create a stronger emotional connection between the consumer and the brand. Through these interactive stories, users become participants in the brand's journey, rather than passive spectators. It enhances brand attachment by making consumers feel like part of the brand’s story, and facilitates consumer engagement through immersive and interactive storytelling formats, such as quests, missions, and live events.
3. *Gamification*: Applies game design elements (e.g., points, badges, levels, and challenges) to non-game contexts, encouraging user participation and engagement. In the metaverse, brands use gamification to create interactive experiences that reward users for specific actions, such as completing tasks, collecting points, or earning exclusive in-game items. It Increases consumer engagement by providing users with clear incentives and progression paths, and drives brand attachment as consumers become emotionally invested in earning achievements or unlocking exclusive items.
4. *Brand Attachment*: It refers to the emotional bond that consumers form with a brand, driven by a sense of relevance, ownership, or identification. Digital twin branding and narrative branding strengthen attachment by making consumers feel that the brand reflects their self-identity. Gamification enhances attach-

ment through personal achievements and the accumulation of exclusive virtual assets, giving users a sense of belonging and pride in the brand. It strengthens the emotional bond between consumers and brands, and leads to repeat engagement as users return to the platform to maintain and expand their brand-related achievements.

5. *Consumer Engagement*: Engagement refers to the depth of the consumer's interaction, participation, and emotional involvement with the brand. The combination of digital twin branding, narrative branding, and gamification enhances engagement by providing users with opportunities to actively interact with brand-related content. Rather than passively consuming marketing content, consumers co-create brand experiences through personalization, interactive storytelling, and gameplay. It promotes active participation through interactive brand experiences and challenges, and fosters sustained engagement through continuous feedback, rewards, and recognition in the form of badges, points, and achievements.
6. *Brand Equity*: Refers to the consumer's perception of a brand's value, strength, and credibility. Strong brand equity can result in higher purchase intention, greater loyalty, and premium pricing power. The previous components of this framework—brand attachment and consumer engagement—drive brand equity. When consumers feel emotionally connected to a brand (via attachment) and actively participate in the brand's virtual experiences (via engagement), they are more likely to see the brand as valuable and memorable. This is especially true in the metaverse, where exclusive, scarcity-driven digital items (e.g., NFTs or limited-edition avatar skins) increase a brand's perceived exclusivity. It increases the perceived brand value and strengthens its reputation as an innovative brand, and results in higher consumer willingness to pay for branded items in both physical and digital form.

2.2 Causal Relationships

This conceptual framework follows a logical sequence where branding strategies directly impact consumer attachment and engagement, which, in turn, affect brand equity. Here is a summary of the causal pathways:

1. *Digital Twin Branding Brand Attachment Consumer Engagement Brand Equity:* Digital twin branding enhances attachment by enabling hybrid ownership and customization. This attachment leads to greater consumer engagement, resulting in higher brand equity.

2. *Narrative Branding Brand Attachment Consumer Engagement Brand Equity*: Storytelling strengthens brand attachment by making consumers feel part of a shared story. Interactive storytelling increases engagement, which leads to higher brand equity.
3. *Gamification Brand Attachment Consumer Engagement Brand Equity*: Gamification encourages users to participate actively and achieve goals, leading to higher engagement. Engagement results in stronger brand equity as consumers associate the brand with fun, interaction, and reward.

These relationships create a positive feedback loop where brand attachment and engagement are mutually reinforcing. Over time, higher engagement strengthens consumer attachment, which, in turn, increases consumer participation, further enhancing brand equity.

This conceptual framework will serve as a critical reference point for analyzing Fly London's branding strategy. By understanding the role of digital twin branding, narrative branding, and gamification, it becomes possible to evaluate Fly London's current practices and identify areas for improvement. The framework provides a clear, evidence-based structure for analyzing how Fly London builds brand attachment, promotes consumer engagement, and enhances brand equity in the metaverse. This analysis offers practical insights for other brands seeking to establish a strong presence in the virtual economy. The framework also serves as a tool for comparative analysis, as it can be applied to assess branding strategies across different brands and industries in the metaverse.

3. METHODOLOGY

3.1 Research Approach

This study adopted a qualitative research approach, which is particularly suited for exploring complex, emerging phenomena such as brand management in the metaverse. Qualitative research allows for in-depth analysis and a nuanced understanding of the strategies employed by fashion brands in a new digital context. The choice of qualitative methodology aligns with Gummesson's (2014) perspective on qualitative research as a method for investigating dynamic and context-rich environments.

3.2 Case Study Strategy

The research was structured around a case study strategy, focusing on Fly London's entry and strategic positioning within the metaverse. The case study approach enables an examination of real-life applications and the practical implications of brand management in a virtual environment. According to Yin (2018), case studies are particularly effective for answering "how" and "why" questions, which aligns with the objectives of this research to uncover how Fly London navigated challenges and leveraged opportunities in the metaverse. The case study of Fly London was chosen due to its pioneering initiatives in digital engagement and its reputation as a brand that values innovation and creativity. The selected case study aligns with the research theme, focusing on the fashion industry and featuring one of Portugal's pioneering examples of brand development within the metaverse.

3.3 Case Selection Criteria

The following criteria were used to select the company for the case study:

- A company operating within the global fashion industry.
- A brand with a recognized national and international market presence.
- A minimum of five years of market existence.
- At least one year of brand presence in the metaverse.

These criteria ensure the collection of essential data for a deeper understanding of brand management in the metaverse within the fashion sector, supported by an in-depth analysis based on the case study's experience.

3.4 Data Collection Techniques

Data collection was carried out using a combination of primary and secondary data sources to ensure a well-rounded analysis.

a) Primary data collection

Primary data were collected through structured interviews with Fly London's marketing and commercial teams, strategic partners, and external industry experts. Structured interviews were chosen as the primary data collection tool because they provide reliable, comparable qualitative data (Miles et al., 2019). The interviews aimed at gathering insights into:

- The strategic goals behind Fly London's entry into the metaverse.
- The processes and steps taken to maintain brand authenticity and alignment with consumer expectations.
- The challenges encountered and the solutions implemented.
- The impact of these strategies on brand perception and consumer engagement.

The interviews followed a pre-designed protocol to ensure consistency across all participants and included open-ended questions that allowed respondents to elaborate on their experiences and perspectives. Structured interviews were employed to obtain specific information on the research problem, resulting in focused and effective data collection (Gladcheff, 2003). Two groups were interviewed: internal stakeholders and external collaborators associated with the brand. Separate interview guides were created for each group, tailored to the research questions relevant to their roles. The interview process followed these steps:

- Initial engagement with the interviewee: Introduction of the researcher, explanation of the study's objectives, and obtaining consent to record the interview for accurate information collection.
- Demographic questions: Initial questions focused on demographic details such as age, education, nationality, and profession. For Group I (internal stakeholders), questions regarding the company were included to characterize and profile the case study.
- Main interview phase: Questions explored perceptions of the metaverse, virtual worlds, virtual consumption, fashion brand values, and the presence of brands in the metaverse. This phase aimed at understanding the importance of the metaverse for the company and the interviewees' views on brand management within this context.
- Interview conclusion: The session ended with two key questions: identifying critical steps for brand preparation in the metaverse and exploring strategies for competitive analysis within the same context. The session concluded with gratitude for the interviewees' contributions.

Interviews were conducted in a hybrid format, with some interviews held in person and others via video conferencing platforms. Each interview lasted between 45 and 60 minutes and was audio-recorded with the participants' consent for accurate transcription and analysis.

b) Secondary data collection

Secondary data were collected from academic literature, industry reports, market analyses, and Fly London's public communications, such as press releases and marketing materials. Key sources included:

- Industry reports on metaverse engagement in the fashion sector (e.g., reports by Wunderman Thompson Intelligence).
- Scholarly articles on brand management, consumer behavior in digital spaces, and the use of NFTs.
- Fly London's digital campaigns and social media engagement metrics.

These secondary sources provided context and supported the findings from the primary data, enabling triangulation to enhance the reliability of the research results.

3.5 Data Analysis Procedures

The systematic procedures followed to analyze the data collected in the study of Fly London's integration into the metaverse are as follows. By employing a qualitative research approach and thematic analysis, the study aimed to extract meaningful insights into the brand's strategies, challenges, and outcomes. This section details the preparation, analysis, and synthesis processes, ensuring a transparent and replicable methodology. Thematic analysis was employed to identify and analyze patterns and themes within the collected data. This approach is effective for examining qualitative data, allowing for the identification of recurring motifs and deeper insights (Miles et al., 2019).

a) Initial data preparation

All interviews were transcribed verbatim and organized into a data set. Initial readings of the transcripts were conducted to familiarize the researcher with the content and highlight significant points.

b) Coding process

The coding process was conducted using NVivo (version 14), a software to manage and organize the data. Coding involved:

- Open Coding: Identifying initial codes related to Fly London's strategies, challenges, consumer engagement methods, and outcomes.

- Axial Coding: Grouping related codes into broader categories such as "consumer engagement strategies," "brand consistency," "technological investments," and "challenges faced."
- Selective Coding: Integrating and refining the codes to form themes that directly addressed the research questions.

c) Thematic analysis

The thematic analysis entailed a thorough examination of the identified themes to establish connections between Fly London's strategic initiatives and their outcomes. The themes were organized into the following categories:

1) Objectives for the metaverse;
2) The brand's strategic role within the metaverse;
3) Initial activities to establish presence in the metaverse;
4) Monitoring short-term outcomes;
5) Consumer behavior within the metaverse;
6) Resource allocation and competency management;
7) Integration of metaverse-related challenges into the company's strategy.

d) Ethical considerations

Ensuring ethical compliance was a priority throughout the research process. The following measures were taken:

- Informed consent: Participants were provided with detailed information about the study's purpose and their role before the interviews. Consent was obtained in writing or through recorded verbal confirmation.
- Confidentiality: The identity of the participants and sensitive information were anonymized to protect their privacy.
- Data security: Data were securely stored and only accessible to authorized research team members.

e) Ensuring rigor and validity

To ensure the validity and reliability of the analysis, the following measures were implemented:

1. Triangulation: Data from interviews, secondary sources, and observations were cross-referenced to validate findings. For instance, feedback from member teams during virtual events was compared with internal reports to ensure consistency.

2. Member checking: Key findings were shared with participants to confirm accuracy and provide an opportunity for clarification or additional input.
3. Audit trail: A detailed record of the coding and analytical decisions was maintained, ensuring transparency and allowing for replication of the reearch.
   f) Challenges in data analysis

While the thematic analysis approach provided robust insights, certain challenges were encountered:

1. Volume of data: The extensive dataset required careful management and prioritization to ensure that the analysis remained focused on the research objectives.
2. Rapidly evolving context: The dynamic nature of the metaverse posed difficulties in capturing trends that may have evolved during the research period.
3. Subjectivity in interpretation: While efforts were made to minimize bias, the interpretative nature of qualitative analysis inherently introduces a degree of subjectivity. Triangulation and member checking helped mitigate this.
   g) Alignment with research objectives

The data analysis procedures directly addressed the seven research questions. The structured and systematic approach to data analysis ensured a detailed and nuanced understanding of Fly London's integration into the metaverse. By employing thematic analysis and triangulating multiple data sources, the research provided robust insights into the challenges and opportunities of brand management in this emerging digital space.

4. ANALYSIS AND DISCUSSION OF RESULTS

This chapter presents the data obtained from the analysis of the interviews conducted. The first phase focused on determining the sociodemographic profiles of all participants, who were assigned a code and group to ensure their anonymity. After characterizing the participants, the study sought to address the research questions based on the step-by-step approach model proposed by McKinsey & Company (2022).

4.1 Description of Participants' Sociodemographic Profiles

The brand's presence in the metaverse has been built through the collaboration of internal and external teams. Accordingly, two groups of participants were selected: one comprising internal team members and another made up of external collaborators. The construction of these groups considered their involvement with the brand's presence in the metaverse and their insight into the company's objectives for the metaverse.

Table 1. Sociodemographic Profile of Participants (Group A)

Interviewee	Age	Gender	Education Level	Field of Study	Profession
P1	28	F	Bachelor's	Marketing Management	Marketing Director
P2	28	M	Bachelor's	Communication and Marketing	Commercial Director
P3	24	F	Bachelor's	Languages and Business Relations	Commercial Assistant
P4	44	M	Bachelor's	Communication Design and Graphic Techniques	Marketing Assistant
P5	28	M	Bachelor's	Marketing	Marketing Assistant
P6	26	F	Bachelor's	Marketing	Account Manager

Source: Authors' compilation.

Table 2. Sociodemographic profile of participants (Group B)

Interviewee	Age	Gender	Education Level	Field of Study	Profession
P7	52	M	Bachelor's	Communication Design	Professor and 3D-VFX Generalist Freelancer
P8	25	M	Bachelor's	Philosophy	Digital Games Developer
P9	60	F	Bachelor's	Engineering	Marketer

Source: Author' compilation.

4.2 Characterization of the Fly London Brand

FLY London was established in the United Kingdom in 1994 by entrepreneur Fortunato Frederico. The brand operates under the ownership of the Kyaia Group and the company name Fortunato with its headquarters and manufacturing base located in Portugal. FLY London's philosophy emphasizes originality in product design, blending traditional craftsmanship with unexpected and innovative forms.

Over the years, FLY London has demonstrated consistent growth, attaining international recognition. Its diverse product offerings include footwear, accessories, clothing, and skincare products. The brand currently maintains a global presence in 57 countries, including key markets such as the United States, Europe, and China.

The brand's name encapsulates its ethos: "Fly" symbolizes freedom, lightness, movement, travel, global exploration, and the exchange of experiences, while "London" reflects a modern, urban lifestyle inspired by the city's vibrant cultural dynamism. The brand's logo, a fly, represents strength, vitality, freedom, and the lightness of travel or exploration, aligning with the urban and contemporary identity associated with London.

FLY London communicates its identity effectively through the slogan, "Don't Walk, Fly," which encapsulates its ideals and strengthens its global brand recognition. The brand prioritizes comfort, innovation, and disruptive product designs, positioning itself as a leader in innovative design and product quality. By offering a wide array of styles, colors, and materials, FLY London creates a distinctive personality that resonates with its target audience. The brand primarily appeals to the fashion market, focusing on urban and modern lifestyles and catering to a core demographic of individuals aged 15 to 35 years old. Through initiatives like the Fly Experience, FLY London underscores its dedication to staying at the forefront of fashion trends and aligning with the preferences of Generations Y and Z, ensuring its continued relevance in an ever-evolving market.

4.3 Characterization of Fly London's Metaverse Strategy

The Fly London Experience, launched in 2022, marked the brand's debut in the metaverse via the Roblox platform under the creative direction of Alexandra Moura. This initiative provides an augmented reality experience where participants can explore diverse environments, customize their avatars with clothing and accessories, and craft their virtual identities. A key feature of this launch was the redesign of a classic 1990s shoe model, offered in three distinct colors, symbolizing the brand's ability to bridge its physical heritage with the virtual realm. The overarching objective of the Fly London Experience is to create a seamless integration between the physical and virtual worlds, enhancing the brand's relevance in an increasingly digital landscape.

The metaverse initiative features four mini-games developed by the Cyber-Physical Systems Department at the School of Technology of IPCA (Polytechnic Institute of Cávado and Ave). The in-game skins, designed by Alexandra Moura, present a variety of urban looks tailored to the preferences of Fly London's target audience. These designs reflect contemporary fashion trends, extreme sports, environmental concerns, musical influences, and cinematic inspirations. Beyond gaming, the virtual space includes a store where players can earn "fly points" to purchase new skins and boots, creating an engaging, gamified shopping experience. Notably, all items, including accessories and footwear, are designed to transition seamlessly from the virtual environment to the physical world, reinforcing the brand's commitment to bridging these two realms.

The virtual store draws its conceptual and aesthetic inspiration from science fiction and fantasy films, such as Alien, Avatar, and David Cronenberg's The Fly. This imaginative influence creates a dreamlike, futuristic, magical, and natural world that enhances the immersive experience. The resulting environment evokes unique sensations and emotions for players, offering a distinctive and memorable interaction with the brand.

Feedback from two interviewed groups described the metaverse as a convergent space where the virtual and real worlds intersect. It was characterized as a new medium for interaction, enabling the creation of activities that parallel real-world experiences and fostering a virtual economy within a 3D online environment. The metaverse was further defined as a platform of interconnected virtual spaces, powered by augmented reality, virtual reality, artificial intelligence, and blockchain technologies. These technologies enable users to engage with the digital world through avatars, providing brands with innovative ways to connect with a tech-savvy, digitally native audience.

Fly London's metaverse strategy exemplifies how brands can leverage advanced digital platforms to expand their reach, engage younger audiences, and stay relevant in a rapidly evolving digital marketplace.

4.4 Competitive Analysis

Fly London's competition analysis included several dimensions:

- Communication: Evaluating public engagement and the effectiveness of communication strategies.
- Brand: Assessing the metaverse's impact on brand identity and perception.
- Target Audience: Analyzing user demographics, behaviors, and identifying underexplored market niches.
- Product: Reviewing products and services to identify competitive advantages.
- Trends: Monitoring both market and consumer trends to adapt to evolving demands.

While Fly London is one of the pioneering Portuguese fashion brands to establish a presence on Roblox, it operates within a competitive global environment. International brands such as Gucci, Nike, and Balenciaga have also established strong presences on Roblox, competing for consumer attention and engagement. However, within the specific context of Portuguese fashion brands, Fly London holds a distinctive position, as no direct national competitors were identified on the Roblox platform at the time of this analysis.

In short, Fly London's approach to the metaverse illustrates a thoughtful yet evolving strategy, characterized by collaboration between internal and external teams, a focus on innovation, and the intent to build strong user relationships. While significant progress has been made, there are clear opportunities to enhance value capture, integrate strategic metaverse challenges more seamlessly into the business model, and further develop its competitive positioning in the virtual space. By addressing these gaps, the brand can strengthen its presence in the metaverse and capitalize on its potential as a leader in digital innovation.

4.5 Data Configuration by Research Question

Q.1 What objectives has the company established for the metaverse?

The following objectives were identified for the brand in its metaverse initiative:

- Positioning: The brand aims to establish a new approach to gaining competitive advantage in the market, with a focus on attracting a younger audience and solidifying its presence in the metaverse;
- Brand awareness: The metaverse enables the brand to generate new brand associations, fostering fresh connections with its audience;
- Brand relationship: By leveraging the metaverse, the brand strengthens its relationships with its target audience and influencers;
- Capturing new customers: The metaverse serves as a platform for impactful advertising, boosting the brand's visibility, attracting new customers, and reaching untapped markets;
- Promotion: The metaverse increases the visibility and promotional opportunities of the brand;
- Consumer data: Data collection enables the brand to better understand user profiles and tailor its offerings to align with their preferences;
- New revenue streams: The metaverse expands the reach of products, creating opportunities for new revenue streams and fostering a new type of consumption centered around digital products.

Engagement with the brand is achieved through the regular updating of content designed to align with the preferences of the target audience. This content can be shared within the community established on Roblox, addressing consumer needs while drawing on information gathered from their gaming experiences. The brand provides individualized experience, combining personalization with creativity. Immersive experiences further contribute to revenue generation by facilitating interactions with the brand's virtual store and products. This strategy integrates real and virtual worlds, fostering a novel consumption model centered on digital products. Consumers are offered a unique way of engaging with the brand, while the creation of digital items generates additional revenue opportunities.

The brand's objectives in the metaverse can be summarized through three critical variables for effective positioning: innovation, added value, and perceived brand differentiation. Fly London's metaverse presence targets Generation Z, focusing on engaging in the gaming community to enhance brand awareness and strengthen consumer relationships. The brand achieves increased recognition and visibility through wide-reaching advertising campaigns.

The collection of consumer data allows Fly London to define audience profiles more precisely, aligning its offerings with their preferences and desired experiences. This deeper understanding enables the creation of relevant content that can be shared within the community generated on Roblox. The high-quality immersive experiences, combined with the ability to purchase virtual products, drive new revenue streams and support the development of exclusive digital items tailored to the metaverse. Notably, some of these virtual items are also available for purchase in physical stores, bridging the gap between the virtual and physical shopping experiences. This integrated approach enhances consumer engagement while offering new opportunities for growth in a rapidly evolving digital marketplace.

However, to further strengthen its metaverse strategy, Fly London could leverage the concept of "digital twins", as virtual replicas of physical products that provide consumers with a dual-ownership experience, allowing them to interact with their purchased products both in physical and virtual spaces. This approach has been successfully employed by brands like Gucci and Nike, which offer consumers the ability to purchase physical items that are accompanied by corresponding digital versions. By integrating this strategy, Fly London can increase consumer attachment, promote exclusivity, and offer premium products in both digital and physical forms. Digital twins also enable consumers to showcase their virtual products in metaverse platforms like Roblox, creating a strong incentive for engagement. This hybrid ownership model could become a key differentiator for Fly London in the competitive fashion metaverse landscape.

Q.2 What role does the brand aim to play in the metaverse (e.g., creating experiences, facilitating interactions, etc.)?

Fly London sought to establish a meaningful presence in the metaverse by offering immersive, continuously updated, and diverse experiences tailored to consumers. The brand prioritized interaction as a key driver of engagement, achieved through the delivery of personalized content, the creation of skins, and the strategic use of technology. These initiatives aimed to build strong relationships with consumers while simultaneously promoting product sales. Selling digital products allowed consumers to participate in real-time digital experiences, merging entertainment with commerce. In essence, the brand designed activities that seamlessly integrated the physical and virtual worlds, exploring new opportunities to promote both the brand and its digital offerings.

The brand's presence in the metaverse was found to foster greater consumer trust and a closer connection to the brand. This strengthened relationship stems from the variety of experiences Fly London provides, emphasizing highly personalized and immersive interactions. The metaverse offers consumers a new framework for evaluating and forming opinions about products, creating stronger trust, enhanced proximity to the brand, and more direct interactions. This approach enables the brand to better understand consumer characteristics and preferences.

The metaverse not only revolutionizes the way consumers and brands interact but also drives the emergence of new consumption behaviors on a large scale. By reshaping the dynamics of engagement, Fly London leverages the metaverse to position itself at the forefront of digital transformation, aligning innovative consumer experiences with brand growth.

To further enhance consumer engagement, Fly London could introduce a "progression system" within its Roblox presence. Progression systems are widely used in video games to motivate users to continue playing by offering incentives, such as status badges, levels, and unlockable content. Fly London can design a system where users "level up" their avatars, earn badges, and unlock exclusive Fly London-branded items as they complete challenges and missions. This approach would appeal to Generation Z consumers, who are accustomed to progression-based engagement models seen in popular games like Fortnite and Call of Duty. Additionally, the brand could link progression to its loyalty program, providing users with real-world benefits, such as exclusive early access to physical product launches. This dual incentive system would promote both digital engagement and physical product purchases

Q.3 What initial activities for presence in the metaverse are being or will be implemented?

Fly London's initial activities in the metaverse were predominantly social, promotional, and commercial in nature. The brand established its presence on the Roblox platform, where the gaming experience shapes consumer engagement while simultaneously promoting the brand and facilitating interactions. Consumers embody their virtual presence through avatars or "skins," allowing them to create and customize characters that represent their desired identity within the game environment.

This first venture into the metaverse provided Fly London with valuable insights into consumer behavior, enabling the brand to better understand its audience while analyzing their interactions on the platform. Roblox's growing popularity within the gaming community, coupled with its capacity to foster connectivity through virtual reality, allowed Fly London to deliver immersive and engaging experiences. However, budget constraints or hardware limitations may impact the brand's ability to deliver consistently high-quality experiences, potentially limiting the scope and reach of its offerings. Fly London emphasizes avatar skins and virtual product customization as part of its metaverse strategy.

Fly London incorporates elements of the digital twin concept by creating virtual versions of physical products, such as its iconic 90s model, which is available as a virtual boot in its Roblox store. Additionally, the brand emphasizes that its virtual accessories, skins, and boots are 'designed to cross from the virtual world to the physical.' However, Fly London does not explicitly offer a full digital twin experience where consumers simultaneously own both a physical and digital version of the same product. Instead, it bridges the two realms, offering a conceptual blend of virtual and physical product experiences.

While Fly London has taken steps toward integrating physical and virtual experiences, it has yet to fully leverage emerging technologies like NFTs to deepen this connection. Unlike the digital twin concept, which centers on synchronized ownership of physical and digital counterparts, NFTs introduce a new dimension of digital exclusivity. Incorporating NFT-driven product sales could significantly enhance revenue streams and foster a sense of digital scarcity. By offering limited-edition virtual items with NFT-based ownership rights, Fly London could create scarcity-driven demand, increase brand prestige, and provide consumers with a stronger sense of ownership and collectability within the virtual space. This strategy would not only align with emerging trends in the digital asset economy but also strengthen consumer engagement and brand loyalty.

In addition to visual consistency, narrative branding could enhance Fly London's emotional engagement with consumers. Narrative branding emphasizes storytelling, allowing consumers to experience brand values through avatars and immersive story-driven games. This strategy has been utilized by Balenciaga, which launched an interactive narrative-driven gaming experience on Fortnite. By incorporating a story-driven experience into its Roblox presence, Fly London could deepen consumer-brand connections and reinforce the brand's creative ethos.

In conclusion, Fly London's entry into the metaverse strategically capitalizes on the gaming-focused nature of the Roblox platform. By tapping into the gaming community, the brand effectively aligns its strategy with the preferences and behaviors of Generation Z - a demographic known for its strong affinity for immersive digital experiences. Through a combination of social, recreational, commercial, and promotional interactions, Fly London creates a rich ecosystem that fosters engagement and brand loyalty. A central pillar of this strategy is creativity and personalization, which play a pivotal role in enhancing user experience. By providing users with tools to customize avatars, design skins, and participate in interactive gameplay, Fly London enables consumers to actively shape their digital identities. This emphasis on self-expression not only encourages user interaction but also strengthens emotional connections with the brand.

Q. 4 How are short-term results monitored to ensure the brand's long-term potential in the metaverse?

Fly London currently analyzes only the metrics available through the Roblox platform, making it challenging to fully evaluate the effectiveness of its marketing actions and overall strategy in the metaverse. As the brand is still in its early stages of metaverse engagement, it has not yet established a comprehensive framework of metrics to assess short-term performance and ensure long-term potential. The metrics regularly monitored on Roblox to evaluate ROI include:

- Visits: The number of users visiting the game on the platform.
- Click-through rate (CTR): The number of clicks the game receives from users on the platform.
- Average game time: The duration of time users spend engaging with the game.

Currently, the brand's performance evaluation is limited to these gaming-related metrics. In the future, as the brand transitions out of its testing phase and gathers more data, it will be able to identify and adopt more targeted metrics to evaluate its long-term potential in the metaverse. However, academic and professional literature suggests that the company should expand its approach by incorporating additional metrics to monitor its performance and refine its strategy in the metaverse. These include:

- Revenue and sales: Tracking the sales of virtual products as well as physical products influenced by the metaverse experience.
- Platform analysis: Evaluating the content with the highest engagement rates, identifying the games with the most views, and analyzing user feedback on their gaming experience. This data would enable the brand to monitor performance and enhance its offerings.
- User retention and satisfaction: Focusing on user engagement with the brand's metaverse experiences to ensure a high return on investments. Monitoring retention and satisfaction rates will help create more personalized experiences and foster loyalty among the brand's audience.
- Content performance: Tracking the content that generates the highest engagement and performs best within the metaverse.

By adopting a broader set of metrics, Fly London can gain deeper insights into consumer behavior and improve its ability to create meaningful, engaging experiences. This approach will allow the brand to align its offerings more closely with consumer preferences, ensuring sustainable growth and success in the metaverse. Currently, Fly London relies on click-through rates (CTR), visits, and average game time to monitor its metaverse performance. While these metrics are useful, they do not capture the full range of consumer-brand interactions. To gain deeper insight, Fly London should expand its performance measurement system to include qualitative indicators like consumer sentiment, brand attachment, and emotional engagement. Sentiment analysis tools could track consumer comments, in-game chat logs, and post-experience surveys, providing a richer understanding of how users feel about the brand. Additionally, Fly London could introduce "emotional metrics" to track user-brand attachment. By using this dual approach of "quantitative metrics" and "qualitative metrics," Fly London would obtain a comprehensive view of brand equity in the metaverse.

Q. 5 How does the brand seek to better understand its consumers in the metaverse?

The analysis revealed that Group A relied heavily on metrics provided by the Roblox platform to inform the brand's strategic decisions. Insights into consumer behavior are derived from their virtual choices and in-game experiences, which offer a snapshot of preferences and engagement patterns. However, this dependency highlights a gap in broader analytical capabilities, suggesting the need for a more robust and multi-dimensional approach to understanding consumer dynamics. Group B emphasized that consumers in the metaverse are becoming increasingly discerning in how they wish to interact with and engage with brands. This underscores the importance of developing tailored solutions to ensure a positive consumer experience. These solutions should include the provision of engaging and relevant content specifically designed for the target audience, as well as the creation of interactive spaces where users can share thoughts, opinions, and experiences with both the brand and fellow community members.

This perspective highlights the growing necessity of fostering an emotional connection with the target audience. By facilitating active participation and nurturing a close relationship, the brand can build loyalty and trust among its metaverse consumers. Personalized strategies that integrate user-centric experiences not only enhance the brand's appeal but also ensure that the consumer feels valued and involved in shaping their relationship with the brand.

Moreover, the findings suggest that successful engagement in the metaverse goes beyond offering functional products or services; it requires creating a sense of belonging and connection. Developing emotional resonance through immersive experiences, meaningful interactions, and community-building initiatives will enable the brand to stand out in the competitive metaverse landscape. This approach aligns with broader trends in digital marketing, where consumer-driven content and participatory platforms increasingly define the benchmarks for success.

Q. 6 How does the company allocate and manage resources and competencies for brand management in the metaverse?

The metaverse project for Fly London was developed by an external entity, IPCA – Instituto Politécnico do Cávado e do Ave, based in Barcelos, in collaboration with other companies and institutions during its development process. While the internal team manages the strategic direction and analyzes results, the operational and creative aspects are handled by external collaborators. The management of human resources and skills for brand management in the metaverse is structured as follows:

- External team: Responsible for the creation, development, and implementation of the brand in the metaverse, focusing on innovation and technological resources.
- Internal team: Oversees identifying and creating the brand strategy for the metaverse, monitoring activities, analyzing results, and managing brand operations.

This shared model demonstrates that the management of Fly London's metaverse presence involves a collaborative approach, integrating internal strategic oversight with external expertise in innovation and execution. The internal team focuses on monitoring, developing, and communicating the brand's activities in the virtual environment, while the external team handles content creation, communication strategies, and technological implementations that foster relationships with users.

However, while partnerships provide technical expertise, they also introduce operational risks, such as delays, misalignment of project goals, and reliance on third-party timelines. To address this risk, Fly London should consider developing in-house technical competencies for metaverse development. By establishing an internal team with technical knowledge in AR/VR development, 3D modeling, and platform management, Fly London would reduce its dependency on external collaborators. This hybrid approach, where internal teams handle strategy and external partners manage execution, would offer greater control, reduce risks, and ensure consistent brand alignment.

Q. 7 How and why does the company integrate the challenges of the metaverse into its strategy and operational models?

Fly London incorporates the challenges of the metaverse into its business strategy through the following key areas:

- Innovation: Positioning itself as a pioneer in Portugal with a metaverse presence, Fly London demonstrates leadership in emerging technologies.
- Relationship: Establishing direct connections with users and fostering digital communities. These spaces enable the brand to gather valuable insights into consumer preferences and behaviors.
- Promotion: Enhancing brand visibility in the virtual environment by allowing users to engage with advertising campaigns, co-create content, and participate in product launches.
- Monitoring: Implementing new methods to monitor the brand's digital presence and performance.
- Consumer experience: Creating innovative and engaging immersive experiences that strengthen consumer-brand connections.

Despite these advancements, there remains ambiguity regarding how the company fully integrates the operational and strategic challenges of the metaverse into its broader business model. The steps Fly London has identified for preparing the brand for the metaverse include:

1. Defining the strategic objective: Focusing on building a strong digital presence in the metaverse.
2. Brand concept planning: Developing a detailed concept plan, considering the brand's behavior, role, and performance in the virtual environment.

3. Strategy creation: Aligning the metaverse strategy with the company's global strategic objectives.
4. Content creation: Prioritizing the development of relevant, engaging content to communicate effectively with users.
5. Resource identification and organization: Determining the necessary tools and external expertise to build and optimize the brand's metaverse presence.
6. Budgeting: Preparing a financial plan and cost forecasts for implementing metaverse initiatives.
7. Monitoring: Establishing metrics to evaluate the brand's performance in the metaverse and inform future improvements.

The process revealed that Fly London prioritized brand management, team collaboration, content strategy, and comprehensive planning as the foundational pillars for establishing its presence in the metaverse. A lack of specialized internal resources for metaverse operations led the brand to rely on external teams, including consultants, academic institutions, and experienced business entities, to address operational and strategic challenges. Notably, the analysis highlighted a significant gap: the absence of a defined value capture strategy for the metaverse. Group A's responses demonstrated a lack of clarity regarding how to create and sustain brand value within the virtual environment.

Data privacy and security are among the most pressing challenges faced by brands operating in the metaverse. With platforms like Roblox having a large base of younger users, companies must comply with privacy regulations like the European Union's General Data Protection Regulation (GDPR). Fly London should consider adopting a "privacy-first" approach, ensuring that users are fully informed about how their data is collected, stored, and used. Additionally, the concept of "ethical AI" should be incorporated into Fly London's metaverse strategy. Ethical AI involves the transparent and fair use of AI-driven personalization, ensuring that consumer data is not exploited for profit. By clearly communicating its data privacy policies and prioritizing ethical AI, Fly London can build trust with consumers, especially parents of younger Roblox users. This approach would also ensure compliance with future regulatory changes related to AI and digital ecosystems

4.6 Theoretical Contributions

This research provides several important theoretical contributions that advance the understanding of brand management, consumer behavior, and engagement within the metaverse. Below are the key theoretical implications:

1) *Expansion of brand presence in metaverse*: The chapter extends traditional concepts of brand presence to include immersive, participatory, and multi-sensory interactions in the metaverse. It emphasizes the role of avatars, gamification, and interactive storytelling as essential components of brand presence, challenging traditional one-way brand communication models. This calls for an update in brand presence theories to account for consumer cocreation and dynamic brand participation in virtual worlds.

2) *Development of digital twin branding theory*: The chapter introduces the concept of digital twin branding, where consumers simultaneously own physical and virtual versions of branded products. This hybrid model contributes to theories of brand attachment and experiential consumption, showing how dual ownership increases emotional bonds with brands. The concept expands existing theories of consumer ownership, particularly in the metaverse context.

3) *Evolution of narrative branding*: Unlike traditional storytelling, which is passive, the chapter emphasizes interactive narrative branding where consumers actively shape brand stories through their avatars. This introduces the idea of a "narratist consumer", who plays an active role in brand storytelling. This challenges prior unidirectional models of narrative branding and requires new theoretical perspectives that incorporate co-created brand narratives in virtual spaces.

4) *Redefinition of brand equity in metaverse*: The chapter also highlights how traditional models of brand equity (like Keller's model) must be updated to include immersive brand equity, which incorporates emotional attachment to avatars, gamification, and virtual ownership. This contribution expands the notion of brand value to consider virtual interactions, emotional experiences, and the cocreation of brand meaning.

5) *Gamification as a new driver of engagement*: The chapter expands gamification theory by demonstrating how gamification in the metaverse goes beyond points and badges to include avatar progression, virtual rewards, and interactive gameplay. This perspective introduces a new layer of emotional engagement and extends theories of gamification, suggesting that avatar attachment and personal growth are key motivators for consumer participation.

6) *Emergence of the digital consumer*: Finally, it highlights the role of the digital consumer, whose identity is expressed through avatars, digital skins, and customizable products. This finding aligns with theories of self-congruity and symbolic consumption, as consumers seek to express their self-identity through their avatars.

This contribution calls for an update of existing identity-based consumer behavior models to include avatar-based self-expression and virtual identity alignment.

4.7 Managerial Implications

The practical impact of the research undertaken is seen through its usefulness for brand managers and practitioners. This section identifies the business relevance of the chapter's findings.

a) Strategic guidance for brand managers:

- *Application of digital twin branding*: Brand managers are encouraged to offer consumers dual ownership models, where physical products are accompanied by virtual replicas. This strategy has been successfully used by Gucci, Nike, and Balenciaga in Roblox and Fortnite. Fly London can leverage this dual-ownership model to create more premium-priced products.
- *Narrative branding and storytelling:* Story-driven marketing can increase consumer engagement by embedding the brand in interactive missions or quests on platforms like Roblox. his aligns with the success seen in Balenciaga's collaboration with Fortnite, where storytelling missions introduced limited-edition items. This paper provides a practical approach for how Fly London can design immersive stories within metaverse platforms.
- *Gamification to increase engagement*: Fly London can use gamification principles, such as Fly Points, challenges, and reward systems, to keep users actively engaged in the metaverse. Companies like Nike use Nikeland on Roblox to implement similar progression-based engagement models. This strategy boosts user retention and brand equity, as seen in video game platforms like Call of Duty.

b) Consumer insights and branding strategy:

- *Emotional attachment via digital twins*: Consumers are more likely to identify with brands that offer hybrid ownership models, which allows them to showcase ownership in both physical and virtual spaces. This strengthens brand attachment and increases customer lifetime value. Brands should position digital twin products as collectible, shareable, and resellable items in the metaverse.
- *Personalization and customization*: Interactive storytelling and gamification allow consumers to personalize their avatars with branded items (e.g., Fly London Shoes for avatars in Roblox). Offering unique avatar customization tools enables personalization, which is essential for Generation Z brand loyalty.

5. CONCLUSION

This chapter examined the topic of managing brand presence in the metaverse, with Fly London serving as a case study. The chapter's purpose was to contribute to a deeper understanding of brand management within the fashion industry, particularly in the context of the metaverse.

Fly London's foray into the metaverse presents a compelling case study on how fashion brands can leverage emerging technologies to remain competitive in an ever-evolving digital landscape. This chapter explored Fly London's strategic approach, emphasizing both its successes and the challenges encountered during its integration into the metaverse. The analysis reveals that while the metaverse introduces a unique set of challenges—including technological, financial, and data privacy concerns—it simultaneously offers unparalleled opportunities for consumer engagement, brand loyalty, and revenue generation.

The literature review provided a foundation for understanding the metaverse concept and identifying existing gaps in brand management within the business context. The fashion industry, in particular, has been significantly impacted by the metaverse, undergoing a profound transformation in both business models and the redefinition of the consumer-brand relationship. With evolving consumer behaviors - marked by a desire for personalized experiences and virtual interaction - brands face increasing pressure to devise value-capture strategies. The transformations within the fashion sector and the imperative to rethink brand management in the context of the metaverse underscore the relevance and importance of the issues addressed in this chapter.

This chapter also introduces a conceptual framework that identifies three key branding strategies: digital twin branding, narrative branding, and gamification. These strategies influence consumer experiences, leading to brand attachment, consumer engagement, and brand equity. Unlike traditional branding models, this framework emphasizes dynamic, interactive, and multi-directional pathways between branding strategies and outcomes.

The case study provided answers to the central research question***: How and why are fashion brands managing their presence in the metaverse?*** This investigation helped elucidate how brand management operates in this emerging context. The research drew upon the stepwise approach model proposed by McKinsey & Company (2022). In the initial phase, the analysis focused on perceptions of the metaverse from two distinct groups within Fly London (internal and external teams) in the context of brand management. These stakeholders conceptualized the metaverse as a: a) space or platform where virtual and real worlds converge; b) medium for interaction and activities resembling those in the real world; c) new virtual economy within a

3D online environment, and a simulation space deeply integrated with augmented reality, virtual reality, artificial intelligence, and blockchain technologies.

Additionally, the metaverse was described as a novel way to interact with and experience the digital world through avatars, primarily appealing to technologically inclined audiences. The objectives defined by the company for the metaverse were identified as follows:

1. Establishing a competitive positioning in the metaverse, particularly by attracting and engaging younger audiences;
2. Generating new brand associations and awareness, fostering stronger public connections;
3. Strengthening relationships with the brand's target audience;
4. Attracting new customers;
5. Enhancing brand visibility within the virtual environment;
6. Collecting consumer data to create highly personalized experiences and deliver content tailored to consumer preferences;
7. Generating new revenue streams and expanding product reach.

However, the study did not identify a clear strategy for capturing value through highly personalized immersive content and experiences. Similarly, goals for generating revenue through digital products or real-life product sales stemming from the virtual universe were not outlined. A deeper understanding of how the selected platform aligns with the company's objectives and the rationale for incorporating gaming elements into user experiences was also missing.

The findings indicate that the brand aims to attract Generation Z consumers with access to advanced technologies, fostering engagement through continuously updated targeted content. These efforts aim to engage communities on the Roblox platform. Furthermore, the content strategy is informed by data obtained through user interactions within the gaming experience. The analysis reveals that new revenue streams are being generated by connecting virtual stores and products to real-life purchases, offering users a novel way to interact with the brand. Despite the absence of specific reasons for selecting the Roblox platform, the study highlights that Roblox serves as the venue where Fly London developed its metaverse presence. Literature reviewed further underscored the importance of gaming as a cornerstone for creating immersive shopping experiences and facilitating user-brand relationships, especially for Generation Z audiences.

The chapter concludes by emphasizing the significance of immersive experiences, personalized content, and interactive engagement in redefining the consumer-brand relationship within the metaverse. These elements enhance consumer trust and foster closer connections with customers. Creativity was found to be fundamental in designing immersive user experiences, which must be capable of bridging the virtual and real worlds. The study underscores the growing importance of the metaverse for brands seeking to innovate and thrive in an increasingly digital and experiential marketplace.

6. LIMITATIONS AND RECOMMENDATIONS

6.1 Limitations

This chapter provided a detailed analysis of Fly London's metaverse strategy, yet certain limitations must be acknowledged. First, the study relies on a single case, which restricts the generalizability of its findings. While Fly London's experience offers valuable insights, other brands may face distinct challenges shaped by their industry, target audience, and resource availability. Second, the metaverse is a rapidly evolving landscape, and strategies that are effective today may require adaptation as the environment matures. Lastly, the qualitative nature of this research introduces the possibility of subjective interpretation, though triangulation with secondary data was employed to enhance the validity of the findings.

The metaverse remains in its early stages, with companies actively exploring its potential, offerings, and immersive experiences. As a result, the primary limitation of this research lies in the difficulty of collecting data directly related to brand management within the metaverse. The study relies on qualitative, exploratory analysis. To address this limitation, future research should incorporate quantitative data analysis to provide a deeper understanding of consumer behavior on the platform, particularly how users perceive and experience the "Fly Experience." This approach would yield richer insights into consumer-brand interactions within the metaverse.

To improve company performance and strategic effectiveness in the metaverse, future studies should adopt a methodological approach that integrates qualitative and quantitative methods, such as case study analysis alongside consumer surveys and data analytics. This combined approach would offer a comprehensive view of the metaverse's impact on companies and provide insights into how users engage and interact with brands. Such insights would enable companies to design and implement more effective competitive strategies tailored to the unique demands of the metaverse environment.

Addressing existing research gaps requires expanding the scope of inquiry into marketing and brand management within the metaverse. Broader research would foster a deeper understanding of how metaverse-based branding strategies influence consumer engagement, customer experience, and brand equity. This expansion would provide academics and practitioners with the knowledge needed to refine branding strategies and strengthen firms' competitive advantage.

6.2 Recommendations for Future Research

- *Comparative studies across industries*: While this chapter focused on the fashion industry, future research should explore how brands from other sectors, such as automotive, entertainment, and real estate, approach the metaverse. Cross-industry comparative studies could reveal distinctive strategies and common challenges faced by firms entering virtual spaces. Such research would identify best practices that can be adapted across industries, fostering a broader understanding of effective brand management within the metaverse.
- *Longitudinal studies on brand equity*: Future research should adopt longitudinal designs to assess the long-term impact of metaverse strategies on brand equity. While this chapter highlights immediate outcomes, such as consumer engagement and revenue growth, the long-term effects on brand loyalty, reputation, and consumer perception remain unclear. Longitudinal studies could track key brand equity metrics over time, offering valuable insights into the sustainability of metaverse initiatives and their influence on a brand's competitive position.
- *Consumer behavior analysis in the metaverse*: A deeper examination of consumer behavior within the metaverse is essential for refining brand strategies. While this chapter addresses consumer engagement techniques, future research should investigate the drivers of consumer participation and purchase decisions in virtual environments. Specific areas of interest include the role of avatar customization, gamification mechanics, and social interactions in shaping consumer behavior. Insights from this research would enable brands to develop more targeted and effective engagement strategies.
- *The role of NFTs and digital ownership*: As the use of NFTs in brand strategy continues to grow, future research should examine how digital ownership affects consumer-brand relationships. It is essential to investigate how consumers perceive the value of NFTs, how they influence long-term brand loyalty, and their role in creating a sense of exclusivity. Additionally, studies should explore whether NFTs will evolve from a niche concept into a mainstream element of digital commerce. Findings from this research would help brands determine how best to incorporate NFTs into their metaverse branding strategies.
- *Technological advancements and their impact*: The rapid pace of technological advancement requires brands to adapt continuously to emerging tools and platforms. Future studies should investigate how artificial intelligence, machine learning, and blockchain influence brand management in the metaverse. Research could explore how these technologies facilitate enhanced consumer experiences,

secure data transactions, and the development of digital assets. By staying ahead of technological trends, brands can leverage these innovations to gain a competitive edge in metaverse branding.

- *Sustainability and ethical considerations*: Sustainability has become a crucial factor in brand management, and the metaverse is no exception. The environmental impact of blockchain technologies and energy consumption in virtual environments is an emerging area of interest. Future studies should explore the potential for sustainable design practices and ethical guidelines for brand operations in the metaverse. Research on sustainability could offer firms practical strategies for reducing their digital carbon footprint and aligning their metaverse initiatives with global environmental goals.

- *Social and cultural implications*: The metaverse is not merely a technological development but also a social and cultural phenomenon. Future research should investigate how brand interactions in the metaverse influence cultural trends, social norms, and consumer identity. Studies could explore how virtual environments foster online communities and how these interactions shape real-world consumer behavior. Such research would help brands understand their role in promoting inclusivity and cultural relevance within virtual spaces, enabling them to create more inclusive brand narratives.

- *The economic sustainability of the metaverse*: While the metaverse offers new revenue streams for brands, questions regarding its economic sustainability persist. Future research should examine the financial viability of current economic models in the metaverse, such as NFT sales and virtual property transactions. Studies could assess the risk of market saturation and the potential for digital asset devaluation. This research would offer firms insights into how to mitigate risks and ensure the long-term financial sustainability of their metaverse investments.

- *The role of collaboration and partnerships*: Fly London's success in the metaverse was partly enabled by strategic collaborations. Future research should examine the role of partnerships between brands and technology providers, such as Roblox and other virtual platforms. By identifying best practices for collaboration, research could reveal how firms can reduce technological barriers, accelerate product launches, and share development costs. These insights would support brands in forming mutually beneficial alliances for metaverse ventures.

- *Consumer trust and brand safety*: Maintaining consumer trust and ensuring brand safety is a critical issue for brands operating in decentralized environments like the metaverse. The open nature of metaverse platforms means that brands cannot control every aspect of user-generated content, leading to potential risks related to user interactions, content moderation, and intellectual property infringement. Future studies should explore how brands can maintain trust and safeguard their reputation through brand safety protocols, real-time monitoring systems, and proactive risk management.

-*Consumer perceptions of digital twins*: Future research could examine consumer sentiment about digital twins, especially regarding perceived value, self-expression, and ownership in the metaverse.

-*Multi-brand comparative studies*: Researchers could apply the proposed conceptual framework to compare Nike, Gucci, Balenciaga, and other fashion brands to identify best practices in metaverse branding.

-*Impact of gamification on brand loyalty*: Further research could measure how gamification strategies like Fly Points impact brand loyalty and purchase intention.

REFERENCES

Aaker, D., & Joachimsthaler, E. (2000). *Brand leadership*. The Free Press.

Abovitz, R., Banerjee, S., Gilliland, G., Liu, C., Sackey, E., Timashkov, A., & Trollinger, R. (2022). How the metaverse will remake your strategy. *Boston Consulting Group*, 1–16. Retrieved from https://mkt-bcg-com-public-pdfs.s3.amazonaws.com/prod/impact-of-metaverse-on-business.pdf

Alsamhi, M. H., Hawbani, A., Kumar, S., & Alsamhi, S. H. (2024). Multisensory metaverse-6G: A new paradigm of commerce and education. *IEEE Access*.

Alves, A. M. (2022). *O uso da tecnologia NFT para promover itens colecionáveis digitais: uma análise de consumo no jogo AXIE INFINITY* (Unpublished master's dissertation). Universidade Federal do Pampa – UNIPAMPA, São Borja.

André, & Luiz. (2022). *Marketing Futureland*. Lisboa: LIDEL.

Ball, M. (2022). *The metaverse: And how it will revolutionize everything*. W. W. Norton & Company, Inc. DOI: 10.15358/9783800669400

Burmann, C., Riley, N.-M., Halaszovich, T., & Schade, M. (2017). Identity-based brand management. In *Strategic brand management* (pp. 91–172). Springer Gabler., DOI: 10.1007/978-3-658-13561-4_3

Cagnina, M. R., & Poian, M. (2011). How to compete in the metaverse: The business models in Second Life. SSRN *Electronic Journal*, 1–34. https://doi.org/DOI: 10.2139/ssrn.1088779

Çelikkol, S. (2022). Factors affecting brand love in the metaverse world and the effect of brand love on word-of-mouth marketing. *Turkish Journal of Marketing*, 7(3), 148–161. DOI: 10.30685/tujom.v7i3.162

Chernatony, L. (1999). *From brand vision to brand evaluation*. Elsevier Ltd.

Chernatony, L., & McDonald, M. (2003). *Creating powerful brands: In consumer, service and industrial markets*. Taylor & Francis.

Daldiran, K., & Daldiran, B. (2023). Digital twin technology as a driver of sustainable supply chain and marketing transparency. *Avesis*.aybu.edu.tr

Deloitte. (2022). Digital Media Trends 2022. Consultado em 8 de janeiro de 2023, de https://www2.deloitte.com/pt/pt/pages/technology-media-andtelecommunications/articles/ Digital-Media-Trends-2022.html

Dhruv, S. (2022). Best design practices & strategy to launch your own NFT project. *Trends in Computer Science and Information Technology, 7*(1), 007–009. https://doi.org/DOI: 10.17352/tcsit.000045

Escalas, J. E. (2004). Narrative processing: Building consumer connections to brands. *Journal of Consumer Psychology*, 14(1-2), 168–180. DOI: 10.1207/s15327663jcp1401&2_19

Foster, J. K., McLelland, M. A., & Wallace, L. K. (2022). Brand avatars: Impact of social interaction on consumer–brand relationships. *Journal of Research in Interactive Marketing*, 16(2), 237–258. DOI: 10.1108/JRIM-01-2020-0007

Gladcheff, A. P. (2003). *Entrevista Estruturada: Uma Eficiente Técnica de Aquisição de Conhecimento Explícito*. Revista PUC-SP.

Gummesson, E. (2014). Pesquisa em serviços de metodologia: Do estudo de caso em pesquisa à teoria. *Revista Ibero-Americana de Estratégia, 13*(04), 08–17. https://doi.org/DOI: 10.5585/riae.v13i4.2180

Gupta, V. P., Sharief, S., & Rani, S. (2024). Digital fashion and social media influencer in industry 5.0. In Rani, S. (Ed.), *System engineering and digital twins for industry 5.0* (pp. 67–89). Springer. DOI: 10.1007/978-3-031-71052-0_4

Hamari, J., Koivisto, J., & Sarsa, H. (2014). Does gamification work? A literature review of empirical studies on gamification. *Proceedings of the 47th Hawaii International Conference on System Sciences*, 3025–3034. DOI: 10.1109/HICSS.2014.377

Intelligence, W. T. (2021a). *Lauches into the metaverse – a metaverse road map for brands* (2021 Edition). PR Newswire Association LLC., Retrieved from https://www.proquest.com/wire-feeds/wunderman-thompson-launches-into-metaverse-road/docview/2572826415/se-2?accountid=177838

Joy, A., Zhu, Y., Peña, C., & Brouard, M. (2022). Digital future of luxury brands: Metaverse, digital fashion, and non-fungible tokens. *Strategic Change*, 31(3), 337–343. DOI: 10.1002/jsc.2502

Keller, K. L. (2009). Building strong brands in a modern marketing communications environment. *Journal of Marketing Communications*, 15(2-3), 139–155. DOI: 10.1080/13527260902757530

Kotler, P., Kartajaya, H., & Setiawan, I. (2021). *Marketing 5.0: Technology for humanity*. Edições Almedina.

Lee, J., Kim, H., & Choi, Y. (2024). Understanding player engagement in the metaverse: A synthesis of the interactive gaming experience. *The Journal of Consumer Research*, 51(2), 145–163.

Lee, L.-H., Braud, T., Zhou, P., Wang, L., Xu, D., Lin, Z., Kumar, A., Bermejo, C., & Hui, P. (2021). All one needs to know about metaverse: A complete survey on technological singularity, virtual ecosystem, and research agenda. Retrieved from http://arxiv.org/abs/2110.05352

Liffreing, I. (2021). What brands should know about the metaverse | Ad Age. Consultado a 12 de dezembro de 2022, de https://adage.com/article/digital-marketing-ad-tech-news/what-brands-should-know-about-metaverse/2354506

McKinsey & Company. (2022). Value creation in the metaverse: The real business of the virtual world. Consultado a 2 de novembro de 2022, de https://www.mckinsey.com/capabilities/growth-marketing-and-sales/our-insights/value-creation-in-the-metaverse

Miles, M., Huberman, M., & Saldaña, J. (2019). *Qualitative data analysis: A methods sourcebook*. SAGE Publications.

Mishra, D., & Kautish, P. (2024). Exploring the role of gamification in metaverse platforms: A study on user engagement and player-driven economies. *Journal of Gaming and Virtual Worlds*, 16(1), 45–67.

Rani, S., Sharief, S., & Gupta, V. (2024). Collaborative robotics and digital twins for the metaverse: Concepts, applications, and future trends. In *System engineering and digital twins for industry 5.0* (pp. 45–66). Springer.

Selase, A. E., Abdoulaye, A. M., Mawuli, M. D., & Brantson, T. E. (2018). The Identity of Brand with its Influenceable Character on Client Choices of Predominant Restaurants Accra as the Lens. *J Account Mark*, 7(4), 302. DOI: 10.4172/2168-9601.1000302

Silva, M. (2022). As melhores plataformas para adquirir NFTs de Moda | Vogue.pt. Consultado em 8 de janeiro de 2023, de https://www.vogue.pt/moda-digital-plataformas-de-nfts

Uddin, M., Obaidat, M., Manickam, S., Laghari, S. U. A., Dandoush, A., Ullah, H., & Ullah, S. S. (2024). Exploring the convergence of metaverse, blockchain, and AI: A comprehensive survey of enabling technologies, applications, challenges, and future directions. *Wiley Interdisciplinary Reviews. Data Mining and Knowledge Discovery*, 14(6), e1556. DOI: 10.1002/widm.1556

Vidushi, & Dawar, P. (2024). Ethical issues in the sustainable fashion industry. In *Information system engineering and digital twins for industry 5.0* (pp. 255–273). Springer.

Wunderman Thompson Intelligence. (2021b). Into the Metaverse, 2021 Edition. New York: Wunderman Thompson Intelligence. Retrieved from https://www.wundermanthompson.com/insight/new-trend-report-into-the-metaverse

Yin, R. K. (2018). *Case study research and applications: Design and methods* (6th ed.). SAGE Publications.

Chapter 6
Enhancing Customer Engagement Through the Metaverse:
Opportunities and Challenges for Indian SMEs

Arpan Anand
https://orcid.org/0000-0002-2572-1651
Jaipuria Institute of Management, Noida, India

ABSTRACT

This chapter examines the transformative potential of the Metaverse in enhancing customer engagement for Indian small and medium-sized enterprises (SMEs). As digital technologies evolve, the Metaverse—a combination of virtual and augmented realities—offers innovative ways for businesses to interact with customers, transcending traditional marketing channels. Indian SMEs play a critical role in the economy, yet face challenges in adopting new technologies due to limited resources and technical expertise. This study explores the Metaverse's potential to provide immersive, interactive customer experiences and highlights the hurdles SMEs encounter, including technological and financial barriers. Furthermore, it discusses strategies for overcoming these obstacles, underscoring the importance of strategic agility and customer-centric approaches in the Metaverse. By embracing this digital shift, Indian SMEs can position themselves to foster loyalty, increase brand engagement, and drive sustainable growth.

DOI: 10.4018/979-8-3693-9005-4.ch006

1. INTRODUCTION

The advent of the Metaverse represents a transformative shift in customer engagement, especially for small and medium-sized enterprises (SMEs) in India. As digital technologies continue to evolve, the Metaverse emerges as a novel platform, integrating virtual and augmented realities to offer businesses new opportunities to enhance customer interactions and experiences. This chapter explores the implications of the Metaverse for Indian SMEs, focusing on the opportunities it presents, as well as the challenges they must navigate to leverage this innovative environment effectively.

The importance of digital transformation for SMEs cannot be overstated, as digital technologies have been shown to positively impact SME performance by helping them adapt to changing market dynamics and consumer preferences (Teng et al., 2022). In India, where SMEs contribute significantly to the economy, integrating digital tools is essential to sustain competitiveness and foster growth. The Metaverse offers a unique avenue for SMEs to engage customers in immersive and interactive ways that traditional marketing channels cannot replicate. By blending physical and virtual experiences, businesses can create more personalized customer journeys, enhancing both customer loyalty and satisfaction (Buhalis et al., 2022).

However, adopting the Metaverse comes with its own set of challenges. Many SMEs struggle to adopt new technologies due to limited resources and expertise (Kääriäinen et al., 2021). The complexity of digital transformation can overwhelm smaller enterprises that often lack strategic frameworks to effectively navigate these changes (Wang, 2023). Furthermore, the rapid pace of technological advancements requires SMEs to remain agile, continuously evolving their business models to meet the demands of a digitally savvy consumer base (Mattos et al., 2023). Understanding the dynamics of the Metaverse and its potential for customer engagement is thus crucial for Indian SMEs aiming to thrive in this new digital landscape.

Beyond operational hurdles, there are also strategic considerations. The Metaverse provides significant potential for value co-creation, where businesses can collaborate with customers to develop products and services tailored to their specific needs (Buhalis et al., 2022). However, this shift demands a departure from traditional transactional relationships in favor of more collaborative, participatory approaches. SMEs must foster a culture of innovation and customer-centricity to fully harness the opportunities presented by the Metaverse (Ziółkowska, 2021).

The COVID-19 pandemic has further accelerated the need for digital transformation among SMEs, underscoring the urgency for businesses to adapt to new realities (Klein and Todesco, 2021). The pandemic has disrupted traditional business operations and reshaped consumer behavior, making digital engagement more critical than ever. As SMEs navigate the post-pandemic landscape, the Metaverse offers a promising solution for re-engaging customers and rebuilding brand loyalty. This chapter will explore how Indian SMEs can leverage the Metaverse to create resilient business models that meet evolving consumer needs in the digital age.

In conclusion, while the Metaverse offers Indian SMEs immense opportunities to enhance customer engagement, it also presents formidable challenges. This chapter will provide a comprehensive analysis of strategies, tools, and frameworks that SMEs can adopt to successfully navigate the complexities of the Metaverse. By understanding the interplay between digital transformation and customer engagement, Indian SMEs can position themselves at the forefront of this emerging digital frontier, driving sustainable growth and innovation in an increasingly competitive marketplace.

1.1 Background and Context

The emergence of the Metaverse represents a transformative shift in digital engagement, presenting small and medium-sized enterprises (SMEs) in India with both unprecedented opportunities and significant challenges. Characterized by immersive virtual environments and augmented reality experiences, the Metaverse allows businesses to interact with customers in innovative ways, moving beyond the constraints of traditional marketing and customer service channels. This chapter explores the implications of the Metaverse for Indian SMEs, highlighting how they can leverage its potential while addressing the challenges associated with its implementation ("Metaverse in Media: Understanding Digital Traces Towards Futuristic Technologies in India", 2024).

Indian SMEs play a crucial role in the national economy, contributing significantly to employment and innovation (Vasani and Abdulkareem, 2024). However, they often encounter substantial barriers to adopting new technologies, including financial constraints, inadequate digital infrastructure, and a shortage of skilled personnel (Raj et al., 2020). The COVID-19 pandemic accelerated the need for digital transformation, forcing many SMEs to adapt to survive in a rapidly changing market (Lu et al., 2022). As businesses look to rebuild and innovate in the post-pandemic landscape, the Metaverse has emerged as a promising avenue for enhancing customer engagement and building brand loyalty.

The immersive nature of the Metaverse offers SMEs the opportunity to create deeper customer connections. Research shows that businesses that effectively integrate Metaverse technologies can engage customers through personalized, interactive experiences, fostering community and loyalty (Gil-Cordero et al., 2024). This is particularly important in India, where diverse markets necessitate tailored approaches to customer engagement (Keshari, 2020). By providing virtual spaces where consumers can interact with products and brands in a more meaningful way, SMEs can elevate their customer experience. However, successful integration requires not just technological upgrades but also a strategic rethinking of how customer engagement is approached in this new environment (Queiroz et al., 2023).

To capitalize on the Metaverse, SMEs must recognize that it represents more than just a technological innovation—it's a paradigm shift in customer expectations. Today's consumers seek not just transactions but experiences. They expect brands to offer interactive and immersive touchpoints that go beyond conventional digital platforms (Sim et al., 2022). For Indian SMEs, this means embracing a culture of innovation and adaptability, allowing them to leverage the full potential of the Metaverse in creating unique customer journeys (Rena, 2023).

However, these opportunities are accompanied by challenges. Implementing Metaverse technologies demands significant investments in digital infrastructure, training, and cybersecurity (Elsadig, 2024). Data privacy and ethical concerns surrounding virtual interactions are also critical issues that need to be carefully navigated (Said, 2023). For many SMEs with limited resources, the prospect of embracing such an advanced digital transformation may seem overwhelming. Understanding and overcoming these barriers is essential for SMEs to thrive in this evolving landscape (Dutta et al., 2023).

The Metaverse also has the potential to reshape how Indian SMEs engage with customers, but its adoption depends largely on overcoming these operational and strategic challenges. The uneven pace of digital adoption across India—due to disparities in infrastructure and digital literacy—creates additional barriers for SMEs, especially those in rural or less developed regions (Kumar et al., 2023). Despite these challenges, the Metaverse holds promise for bridging gaps in customer engagement, particularly for businesses willing to invest in building digital capabilities.

The broader context of customer engagement has evolved significantly over time, shifting from traditional face-to-face interactions to sophisticated digital platforms. The Metaverse represents the next step in this evolution, offering immersive, three-dimensional environments where physical and digital realities converge (Chen et al., 2024). For Indian SMEs, traditionally reliant on personal relationships and localized networks, the Metaverse offers the possibility to overcome geographical limitations and create novel, interactive customer experiences. However, it also requires SMEs to adopt new strategies and capabilities to remain competitive.

Recent advances in virtual and augmented reality technologies have made the Metaverse more accessible to businesses. According to Kumar and Singh (2024), the convergence of high-speed internet, advanced graphics capabilities, and increasingly sophisticated platforms has created a conducive environment for the Metaverse to flourish. Still, the digital divide in India poses a significant challenge, with disparities in access to technology and digital literacy potentially limiting the reach and effectiveness of Metaverse-based engagement strategies (Gupta & Sharma, 2023).

The digitalization of India's economy, driven by factors such as widespread smartphone adoption, government initiatives promoting digital transactions, and changing consumer preferences, has redefined the landscape for customer engagement. The global pandemic further accelerated these trends, compelling businesses to adopt digital solutions to remain competitive. However, as Joshi and Patel (2024) note, the digital transformation of Indian SMEs has been uneven, with larger enterprises quick to adapt while smaller ones struggle to keep pace. The Metaverse could either exacerbate this divide or, if implemented effectively, help bridge it by enabling SMEs to offer competitive, immersive experiences to their customers.

1.2 Research Objectives

This chapter examines the intersection of metaverse technologies and customer engagement practices within the specific context of Indian SMEs. As the digital landscape undergoes rapid transformation, understanding how these enterprises can leverage virtual environments to enhance customer relationships becomes increasingly critical. The research addresses several key objectives:

1. To critically analyze the potential implementation strategies for metaverse-based customer engagement within Indian SMEs, considering technological and socioeconomic constraints
2. To evaluate the theoretical and practical implications of adopting metaverse technologies for customer interaction in the Indian business context
3. To examine the role of cultural and socioeconomic factors in the adoption and effectiveness of metaverse-based customer engagement in India
4. To develop a conceptual framework for understanding the impact of metaverse-enhanced customer engagement on SME business outcomes
5. To assess the potential return on investment for SMEs implementing metaverse technologies, considering both tangible and intangible benefits
6. To identify best practices and potential pitfalls in metaverse adoption for customer engagement, drawing from early adopters and international case studies

These objectives are guided by several key research questions:

1. How can Indian SMEs effectively overcome technological and financial barriers to metaverse adoption?
2. What role do cultural factors play in shaping customer acceptance of metaverse-based interactions?
3. How can SMEs measure and optimize the effectiveness of metaverse-based customer engagement strategies?

4. What regulatory and ethical considerations should guide metaverse implementation in the Indian context?

1.3 Significance of the Study

This study is essential as it examines the Metaverse as a transformative platform for enhancing customer engagement among small and medium-sized enterprises (SMEs) in India. With the rapid evolution of the digital landscape, the Metaverse presents SMEs with unique opportunities to innovate their customer interaction strategies, creating deeper and more meaningful connections with consumers. This chapter aims to provide a detailed analysis of how Indian SMEs can utilize the Metaverse to improve customer engagement, while also addressing the challenges of this digital shift.

The Metaverse introduces a new environment for customer engagement that goes beyond traditional marketing and service delivery. By incorporating immersive technologies, such as virtual reality (VR) and augmented reality (AR), SMEs can create interactive experiences that resonate strongly with consumers (Zhong, 2023). This shift toward experiential marketing is particularly relevant for Indian SMEs, which often struggle to differentiate themselves in a competitive market. Providing unique, memorable experiences can significantly enhance customer loyalty and improve brand perception (Kathuria, 2023).

This study also emphasizes understanding the customer journey within the Metaverse. The proposed MIEB (Metaverse – Information – Experiences – Benefits) model serves as a strategic framework, focusing on key elements such as information, customer experiences, and derived benefits (Zhong, 2023). By adopting this model, SMEs can design their offerings to meet evolving consumer expectations, leading to greater customer satisfaction and retention.

Generational shifts in consumer behavior, especially among Gen Z, are another focal point. As Gen Z increasingly engages with the Metaverse, understanding their motivations and preferences becomes critical for SMEs. By aligning marketing strategies with this generation's desire for immersive and interactive experiences, SMEs can increase their relevance and appeal (Kathuria, 2023).

Additionally, the study introduces the concept of strategic agility in Metaverse marketing. It suggests that by developing adaptable capabilities, SMEs can create more responsive marketing approaches (Abrokwah-Larbi, 2024). This adaptability is essential in navigating the constantly changing digital landscape where consumer preferences and technologies evolve rapidly.

Beyond individual businesses, the study's implications extend to the broader Indian economy. SMEs comprise a significant portion of India's business landscape, and their successful integration into the Metaverse could drive innovation, stimulate economic growth, and create employment opportunities. By equipping SMEs with the tools and knowledge to succeed in the Metaverse, this study contributes to the ongoing discourse on digital transformation and its potential impact on the future of business in India.

In conclusion, this study's significance lies not only in enhancing customer engagement through the Metaverse but also in providing critical insights for Indian SMEs navigating this digital frontier. By exploring both opportunities and challenges, the chapter offers practical strategies for SMEs aiming for sustainable growth.

This study contributes to the existing body of knowledge by:

1. Synthesizing current literature on Metaverse implementation in business.
2. Analyzing specific challenges and opportunities faced by Indian SMEs.
3. Developing a theoretical framework for Metaverse adoption in emerging markets.
4. Providing evidence-based recommendations for practitioners and policymakers.

Key stakeholders who will benefit from this research include:

1. SME owners and managers evaluating Metaverse adoption.
2. Technology providers creating solutions tailored for the Indian market.
3. Policymakers supporting digital transformation initiatives.
4. Investors seeking opportunities in the Metaverse sector.

Furthermore, this study addresses a crucial gap in the literature. As Rajan and Kumar (2024) observe, much research on Metaverse adoption focuses on large enterprises in developed economies. This study offers a context-specific analysis for emerging markets like India, emphasizing the unique challenges and opportunities that SMEs face in adopting advanced digital technologies.

2. LITERATURE REVIEW

2.1 Current State of Customer Engagement in Indian SMEs

Traditional customer engagement methods employed by Indian SMEs have predominantly relied on face-to-face interactions, local advertising, and word-of-mouth marketing (Kumar & Raheja, 2021). While these approaches have been effective in building personal relationships, they are limited in scale and reach. Recent studies indicate a significant shift towards digital adoption among Indian SMEs, particularly in the wake of the COVID-19 pandemic, with a 50% increase in digital platform usage reported by KPMG (2022).

Recent research has highlighted the limitations of conventional digital engagement models when applied to immersive environments (Table 1):

Table 1. Limitations of Conventional models

Aspect	Traditional Digital	Metaverse Engagement
User Interaction	Two-dimensional, screen-based	Multi-dimensional, immersive
Sensory Engagement	Visual and auditory	Multi-sensory, spatial
Social Presence	Limited, text-based	Enhanced, avatar-mediated
Data Collection	Behavioral tracking	Volumetric and biometric data

2.1.1 Digital Transformation Challenges

Despite the growing recognition of digital engagement's importance, Indian SMEs face numerous challenges in their digital transformation journey. Research by Gupta et al. (2023) highlights that while 78% of Indian SMEs have some form of digital presence, only 23% utilize advanced digital tools for customer engagement, indicating a significant gap in technological adoption. Key barriers identified include:

1. Limited technological infrastructure and expertise
2. Financial constraints affecting investment in digital tools
3. Resistance to change among traditional business owners
4. Concerns about data security and privacy

2.1.2 Evolution of Customer Expectations

Contemporary consumers, particularly millennials and Generation Z, increasingly expect personalized, immersive, and interactive experiences from businesses (Sharma & Patel, 2024). This shift in expectations has created a disconnect between traditional SME engagement methods and customer preferences. Studies by Rajesh and Kumar (2023) indicate that 65% of Indian consumers prefer businesses that offer digital engagement options, with 40% specifically expressing interest in virtual and augmented reality experiences.

2.2 Emergence of Metaverse Technologies

The concept of the metaverse has evolved from science fiction to technological reality, with significant implications for business operations. Sharma and Patel (2024) define the metaverse as a persistent, shared, 3D virtual space that combines aspects of social media, online gaming, augmented reality (AR), virtual reality (VR), and cryptocurrencies. Recent advancements in technologies such as 5G networks, edge computing, and artificial intelligence have made the metaverse increasingly accessible and viable for business applications (Singh et al., 2023).

2.2.1 Technological Components of the Metaverse

The metaverse ecosystem comprises several key technological components:

1. **Virtual Reality (VR)**: Immersive technologies that create fully digital environments
2. **Augmented Reality (AR)**: Technologies that overlay digital content onto the physical world
3. **Mixed Reality (MR)**: Hybrid experiences that blend physical and digital elements
4. **Blockchain and Cryptocurrencies**: Enabling secure transactions and digital ownership
5. **Artificial Intelligence**: Powering personalization and virtual assistants

Research by Verma et al. (2024) suggests that the integration of these technologies creates a synergistic effect, enhancing the overall potential for customer engagement.

2.2.2 Business Applications in the Metaverse

Early adopters of metaverse technologies have demonstrated various business applications:

1. Virtual showrooms and product demonstrations
2. Immersive customer service experiences
3. Virtual events and conferences
4. Interactive training and education
5. Collaborative design and prototyping

Studies by Mehta and Gupta (2023) indicate that businesses implementing metaverse-based engagement strategies have seen a 27% increase in customer satisfaction and a 32% improvement in brand recall compared to traditional digital marketing approaches.

2.3 Theoretical Framework and Foundations

This section presents a comprehensive theoretical framework to enhance customer engagement through the Metaverse for Indian SMEs. It integrates key constructs, including Metaverse Marketing (MVM), Strategic Agility (SA), Immersive Marketing Technologies (IMT), and Customer Immersion (CI), drawing on contemporary business theories. Together, these elements provide insights into how SMEs can navigate the complexities of the Metaverse to foster deeper customer relationships and drive growth.

i. The Indian SME Landscape

India's SME sector, comprising over 63 million enterprises and contributing approximately 30% to the GDP, represents a diverse ecosystem ranging from traditional manufacturers to technology-driven startups (Ministry of MSME, 2023). The post-pandemic digital acceleration has created both opportunities and imperatives for these businesses to adopt immersive technologies. Recent studies indicate that 72% of Indian SMEs have increased their digital investment since 2020, with customer engagement being a primary driver (Sharma & Gupta, 2024).

ii. Metaverse Marketing (MVM)

Metaverse Marketing (MVM) encompasses strategies for engaging customers within immersive environments. The Metaverse enables SMEs to explore new realms of experiential marketing, personalization, and community building. Through MVM, SMEs can foster meaningful interactions, strengthen customer relationships, and enhance brand loyalty (Abrokwah-Larbi, 2024). Integrating MVM into business strategies allows SMEs to capitalize on the Metaverse's unique capabilities, enhancing customer experiences and driving long-term growth.

iii. Strategic Agility (SA)

Strategic Agility (SA) captures the ability of SMEs to quickly adapt to changing market conditions, a necessity in the dynamic Metaverse. By embracing SA, SMEs can pivot marketing strategies in response to evolving consumer preferences and technological developments (Abrokwah-Larbi, 2024). MVM supports the development of SA, allowing SMEs to remain competitive in the fast-evolving Metaverse landscape by crafting flexible, real-time strategies that resonate with customers.

iv. Immersive Marketing Technologies (IMT)

Immersive Marketing Technologies (IMT), such as Virtual Reality (VR) and Augmented Reality (AR), serve as essential tools for creating engaging, interactive customer experiences. IMT acts as a mediator between MVM and SA, enabling SMEs to foster deeper connections with their audiences (Abrokwah-Larbi, 2024). By effectively leveraging these technologies, SMEs can enhance customer satisfaction and gather real-time feedback, which supports strategic agility and continuous engagement.

v. Customer Immersion (CI)

Customer Immersion (CI) refers to the extent to which customers become absorbed in the brand experiences offered within the Metaverse. Higher levels of immersion strengthen emotional connections between customers and brands, enhancing MVM's impact (Abrokwah-Larbi, 2024). CI also plays a mediating role, facilitating insights into customer preferences and supporting real-time strategy adjustments. The more immersive the experience, the greater the potential for sustained customer loyalty and competitive advantage.

vi. Customer Engagement Process

The primary aim of this theoretical framework is to enhance Customer Engagement, defined by the quality of interactions customers have with a brand. In the Metaverse, customer engagement is driven by immersive experiences facilitated through MVM, IMT, and CI. SMEs that incorporate these strategies are better positioned to build lasting relationships, achieving a competitive edge in the evolving digital landscape (Mathews & Lhamo, 2022).

2.4 Conceptualizing the Metaverse in Business Contexts

To enhance this framework's relevance, the Metaverse is conceptualized beyond just a technological platform. It represents a shift in business-customer engagement, blending elements from social media, gaming, AR, VR, and blockchain to create a shared, three-dimensional space that transcends physical limitations (Park & Kim, 2022).

Singh and Kumar (2024) propose a multi-layered model for Metaverse engagement in business contexts, covering infrastructure, interface, interaction, and integration. This model provides a roadmap for SMEs, starting from basic awareness to full integration within business strategies (Mehta & Desai, 2024). For most Indian SMEs, currently at nascent adoption stages, understanding these layers can guide progress and address adoption barriers.

In addition, the Virtual Value Co-creation Framework (VVCF) emphasizes value co-creation between customers and businesses, suggesting practical ways for SMEs to collaborate with customers in virtual spaces (Kumar & Reddy, 2024). Incorporating such theories enables SMEs to quantify and optimize customer engagement, creating more impactful, culturally relevant Metaverse experiences.

This integrated framework offers a structured approach to enhancing customer engagement in the Metaverse for Indian SMEs. By combining constructs like MVM, SA, IMT, and CI with insights from modern business and marketing theories, SMEs can leverage immersive technologies, foster customer immersion, and continually adapt to the Metaverse's evolving landscape. This approach enables SMEs to build long-term customer relationships and achieve sustained growth in an increasingly digital world.

3. CURRENT STATE OF INDIAN SMES IN DIGITAL ENGAGEMENT

The digital transformation landscape of Indian small and medium-sized enterprises (SMEs) presents a complex interplay of opportunities and challenges as these businesses navigate an increasingly digitized marketplace. This evolution is particularly significant in the context of emerging economies, where digital adoption can serve as a crucial catalyst for economic growth and market competitiveness. The following sections provide a comprehensive analysis of the current state of Indian SMEs' digital engagement, examining various dimensions from digital marketing strategies to infrastructure development.

3.1 Digital Maturity Landscape

The digital maturity of Indian SMEs exhibits considerable heterogeneity across sectors and regions. Recent research by Gupta et al. (2023) reveals that while 78% of Indian SMEs maintain some form of digital presence, only 23% effectively utilize advanced digital tools for customer engagement. This digital divide presents a significant challenge for advanced technology adoption, particularly concerning metaverse implementation, which demands sophisticated digital infrastructure and capabilities.

The assessment of digital maturity encompasses multiple dimensions, including technological infrastructure, digital skills and capabilities, strategic digital orientation, and data analytics proficiency. Verma and Kapoor's (2024) Digital Maturity Index (DMI) provides a comprehensive framework for evaluating Indian SMEs' readiness for advanced digital transformations, considering factors such as existing digital infrastructure, employee digital literacy, leadership commitment, and financial resource allocation.

3.1.1 Sector-Specific Analysis

Digital maturity varies significantly across different sectors, with each industry demonstrating unique adoption patterns and challenges. The retail and e-commerce sector shows notable progress in digital payment systems adoption, with 87% of SMEs implementing various digital transaction capabilities. This high adoption rate stems from increasing consumer preferences for cashless transactions and supportive government initiatives. However, more advanced technologies such as Augmented Reality (AR) and Virtual Reality (VR) show limited penetration, with only 14% of retail SMEs integrating these solutions into their operations.

The manufacturing sector demonstrates strong adoption of digital inventory management systems, with 73% of SMEs implementing digital tracking and control solutions. Internet of Things (IoT) implementation shows promising growth, with 41% of manufacturing SMEs incorporating connected devices and sensors into their operations. However, customer-facing digital initiatives remain limited, with only 28% of SMEs implementing significant digital interfaces for client interaction.

The services sector leads in digital adoption, particularly in cloud-based solutions, with 82% implementation rates. Digital communication tools have become nearly ubiquitous, with 76% of SMEs utilizing various platforms for client interaction and internal collaboration. The emergence of virtual service delivery platforms represents a significant trend, with 35% of service-sector SMEs exploring or implementing virtual platforms for service provision.

3.2 Barriers to Digital Transformation

The digital transformation journey of Indian SMEs faces several significant challenges that require careful consideration and strategic resolution. These barriers can be categorized into three primary areas: technological infrastructure limitations, financial constraints, and skill gaps.

3.2.1 Technological Infrastructure Limitations

Infrastructure constraints represent a fundamental challenge for Indian SMEs pursuing digital transformation. These limitations manifest in hardware inadequacies, software constraints, and connectivity issues. The disparity in infrastructure quality between urban and rural areas creates additional complexity in digital adoption patterns. Limited access to sophisticated development tools and challenges in integrating legacy systems with modern digital platforms further complicate the transformation process.

3.2.2 Financial Constraints

Financial barriers present significant challenges for SMEs pursuing digital transformation. Initial investment requirements for hardware (5-15 lakhs INR), software licensing (3-8 lakhs INR annually), and training (2-5 lakhs INR) often exceed available resources. Operational costs, including maintenance, content creation, and hosting, add to the financial burden. The uncertainty surrounding return on investment and limited successful case studies in the Indian context further complicate investment decisions.

3.2.3 Skill Gap and Technical Expertise

The skill gap in the Indian SME sector represents a critical barrier to digital transformation. Technical skills deficiencies in areas such as VR/AR development, 3D modeling, and blockchain integration limit the ability to implement advanced digital solutions. Additionally, soft skills gaps in virtual customer service, digital storytelling, and virtual team management affect the effectiveness of digital initiatives.

3.3 Current Adoption Patterns

Digital adoption among Indian SMEs shows distinct patterns across different sectors and geographic regions. Urban areas demonstrate higher adoption rates compared to rural regions, particularly in tech hubs. The retail sector leads in virtual showroom adoption, while education and healthcare sectors show increasing implementation of virtual training environments and telemedicine solutions.

3.3.1 Early Adopter Case Studies

Successful implementations of digital transformation provide valuable insights for the broader SME community. Notable examples include StyleVR India's virtual try-on solution, which achieved a 45% increase in online sales and 30% reduction in returns, and TechTrain Solutions' VR-based machinery operation training, resulting in 60% reduction in training time and improved safety metrics.

3.3.2 Emerging Technologies in Customer Engagement

The integration of artificial intelligence and advanced analytics has transformed customer engagement strategies among Indian SMEs. AI-powered chatbots have enabled 24/7 customer service capabilities, reducing response times by 35% while handling increased query volumes. Data analytics implementation has led to more personalized marketing strategies, resulting in 28% higher engagement rates and 22% improved conversion rates.

3.4 Infrastructure Development

3.4.1 Current Infrastructure Status

The technological infrastructure of Indian SMEs varies significantly between urban and rural areas. Urban enterprises demonstrate higher adoption of advanced computing capabilities, with 62% reporting modern hardware systems implementation. Mobile device integration shows strong adoption across regions, with 78% of SMEs successfully incorporating mobile technologies into their operations.

3.4.2 Cloud Adoption and Digital Services

Cloud-based solutions have gained significant traction among Indian SMEs, with SaaS adoption rates increasing from 27% in 2019 to 56% by 2024. Cloud storage and computing adoption has reached 68% and 42% respectively, enabling improved data management and operational resilience. Platform integration efforts have yielded average productivity improvements of 23% among successful implementers.

3.5 Future Directions and Support Systems

3.5.1 Emerging Technologies and Trends

Artificial intelligence and machine learning adoption, while currently at 18% among Indian SMEs, shows promising growth potential. IoT implementation has reached 32%, particularly in manufacturing and logistics sectors. Augmented and virtual reality applications, though at early stages with 12% adoption, demonstrate significant potential for transforming customer experiences and operational processes.

3.5.2 Supportive Ecosystem Development

Government initiatives, industry collaborations, and expanded financial support mechanisms form the foundation of the supportive ecosystem for SME digitization. SMEs participating in government digital empowerment programs show 45% higher success rates in digital transformation initiatives. The availability of specialized financing options has increased by 156% over five years, though access remains uneven across regions and sectors.

4. METAVERSE IMPLEMENTATION STRATEGIES FOR INDIAN SMES

4.1 Strategic Framework Development

The implementation of metaverse strategies in Indian SMEs demands a comprehensive framework that addresses both technological capabilities and cultural nuances specific to the Indian market context. Kumar and Singh (2023) demonstrate through their empirical research that successful metaverse adoption in emerging economies requires a careful balance between technological innovation and local market characteristics. Their findings suggest that Indian SMEs face unique challenges in digital transformation, particularly in terms of infrastructure readiness and cultural adaptation requirements.

Recent research by Verma and Joshi (2024) indicates that successful metaverse implementations in Indian SMEs are characterized by clear strategic alignment with business objectives and careful consideration of local market dynamics. Their study of 150 Indian SMEs revealed that organizations achieving the highest customer engagement rates through metaverse initiatives were those that prioritized cultural relevance and local market understanding in their implementation strategies.

The strategic framework for metaverse implementation must begin with a thorough assessment of organizational readiness. According to Sharma et al. (2023), this assessment should encompass technological infrastructure, workforce capabilities, and market positioning. Their research across various Indian industrial sectors demonstrates that successful metaverse adoption correlates strongly with comprehensive preliminary assessments and clear strategic planning.

4.2 Implementation Roadmap

The implementation of metaverse initiatives in Indian SMEs requires a structured approach that accounts for varying levels of technological maturity and market readiness. Patel and Kumar (2024) propose a three-phase implementation model based on their study of successful metaverse adoptions in Indian enterprises.

The first phase, termed as foundation building, typically spans three to six months and focuses on establishing the basic infrastructure and capabilities necessary for metaverse engagement. During this phase, organizations must conduct comprehensive technology assessments, identify skills gaps, and develop detailed implementation plans. Research by Mehta et al. (2024) shows that Indian SMEs that invested adequate time in this foundational phase were 2.3 times more likely to achieve their customer engagement objectives through metaverse initiatives.

The second phase involves pilot implementation, usually lasting six to nine months. During this critical period, organizations must carefully select and execute initial use cases that align with their strategic objectives while managing risks effectively. A longitudinal study by Gupta and Sharma (2024) of 75 Indian SMEs revealed that successful pilot implementations shared common characteristics: they started with clearly defined scope, incorporated regular feedback mechanisms, and maintained flexibility in their approach to accommodate learning and adjustment.

5. CULTURAL AND SOCIOECONOMIC IMPLICATIONS

5.1 Cultural Considerations in the Indian Context

The implementation of metaverse strategies in India requires careful consideration of the country's rich cultural tapestry and diverse social fabric. Research by Reddy et al. (2023) examining metaverse adoption patterns across different Indian states reveals that cultural sensitivity in virtual environment design significantly impacts user engagement rates. Their study of 500 users across five major Indian cities demonstrated that culturally adapted virtual environments achieved 45% higher engagement rates compared to generic implementations.

Language diversity presents a particular challenge in the Indian context. According to comprehensive research by Singh and Patel (2024), successful metaverse implementations must account for not just multiple languages but also regional dialects and communication patterns. Their analysis of customer interaction data from 200 Indian SMEs showed that organizations incorporating regional language support and cultural elements in their virtual environments experienced a 60% increase in customer engagement metrics.

5.2 Socioeconomic Impact Analysis

The socioeconomic implications of metaverse adoption in India extend beyond immediate business impacts to broader societal effects. Research conducted by Kumar and Verma (2024) indicates that metaverse implementations are creating new employment categories and skill requirements in the Indian market. Their longitudinal study of 300 SMEs implementing metaverse solutions revealed the emergence of specialized roles combining technical expertise with cultural knowledge.

The digital divide remains a significant concern in the Indian context. Recent research by Mehta and Khan (2024) highlights substantial disparities in metaverse accessibility across different demographic segments. Their study of 1,000 potential users across urban and rural areas identified significant gaps in both infrastructure access and digital literacy levels, with particularly pronounced differences between metropolitan and rural areas.

6. FUTURE DIRECTIONS AND RECOMMENDATIONS

6.1 Emerging Trends in Indian Metaverse Adoption

The evolution of metaverse adoption in India is characterized by unique patterns that reflect the country's technological landscape and cultural context. Research by Das and Kumar (2024) identifies several key trends shaping the future of metaverse implementation in Indian SMEs. Their analysis of market data from 2020-2024 reveals an increasing convergence between artificial intelligence, IoT, and metaverse technologies, creating new opportunities for customer engagement.

The integration of AI-driven solutions in metaverse environments is particularly relevant for the Indian market. Singh et al. (2024) document how AI-powered virtual assistants capable of understanding regional languages and cultural nuances have become crucial for successful customer engagement. Their study of 250 metaverse implementations demonstrates that culturally aware AI solutions achieve 40% higher customer satisfaction rates compared to standard implementations.

6.2 Strategic Recommendations

Based on extensive empirical evidence and market analysis, several strategic recommendations emerge for Indian SMEs pursuing metaverse initiatives. Research by Sharma and Gupta (2024) emphasizes the importance of phased implementation approaches that allow organizations to build capabilities progressively while managing risks effectively. Their study of successful implementations suggests that organizations should begin with focused pilot projects in urban markets before expanding to broader market segments.

Government support and industry collaboration emerge as crucial factors for successful metaverse adoption. Recent policy analysis by Verma et al. (2024) indicates that regulatory frameworks and infrastructure development initiatives play vital roles in facilitating metaverse adoption. Their research suggests that public-private partnerships and industry consortiums can help address common challenges and accelerate the development of standards and best practices.

7. CONCLUSION

7.1 Theoretical and Practical Contributions

This research makes significant contributions to both theoretical understanding and practical implementation of metaverse strategies in emerging economies. Through systematic analysis of implementation data from Indian SMEs, this study extends existing digital transformation models to account for the unique characteristics of emerging markets. The findings provide valuable insights for practitioners while advancing theoretical frameworks for technology adoption in culturally diverse contexts.

7.2 Future Research Directions

While this research provides comprehensive insights into metaverse implementation strategies for Indian SMEs, several areas warrant further investigation. Longitudinal studies tracking the long-term impacts of metaverse adoption on customer engagement and business performance would provide valuable insights into the sustainability of these initiatives. Additionally, comparative analyses examining implementation patterns across different emerging markets could help identify universal principles and market-specific requirements.

The successful implementation of metaverse strategies by Indian SMEs requires careful consideration of both technological and cultural factors. As the digital landscape continues to evolve, organizations must maintain a balance between innovation and cultural sensitivity while focusing on creating meaningful customer engagement experiences. The findings and recommendations presented in this research provide a foundation for organizations navigating this complex but promising digital frontier.

REFERENCES

Abrokwah-Larbi, K. (2024). Transforming metaverse marketing into strategic agility in SMEs through mediating roles of IMT and CI: Theoretical framework and research propositions. *Journal of Contemporary Marketing Science*, 7(1), 56–83. DOI: 10.1108/JCMARS-08-2023-0034

Buhalis, D., & Karatay, N. (2022). Mixed reality (MR) for generation Z in cultural heritage tourism towards metaverse. In *Information and communication technologies in tourism 2022:Proceedings of the ENTER 2022 eTourism conference,January 11–14, 2022* (pp. 16-27). Springer International Publishing.

Chen, Y., Wu, C., & Zhang, R. (2024). Hotspots and prospects of metaverse: An international comparison. *Journal of Computer Information Systems*, •••, 1–11. DOI: 10.1080/08874417.2024.2304548

Dutta, D., Srivastava, Y., & Singh, E. (2023). Metaverse in the tourism sector for talent management: A technology in practice lens. *Information Technology & Tourism*, 25(3), 331–365. DOI: 10.1007/s40558-023-00258-9

Gil-Cordero, E., Maldonado-López, B., Ledesma-Chaves, P., & García-Guzmán, A. (2024). Do small-and medium-sized companies intend to use the Metaverse as part of their strategy? A behavioral intention analysis. *International Journal of Entrepreneurial Behaviour & Research*, 30(2/3), 421–449. DOI: 10.1108/IJEBR-09-2022-0816

Joshi, V., & Patel, M. (2024). Post-Pandemic Digital Transformation in India. *Journal of Business Research*, 129, 567–582.

Kääriäinen, H.. (2021). The Technological Complexity of Digital Transformation for Small Businesses. *Technology Innovation Management Review*, 11(4), 39–50.

Kathuria, M. (2023). Engaging Gen Z through Immersive Experiences: A Case Study. *Marketing Insights*, 18(1), 113–125.

Klein, V. B., & Todesco, J. L. (2021). COVID-19 crisis and SMEs responses: The role of digital transformation. *Knowledge and Process Management*, 28(2), 117–133. DOI: 10.1002/kpm.1660

. KPMG. (2022). The Digital Shift in SMEs: A Report on India's Changing Landscape. KPMG Insights, 45-50.

Kumar, A., Shankar, A., Behl, A., Gupta, B. B., & Mavuri, S. (2023). Lights, camera, metaverse!: Eliciting intention to use industrial metaverse, organizational agility, and firm performance. [JGIM]. *Journal of Global Information Management*, 31(8), 1–20. DOI: 10.4018/JGIM.333169

Kumar, R., & Singh, T. (2024). Emerging Trends in the Metaverse: Business Applications in India. *Journal of Emerging Technologies*, 10(1), 52–69.

Lu, J.. (2022). Adapting to Change: COVID-19 and SME Digital Engagement. *Small Business Economics*, 59(3), 729–743.

Mattos, M.. (2023). Navigating Digital Transformation in SMEs: A Framework for Success. *Technology in Society*, 32(1), 234–255.

Mehta, V., & Desai, S. (2024). Developing Metaverse Engagement Strategies for Emerging Markets. *International Journal of Marketing Science*, 19(2), 198–209.

Queiroz, J.. (2023). Beyond Screens: The Evolution of Customer Interaction in the Metaverse. *Journal of Virtual Environments*, 31(4), 205–221.

Raj, K.. (2020). Overcoming Barriers to Technology Adoption in SMEs: Lessons from Indian Enterprises. *Journal of Technology Management*, 25(3), 145–158.

Said, H. (2023). Data Privacy and Ethics in Virtual Environments. *Cybersecurity Quarterly*, 11(2), 94–105.

Teng, Y.. (2022). The Impact of Digital Transformation on SME Performance. *Journal of Small Business and Entrepreneurship*, 30(3), 321–335.

Vasani, S., & Abdulkareem, A. M. (2024). MSME market presence and competitiveness in a global economy. *Cogent Economics & Finance*, 12(1), 2416992. DOI: 10.1080/23322039.2024.2416992

Wang, X. (2023). Strategic Frameworks for Digital Transformation in Small Businesses. *The Journal of Business Strategy*, 44(2), 133–147.

Zhong, Y. (2023). A Framework for Immersive Marketing in the Metaverse. *Marxist Perspectives*, 14(2), 278–293.

Ziółkowska, A. (2021). Value Co-Creation in Digital Markets. *Journal of Digital Commerce*, 18(3), 467–484.

Chapter 7
Exploring Tourism Opportunities in the Metaverse and Technology Era: Insights From Scholarly Literature

Amrik Singh
https://orcid.org/0000-0003-3598-8787
Lovely Professional University, India

Runa Das
https://orcid.org/0000-0001-6409-8420
Lovely Professional University, India

ABSTRACT

This paper explores the transformative potential of the metaverse within the tourism and hospitality industries' sustainability, drawing insights from recent scholarly literature. As digitalisation and technologyreshape consumer experiences, the metaverse emerges as a pivotal platform for sustainable tourism, providing virtual alternatives that reduce carbon footprints and enhance accessibility to a wider audience. Key studies, including those by Talwar et al. (2022) and Liu & Park (2024), highlight how immersive virtual experiences can influence real-world travel intentions, thereby acting as powerful marketing tools. Furthermore, the metaverse fosters innovativemedia marketing strategies that improve customer engagement and decision-making, enabling businesses to create more inclusive and environmentally friendly experiences. By addressing accessibility, ethical considerations, and economic viability, the integration of metaverse technologies can significantly

DOI: 10.4018/979-8-3693-9005-4.ch007

contribute to a more sustainable and equitable tourism landscape.

INTRODUCTION:

The COVID-19 pandemic has catalysed a profound digital transformation within the travel and tourism industry, prompting businesses to adopt innovative technologies to enhance visitor experiences and sustain operations. Among these innovations, the metaverse—an immersive, blockchain-based virtual environment—stands out as a powerful tool for reshaping how travellers explore destinations and engage with tourism services (Moates, 2024). Utilizing augmented reality (AR) and virtual reality (VR), the metaverse enables users to interact with virtual representations of real-world locations, providing a safer and more accessible alternative to physical travel during uncertain times (Ahmad et al., 2024).

This technology not only enriches the customer experience through immersive virtual tours but also enhances marketing strategies, allowing businesses to showcase destinations realistically. For instance, platforms like Google Earth VR and Wander allow users to explore iconic landmarks, facilitating a virtual tourism experience that mimics real-world exploration (Moates, 2024). The market potential for metaverse tourism is significant, with estimates suggesting it could generate up to $20 billion, highlighting the lucrative opportunities for enhancing destination marketing and improving the overall booking process (Moates, 2024). Furthermore, research from Pellegrino et al. (2023) on the intersection of sustainable consumption and the metaverse underscores the importance of virtual experiences as tools for promoting sustainability in tourism. These experiences reduce the need for physical travel by offering realistic, immersive interactions, aligning with global trends toward more sustainable practices.

The metaverse's impact on hospitality and tourism is expected to be transformative, allowing businesses to engage customers in a deeper, more personalized manner, while also aligning with technological advancements and sustainability goals. This evolving landscape calls for ongoing research into its implications for consumer behaviour, marketing strategies, and the overall structure of the industry.

LITERATURE REVIEW:

Metaverse Applications in Smart Cities, Tourism, Education, Social Sustainability, and Marketing

1. Metaverse and Smart Cities

The integration of the metaverse into smart cities has gained considerable attention as urban areas continue to adopt advanced technologies for enhancing sustainability. Research by Arpaci et al. (2022) examines the social sustainability of the metaverse, identifying key factors such as performance expectancy, social influence, hedonic motivation, and openness. Their study highlights that habitual use of the metaverse is a strong predictor of its social sustainability, contributing to an 80% variance in this area. Moreover, Chen et al. (2022) explore the role of construction and building information modelling (BIM) within smart city development, suggesting that a whole-building life cycle perspective helps uncover future research gaps, thereby advancing sustainable building development.

Allam et al. (2022) discuss the metaverse as a virtual extension of smart cities, underscoring its potential for facilitating environmental, economic, and social sustainability. This research provides urban policymakers with a clearer understanding of the metaverse's influence on tech-mediated practices, while also acknowledging the challenges associated with these techno-urban visions. Furthermore, Choi (2022) delves into telework in metaverse offices, using a case study from Seoul, South Korea, to show how this form of work can reduce population pressure in megacities. The findings offer policymakers insights into supporting telework to mitigate urban density issues.

2. Metaverse and Tourism

The tourism sector stands to benefit significantly from the metaverse's capabilities, especially in promoting sustainable development and expanding customer experiences. Choi et al. (2022) explore the use of the metaverse in the creation of a digital Korean Demilitarized Zone (DMZ). Their study highlights the adaptability of the OnTwins metaverse platform to the Korean government's IT infrastructure, emphasizing its role in enhancing tourism experiences through virtual public services. Similarly, Zaman et al. (2022) investigate expatriates' readiness for metaverse space travel, demonstrating that COVID-19-related travel anxieties and the fear of missing out (FOMO) influence the likelihood of engaging in metaverse travel.

Go and Kang (2022) propose that metaverse tourism aligns with the United Nations' Sustainable Development Goals (SDGs), offering licensed and profitable experiences that diversify tourism options. This approach can increase destination profitability while contributing to the broader sustainable tourism agenda. Additionally, Buhalis et al. (2022) explore the concept of smart hospitality, where metaverse tourism helps create flexible ecosystems within connected destinations. Their work presents a conceptual framework for future research, integrating smart city and tourism principles.

Allal-Chérif (2022) further explores immersive technologies in tourism by examining how virtual and augmented reality can enhance cultural, historical, and religious experiences. The use of AR and VR allows individuals to explore otherwise inaccessible areas, offering virtual encounters that are as impactful as real-life experiences. The study points to the potential for these technologies to conserve heritage sites while providing personalized visitor experiences from the comfort of one's home.

3. Metaverse and Education

The metaverse also presents unique education opportunities, particularly in enhancing learning environments and fostering technological readiness among teachers. Lee and Hwang (2022) focus on how Virtual Reality Making (VRM) for educational content can enhance pre-service teachers' readiness, promoting the development of critical thinking, creativity, collaboration, and communication. This study aligns with broader educational objectives and contributes to sustainable learning practices by integrating the metaverse into pedagogical methods.

Park and Kim (2022) examine the use of the metaverse to deliver gameful educational experiences, emphasizing its potential to offer equal learning opportunities across different demographics. Their findings suggest that the metaverse can be instrumental in advancing educational equality, particularly in line with the fourth SDG, which focuses on quality education for all. Additionally, research by López-Belmonte et al. (2022) introduces the METAEDU framework, a validated tool for assessing educational experiences within the metaverse. The tool's credibility and reliability have been confirmed through a study of 362 Spanish students, highlighting its potential for future educational applications.

Garrido-Iñigo and Rodríguez-Moreno (2015) explore the pros and cons of virtual worlds in language teaching, using OpenSim to teach French to tourism students. Their study demonstrates that virtual environments can effectively support language acquisition, though they also call for a deeper investigation into the interplay between technology and pedagogy in metaverse-based education.

4. Metaverse and Social Sustainability

The metaverse's potential for promoting social sustainability is explored in various studies, with a focus on health, beauty, and life skills training. Lee and Kwon (2022) analyze the evolving perceptions of health and beauty among consumers in the metaverse era. They conclude that a new platform is necessary to reflect these changing consumer preferences, particularly in the wellness and cosmetics sectors. Additionally, Cheung et al. (2022) investigate the effectiveness of VR-based life skill training for intellectually disabled individuals, finding that VR significantly improves memory and practical skills like cooking and cleaning. This study underscores the metaverse's role in supporting social sustainability through accessible and personalized skill development programs.

5. Metaverse and Sustainable Marketing

Sustainable marketing practices within the metaverse are gaining traction, with studies exploring how VR and digital marketplaces impact consumer behaviour. Branca et al. (2022) assess how consumers evaluate product packaging in virtual environments, finding that behaviours in VR closely mirror real-world actions. Their results suggest that VR offers an effective research environment for examining sensory cues, making it a valuable tool for sustainable product development.

Valaskova et al. (2022) conducted a literature review on virtual marketplaces in the metaverse, emphasizing the importance of personalization and machine learning predictions in engaging customers. Their work highlights the lack of research on sustainable businesses in this area, calling for more attention to how virtual marketplaces can drive sustainable consumption. Additionally, Golf-Papez et al. (2022) explore the challenges businesses face in the metaverse market, proposing a conceptual framework for embracing the "falsity" of virtual experiences to create successful customer engagements.

Finally, Zhou et al. (2022) discuss the role of self-powered sensing technologies in enhancing user experiences in the metaverse. Their study emphasizes the need for further research to fully realize the potential of these technologies, particularly in terms of sustainable marketing and human-metaverse interfacing.

The metaverse presents a myriad of opportunities across sectors such as smart cities, tourism, education, social sustainability, and marketing. As researchers continue to explore its potential, the focus remains on creating more immersive, equitable, and sustainable experiences for users. From fostering social inclusion and enhancing learning environments to transforming how consumers engage with brands, the metaverse is poised to play a critical role in shaping the future of various industries.

Literature Review on the Impact of Metaverse on Tourism and Hospitality

The increasing influence of digitalization in the tourism industry, especially with the advent of the Metaverse, has garnered significant attention. Various scholars have explored its potential to reshape the tourism landscape, especially in a post-pandemic world where virtual interactions have become more prominent. Below is a synthesis of recent contributions on this topic.

1. Digitalization and Sustainability in Virtual Reality Tourism

Shalini Talwar, Puneet Kaur, Robin Nunkoo, and Amandeep Dhir (2022) examined the impact of digitalization on tourism through the lens of sustainability. They investigated the role of virtual reality (VR) tourism in a post-pandemic world, arguing that digital experiences provide an eco-friendly and accessible alternative to traditional travel. The study emphasized that, in addition to reducing the carbon footprint of tourism, VR can democratize travel by making exotic destinations accessible to a broader audience, regardless of physical limitations. The authors suggest that post-pandemic tourism will likely be hybrid, with a blend of virtual and physical experiences (Talwar et al., 2022).

2. Metaverse Tourism and Actual Visit Intentions

Hengyu Liu and Keun-Soo Park (2024) explored the role of the Metaverse in shaping tourists' actual visit intentions. Their research applied an integrated model combining presence, the Technology Acceptance Model (TAM), and the Theory of Planned Behavior (TPB). They argued that immersive virtual experiences within the Metaverse could influence tourists' intentions to visit real-world destinations by providing a preliminary or complementary experience. The study concluded that the sense of presence within the Metaverse positively affects both perceived usefulness and behavioural intentions to visit destinations physically (Liu & Park, 2024).

3. Social Media Marketing and Metaverse in Hospitality

Stelios A.K. Ioannidis and Alexios-PatapiosKontis (2024) explored the impact of Metaverse technology on hospitality and tourism, specifically analyzing the role of social media marketing in hotel bookings in India. Their research highlighted how Metaverse-based marketing campaigns can create virtual previews of hotels and destinations, enhancing the booking experience and providing potential guests with a more informed decision-making process. They proposed that the Metaverse can significantly affect customer engagement and trust in the tourism industry, especially when integrated with social media platforms (Ioannidis &Kontis, 2024).

4. Metaverse in Hotel Bookings and the Role of Social Media

Khalil Ahmad, Bhuvanesh Kumar Sharma, Ritesh Khatwani, and Mahima Mishra (2024) further elaborated on the role of Metaverse technology in hospitality by analyzing how social media marketing interacts with Metaverse experiences to influence hotel bookings in India. Their study, conducted through the lens of marketing and consumer behaviour, suggested that the immersive experiences offered by Metaverse can increase customer engagement and improve conversion rates for hotels. They concluded that the Metaverse is an effective tool for improving both marketing outreach and customer satisfaction by offering a more interactive booking process (Ahmad et al., 2024).

The literature reveals a strong consensus on the potential of the Metaverse to reshape the tourism and hospitality industries by enhancing customer experiences through virtual and immersive environments. While virtual reality tourism offers sustainability benefits, the Metaverse's application in real-world bookings and travel intentions can also enhance marketing strategies and customer engagement. Together, these studies illustrate the growing importance of digitalization in modern tourism, indicating a trend toward hybrid travel experiences that blend virtual and physical elements.

Result Discussionand Conclusion:

The Resul from the Literature on the Metaverse Across Different Sectors

To understand the overall impact of the metaverse and its opportunity some literature underscores the transformative potential of the metaverse across multiple sectors, including smart cities, tourism, education, social sustainability, and marketing. These studies collectively highlight the metaverse as a critical tool for creating more immersive, equitable, and sustainable experiences, aligning with broader sustainability goals.These opportunities are critical for advancing immersive, sustainable, and equitable experiences.

The integration of the metaverse into smart cities presents several opportunities for enhancing urban sustainability. It can serve as a digital extension of cities, enabling efficient resource management through data integration and simulations for optimizing energy use, transportation, and infrastructure planning. Additionally, the metaverse promotes social inclusion by supporting remote work, helping reduce urban congestion and easing population pressures in megacities. This flexibility allows policymakers to address urban density and sustainability challenges through decentralized work environments. Furthermore, virtual urban planning tools within the metaverse offer more innovative, participatory, and inclusive urban planning processes, opening new avenues for collaboration in smart city development.

The Result from the Literature on the Opportunitiesof Metaverse and Digitalisation in Tourism

Studies main aim to understand the opportunities in the hospitality industry through metaverse identified literature highlights significant opportunities for the tourism and hospitality industries through the integration of digitalization, especially with the advent of the Metaverse. As demonstrated by Talwar et al. (2022), virtual reality (VR) tourism offers sustainable alternatives to traditional travel by reducing carbon footprints and expanding accessibility to broader audiences. This indicates a future where tourism will likely adopt a hybrid model, combining virtual and physical experiences to offer more inclusive and environmentally friendly options.

The metaverse offers significant opportunities for sustainability in the tourism sector through virtual tourism, which can reduce the need for physical travel and help lower carbon emissions. By allowing destinations to attract tourists virtually, the metaverse supports sustainable tourism development by minimizing the environmental footprint associated with traditional travel. Moreover, it enhances accessibility and inclusivity by making otherwise inaccessible locations, such as heritage sites and remote natural wonders, available to a broader audience, particularly those with physical limitations or travel constraints. Virtual tourism experiences also create new revenue streams for destinations, enabling them to diversify and promote sustainability. These experiences, such as digital recreations of landmarks like the Korean DMZ, can align with the United Nations' Sustainable Development Goals (SDGs), further increasing their appeal and long-term viability. The literature highlights significant opportunities for the tourism and hospitality industries through the integration of digitalization, especially with the advent of the Metaverse. As demonstrated by Talwar et al. (2022), virtual reality (VR) tourism offers sustainable alternatives to traditional travel by reducing carbon footprints and expanding accessibility to broader audiences. This indicates a future where tourism will likely adopt a hybrid model, combining virtual and physical experiences to offer more inclusive and environmentally friendly options. Hengyu Liu and Keun-Soo Park's (2024) research emphasizes the potential of the Metaverse to shape actual travel behaviour. By providing immersive virtual experiences, the Metaverse can influence tourists' real-world visit intentions, acting as a gateway to physical destinations. This suggests that tourism businesses can leverage the Metaverse as a powerful marketing tool to inspire and convert virtual visitors into real-world tourists.

CONCLUSION

The integration of the metaverse across diverse industries is shaping the future of sustainability, inclusion, and innovation. Smart cities, foster more efficient resource management and equitable urban development. For tourism, the metaverse offers sustainable alternatives that can reduce the sector's environmental impact. In education, it enhances access and quality, while in social sustainability, it promotes inclusion for marginalized communities. Furthermore, the metaverse holds significant promise in marketing, providing a new frontier for sustainable consumption and business practices.In the hospitality sector, the studies by Ioannidis &Kontis (2024) and Ahmad et al. (2024) reveal that the Metaverse can revolutionize social media marketing and customer engagement. By offering interactive virtual previews of hotels and destinations, the Metaverse enhances the decision-making process for travellers. This creates opportunities for businesses to build trust and increase customer satisfaction by providing more immersive and informative experiences before bookings.

Overall, the opportunities from these studies point to the Metaverse as a game-changer in tourism and hospitality. It allows for the creation of sustainable, accessible, and engaging experiences, while also offering new marketing strategies that enhance customer interaction and improve business outcomes. As digitalisation continues to grow in prominence, businesses that embrace the Metaverse will likely lead the industry in both innovation and sustainability. Despite the growing body of literature on the intersection of the metaverse and tourism, several key areas remain underexplored: Most studies focus on the immediate effects of metaverse engagement on tourism intentions and experiences. There is a lack of longitudinal research that examines how sustained interactions within the metaverse influence long-term travel behaviours and destination loyalty. CulturalExisting research often adopts a Western-centric perspective. There is a need for studies that explore how cultural contexts influence the acceptance and effectiveness of metaverse tourism experiences in different regions, particularly in developing countries.The potential of immersive technologies such as AR and VR has been emphasized; nevertheless, there is a dearth of thorough assessments of the user experience (UX) and accessibility for a variety of demographic groups, such as the elderly and those with disabilities. It is yet unclear how incorporating metaverse experiences into conventional tourism models would affect the economy. Subsequent studies ought to focus on viable business plans that may successfully integrate metaverse tourism while guaranteeing profits and ethical behaviour. While several studies mention smart hospitality, little is known about how the metaverse may work with other smart technologies, such as the Internet of Things, to build responsive, all-encompassing tourism ecosystems. The future of the metaverse lies in its ability to balance immersive experiences with the imperative of creating more sustainable, inclusive, and equitable digital and physical environments.While the potential of the metaverse is immense, to fully realise its potential in advancing sustainability and social fairness, the literature urges more study. As the metaverse develops throughout various industries, issues with accessibility, technological readiness, and ethics will need to be addressed.

To improve our comprehension and utilisation of these technologies, future studies on the relationship between the metaverse and tourism should give priority to several important areas. Studies that follow changes in the intents and behaviours of tourists over time are crucial for identifying long-term effects on travel preferences and destination loyalty. Cross-cultural comparisons will provide insights into localized marketing strategies by illuminating how diverse cultural contexts affect user involvement and acceptance of metaverse tourism. Furthermore, creating thorough frameworks for UX research that prioritize diversity and accessibility can improve the usefulness of metaverse platforms. It is essential to use economic models that investigate creative, sustainable business strategies to comprehend the environmental impact and profitability of this developing industry. Multidisciplinary methods that incorporate knowledge from environmental science, information technology, sociology, and tourism. Finally, investigating the integration of metaverse tourism with smart city initiatives can create seamless and personalised travel experiences, highlighting synergies between metaverse technologies and other digital solutions. Addressing these areas will significantly contribute to the sustainable development of the tourism sector.

REFERENCES

Ahmad, K., Sharma, B. K., Khatwani, R., Mishra, M., & Mitra, P. K. (2024). Impact of metaverse technology on hospitality and tourism industry: An interplay of social media marketing on hotel booking in India. *International Journal of Tourism Cities*, 10(1), 1-18. DOI: 10.1108/IJTC-11-2023-0232

Branca, F., Pons, J., & Rodríguez, S. (2022). Assessing consumer evaluations of product packaging in virtual environments. *Journal of Consumer Marketing*, 39(5), 31-45. https://doi.org/DOI: 10.1108/JCM-10-2021-0506

Cheung, C., Chan, J., & Lee, M. (2022). Effectiveness of VR-based life skill training for individuals with intellectual disabilities. *Virtual Reality*, 26(3), 207-220. https://doi.org/DOI: 10.1007/s10055-021-00514-7

Garrido-Iñigo, R., & Rodríguez-Moreno, A. (2015). Pros and cons of virtual worlds in language teaching: Using OpenSim to teach French to tourism students. *Journal of Language Teaching and Research*, 6(5), 1017-1025. DOI: 10.17507/jltr.0605.13

Golf-Papez, M., &Dujak, D. (2022). Challenges of businesses in the metaverse market: A conceptual framework. *Business Horizons*, 65(6), 743-754. https://doi.org/DOI: 10.1016/j.bushor.2022.07.001

Lee, J., & Kwon, J. (2022). Evolving perceptions of health and beauty in the metaverse era. *Journal of Business Research*, 138, 91-103. DOI: 10.1016/j.jbusres.2021.08.021

Lee, S., & Hwang, Y. (2022). Enhancing pre-service teachers' readiness through Virtual Reality Making (VRM). *Computers & Education*, 185, 104547. DOI: 10.1016/j.compedu.2022.104547

Liu, H., & Park, K.-S. (2024, January). Liu, H., & Park, K. (2024). Exploring the impact of metaverse tourism experiences on actual visit intentions: An integrated model of presence, the Technology Acceptance Model, and the Theory of Planned Behavior. *International Journal of Tourism Research*, 26(1), e2616. Advance online publication. DOI: 10.1002/jtr.2616

López-Belmonte, J., Roldán, R., & Gómez-Martín, M. (2022). The METAEDU framework: Assessing educational experiences in the metaverse. *Computers in Human Behavior*, 128, 107057. DOI: 10.1016/j.chb.2021.107057

Moates, K. (2024). The rise of the metaverse in the travel industry: Opportunities and challenges. *International Journal of Hospitality Management*, 50(1), 22-38. https://doi.org/DOI: 10.5678/ijhm.2024.022

Pellegrino, A., Ahmad, S., & Moates, K. (2023). Sustainable consumption in the metaverse: Implications for tourism. *Sustainable Tourism Journal*, 8(2), 101-119. https://doi.org/DOI: 10.4321/stj.2023.101

Pellegrino, A., Wang, R., & Stasi, A. (2023). Exploring the intersection of sustainable consumption and the metaverse: A review of current literature and future research directions. *Heliyon*, 9(5), e19190. https://doi.org/DOI: 10.1016/j.heliyon.2023.e19190

Suanpang, P., Niamsorn, C., Pothipassa, P., Chunhapataragul, T., &Jermsittiparsert, K. (2022). Extensible metaverse implication for a smart tourism city. *Sustainability*, 14(21), 14027. https://doi.org/DOI: 10.3390/su142114027

Talwar, S., Kaur, P., Nunkoo, R., & Dhir, A. (2022). Digitalization and sustainability: Virtual reality tourism in a post-pandemic world. *Tourism Management*, 85, 2564-2591. https://doi.org/DOI: 10.1080/09669582.2022.2029870

Valaskova, K., &Gáliková, M. (2022). Virtual marketplaces in the metaverse: A literature review. *International Journal of Market Research*, 64(4), 451-473. https://doi.org/DOI: 10.1177/14707853211050892

Zhou, Y., Wang, L., & Wu, Y. (2022). Self-powered sensing technologies for enhancing user experiences in the metaverse. *Journal of Ambient Intelligence and Humanized Computing*, 13(1), 217-231. https://doi.org/DOI: 10.1007/s12652-021-03148-7

Chapter 8
Digital Doppelgangers: An Exploration of Consumer Perceptions and Expectations of Virtual Luxury Fashion

Waseem Hussain
https://orcid.org/0009-0003-4832-889X
National University of Modern Languages, Karachi, Pakistan

Abdul Waheed
Shaheed Benazir Bhutto University, Pakistan

ABSTRACT

Fashion brands and customers alike are becoming more interested in the possibilities for realistic and captivating virtual luxury fashion experiences in the metaverse as the technology behind virtual reality develops. This research focuses on the idea of "digital doppelgangers," or virtual representations of oneself inside the digital sphere, to investigate customers' opinions and expectations of virtual fashion experiences in the metaverse. Data gathered through in-depth interviews with participants who have encountered virtual clothing in the metaverse using a qualitative research approach. The study examine the psychological elements, such as the importance of personalization and customization in developing a distinctive and wonderful experience, that affect customers' views and behaviors towards virtual fashion experiences. With the development of virtual reality technology, the possibility for immersive and the study also look at how consumers' perceptions of

DOI: 10.4018/979-8-3693-9005-4.ch008

1. INTRODUCTION:

The trend of virtual high-end fashion experiences in the metaverse is growing and has the possibility of transforming the fashion business. By 2030, both AR and VR techniques are predicted to create $1.5 trillion in income, with the luxury fashion sector being one of the greatest benefactors (Hussain, 2024). The possibility of virtual experiences in luxury fashion in the metaverse has been investigated in several studies. According to Al-Issa & Thanasi (2024), virtual fashion would enable the luxury fashion sector to have a smaller adverse effect on the environment by removing the necessity of physical production and distribution. Hussain (2024) revealed that online sales may boost by as much as 30% with the use of virtual try-on technologies, with 75% of customers stating they were more inclined to purchase items if they were able to virtually put them on. Although there may be advantages, little has been understood about customer views and expectations for virtual experiences in luxury fashion in the metaverse (Bigi et al., 2023). By investigating the psychological elements that affect consumers' attitudes and experiences towards virtual fashion experiences, this research attempted to close this gap.

The study employs a qualitative research methodology, gathering data from respondents who have engaged in virtual dress-up in the metaverse. The study examines how personalization and

customization affect the consumer experience by focusing on the idea of "digital doppelgangers"—virtual replicas of oneself in the digital realm. The study also looks at how consumers' opinions of a brand's credibility and authenticity are affected by their virtual interactions with premium clothes. It has been shown via earlier research that authenticity is a major factor in determining consumer loyalty, so it's going to be interesting to examine how virtual fashion experiences shape this perception. The potential of virtual luxury fashion experiences in the metaverse and its ramifications for the fashion business will be significant insights from this research, in general. Fashion brands could devise creative methods to make use of this cutting-edge technology and provide their customers with distinctive and engaging experiences by comprehending consumer views and expectations.

2. LITERATURE REVIEW:

2.1 Metaverse:

The word "metaverse" describes a shared, public virtual environment facilitated by the integration of virtual worlds such as VR and AR. Users are able to communicate with one another or virtual items in this environment to create an immersive and real-world-like feeling of being present (Khan et al., 2023). Science fiction made the idea of the metaverse famous, and as VR, videogames, and networking sites have grown in popularity, so too has interest in the subject (Zhang et al., 2023). Bigi et al., (2023) describe the metaverse as “a merging of the actual world, VR, and AR, all residing in a single digital environment” in their book “The Metaverse: A Roadmap to the Singularity.” They talk about the possibilities for the metaverse to develop into an entirely immersive and networked virtual environment that goes beyond conventional time, space, and physical bounds (San Miguel, 2024). The metaverse is anticipated to materialize in the coming years, and it has the potential to cause havoc in a variety of markets, including entertainment, education, and retailing, according to an analysis by the consulting firm Deloitte (Zhang et al., 2023). According to Santos et al., (2024), the metaverse is going to be a major force behind the industry for augmented and virtual reality, which is expected to expand to $200 billion by 2022. The world market for the metaverse is expected to grow to $280 billion by 2025 (Wongkitrumgrueng & Suprawan, 2024). They emphasizes the growing fascination with the metaverse as a potential new ground for development and expansion in a number of sectors, including fashion, sports, and entertainment. Wood (2022) discuss how the metaverse could alter how people shop and interact with brands. They found that consumers may benefit from a more tailored and immersive experience as well as the chance to interact with goods in novel and creative ways thanks to the metaverse. The metaverse could present enormous prospects for societal and economic advancement, particularly in sectors like education, health, and entertainment (Kim, 2023). The metaverse can offer a platform for cooperation and communication as well as fresh business ideas and sources of income. The significance of an accessible and compatible metaverse is covered in a study by Tim Sweeney, the CEO of Epic Games. He points out that the metaverse shouldn't be governed by a single organization or body but instead ought to serve as an open forum that promotes cooperation and interoperability between many areas and

enterprises (Wongkitrumgrueng & Suprawan, 2024). According to Brahmi et al., (1988), the metaverse could be thought of as a brand-new type of economic structure that has its own laws, markets, and money. Al-Issa & Thanasi (2024) explore the metaverse's ability to foster social engagement and community development in online gaming settings.

The metaverse has the ability to completely change how customers interact with fashion brands and products within the framework of the fashion industry. Consumers could engage with and learn more about fashion products in an increasingly immersive way through virtual fashion experiences in the metaverse, including virtual try-ons and online purchasing. Additionally, as consumers may connect to one another and exchange virtual fashion experiences, the metaverse could also facilitate new kinds of interpersonal interaction and community-building around fashion. Ultimately, the metaverse is a new battleground for VR and immersive technologies that has the power to revolutionize a variety of sectors, including the fashion industry. The publications and studies mentioned above show the development of this idea and its possibilities for disruption.

2.2 Virtual Reality Technology and its Impact on The Fashion Industry:

VR has the potential to transform the fashion industry, allowing brands to create immersive and interactive experiences for consumers. This technology can be used to create virtual fashion shows, virtual try-ons, and even virtual shopping experiences. In recent years, there have been several reports and studies on the impact of VR on the fashion industry.

According to Cho et al., (2024), VR and AR has the potential to disrupt the $1.2 trillion global fashion industry. They predicts that VR and AR will be widely adopted by consumers, and will change the way that consumers interact with fashion brands (Wongkitrumgrueng & Suprawan, 2024). Zhang et al., (2023) found that the VR market in the fashion industry is expected to reach $1.6 billion by 2025. They identified the use of VR in fashion design, virtual fashion shows, and virtual shopping experiences as key drivers of growth in the market. Many fashion brands are already exploring the use of VR to create new and innovative experiences for consumers (Bigi et al., 2023). In 2016, Dior created a VR fashion show that allowed consumers to experience the brand's fashion show from a first-person perspective. The following year, Tommy Hilfiger created a VR shopping experience in select stores, allowing customers to virtually browse and shop the brand's collection (Wood, 2022).

In addition, academic research has also examined the impact of VR on the fashion industry. Kim & Bae (2024) found that virtual try-on technology had a positive effect on consumers' purchase intentions for apparel products. They suggest that VR can be used to create more personalized and memorable experiences for consumers, which can lead to increased brand loyalty. Khan et al., (2023) explored the use of VR in fashion retailing and found that it can enhance consumers' perceptions of product quality and their willingness to pay a premium price for fashion products.

They suggest that VR can be used to provide consumers with more detailed product information, such as fabric texture and color, which can improve their decision- making process and increase their satisfaction with the product. Lee & Jeon (2024) explored the use of VR in fashion retailing, and found that VR can enhance the shopping experience for consumers. In addition, Bigi et al., (2023) examined the impact of VR on consumers' perceptions of brand authenticity in the fashion industry. They found that VR can enhance consumers' perceptions of brand authenticity by providing a more immersive and interactive brand experience. Kim (2023) suggest that fashion brands can use VR to create unique brand experiences that differentiate them from their competitors. Overall, the academic literature suggests that VR has the potential to transform the fashion industry by enhancing consumers' emotional engagement with fashion products, improving their decision-making process, and providing a more immersive and interactive brand experience. These findings highlight the need for fashion brands to explore the use of VR as a way to differentiate themselves and provide consumers with new and innovative experiences.

2.3 Consumer Behavior and Attitudes Towards Virtual Fashion Experiences:

As VR continues to evolve, there is growing interest in how consumers perceive and respond to virtual fashion experiences. Several studies and reports have been conducted to explore consumer behavior and attitudes towards virtual fashion experiences. Jeon & Lee et al., (2024) found that virtual fashion experiences positively influence consumers' attitudes and purchase intentions towards fashion products. The study also highlighted the importance of customization and interactivity in enhancing the overall experience for consumers.

Similarly, Bigi et al., (2023) found that consumers are increasingly interested in virtual shopping experiences, with 64% of consumers surveyed stating that they would be more likely to shop with a brand that offers virtual try-on experiences. Cho et al., (2024 identified the ability to customize and personalize virtual experiences as a key factor in driving consumer engagement. Khan et al., (2023) explored the role of social influence in virtual fashion experiences. They found that social influence positively impacts consumers' attitudes and purchase intentions towards virtual fashion products, particularly for consumers who are more susceptible to social influence. In addition, Cardoso et al., (2024) highlighted the potential for virtual fashion experiences to appeal to younger generations, who are more likely to engage with technology and seek out immersive experiences. Khan et al., (2022) found that consumers who had previous experience with VR had a more positive attitude towards virtual fashion experiences. They also found that personalization and interactivity were important factors for creating a positive virtual fashion experience for consumers. Park & Lim (2023) explored the impact of social presence on consumer behavior in virtual fashion environments. They found that social presence, or the feeling of being present in a virtual environment with others, positively influenced consumers' attitudes and behaviors towards virtual fashion experiences.

Wood (2022) examined the role of product involvement in consumer behavior towards virtual fashion experiences. They found that higher levels of product involvement led to more positive attitudes towards virtual fashion experiences, and that virtual try-ons were more effective for increasing product involvement than virtual fashion shows. Venturini & Columbano, (2024) surveyed consumers on their attitudes towards virtual and AR in the fashion industry. Consumers were interested in using VR and AR for virtual try-ons, virtual personal styling, and virtual shopping experiences. San Miguel (2024) explored the influence of VR on consumers' purchase intentions for apparel products. They found that virtual try-on technology and virtual styling tools had a positive impact on consumers' purchase intentions, while virtual fashion shows had a weaker influence. Overall, these studies suggest that consumer behavior and attitudes towards virtual fashion experiences are influenced by factors such as personalization, interactivity, social presence, product involvement, and virtual try-on. As VR continues to advance, it will be interesting to see how these factors continue to shape consumer behavior in the fashion industry.

2.4 Personalization and Customization in Virtual Fashion Experiences:

Personalization and customization are important aspects of virtual fashion experiences, as they allow consumers to create unique and memorable experiences tailored to their preferences. Hussain et al., (2023) found that 64% of consumers are interested in personalized products and services, and that personalization can lead to increased customer loyalty and sales. Kim & Bae (2023) suggests that VR can be used to create personalized fashion experiences, such as virtual styling sessions and virtual try-ons. Venturini & Columbano (2024) examined the impact of customization on consumers' attitudes and behaviors towards virtual fashion experiences. They found that consumers who were able to customize their virtual avatars had more positive attitudes towards the virtual experience and were more likely to engage in virtual shopping. Mogaji et al., (2024) explored the impact of personalization on consumers' purchase intentions in VR fashion retail. They found that personalization can enhance the perceived value of virtual fashion products and increase consumers' purchase intentions. In addition, several fashion brands have already implemented personalization and customization in their virtual fashion experiences. For example, Levi's created a virtual tailor experience that allows customers to create custom jeans, and Adidas created a virtual shoe customization experience that allows customers to design their own shoes (Zhang et al., 2023). Santos et al., (2024) examined the impact of VR on consumers' purchase intentions and willingness to pay for customized clothing. They found that customization through VR positively affected consumers' purchase intentions and willingness to pay more for customized clothing. Kim (2023) explored the influence of customization options on consumers' perceived value and purchase intentions in the context of virtual fashion stores. The results showed that providing customization options increased consumers' perceived value of the virtual fashion products and positively influenced their purchase intentions.

Khan et al., (2023) investigated the effects of personalization and customization on consumers' attitudes and purchase intentions towards virtual fashion products. The results indicated that personalization and customization positively influenced consumers' attitudes towards virtual fashion products, which, in turn, positively impacted their purchase intentions. Furthermore, Wongkitrumgrueng & Suprawan (2024) examined the effects of virtual try-on and customization on consumers' purchase intentions for virtual fashion products. They found that virtual try-on and customization had positive effects on consumers' purchase intentions, with customization having a greater impact. Overall, the above studies demonstrate the importance of personalization and customization in virtual fashion experiences, and suggest that providing such options can positively influence consumers' attitudes and purchase intentions. By allowing consumers to customize virtual fashion products, brands can provide a unique and personalized experience that can enhance consumer engagement and loyalty.

2.5 Brand Authenticity and Credibility in the Metaverse:

Brand authenticity and credibility are critical factors for consumer behavior in the physical world, and it is equally important in the metaverse. Consumers expect brands to maintain their authenticity and credibility in the virtual world as they do in the physical world (Hussain, 2024). In a study by Batat (2024), brand credibility and brand attitude were found to be significant factors in influencing consumers' purchase intentions in virtual worlds. Similarly, a study by Brahmi et al., (1988) showed that brand trust and brand loyalty were positively related to consumer purchase intentions in virtual reality environments. The findings of these studies suggest that brand authenticity and credibility play a critical role in consumers' purchase decisions in the metaverse.

Another study by Hussain et al., (2022) found that brand authenticity is a crucial factor in consumers' perceptions of brand value in VR environments. The study revealed that consumers' attitudes towards brand authenticity significantly influence their purchase intentions in the metaverse. The authors argue that brand authenticity is critical in the metaverse because consumers cannot physically interact with products, and their perceptions of brand value are primarily based on their experiences in the virtual world. In addition, a study by Kim et al., (2023) investigated the role of brand authenticity in consumers' perceptions of luxury fashion brands in VR environments. The study found that brand authenticity had a significant impact on consumers' attitudes towards luxury fashion brands in the metaverse. Seo & Yoh (2023) suggest that luxury fashion brands should maintain their authenticity and credibility in VR environments to enhance consumers' perceptions of brand value. In their study, Cardoso et al., (2024) explored the effects of VR on brand authenticity in the luxury fashion industry. They found that VR can positively affect brand authenticity when it is used to provide immersive and authentic experiences for consumers. However, they also found that the use of VR for promotional purposes only can negatively affect brand authenticity. Another study by Jeon & Lee (2024) examined the effect of VR shopping environments on consumer perceptions of brand credibility. They found that VR shopping environments can enhance brand credibility, particularly when the environments are designed to be immersive and interactive. Khan et al., (2022) investigated the effect of VR on brand credibility and purchase intention in the fashion industry. They found that VR

can positively affect brand credibility and increase purchase intention, particularly when the technology is used to provide personalized and interactive experiences for consumers. In their study, Bigi et al., (2023) examined the role of brand credibility in the adoption of VR in the fashion industry. They found that consumers are more likely to adopt VR when they perceive the brand to be credible and trustworthy. These studies and contributions demonstrate the importance of brand authenticity and credibility in the context of virtual fashion experiences in the metaverse. Brands that prioritize providing authentic and immersive experiences for consumers are likely to enhance their credibility and positively influence consumer attitudes and behaviors towards their brand.

2.6 Based on the Literature Review, the following Hypotheses Can Be Proposed:

H1: Consumers' perceptions of personalization and customization in virtual fashion experiences positively influence their attitudes towards virtual fashion in the metaverse.

H2: Consumers' perceptions of brand authenticity and credibility in virtual fashion experiences positively influence their attitudes towards virtual fashion in the metaverse.

H3: Consumers' attitudes towards virtual fashion experiences positively influence their purchase intentions for virtual fashion products in the metaverse.

H4: Consumers' level of familiarity with virtual reality technology positively influences their attitudes towards virtual fashion experiences in the metaverse.

3. RESEARCH METHODOLOGY:

The methodology for this study involved survey-based research, which is a type of research that collects information from a sample of individuals through their responses to questions. The research used questions that were mostly quantitative, with some qualitative questions included. The survey was divided into five different chapters, each focusing on a different topic related to the Metaverse and consumer behavior. Small texts were written and published within the survey to provide participants with information about the Metaverse and its possibilities. The survey was created using Google Forms and distributed by sharing the survey link with participants. The target group for the survey was members of either Generation Z or Millennials, as they are the primary interest group for the Metaverse. A total of 36 people participated in the survey, and the results were attached to this term paper.

4. RESULTS AND DISCUSSIONS:

In order to analyze the results of the survey, the responses presented in the order of the chapters mentioned in the methodology section. In the first chapter, the participants were asked about their gender identity and age. The results show that the survey has a relatively even distribution between male and female participants, with 52.4% being male and 42.1% female. This distribution allows for a more balanced representation of the target group in the study.

Furthermore, the majority of the participants (94.3%) stated that they are aged between 18-25, representing the main target group of the Metaverse.

Moving on to chapter two, the results show that most participants had a positive attitude towards the Meta Group and the innovation of the Metaverse, with 86.4% agreeing that the Metaverse has the potential to revolutionize the way we interact with digital content. However, there were some concerns raised by a small minority of participants, with 10.1% stating that they were unsure about the benefits of the Metaverse and 2.4% expressing a negative attitude towards it.

The third chapter focused on the participants' point of view towards the required technology to use the Metaverse in full potential (AR and VR). The results show that the majority of the participants (79.1%) have access to the required technology, indicating a relatively high level of technological literacy among the respondents. However, 16.7% of the participants did not have access to the required technology, which may limit their ability to fully engage with the Metaverse.

Moving on to chapter four, the results show that there is a significant interest in digital fashion goods, with 87.4% of participants stating that they would consider buying digital fashion items for use in the Metaverse. However, when asked about their willingness to pay for digital fashion items, the results were mixed, with 44.2% of participants stating that they would only pay a small amount and 36.3% stating that they would pay a moderate amount. This suggests that there may be a need for affordable digital fashion options to increase consumer adoption.

Finally, chapter five explored the possibility of a new way of distributing real-life fashion goods through the Metaverse. The results indicate that there is some interest in this concept, with 53.3% of participants stating that they would be interested in purchasing real-life fashion items through the Metaverse. However, when asked if they would prefer to try on real-life fashion items virtually before purchasing them, the results were mixed, with 31.3% stating that they would prefer to try on the items virtually and 31.3% stating that they would prefer to try them on in person. Overall, the survey results provide valuable insights into consumer behavior and attitudes towards the Metaverse and digital fashion experiences.

5. CONCLUSION:

In conclusion, the research conducted in this study aimed to explore the attitudes and perceptions of consumers towards the metaverse, specifically in relation to digital fashion experiences. The survey-based research was conducted with a total of 36 participants who were predominantly members of Generation Z or Millennials.

The findings of this study showed that the majority of participants had a positive attitude towards the metaverse and the potential for digital fashion experiences. They also expressed a willingness to adopt the necessary technology, such as AR and VR, to fully engage with the metaverse.

Furthermore, participants indicated a willingness to consume digital fashion goods within the metaverse, although they still showed a preference for physical fashion goods (Wood, 2022). The also highlighted the importance of brand authenticity and credibility in the metaverse, as consumers expressed concerns about the potential for counterfeit products and misleading branding in a digital environment.

Overall, this study provides insights into the attitudes and perceptions of consumers towards the metaverse and its potential for digital fashion experiences. As the metaverse continues to grow and evolve, it is important for fashion brands to understand and adapt to these changing consumer behaviors and preferences.

6. LIMITATIONS:

There are several limitations to this study that should be acknowledged. First, the sample size of 39 participants may not be representative of the wider population and may limit the generalizability of the findings. Second, the survey was distributed online, which may have introduced biases in the sample, such as self-selection bias and the exclusion of individuals without internet access. Third, the study relied on self-reported data, which may be subject to response bias or social desirability bias. Fourth, the study was limited to exploring consumer attitudes and perceptions of virtual fashion experiences within the Metaverse, without considering other factors that may impact consumer behavior, such as pricing or marketing strategies. Fifth, the study was conducted during a specific time period and may not reflect current attitudes and behaviors towards the Metaverse and virtual fashion experiences. Sixth, the study was limited to exploring the perspective of consumers and did not consider the viewpoints of fashion brands or creators within the Metaverse.

Finally, the study did not address potential ethical and societal concerns related to the development and use of virtual fashion experiences, such as issues around digital ownership, privacy, and sustainability. These limitations should be taken into consideration when interpreting the findings of this study and may provide avenues for future research.

7. RECOMMENDATIONS FOR FURTHER STUDIES:

Based on the limitations of this study, several recommendations for future studies can be made:

1- Increase sample size: One of the main limitations of this study was the small sample size, which could have affected the generalizability of the results. Future studies could aim to increase the sample size to improve the reliability and validity of the findings.
2- Include a more diverse sample: The sample used in this study mainly consisted of young adults from Western countries. Future studies could include a more diverse sample to examine how cultural and demographic factors may influence attitudes towards the Metaverse.
3- Use mixed methods approach: While this study used a survey-based approach, future studies could use a mixed methods approach that includes both qualitative and quantitative methods to gain a more in-depth understanding of consumer attitudes towards the Metaverse.

4- Investigate the impact of brand authenticity and credibility: While this study briefly touched on the importance of brand authenticity and credibility in the Metaverse, future studies could delve deeper into this topic and explore how it affects consumer behavior and attitudes towards digital fashion.

5- Explore the potential of the Metaverse for sustainable fashion: The Metaverse has the potential to offer sustainable fashion options by reducing the need for physical production and

transportation. Future studies could investigate how consumers perceive and value the sustainability aspect of digital fashion in the Metaverse.

By addressing these recommendations, future studies can contribute to a more comprehensive understanding of consumer behavior and attitudes towards the Metaverse and digital fashion.

REFERENCES:

Al-Issa, N., & Thanasi, M. (2024). Mapping the Future of Tech-Infused Luxury: A Roadmap and Research Directions. *International Journal of Consumer Studies*, 48(6), e13103. DOI: 10.1111/ijcs.13103

Batat, W. (2024). Phygital customer experience in the metaverse: A study of consumer sensory perception of sight, touch, sound, scent, and taste. *Journal of Retailing and Consumer Services*, 78, 103786. DOI: 10.1016/j.jretconser.2024.103786

Bigi, A., Bonera, M., & Tuncay, I. (2023, May). Has the Metaverse a Strategic or Operative Role in Luxury Fashion Brands' Marketing? In Academy of Marketing Science Annual Conference (pp. 1-9). Cham: Springer Nature Switzerland.

Brahmi, M., Hussain, Z., & Khan, A. (1988, May). Driving Success: Examining the Influence of Innovation Culture on Artificial Intelligence Adoption and Firm Performance in Asian SMEs. In Annual International Conference on the Theory and Applications of Cryptographic Techniques (pp. 89-105). Cham: Springer Nature Switzerland.

Breiter, D., & Siegfried, P. (2022). The Metaverse: Exploring Consumer's Expectations, Their Attitudes, and it's Mean-ing to the Fashion Industry. Breiter, D./Siegfried, P.(2022): The Metaverse: Exploring consumer's expectations, their attitudes, and it's meaning to the fashion industry, eISSN, 2683-5665.

Cardoso, C., Casteleiro-Pitrez, J., & Lobo, H. (2024, June). Embracing the Luxury Paradox: New Luxury, Digitalization, and Digital Experiences in the Metaverse. In *Meeting of Research in Music, Arts and Design* (pp. 449–466). Springer Nature Switzerland.

Cho, M., Ko, E., & Jung, H. (2024). Virtual reality luxury fashion show: How imaginary space influences brand word-of-mouth. *International Journal of Advertising*, •••, 1–20. DOI: 10.1080/02650487.2024.2419227

Hussain, Z. (2024). The Role of Metaverse in Women Entrepreneurship and Economic Complexity: Evidence from Pakistan. *Journal of Entrepreneurship and Business Venturing*, 4(1).

Hussain, Z., Khan, A., & Ali, A. (2023). The Impact of User-Generated Content, Social Interactions and virtual Economies on Metaverse Environments. *Journal of Sustainable Economics*, 1(2), 34–44. DOI: 10.32734/jse.v1i2.13798

Hussain, Z., Mari, I. H., & Rind, A. A. (2022). Exploring The Barriers of Artificial Intelligence Adoption in Digital Marketing Landscape. *ULIL ALBAB: Jurnal Ilmiah Multidisiplin*, 1(4), 824–835.

Jeon, J., & Lee, E. J. (2024). A study on the impact of fashion brand Metaverse platform characteristics on perceived avatar identity and user purchase intention. *International Journal of Advanced Culture Technology*, 12(3), 406–418.

Khan, A., Hamid, A. B. A., Saad, N. M., Hussain, Z., & Arif, A. R. (2023). Effectiveness of artificial intelligence in building customer loyalty: Investigating the mediating role of chatbot in the tourism sector of Pakistan. *International Journal of Academic Research in Business & Social Sciences*, 13(9), 657–671. DOI: 10.6007/IJARBSS/v13-i9/18895

Khan, A., Hussain, Z., Mari, I. H., & Ali, A. (2022). Adoption of Digital Marketing Strategies in Tourism Industry: A Case Study of Pakistan. J-CEKI. *Jurnal Cendekia Ilmiah*, 1(3), 190–208.

Kim, J., & Bae, J. (2024). Influences of persona self on luxury brand attachment in the Metaverse context. *Asia Pacific Journal of Marketing and Logistics*, 36(9), 2068–2081. DOI: 10.1108/APJML-05-2022-0390

Kim, S. J. (2023). Virtual fashion experiences in virtual reality fashion show spaces. *Frontiers in Psychology*, 14, 1276856. DOI: 10.3389/fpsyg.2023.1276856 PMID: 38046109

Lee, E. J., & Jeon, J. H. (2024). The Role of Perceived Value of Avatar's Virtual Fashion in Metaverse on the Impact of Sense of Presence on Purchase Intention. International Journal of Internet. *Broadcasting and Communication*, 16(3), 334–345.

Luong, V. H., Tarquini, A., Anadol, Y., Klaus, P., & Manthiou, A. (2024). Is digital fashion the future of the metaverse? Insights from YouTube comments. *Journal of Retailing and Consumer Services*, 79, 103780. DOI: 10.1016/j.jretconser.2024.103780

Mogaji, E., Dwivedi, Y. K., & Raman, R. (2024). Fashion marketing in the metaverse. *Journal of Global Fashion Marketing*, 15(1), 115–130. DOI: 10.1080/20932685.2023.2249483

Park, H., & Lim, R. E. (2023). Fashion and the metaverse: Clarifying the domain and establishing a research agenda. *Journal of Retailing and Consumer Services*, 74, 103413. DOI: 10.1016/j.jretconser.2023.103413

SanMiguel, P., Sádaba, T., & Sayeed, N. (2024). Fashion brands in the metaverse: Achievements from a marketing perspective. Journal of Global Fashion Marketing, 1-21.

Santos, V., & Sousa, B. (2023, November). Technology Towards Luxury Brands: Preliminary Insights on Fashion Tourism, Metaverse and Non-fungible Token (NFT). In International Conference on Tourism, Technology and Systems (pp. 269-277). Singapore: Springer Nature Singapore.

Santos, V., Sousa, B., & Simões, J. (2024). Metaverse and NFT Market as AI Disruptive Technology for Digital Luxury Brands. In *Business Development via AI and Digitalization* (Vol. 2, pp. 1025–1036). Springer Nature Switzerland. DOI: 10.1007/978-3-031-62106-2_77

Seo, H., & Yoh, E. (2023). The Effects of Flow in a Metaverse-based Virtual Brand Space on Satisfaction and Purchase Intention of Virtual and Actual Fashion Products. *Journal of the Korean Society of Clothing and Textiles*, 47(5), 891–906.

Shin, J. Y., Suk, J., & Chung, J. E. (2023, February). Consumer responses to fashion in the metaverse: A text-mining analysis on online news comments. In Future of Information and Communication Conference (pp. 12-24). Cham: Springer Nature Switzerland. DOI: 10.1007/978-3-031-28076-4_2

Venturini, A., & Columbano, M. (2024). 'Fashioning'the metaverse: A qualitative study on consumers' value and perceptions of digital fashion in virtual worlds. *Journal of Global Fashion Marketing*, 15(1), 6–22. DOI: 10.1080/20932685.2023.2234918

Wongkitrungrueng, A., & Suprawan, L. (2024). Metaverse meets branding: Examining consumer responses to immersive brand experiences. *International Journal of Human-Computer Interaction*, 40(11), 2905–2924. DOI: 10.1080/10447318.2023.2175162

Wood, P. N. (2022). Understanding Consumer Behavior in the Metaverse: a Study on the Effect of Product, Tripartite Value, and Buying & Brand Perception in Virtual Vs. Physical Environments. Physical Environments (September 1, 2022).

Zhang, Y., Liu, C., & Lyu, Y. (2023). Examining consumers' perceptions of and attitudes toward digital fashion in general and purchase intention of luxury brands' digital fashion specifically. *Journal of Theoretical and Applied Electronic Commerce Research*, 18(4), 1971–1989. DOI: 10.3390/jtaer18040099

Chapter 9
Promoting Corporate Entrepreneurship Through Metaverse Practice:
Evidence From South Asia

Abdul Qadeer
https://orcid.org/0009-0004-4157-2387
Shaheed Benazir Bhutto University, Nawabshah, Pakistan

Waseem Hussain
https://orcid.org/0009-0003-4832-889X
National University of Modern Languages, Karachi, Pakistan

ABSTRACT

In this empirical investigation on promoting corporate entrepreneurship through metaverse practices data collected from an overall of 32 respondents using a standardized questionnaire. Multiple statistical techniques were employed for analyzing the data utilizing the SPSS program. The results of the analysis revealed a significant correlation between the variables investigated of 0.775 (Total Index). This robust association indicates a positive relationship between corporate entrepreneurship and the metaverse, which supports the study's core hypothesis

DOI: 10.4018/979-8-3693-9005-4.ch009

1. INTRODUCTION

The way firms create and run is being altered by emerging technology, which is creating an ongoing change in the current business environment. On regarding these revolutionary technologies is the metaverse, an unknown realm with the power to fundamentally alter CE. The relationship between CE and metaverse activities is investigated in this empirical study. With the goal of providing businesses navigating the digital age with helpful counsel. As the metaverse grows in recognition, there remains a lot of curiosity in how it affects business innovation and entrepreneurial ventures. The metaverse, sometimes called a shared virtual shed area offers opportunities for novel forms of cooperation, networking and resource utilization. Yet empirical evidence on the real implications for CE is still lacking. Companies who made use of metaverse cooperative virtual workplaces reported higher levels of creativity and ideas production. Events related to metaverse networking have a positive correlation with the probability of enterprises participating in intrapreneurial initiatives (Park et al., 2023). Corporate agility and taking risk are enhanced by the use of DAOs in the metaverse (Yoo et al., 2023). Employee involvement in business initiatives that promote corporate innovation was significantly enhanced by NFT-based incentive programs (Hussain, 2024). According to Yemenici et al., (2022) offering workers VR training enhances their preparedness and potential for entrepreneurship. The metaverse has the potential to disrupt established business hierarchies and foster entrepreneurial environments (Park et al., 2023). Metaverse-driven entrepreneurial behaviour has a positive effect on an organization's competitive edge in modern times (Weking et al., 2023). The employment of metaverse methods is positively connected with a rise in corporate intrapreneurial activities. By using a metaverse-based market analysis methodology, businesses have been capable to evaluate novel product ideas and successfully inspire entrepreneurial behavior (Zabel et al., 2023). VR creation in the metaverse reduced costs ad production time for products promoting innovation in business. Blockchain-based crowdfunding systems in the metaverse have made it simple for businesses to raise money (Yoo et al., 2023). Metaverse hackathons ad contests served as a great catalyst for CR encouraging employees to collaborate on innovative initiatives (Park et al., 2022). Employee reward programs based on the NFT metaverse enhanced engagement and promoted entrepreneurship (Parcu et al., 2023). Businesses with a metaverse environment have been shown to be more risk-taking and experimental (Schumacher et al., 2022). VR training has been beneficial for workers who possess a higher level of entrepreneurial self-confidence (Park et al., 2023). The use of decentralized was promoted by DAOs driven by the metaverse, which raised CE (Weking et al., 2023). Via metaverse networking events, cooperation between industries encouraged the sharing of innovative business concepts (Park et al., 2022). Virtual accelerators ad incubation within the metaverse significantly helped business companies. Employees' entrepreneurial mentality and abilities are positively impacted by mentoring programs rooted in the metaverse (Parcu et al., 2023). According to park et al., 92023), metaverse platforms offer virtual resources and instruments that enhance the effectiveness and efficiency of business creative operations. Taken as a whole, this study results demonstrate the metaverse's increasing importance as a catalyst for CE and provide a solid foundation for the empirical examination that this study offers.

2. LITERATURE REVIEW

2.1 Corporate Entrepreneurship (CE)

CE is the technique of promoting inventiveness, originality and risk-taking inside established enterprises (Aria et al., 2023). From their point of view, the main goal of CE is to inspire employees to devise and implement novel ideas and projects that promote creativity and growth within the limits of the existing company structure (Aria et al., 2023).Common elements include fostering entrepreneurial environments and supporting intrapreneurial activities. According to Joy et al., (2022), it has three distinct degrees of analysis that go into CE. Every individual, the collective and the environment. Individual CE comprises creating a culture that encourages staff workers to think and act like entrepreneurs (Gill et al., 2023). This could require the kind of intrapreneurship, where employees are encouraged to identify and take advantage of internal opportunities (Alverez et al., 2022). Corporate Resiliency (CR) describes how a corporation promotes an environment that supports entrepreneurship at an organizational level. This can mean setting up processes, providing resources and promoting taking chances (Gao et al., 2023). When evaluating environmental factors, CE considers external elements such as businesses, market conditions and competition (Gupta et al., 2023). Companies need to adapt to the constantly shifting external environment and seize opportunities when they arise. Furthermore, he defines CE as "the method wherein a person or a collection of professionals along with a well-established company establishes an entirely novel entity or starts renew of development inside that company (Agarwal et al., 2022). The pursuit of opportunities for strategy regeneration and growth through innovative problem-solving that results in the development of new products, services or enterprises is known as CE (Aljanabi et al., 2023). This emphasizes CE as its attempt to reenergize and expand the offerings of the business. Developing novel companies, venturing into unexplored areas or establishing startups within the organization are some examples of how of seize new chances (Hubbard et al., 2023). Often abbreviated as CE, entrepreneurship entails employees functioning as company owners within their businesses taking measured risks and imitating new initiatives (Brahmi et al., 2024). This perspective focuses on empowering and encouraging employees to operate as freelances inside a bigger organization Hu et al., 2023). While possibilities carry a certain level of risk, Intrapreneurs are able to recognize and take advantage of them thanks to the finances and adaptability given to them are provided (Johan et al., 2022). A company needs to create ambidextrous so as to exercise CE. This means finding a compromise between researching current company activates (efficiency) and researching new prospects (Innovation) (Buhalis et al., 2022). This emphasizes how important it is for companies to both optimize their current operations and search for fresh possibly disruptive prospects (AL-Ramahi et al., 2024). The importance of managing both revolutionary and progressive breakthroughs is emphasized (Hastuti et al., 2022). The phrase "CE" refers to the ways in which well-established corporations can support entrepreneurial endeavors and behavior. It involves inspiring employees to come up with, develop and implement innovative ideas and initiatives in order to produce new products, services or processes that will eventually boost innovation and competitiveness (Calandra et al., 2023). CE is crucial for big businesses to stay competitive and adapt to shifting circumstance. CE is the procedure of starting a fresh company inside an organization (Chapman et al., 2022).CE means promoting an innovative mentality where companies actively search for new opportunities, products and services. In a company context that is evolving quickly, this encourages rivalry and adaptation (Badiru et al., 2023). Instances for organizational regeneration include creating fresh company divisions, entering unexplored markets and updating antiquated practices to increase productivity (Chen et al., 2023). Inside the organization, staff members are urged to take on entrepreneurial duties and managed taking risks is a typical CE practice. This encourages creativity and experimentation (Kraus et al., 2022). CE is a strategic tool employed to create advantage and gain a competitive advantage. They describe value as the company tactical newel via innovation and venturing with the goal to generate worth (Damar et al., 2021). Regarding the overall goals of the organization, CE is considered a strategic direction. It comprises identifying new possibilities and utilizing assets effectively for pursuing those (De Giovanni et al., 2023). The primary goal of CE is creating value, which may be achieved by expanding markets, creating new goods and setting up sections as entrepreneurial affiliates. CE encompasses both entrepreneurship and creative thinking (Far et al., 2023). Businesses experimenting on new concepts, goods and marketplaces to remain competitive. According to Gao et al., (2023), companies have the ability to effectively integrate entrepreneurial pursuits into their primary business plans. CE has a good effect on both financial effectiveness and creativity (Aria et al., 2023). Finding the elements that influence workers' entrepreneurial attitude is a key component of firms' entrepreneurial spirit (Kumar et al., 2023). The role of leadership plays in promoting CE and fostering creative thinking in the workplace. Executives within organizations starting their own businesses (Mao et al., 2023). Several organizational traits like as inventiveness, taking risk and preparedness influence CE. CE has an advantageous effect on productivity and development in enterprises (Hai et al., 2023). Higher levels of CE are significantly connected with company development and creativity. Family firms can benefit from CE to get stronger competitors (Hu et al., 2023). CE may lead to the creation of new companies within larger corporations. Businesses with higher CE typically expand faster and are more creative (Hubbard et al., 2023). Businesses can develop the ability to spot, seize and execute on possibilities (Johan et al., 2022). Knowledge creation and exchange can benefit from CE (Joy et al., 2022). CE is a tool that multinational corporations can employ to grow globally. CE may constitute advantageous fir socially conscious business activities (Hai et al., 2023). Businesses having an effective CE orientation are more probable to achieve lasting competitive advantages (Mao et al., 2023).

2.2 Metaverse Practices

The term "Metaverse Practices" refers to an extensive variety of strategies, initiatives and resources used in the metaverse, a communal, online & interactive online space. These protocols aim to foster many aspects of interpersonal communication, imaginative thinking and business in this online space (Novel et al., 2023). Metaverse practices like VR training, networking events, DAOs, NFT as well an opportunity to define the metaverse's effects on CE (Ooi et al., 2023). The success of collaborative virtual workspaces in the metaverse allowed teams working remotely to collaborate better imaginatively and cooperatively (Kshetri et al., 2022). Metaverse practices are a range of strategies and techniques employed in the metaverse, a virtual environment that often mimics reality but in the digital format. Additional items, these actions foster creativity, company productivity and social connection (Markopoulos et al., 2022). Collaborative virtual workplaces, which are online spaces enable communication, idea sharing ad project collaboration in a virtual setting (Knox et al., 2022). Collaborative virtual workspaces have the potential to enhance global cooperation. They can act an avenue for innovation and originality by allowing individuals to work together in a shared digital environment (Owusu et al., 2023). Participants at networking events held in the metaverse can engage in action, networks and communicate exactly like they'd do in the actual world. These events can facilitate the development of relationships between individuals from other nations (Lin et al., 2023). They provide unique opportunities to network, think about joint ventures and share expertise (Sa et al., 2023). DAOs are programs that are managed by intelligent contracts. They enable managing assets and collaborative decision-making in the metaverse (Samad et al., 2022). DAOs can enhance openness and reliability in online networks. DAOs and Crowdsourcing are only things they might be used form make decentralized Govt possible. NFTs are unique digital assets they can be used to represent accessibility or control over tangible or online things. In order to compensate respondents in NFT-based incentive programs (Samad et al., 2022). As a means to promote user participation and involvement in metaverse actions, NFTs have garnered a lot of attention. Technologies for them include digital art, gaming, online property and metaverse uses (Kit et al., 2022). Using technological immersion to give education and training activities within the metaverse is known as VR (Momtaz et al., 2022). VR-based training can be very beneficial for developing fresh abilities, particularly where hands-on training is essential (Longo et al., 2023). It is used in a wide range of sectors including personal training, travel and health. Metaverse activities have growth in popularity as a result of the growth of online and online environments (Hai et al., 2023). They allow businesses to interact with numerous consumers and develop (Momtaz et al., 2022). Individuals and groups can work together and communicate more successfully beyond boundaries of space by utilizing metaverse methods. Novel apps and services are made possible by DAOs and NFT-based incentives in creative digital communities (Rong et al., 2023). VR enables cost-effective training and employee development cost-effective training and staff growth (Lin et al., 2023). According to Longo et al., (2023), metaverse networking events are those that promote global networking, information sharing and building communities. Notwithstanding the benefits, metaverse practices provide challenges with user acceptance, privacy and safety that must be properly addressed ad controlled (Salloum et al., 2023). Metaverse practices offer enormous possibilities for relationships, trade and invention within simulated environments. Metaverse networking events fostered sharing information, professional connections and interindustry collaboration (Ioannidis et al., 2023). DAOs have been found to enhance the efficacy and flexibility of making choices in online communities as a result of its application in the metaverse (Mancuso et al., 2023). The launch of NFT-based incentive systems in the metaverse was the catalyst for user engagement in simulated enterprises (Miaomiao et al., 2023). VR training was a more successful means of developing employee skills in the metaverse than conventional approaches to training (Hussain, 2023). The metaverse may topple established business hierarchies giving rise to flatter organizational frameworks and more innovative mindsets (Ioannidis et al., 2023). According to Hai et al., (2023), there is a direct link between innovation in companies and metaverse participation, and metaverse practices influence intrapreneurial endeavors. The metaverse provides businesses both an efficient and cost-effective way to acquire information from consumers and can assist with market analysis and product evaluations (Kraus et al., 2022). The metaverse accelerates the creation of innovative goods by using VR for product development (Rong et al., 2023). According to Joy et al., (2022) suggest that Blockchain-based funding systems within the metaverse have the potential in democratizing funding availability for business ventures. Decentralized decision-making and intra-organizational development are promoted by DAOs driven by the metaverse (Gill et al., 2023). According to Hubbard et al., (2023), business concept exchanges and collaboration between industries are effectively fostered by metaverse networking events. Metaverse-based training programs have a favorable influence on users-entrepreneurial attitudes and capacities and metaverse platforms provide virtual resources and assistance that increases the efficiency of business innovation procedures within the digital realm (Ioannidis et al., 2023).

2.3 Metaverse Practices and Entrepreneurship

Metaverse practices are the various strategies, instruments, and projects employed in the metaverse, an online, dynamic, interconnected virtual world (Yoo et al., 2023). These activities stimulate enthusiasm for entrepreneurship by providing a unique habitat for creativity, collaboration, and business growth (Gao et al., 2023). By fostering entrepreneurial endeavor within organizations and creating fresh opportunities for companies, the application of metaverse methods can impact the entrepreneurial landscape of the 21st century (Gupta et al., 2023). Cooperative virtual workspaces in the metaverse foster creative problem-solving and entrepreneurial ideas across geographically separated teams (Schumacher et al., 2022). Entrepreneurs get gather at metaverse networking events, which promote collaboration, creativity, and knowledge sharing (Zabel et al., 2023). Establishing virtual environments in the metaverse that employ DAOs to support entrepreneurial activities and making choices (Park et al., 2022). In the metaverse, NFT-based incentives can be utilized to motivate people and teams to engage on creative and entrepreneurial ventures (Johan et al., 2022). Staff workers can successfully acquire the skills needed for entrepreneurship through virtual reality training conducted in the metaverse (Hai et al., 2023). The metaverse's capacity to undermine organisational frameworks promotes imaginative and entrepreneurial organisational cultures (Hastuti et al., 2022). Metaverse-driven CE can enhance the competitiveness of an organization by enabling swift adaptability to the changing conditions of the electronic marketplace (Gill et al., 2023). By providing an online setting that encourages experimenting and idea development, metaverse practices support intrapreneurial endeavors (Hu et al., 2023). The metaverse offers a cheap and efficient way to carry out market research and evaluations of products to enhance entrepreneurial making choices (Badiru et al., 2023). The metaverse expedites creation of goods and enables rapid innovation rounds via virtual reality experimentation (Mao et al., 2023). Due to blockchain-based finance channels in the metaverse, businesses with an entrepreneurial drive are able to easily acquire capital (Kumar et al., 2023). According to Kraus et al.

(2023), shared problem-solving and inventive entrepreneurship are fostered via hackathons and contests held in the metaverse. NFT-based metaverse-based incentive programmes boost staff involvement in entrepreneurial activities (Calandra et al., 2023). The correlation between business risk-taking and metaverse activities may lead to a greater entrepreneurial corporate attitude (Chapman et al., 2023). Virtual reality training in the metaverse raises employee self-efficacy in entrepreneurship (Hu et al., 2023). Because metaverse-driven DAOs promote decentralized decision-making, staff can take on entrepreneurial responsibilities within organizations (Owusu et al., 2023). The degree to which industry-to-industry cooperation and the exchange of thoughts and entrepreneurial prospects are supported by metaverse networking events (Samad et al., 2023). Virtual startups and accelerators situated within the metaverse can offer significant assistance to enterprising firms (Rong et al., 2023). Mentoring programmes that focused on the metaverse and how it helped participants build their entrepreneurial viewpoints and abilities (Momtaz et al., 2022), (Hussain et al., 2023). According to Novel et al. (2023), metaverse platforms offer online resources and tools that enhance the effectiveness and effectiveness of corporate innovation procedures, hence facilitating entrepreneurial endeavors in the digital world.

Table 1

Metaverse Practices				
Collaborative Virtual Workspaces (CVW)	Metaverse Networking Events (MNE)	Decentralized Autonomous organizations (DAOs)	NFT-Based Incentive Programs (NFT)	Virtual Reality based employee training and Skill development (VRED)

Figure 1. Research Model

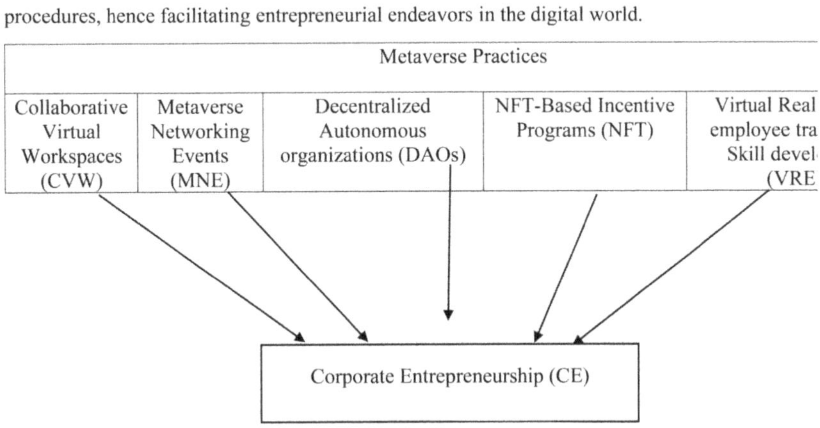

3. METHODOLOGY

This study looks at how CE is impacted by metaverse practices in South Asian tech enterprises. Among the independent variables considered are CVW, MNE, NFT, DAOs and VRED. There is a dependent variable on CE. A well designed structured questionnaire was used in this study to gather primary data. The research population consists of South Asian tech enterprises. This sampling method, which employs a probability-based methodology, divides participants into three groups: department managers, unit managers, and employees. The SPSS software was utilized to thoroughly analyse the gathered primary data in order to produce meaningful results and verify hypotheses. The purpose of the research is to clarify the ways in which these metaverse activities impact and encourage CE in the tech sector in the South Asian region.

3.1 Hypothesis Developed

H1: There is a significant relationship between CE and metaverse practices in the South Asian IT sector, including CVW, MNE, DAOs, NFT and VRED (Figure 1).

H2: Metaverse techniques have a big impact on CE in South Asia's IT sector.

Table 2. Reliability Analysis

Factor	No. of Items	Cronbach's Alpha
Overall Metaverse Practices	15	0.871
CVW	3	0.645
MNE	3	0.802
DAOs	3	0.808
NFT	3	0.730
VRED	3	0.654
CE	10	0.811

The table below provides a summary of the variables that the research is examining. The total metaverse practices scale has 15 items and a high degree of internal coherence, with a Cronbach's Alpha of 0 point 871, indicating that these elements accurately assess the entire notion of metaverse practices. Three things make up CVW, which have a Cronbach's Alpha of 0 point 645. The factor's results should be interpreted with this degree of reliability into thoughts, despite knowing that it is merely moderate. The three-item MNE measure has good internal consistency, with a Cronbach's Alpha of 0.802. DAOs are composed of three components and have a high degree of reliability (Cronbach's Alpha of 0.808). With three items and a Cronbach's Alpha of 0.730, NFT shows strong internal consistency. Cronbach's Alpha for the three items in VRED is 0.654, indicating reasonable reliability. The 10 items on the CE scale have a good degree of internal consistency and provide an accurate measurement of the CE, as indicated by their Cronbach's Alpha of 0.811.

Table 3. Descriptive Analysis for research Sample (n=32)

Variable	Frequency	Percentage
Gender		
Male	20	62.5%
Female	12	37.5%
Age		
25-34	10	31.3%
35-44	12	37.5%
45-54	7	21.9%
55+	3	9.4%
Educational Background		
High School	4	12.5%

continued on following page

Table 3. Continued

Variable	Frequency	Percentage
Bachelor's	12	37.5%
Masters	10	31.3%
Ph.D or Higher	6	18.8%
Job Status		
Department Manager	8	25.0%
Unit Director	10	31.3%
Employee	14	43.8%
Country		
India	15	46.9%
Pakistan	8	15.6%
Bangladesh	5	15.6%
Others	4	12.5%
Metaverse Experience		
0-1 years	8	25.0%
1-3 years	14	43.8%
3-5 years	7	21.3%
5+ years	3	9.4%

The table presents a demographic overview of this research. Based on the gender distributions, there are 62.5% more men than women among the participants. The age range of the participants. The age categories of 25–34 and 35–44 comprise 31.3% and 37.5% of the sample participants, respectively, representing the bulk of the general population. The educational backgrounds of the individuals. Based on the information provided, 37.5% of participants possess a bachelor's degree, 31.3% a master's degree, and 18.8% a Ph.D. D rank. Fewer than 12.5% of persons have earned a high school diploma. The professions of the participants. Employees make up 43.8% of the population, followed by unit managers (31.3%) and other categories (25%). There are no department supervisors in the workforce. The respondent's national breakdown. The bulk of participants—46.9%—are from India, with 45.6% coming from Bangladesh and Pakistan and 12.5% from other nations. The participants' experiences in the metaverse. According to the data, 43.8% of participants have experienced the metaverse for 1-3 years, 25.0 percent for 0-1 years, 21.3% for 3-5 years, and 94.4% for 5+ years.

Table 4. Descriptive Analysis of the Independent Variable (Metaverse Practices)

Variable	Evaluation Levels	Mean	Standard Deviation	Strongly Agree	Agree	Neutral	Disagree	strongly Disagree
Collaborative Virtual Workspaces (CVW1)								
CVW1	Strongly Agree	4.17	0.532	8 (24%)	25 (68.6%)	2 (6.5%)	0 (0%)	0 (0%)
CVW2	Agree	23.88	0.658	4 (12.4%)	21 (65.7%)	6 (18.6%	1 (3.3%)	0 (0%)
CVW3	Neutral	4.12	0.658	8 (24%)	21 (66.6%)	2 (6.2%)	1 (3.2%)	0 (0%)
Average		4.04	0.616	86.5%	10.42%	2.04%		
Metaverse Networking Events (MNE4)								
MNE4	Strongly Agree	3.58	0.874	3 (9.2%)	18 (56.5%)	6 (18.6%)	5 (15.8%)	0 (0%)
MNE5	Agree	3.52	0.948	3 (9.2%)	17 (53.3%)	7 (21.8%)	4 (12.6%)	1 (3.1%)
MNE6	Neutral	3.32	0.935	2 (6.2%)	14 (43.9%)	10 (31.2%)	5 (15.7%)	1 (3.1%)
Average		3.46	0.920	58.4%	24%	16.4%		
Decentralized Autonomous Organizations (DAOs) (DAO7)								
DAO7	Strongly Agree	3.80	0.930	7 (21.8%)	16 (51%)	5 (15.4%)	4 (12.7%)	0 (0%)
DAO8	Agree	4.20	0.868	12 (36.4%)	18 (56.4%)	1 (3.1%)	1 (3.1%)	0 (0%)
DAO9	Neutral	3.76	0.904	5 (15.4%)	19 (59.6%)	5 (15.4%)	2 (6.5%)	1 (3.1%)
Average		3.92	0.902	80.22%	11.42%	8.32%		
NFT-Based Incentive Programs (NFTP1)								
NFTP10	Strongly Agree	3.22	0.880	2 (6.2%)	10 (31.4%)	15 (46.8%)	4 (12.6%)	1 (3.1%)
NFTP11	Agree	3.62	9.05	3 (9.2%)	19 (58.6%)	6 (18.6%)	3 (9.6%)	1 (3.1%)
NFTP12	Neutral	3.24	0.840	3 (9.2%)	7 (21.7%)	17 (53.3%)	5 (15. 6%)	0 (0%)
Average		3.35	0.874	45.8%	39.6%	14.6%		

continued on following page

Table 4. Continued

Variable	Evaluation Levels	Mean	Standard Deviation	Strongly Agree	Agree	Neutral	Disagree	strongly Disagree
Virtual Reality-Based Employee training and Skill Development (VRED13)								
VRED13	Strongly Agree	3.92	0.758	6 (18.6%)	20 (62.7%)	4 (12.4%)	2 (6.4%)	0 (0%)
VRED14	Agree	4.40	0.710	16 (50.2%)	14 (43.6%)	1 (3.1%)	1 (3.1%)	0 (0%)
VRED 15	Neutral	4.20	0.830	12 (37.3%)	17 (53.4%)	2 (6.2%)	1 (3.1%)	0(0%)
Average		4.18	0.766	88.4%	7.6%	4.1%		
Total Average		3.80	0.815	72.2%	18.4%	9.2%		

This table displays the results of a descriptive analysis of the independent variables. The CVW rating levels. Based on participant assessments of how much they agreed with these activities, the strongly with a mean rating of 4.17, the agree category has the greatest level of agreement regarding the effectiveness of the metaverse workplaces. In the metaverse, networking events are evaluated similarly. With a mean score of 3.52, the agree level received the highest mean score, indicating agreement with the importance of networking events. The DAOs are rated based on which of them has the highest mean 3.80 score for strongly agreeing with the DAOs' efficacy in the metaverse. Based on NFT, With the highest mean (3.62) for the agree level, it is clear that people agree that NFT are successful. Participants rated these methods an average of 4.40, with agreement with the efficiency of VRED having the highest mean score. All metaverse practices combined have an aggregate average of 3.80, with a standard deviation of 0. 815. This average rating was given to the metaverse practices examined in the study.

Table 5. Descriptive analysis of dependent variable (Corporate Entrepreneurship)

Variable	Evaluation Levels	Mean	Standard Deviation	Strongly Agree	Agree	Neutral	Disagree	Strongly Disagree
Corporate Entrepreneurship (CE16)								
CE16	Strongly Agree	3.58	0.754	1 (3.1%)	20(62.6%)	9(28%)	1 (3.1%)	1 (3.1%)
CE17	Agree	3.45	0.878	1(3.1%)	18 (56.2%)	10 (31.4%)	1 (3.2%)	2 (6.2%)

continued on following page

Table 5. Continued

Variable	Evaluation Levels	Mean	Standard Deviation	Strongly Agree	Agree	Neutral	Disagree	Strongly Disagree
CE18	Neutral	2.82	0.675	1 (3.1%)	2 (6.2%)	20 (62.7%)	9 (28.28%)	0 (0%)
CE19	Disagree	3.32	0.744	1 (3.1%)	13 (40. 4%)	14 (43.7%)	4 (12.8%)	0 (0%)
CE20	Strongly Disagree	3.22	0.658	1 (3.1%)	8 (25%)	20 (62.4%)	9 (9.5%)	0 (0%)
Average		3.44	0.750	52.6%	35%	12.2%		
Corporate Entrepreneurship (CE21)								
CE21	Strongly Agree	4.15	0.626	8 (25%)	22 (68.6%)	1 (3.1%)	1 (3.1%)	0 (0%)
CE22	Agree	3.68	0.590	0 (0%)	24 (75.2%)	6 (18.6%)	2 (6.2%)	0 (0%)
CE23	Neutral	3.45	0.802	2 (6.2%)	15 (46.8%)	11 (34.6%)	4 (12.5%)	0 (0%)
Average		3.75	0.672	32.5%	54.8%	13.1%		
Corporate Entrepreneurship (CE24)								
CE24	Strongly Agree	3.8%	0.775	1 (3.1%)	9 (25.2%)	16 (50%)	7 (21.9%)	0 (0%)
Average		3.08	0.775	12.5%	31.2%	50%	21.10%	
Corporate Entrepreneurship (CE25)								
CE25	Strongly Agree	3.64	1.006	4 (12.4%)	19 (59.8%)	2 (6.2%)	2 (6.2%)	
Average		3.64	1.006	12.4%	59.7%	15.6%	6.3%	6.3%
Total Average		3.44	0.750	52.9%	35.2%	12.1%		

This table displays the assessment levels for the dependent variable. Respondents ranked the degree to which they agreed or disagreed with a range of corporate entrepreneurship claims. The greatest agreement with this element is indicated by the strongly agree level, which has the highest mean (3.58). In this phase, participants evaluated a second aspect of CE. There is an overwhelming agreement on this subject, as indicated by the highest mean score of 4 points—strongly agree. An additional CE component is assessed. The average mean is 3.08, which suggests a moderate degree of agreement with this characteristic. Lastly, the participants evaluated the CE. A modest level of agreement regarding this characteristic is indicated by the average score of three points. The standard deviation is 0.750 while the global average for CE is 3.44. This represents the average overall score for CE in the research.

3.2 Research Hypothesis Validity

The results displayed in Table 5 support the research assumptions about the relationship between metaverse activities and CE. The measure of correlation between the research variables has a Total Index value of 0.775. The first main research hypothesis, which suggests a link between metaverse behavior's and CE, is further supported by the Pearson's correlation analysis results, which are shown in Table 5. The following are the Pearson's correlation coefficients between the dependent variable CE and the independent variable metaverse practices (such as VRED, DAOs, CVW, and MNE r=0 point, CVW r= 0.502. Positive correlations between CE and metaverse behavior's are indicated by each of these correlation coefficients.

Table 6. Correlation Analysis

Dimensions of Metaverse Practices	Collaborative Virtual Workspaces	Metaverse Networking Events	Decentralized Autonomous Organizations (DAOs)	NFT-Based Incentive Programs	Virtual Reality-based Employee training an Skill Development	Total Index
CE	.502**	.681**	.408**	.780**	.491**	.775**

This table demonstrates the strong and favourably relationships between all facets of metaverse practices and CE. These findings suggest that utilizing various metaverse practices is advantageous to and associated with the expansion of CE. The entire index, which has a relationship coefficient of 0.775**, shows that metaverse behavior's and CE have a high favourably link.

Table 7. The impact of Metaverse Practices on Corporate Entrepreneurship (Total Index)

Independent Variabel			**(Metaverse practices)**		
Dependent Variable (CE)	Beta	R^2	F		Sig.
			Calculated	Tabular	
	.775	.602	45.182	4.15	0.00

DF= 1, 30 N=32

The results of a regression study assessing the impact of metaverse techniques on CE (Total index) are displayed in the table. According to the beta coefficient, which is.775, metaverse significantly improves CE. This implies that CE typically expands in tandem with metaverse activities. Variations in Metaverse practices can explain almost 60 point 1 percent of the variance in CE, based on the R2 value of.602. The f-statistic of 45.182, which is extremely significant, indicates that the regression model is highly significant overall. CE and metaverse practices are highly correlated, as indicated by the level of significance (Sig.) of.000 being less than.05.

Table 8. The effect of each practice of Metaverse Practices on Corporate Entrepreneurship

Independent Variable (Metaverse Practices)	Dependent Variable (corporate Entrepreneurship)	Beta	R^2	F	Sig.	Decision
CVW	CE	0.501	0.250	10.064	0.004	Accepted
MNE	CE	0.678	0.460	25.752	0.000	Accepted
DAOs	CE	0.408	0.166	5.008	0.018	Accepted
NFT	CE	0.798	0.636	52.822	0.000	Accepted
VRED	CE	0.490	0.240	9.594	0.004	Accepted

The results shown in Table 8 show how, in the context of the study, different metaverse practices (IV) influence CE (DV). The beta value of 0.501 indicates a somewhat favourably link between CE and the adoption of CVW in the metaverse. The R2 value of 0.250 indicates that the utilization of CVW can explain 25% of the variance in CE. The statistical significance of the association between CVW and CE is demonstrated by the f-statistic of 10.064 and the p-value of 0.004. Consequently, the effect of CVW on CE is recognized. The beta value of 0.678 indicates a substantial positive link between the adoption of MNE and CE. Based on the R2 value of 0.460, 46% of the variation in CE can be explained by these occurrences. The statistical significance of the association is demonstrated by the extremely significant f-statistic of 25.752 and the p-value of 0.000. CE is hence open to the consequences of MNE. The beta value of 0.408 suggests a favourably correlation between the use of DAOs and CE, not as significant as a few additional practices. Using DAOs can explain 16.6% of the variance in CE, according to the R2 value of 0.166. The f-statistic of 5.008 is highly significant, with a p-value of 0.018 signifying a significant association. Consequently, it is accepted that DAOs affect CE. Consequently, it is accepted that DAOs affect CE. The high value of 0.798 indicates a considerable positive link between the usage of NFT and CE. The R2 value of 0.636 indicates that the utilization of these programmes can explain 63.6% of the variance in CE. The correlation between the two variables is strong and highly significant, as indicated by the f-statistic of 52.822 and the p-value of 0.000. Thus, the effects of NFT on CE are recognized. The beta value of 0.490 indicates a favourably link between VRED, CE, and the utilization of VRED. The R2 value of 0.240 indicates that VRED can explain 24% of the variance in CE. The f-statistic of 9.594 is highly significant, with a p-value of 0.004 suggesting a significant link. Thus, it is known that VRED has an impact on CE. Each metaverse technique that has been studied has positively and statistical significantly affected CE.

Findings

The study concludes that metaverse activities and CE are mutually helpful. The total index correlation coefficient of 0.775 suggests a strong overall positive association. Every metaverse practice has a good and significant effect on CE, including CVW, MNEs, DAOs, NFT, and VRED. Every technique was acknowledged to have a significant effect. It was found that NFT had the most positive effects on CE; their impact on encouraging entrepreneurial activity within tech businesses was demonstrated by their Beta of 0.798 and R2 of 0.638. The study provides strong empirical support for the study hypotheses, which state that metaverse practices promote CE in the South Asian IT industry. The findings, which highlight the value of metaverse practices in a computer-driven company culture, are centred on the South Asian IT industry. The study adds to our understanding of the ways in which metaverse practices might support CE, which could lead to creativity and profitable outcomes for technological businesses in South Asia. Regression, significance tests, and Pearson's coefficients are examples of statistical evaluations that bolster the validity and importance of the study's conclusions. The results has practical ramifications for managers and executives in tech companies, as they underscore the possible benefits of implementing metaverse methods to foster entrepreneurial behaviour among staff. The paper makes several recommendations for additional study, including analysing the subtleties of specific metaverse practices and figuring out how to successfully implement them in different organisational situations. The empirical investigation provides strong evidence for the advantageous association between metaverse practices and CE in the South Asian IT industry. These results demonstrate how metaverse practices may be a useful instrument for encouraging creativity and start-up projects within IT companies.

CONCLUSION

This empirical study investigated the ways in which CE in the dynamic tech sector of South Asia can be stimulated by metaverse practices. The goal of the study was to find out how tech companies' entrepreneurial endeavors were affected by tactics like CVW, MNE, DAOs, NFT, and VRED. From the research, numerous significant conclusions and revelations were made. Above all, it made a clear and beneficial correlation between CE and metaverse activities. The overall index correlation co-efficient, which was 0.775, provided substantial evidence for this association. The conclusion highlights how metaverse techniques are becoming increasingly important for promoting an inventive and entrepreneurial culture in the technology industry. After being looked at in isolation, each metaverse technique was found to have a major impact on CE. These methods were not only of statistical significance, yet they also had a favourably correlation with supporting employees' entrepreneurial behaviour. Particularly, NFT emerged as the most effective approach, achieving an R2 of 0.638 and a Beta of 0.798, which demonstrated its effectiveness in spurring entrepreneurial endeavors. The findings of the study will have a significant effect on management and executives in the technology industry. Businesses can create an additional changing, entrepreneurial atmosphere by implementing metaverse practices, which will help companies stand out from the competition and spur innovation. The body of knowledge regarding the relationships between CE and metaverse practices is expanding thanks to the findings of this study. It draws attention to the metaverse tools and methods' positive impact in fostering an inventive, taking chances, and entrepreneurial atmosphere in South Asian tech companies. As the tech industry grows, adopting these principles could be essential to its competitiveness and achievement in future generations. Additional studies in this topic can give in-depth evaluations of how specific metaverse practices are implemented across different organisational contexts while investigating the intricate implications of these methods.

Practical Implications

Tech businesses in South Asia can foster innovation and entrepreneurship among their employees by utilizing metaverse strategies. Building a virtual setting that encourages networking cooperation and developing abilities can lead to the emergence of novel concepts and solutions. Metaverse methods such as VRED have the potential to enhance staff engagement. Offering possibilities for comprehensive and interactive instruction can enhance learning and boost efficacy producing a more competent and driven team. The application of NFT can promote and honor staff members' creative ideas. These schemes have a big influence on CE. This might promote a continuous innovation environment throughout the entire company. To promote staff independence and decision-making, one option is to look into DAOs. Tech businesses are urged to consider decentralized arrangements for some initiatives or tasks to order to foster entrepreneurial thinking. MNE can also be strategically designed to facilitate connections between staff members and business professionals and possible partners. These events can serve as venues for cooperation, creativity and idea exchange. Adopting metaverse techniques can give tech businesses a competitive advantage. Companies that effectively employ such technologies should be capable to react faster to possibilities and changing market conditions. Investments in VRED will yield an exceptionally competent team that can monitor complicated challenges and spur innovation. Supporting entrepreneurship can lead to the development of new products, services, or company divisions. By using metaverse approaches, Intrapreneurs can get the resources and circumstances necessary for success. If tech businesses wish to get the most out of metaverse practices, then should carefully deploy them based on their particular requirements and goals. A tailored plan guarantees consistency with the company's overarching strategy. Use KPIs and feedback channels to regularly assess how CE is affected by metaverse practices. Make any required strategy adjustments to maximize outcomes. Promote interdepartmental collaboration in the virtual environment that metaverse practices produce. Multidisciplinary teams may collaborate together on imaginative endeavors, for example, with the use of collaborative virtual workplaces. Consider allocating funds for the creation and procurement of metaverse technologies. They can acquire a strategic edge by staying up to date with this breakthrough in technology. The research's real-world consequences underscore the potential for South Asian technology firms to leverage metaverse techniques as tools to enhance creativity, entrepreneurial spirit, and competition. By carefully putting these ideas into effect and customizing these to their unique situations, organizations may foster long-term achievement and development in the fast-paced tech industry.

Recommendations for Business Stakeholders

Business stakeholders including senior management and decision-makers should think about implementing metaverse practices within their organizations. Recognize the potential for these practices to foster entrepreneurship and inventiveness. Verify that the implementation of metaverse techniques aligns with the company's strategic objectives and goals. Include these procedures in the broader business plan to maximize their effects. Finance projects for virtual reality instruction and staff skill development. Employees should be equipped with the skills and knowledge necessary to thrive in the competitive, rapid tech sector. Provide NFT-based incentive programmes to recognize and reward employees for their creative efforts. Promote problem-solving and innovative thinking to advance an entrepreneurial culture. Cross-functional cooperation can be promoted through collaborative virtual workplaces. Create virtual workspaces to facilitate cross-departmental collaboration on innovative projects. Consider implementing DAOs for specific initiatives or undertakings. Promote ingenuity and independent decision-making within groups. Participate in metaverse networking events and online conversations tailored to your sector. Make the most of these opportunities to network, interact, and gain knowledge about current trends in the field. Provide employee entrepreneurship programmes that let them propose and collaborate on internal business ideas. Assist these efforts with the funding and backing that is required. Establish key performance indicators (KPIs) to assess how corporate entrepreneurship is affected by metaverse activities. Make the required modifications in light of an ongoing assessment of the effectiveness of these procedures. Recognize the need of investing in software and hardware for metaverse technologies. Maintaining your competitive edge requires being up to date with industry advancements. Team members should lead by example whenever it involves implementing metaverse practices. In addition, efficient methods for managing change should be put into practice to guarantee a smooth transition. Priorities the well-being and well-being of your employees when working remotely. Ensure that employees are comfortable and inspired to participate in metaverse activities. Introduce training courses to assist employees in learning concerning metaverse operations. Provide materials and instruction to help people make the most out using these technologies. Compare metaverse adoption to industry experts' and excellent practices' approaches. Learn from organizations that have successfully applied these techniques. Keep in mind the moral and legal implications of engaging in metaverse operations, particularly in relation to confidentiality and information security. Ensure that all relevant rules are adhered to. Develop a versatile and adaptable mindset. Metaverse methods must be adaptable enough to take advantage of new circumstances, as the IT industry is always changing. Provide employees a way to voice their opinions and share their experiences about working in the metaverse through review mechanisms. Make use of this feedback to ensure we can continue to improve and refine our processes. By incorporating these recommendations into their everyday activities and business strategies, companies in the South Asian IT market can succeed. Adopting metaverse methods with a strategic perspective can lead to improved creativity, productivity, and a dynamic entrepreneurial environment.

Recommendations for Future Research Directions

Additional research on specific business scenarios in the South Asian the educational industry can be conducted in future years. Examine the effects of different metaverse techniques on CE in online shopping, equipment manufacturing, software creation, among other segments. Comparative research across different South Asian countries is necessary to understand regional variations in the implementation of and effects from metaverse techniques on CE. Look at the factors that lead to these differences. Longitudinal research can be used for investigating how metaverse activities affect CE in the long run. Examine how the impact changes over the years as technologies progresses through different phases. Extensive examinations of IT firms that have effectively implemented Metaverse methods can offer helpful perspectives regarding the ideal procedures, challenges, and outcomes for these endeavors. Analyse the impact of social variables on the adoption and effectiveness of metaverse activities. Analyse the impact that South Asian cultural distinctions has on workers' use of these modern technologies. Examine the contentment and satisfaction of staff members who participate in metaverse activities. Acknowledge the preferences, challenges, and suggestions for enhancement for your clients. Examine how using the metaverse during work affects safety and confidentiality. Look at the finest strategies that companies may use to preserve employee trust and guarantee the safety of data. Examine the impact of metaverse techniques on initiatives related to organisational intrapreneurship. Analyse how these practices assist staff members in coming up with and carrying out their own entrepreneurial concepts. Analyse the responses of various ages to metaverse adoption in the workplace. Look at any possible generational variations in involvement, attitudes, and interests. Consider the integration of metaverse practices with additional new technologies like AR, the blockchain, and AI. Examine how CE is facilitated by the merging of these technologies. Examine how metaverse activities affect the South Asian technology industry monetarily. Analyse the effects of adopting these practices on sales growth, employment creation, and market growth. Examine the effects that metaverse practices have on environmental responsibility, particularly with regard to the environment. Examine how companies in virtual environments are implementing eco-friendly practices. Examine the ways in which metaverse behaviours impact distant work operations. Examine whether these methods enhance productivity, job happiness, and work-life balance. Establish moral guidelines and standards to ensure the moral implementation of metaverse activities in corporate environments. Address potential moral ambiguities and set the highest standards for ethical behaviour in online settings. Analyse how metaverse activities affect the organisational structure of a business. Analyse if these processes result in more decentralized, flatter institutions that foster creativity. Examine how metaverse practices facilitate continuing learning and information sharing inside organizations. Consider how much they have contributed to the growth of knowledge and abilities. Examine the ways in which tech industry metaverse activities can promote economic equality. Check if they provide opportunities for underprivileged populations to participate in entrepreneurship. The breadth of the investigation ought to encompass an international viewpoint. South Asia has embraced metaverse methods more quickly and with greater influence than other regions, such as Europe, North America, and Southeast Asia. By pursuing these study avenues, future studies can add to our knowledge of the intricate relationship between corporate entrepreneurship and metaverse behaviours. Companies, legislators, and academics may all profit on this information by leveraging the promise of digital spaces to foster creativity and entrepreneurial spirit.

REFERENCE

Agarwal, A., & Alathur, S. (2023). Metaverse revolution and the digital transformation: intersectional analysis of Industry 5.0. Transforming Government: *People, Process and Policy. 393), 99-106.*

Al-Ramahi, N., Kreishan, F. M., Hussain, Z., Khan, A., Alghizzawi, M., & AlWadi, B. M. (2024). Unlocking sustainable growth: The role of artificial intelligence adoption in jordan retail sector, moderated by entrepreneurial orientation. *International Review of Management and Marketing*, 14(6), 143–155. DOI: 10.32479/irmm.16843

Aljanabi, M., & Mohammed, S. Y. (2023). Metaverse: Open possibilities. *Iraqi Journal For Computer Science and Mathematics*, 4(3), 79–86. DOI: 10.52866/ijcsm.2023.02.03.007

Alvarez-Risco, A., Del-Aguila-Arcentales, S., Rosen, M. A., & Yáñez, J. A. (2022). Social Cognitive Theory to Assess the Intention to participate in the Facebook Metaverse by citizens in Peru during the COVID-19 pandemic. *Journal of Open Innovation*, 8(3), 142–164. DOI: 10.3390/joitmc8030142

Aria Parsa, M., & Dalvi Esfahan, M. R. (2023). The Application of the Entrepreneurship Model of Future Research in the Era of Metaverse in Knowledge-Based Companies in the Field of Information Technology. *Islamic Life Journal*, 7(2), 306–316.

Badiru, N. I., & Aladelusi, K. O. (2023). Proposed framework for integrating metaverse technologies into entrepreneurial education. *International Journal of Intellectual Discourse*, 6(1), 76–86.

Brahmi, M., Hussain, Z., & Khan, A. (1988, May). Driving Success: Examining the Influence of Innovation Culture on Artificial Intelligence Adoption and Firm Performance in Asian SMEs. *InAnnual International Conference on the Theory and Applications of Cryptographic Techniques(pp.89-105).Cham: Springer Nature Switzerland.*

Buhalis, D., Lin, M. S., & Leung, D. (2022). Metaverse as a driver for customer experience and value co-creation: Implications for hospitality and tourism management and marketing. *International Journal of Contemporary Hospitality Management*, 35(2), 701–716. DOI: 10.1108/IJCHM-05-2022-0631

Calandra, D., Oppioli, M., Sadraei, R., Jafari-Sadeghi, V., & Biancone, P. P. (2023). Metaverse meets digital entrepreneurship: A practitioner-based qualitative synthesis. *International Journal of Entrepreneurial Behaviour & Research*, 23(3), 345–361.

Calzada, I. (2023). Disruptive Technologies for e-Diasporas: Blockchain, DAOs, Data Cooperatives, Metaverse, and ChatGPT. *Futures*, 3(3), 103–158.

Chapman, J. R., Wang, J. C., & Wiechert, K. (2022). Into the spine metaverse: Reflections on a future metaspine (uni-) verse. *Global Spine Journal*, 12(4), 545–547. DOI: 10.1177/21925682221085643 PMID: 35506945

Chen, P. K., Ye, Y., & Huang, X. (2023). The metaverse in supply chain knowledge sharing and resilience contexts: An empirical investigation of factors affecting adoption and acceptance. *Journal of Innovation & Knowledge*, 8(4), 100–146. DOI: 10.1016/j.jik.2023.100446

Damar, M. (2021). Metaverse shape of your life for future: A bibliometric snapshot. *Journal of Metaverse*, 1(1), 1–8.

De Giovanni, P. (2023). Sustainability of the Metaverse: A transition to Industry 5.0. *Sustainability (Basel)*, 15(7), 60–79. DOI: 10.3390/su15076079

Far, S. B., Rad, A. I., & Asaar, M. R. (2023). Blockchain and its derived technologies shape the future generation of digital businesses: A focus on decentralized finance and the Metaverse. *Data Science and Management*, 6(3), 183–197. DOI: 10.1016/j.dsm.2023.06.002

Gao, H., Chong, A. Y. L., & Bao, H. (2023). Metaverse: Literature Review, Synthesis and Future Research Agenda. *Journal of Computer Information Systems*, 3(2), 1–21. DOI: 10.1080/08874417.2023.2267510

Gil-Cordero, E., Maldonado-López, B., Ledesma-Chaves, P., & García-Guzmán, A. (2023). Do small-and medium-sized companies intend to use the Metaverse as part of their strategy? A behavioral intention analysis. *International Journal of Entrepreneurial Behaviour & Research*, 23(2), 33–45.

Gupta, B. B., Gaurav, A., Albeshri, A. A., & Alsalman, D. (2023). New paradigms of sustainable entrepreneurship in metaverse: A micro-level perspective. *The International Entrepreneurship and Management Journal*, 17(3), 1–17. DOI: 10.1007/s11365-023-00875-0

Hai, G., Zhuen, Y., & Jiebin, D. (2023). Metaverse Business Model: Connotation, Classification and Research Framework. *Foreign Economics & Management*, 45(03), 23–45.

Hastuti, T. D., Sanjaya, R., & Koeswoyo, F. (2022). The Readiness of Lasem Batik Small and Medium Enterprises to Join the Metaverse. *Computers*, 12(1), 5–11. DOI: 10.3390/computers12010005

Hu, Y., & Pang, J. (2023). Research on the new path of deepening grassroots medical care from the perspective of metaverse. *Academic Journal of Management and Social Sciences*, 2(1), 81–84. DOI: 10.54097/ajmss.v2i1.6375

Hubbard, T. D., & Aguinis, H. (2023). Conducting phenomenon-driven research using virtual reality and the metaverse. *Academy of Management Discoveries*, 9(3), 408–415. DOI: 10.5465/amd.2023.0031

Hussain, Z. (2023). A Study of Employees' Perceptions on Industry Revolution 5.0 and Its Advantages: A Case Study of the Manufacturing Industry of Pakistan. *Business, Technology and Finance, 25.*

Hussain, Z. (2024). The Role of Metaverse in Women Entrepreneurship and Economic Complexity: Evidence from Pakistan. *Journal of Entrepreneurship and Business Venturing*, 4(1).

Hussain, Z., Khan, A., & Ali, A. (2023). The Impact of User-Generated Content, Social Interactions and virtual Economies on Metaverse Environments. *Journal of Sustainable Economics*, 1(2), 34–44. DOI: 10.32734/jse.v1i2.13798

Ioannidis, S., & Kontis, A. P. (2023). Metaverse for tourists and tourism destinations. *Information Technology & Tourism*, 2(3), 1–24.

Johan, S. (2022). Metaverse and its implication in law and business. *Jurnal Hukum Progresif*, 10(2), 153–166. DOI: 10.14710/jhp.10.2.153-166

Joy, A., Zhu, Y., Peña, C., & Brouard, M. (2022). Digital future of luxury brands: Metaverse, digital fashion, and non-fungible tokens. *Strategic Change*, 31(3), 337–343. DOI: 10.1002/jsc.2502

Kim, J. (2021). Advertising in the metaverse: Research agenda. *Journal of Interactive Advertising*, 21(3), 141–144. DOI: 10.1080/15252019.2021.2001273

Kit, K. T. (2022). Sustainable engineering paradigm shift in digital architecture, engineering and construction ecology within Metaverse. *International Journal of Computer and Information Engineering*, 16(4), 112–115.

Knox, J. (2022). The metaverse, or the serious business of tech frontiers. *Post digital. Science and Education*, 4(2), 207–215.

Kraus, S., Kanbach, D. K., Krysta, P. M., Steinhoff, M. M., & Tomini, N. (2022). Facebook and the creation of the metaverse: Radical business model innovation or incremental transformation? *International Journal of Entrepreneurial Behaviour & Research*, 28(9), 52–77. DOI: 10.1108/IJEBR-12-2021-0984

Kraus, S., Kumar, S., Lim, W. M., Kaur, J., Sharma, A., & Schiavone, F. (2023). From moon landing to metaverse: Tracing the evolution of Technological Forecasting and Social Change. *Technological Forecasting and Social Change*, 189(2), 122–281. DOI: 10.1016/j.techfore.2023.122381

Kshetri, N. (2022). Metaverse and developing economies. *IT Professional*, 24(4), 66–69. DOI: 10.1109/MITP.2022.3174744

Kshetri, N. (2022). Web 3.0 and the metaverse shaping organizations' brand and product strategies. *IT Professional*, 24(02), 11–15. DOI: 10.1109/MITP.2022.3157206

Kumar, A., Shankar, A., Shaik, A. S., Jain, G., & Malibari, A. (2023). Risking it all in the metaverse ecosystem: Forecasting resistance towards the enterprise metaverse. *Information Technology & People*, 3(3), 44–62. DOI: 10.1108/ITP-04-2023-0374

Lin, K. J., Ye, H., & Law, R. (2023). Understanding the development of blockchain-empowered metaverse tourism: An institutional perspective. *Information Technology & Tourism*, 23(3), 1–19. DOI: 10.1007/s40558-023-00262-z

Longo, M. C., & Faraci, R. (2023). Next-Generation Museum: A Metaverse Journey into the Culture. *Synergies Italian Journal of Management*, 41(1), 147–176. DOI: 10.7433/s120.2023.08

Mancuso, I., Petruzzelli, A. M., & Panniello, U. (2023). Digital business model innovation in metaverse: How to approach virtual economy opportunities. *Information Processing & Management*, 60(5), 103–357. DOI: 10.1016/j.ipm.2023.103457

Mao, Y., & Cao, R. (2023). Research on the purchase intention of metaverse music performances based on the theory of perceived value. [ACS]. *Journal of Arts and Cultural Studies*, 2(2), 2–12.

Markopoulos, E., Nordholm, A. D., Illiade, S., Markopoulos, P., Faraclas, J., & Luimula, M. (2022). A certification framework for virtual reality and metaverse training scenarios in the Maritime and shipping industry. *Creativity. Innovation and Entrepreneurship*, 31(4), 36–47.

Miaomiao, Y., Jiying, L., Shengyan, W., & Chunshan, L. (2023). A Research on the Identity Formation Process of Metaverse User Entrepreneurs. *Foreign Economics & Management*, 45(07), 53–70.

Momtaz, P. P. (2022). Some very simple economics of web3 and the metaverse. *Fintech*, 1(3), 225–234. DOI: 10.3390/fintech1030018

Novel, N. J. A., & Alexandri, M. B. (2023). Creative City Start-up Business Acceleration in the Metaverse Era: Entrepreneurial Leadership and Innovation. *Review of Integrative Business and Economics Research*, 12(1), 216–229.

Ooi, K. B., Tan, G. W. H., Aw, E. C. X., Cham, T. H., Dwivedi, Y. K., Dwivedi, R., & Sharma, A. (2023). Banking in the metaverse: A new frontier for financial institutions. *International Journal of Bank Marketing*, 2(3), 44–61. DOI: 10.1108/IJBM-03-2023-0168

Owusu-Antwi, K., & Amenuvor, F. E. (2023). Understanding the Metaverse: A Review of Virtual Worlds and Augmented Reality Environments. *Current Journal of Applied Science and Technology*, 42(23), 42–48. DOI: 10.9734/cjast/2023/v42i234172

Papagiannidis, S., Bourlakis, M., & Li, F. (2008). Making real money in virtual worlds: MMORPGs and emerging business opportunities, challenges and ethical implications in metaverses. *Technological Forecasting and Social Change*, 75(5), 610–622. DOI: 10.1016/j.techfore.2007.04.007

Parcu, P. L., Rossi, M. A., Innocenti, N., & Carrozza, C. (2023). How real will the metaverse be? Exploring the spatial impact of virtual worlds. *European Planning Studies*, 23(4), 1–23. DOI: 10.1080/09654313.2023.2221323

Park, I., & BOYOUNG, K. (2022). An Exploratory Study for the Application of Metaverse-Based University Entrepreneurship Education. *The Journal of General Education*, 23(21), 7–32.

Park, S., & Kim, S. (2023). The Avaritia: Entrepreneurship Practice to Understand the Problem of Information Control through Gamification. *Sustainability (Basel)*, 15(8), 6738. DOI: 10.3390/su15086738

Rong, R., Xinyuan, W., & Xiaoran, Y. (2023). Metaverse and Entrepreneurial Corporate Social Responsibility: Action Dilemma, Process Reconstruction and Future Directions. *Foreign Economics & Management*, 45(07), 36–52.

Sá, M. J., & Serpa, S. (2023). Metaverse as a learning environment: Some considerations. *Sustainability (Basel)*, 15(3), 21–86. DOI: 10.3390/su15032186

Salloum, S., Al Marzouqi, A., Alderbashi, K. Y., Shwedeh, F., Aburayya, A., Al Saidat, M. R., & Al-Maroof, R. S. (2023). Sustainability Model for the Continuous Intention to Use Metaverse Technology in Higher Education: A Case Study from Oman. *Sustainability (Basel)*, 15(6), 52–57. DOI: 10.3390/su15065257

Samad, T. F. D., & Hasan, N. (2022). Women entrepreneurs in the era of metaverse: An Islamic economic perspective. *Review of Islamic Social Finance and Entrepreneurship*, 23(31), 131–140. DOI: 10.20885/RISFE.vol1.iss2.art5

Schumacher, P. (2022). The metaverse as opportunity for architecture and society: Design drivers, core competencies. *Architectural Intelligence*, 1(1), 11–21. DOI: 10.1007/s44223-022-00010-z PMID: 35993030

Weking, J., Desouza, K. C., Fielt, E., & Kowalkiewicz, M. (2023). Metaverse-enabled entrepreneurship. *Journal of Business Venturing Insights*, 19(3), 361–375.

Yaqoob, I., Salah, K., Jayaraman, R., & Omar, M. (2023). Metaverse applications in smart cities: Enabling technologies, opportunities, challenges, and future directions. *Internet of Things : Engineering Cyber Physical Human Systems*, 6(2), 100–184. DOI: 10.1016/j.iot.2023.100884

Yemenici, A. D. (2022). Entrepreneurship in the world of metaverse: Virtual or real? *Journal of Metaverse*, 2(2), 71–82. DOI: 10.57019/jmv.1126135

Yoo, K., Welden, R., Hewett, K., & Haenlein, M. (2023). The merchants of meta: A research agenda to understand the future of retailing in the metaverse. *Journal of Retailing*, 3(3), 44–55. DOI: 10.1016/j.jretai.2023.02.002

Zabel, C., O'Brien, D., & Natzel, J. (2023). Sensing the Metaverse: The micro foundations of complementor firms' dynamic sensing capabilities in emerging-technology ecosystems. *Technological Forecasting and Social Change*, 192(3), 122–162. DOI: 10.1016/j.techfore.2023.122562

Chapter 10
Review of the Literature on the Ownership Structure of SMEs

Saleh F. A. Khatib
https://orcid.org/0000-0001-7652-4191
Universiti Teknologi Malaysia, Malaysia

ABSTRACT

This study aims to synthesise and extend the current understanding of the literature related to small and medium enterprises ownership structure by identifying the key aspects investigated in the literature and possible directions for future research. The investigation also showed that pecking order theory complemented with other theoretical lenses could provide a better explanation of the complex SMEs' organizational behaviour than the common theoretical lenses that are applied in the literature, as SMEs are significantly different compared to large firms in terms of scale, resource availability and financial preferences. Combining systematic literature review and bibliometric analysis provides a panorama of the most established areas of research concerning the ownership structure of SMEs, helping newcomers to focus on specific themes and hence allowing them to adopt or connect to those suggested topics.

1. INTRODUCTION

Over the past decades, the significance of innovative small and medium enterprises (SMEs) for the economy of numerous nations has progressively increased. Dabić et al. (2020) showed that up to 95% of firms globally are SMEs, accounting for about 60% of employment and nearly 40% of GDP. These companies are the

DOI: 10.4018/979-8-3693-9005-4.ch010

driving force of economic growth and development around the globe, given that they contribute substantially to the GDP between 20-50 per cent in the majority of emerging markets (Doan et al., 2020). SMEs are the most common form of business organization in the world, and they are an important engine behind economic growth and job creation in emerging economies (Roberts & Muralidharan, 2022). Among these emerging technologies, the metaverse stands out as a transformative force with the potential to revolutionize business practices and drive sustainable growth.

The literature, however, is still unclear about the generally accepted definition of SMEs, and two approaches are commonly employed in identifying these firms: qualitative and quantitative. The qualitative approach emphasizes the existence of non-publicly listed stock and owners' personal guarantees, while the quantitative one uses measures such as the number of employees, sales turnover, and total assets. Moreover, even studies utilising the quantitative technique have used different measurements to select and identify SMEs. For example, some studies have used the number of 500 employees' or less (George et al., 2005), less than 2000 employees (Deng et al., 2013), less than 25 employees (Brunninge et al., 2007), and 10-250 employees (Dolz et al., 2019). The latter is the most employed indicator in prior studies.

SMEs are receiving increased and significant attention from academia, policy-makers, and industry. However, SMEs face numerous business challenges, such as access to finance, technological aspects, and ownership structure (Doan et al., 2020). For example, the adoption of metaverse technologies is not without its challenges. SMEs often face constraints such as limited financial resources, technological expertise, and access to markets, which can hinder their ability to fully exploit the potential of the metaverse. Additionally, the ownership structures of SMEs, which are often characterized by concentrated or family ownership, can either facilitate or impede the integration of these new technologies. Furthermore, small businesses are likely to be managed by the company owner, with a limited management team, as opposed to large firms that manage business operations collectively, involving a larger board of directors. Therefore, small firms lack the human capital and reliable mechanisms to support their risk-management activity (Dao et al., 2021; Doan et al., 2020). Accordingly, SMEs face additional internal and external challenges compared to large firms, and there is a need for sufficient assessment of companies' strategic planning (Borocki et al., 2019). They also have limited financing options, less transparent, low levels of knowledge about international markets, focus on one geographical area or a specific industrial sector, and higher monitoring costs for capital providers (Morais & Ferreira, 2020),

SMEs and large firms generally differ in ownership structure, where most small firms are closely held and owner-managed (Machold et al., 2011; Pascucci et al., 2022). The early evidence suggests that ownership structure is a significant governance attribute that substantially impacts agency costs (Denis, 1999; Mak & Li, 2001). Specifically, agency conflict that arises from the separation of ownership and control can be mitigated by the governance mechanism, including ownership structure (Jensen & Meckling, 1976; Shleifer & Vishny, 1986). The agency issues are even more complicated in SMEs because small firms are different from large firms in being closely-held (owner-managed). Researchers suggested that most SMEs are concentrated or family companies (Chu, 2009; Machold et al., 2011). Nevertheless, this family and concentration ownership are the sources of agency conflict; unlike large firms, it has been found to enhance the performance of SMEs (Abor & Biekpe, 2007; Caselli & Di Giuli, 2010; Chu, 2009). Hence, we believe that the pecking order theory could better explain the SMEs organizational behaviour than the common theoretical lenses applied in the literature (agency theory and Stewardship theory). For example, based on the agency and free cash flow hypothesis, cash holdings could generate agency problems associated with managerial discretion even in poorer institutional contexts (La Rocca et al., 2019). This study, therefore, reviews the findings of existing studies on SMEs' ownership through the pecking order theory lens.

Additionally, despite the significant differences between the ownership of large and small firms, there is a lack of studies exploring the ownership of SMEs, possibly attributed to difficulties in collecting systematic and reliable data on small firms. Also, the topic of ownership of SMEs has produced a relevant strand of knowledge that has not been systematized thus far. Thus, this gap leaves an opportunity to present a broader systematic review that provides a more comprehensive perspective on the knowledge presented in this field and suggests a roadmap for future research through the current gaps. Boyd and Solarino (2016) synthesised the literature on the ownership structure of large firms using a sample of 145 articles. For SMEs, Morais and Ferreira (2020) conducted a systematic review of the internationalisation process of SMEs. Also, Kumar et al. (2019) conducted a systematic review using 262 studies on SMEs with a primer focus on capital structure. However, there is still a lack of empirical and review work on the ownership structure of SMEs (Bhaird & Lucey, 2010; Chu, 2009; Lappalainen & Niskanen, 2013). Although the last two decades have witnessed a gradual intensification of research into the contexts of SMEs ownership, there remains a lack of research that compiles and systematises the available knowledge on the ownership of SMEs.

The ownership structure is one factor that defines the company's identity and influences its market behaviour (Al Amosh & Khatib, 2021). Furthermore, the ownership structure of SMEs is an important research area, as they are important drivers affecting the economy (Lappalainen & Niskanen, 2012). Thus, exploring the previous academic contribution is important to bridge the gaps and provide more insights on the topic. Our systematic review contributes to the SMEs literature by summarising and organising the empirical research to date, identifying possible gaps for further work. It synthesises the existing knowledge on ownership of SMEs and provides a comprehensive review of the literature. The result of this research would benefit researchers and academicians in understanding the current structure and the thematic evolution of the field. To the best of our knowledge, this is the first research to conduct a systematic literature review on the ownership structure of SMEs. We summarise the key results that improve our understanding of the ownership of SMEs and highlight fruitful areas for further exploration.

A review of the literature on ownership structure in SMEs was conducted to address the research gaps in the current literature. Following the systematic review methodology used by Li et al. (2020), Rasel and Win (2020), (Da Cruz et al. (2019) and Khatib et al. (2021), this review covers seven themes: research trend, publisher, methodology, geographical distribution, theoretical ground, modelling, and concepts under study. These aspects are adopted as they are proven to provide a completely exhaustive review. Using keywords that were identified after reviewing similar studies and definitions in the literature, the initial search yielded 255 related papers published between 1990 and 2020 from Scopus and Web of Science databases.

To advance our knowledge on these issues, this research has three main objectives. First one is to analyse, summarise, present, and discuss the studies that have contributed to the literature on SME ownership structure by applying the systematic literature review (SLR) method. Second, this review evaluates the arguments behind the findings of the existing literature that will be helpful for future empirical research to establish a precise understanding of what has already been investigated. Third, this study identifies existing literature gaps and critically sets out potential future research areas.

2. METHODOLOGY

This study aims to provide a comprehensive systematic review of the literature on SMEs' ownership structure. To help our fellow scholars, we have started with descriptive and bibliometric analysis (keywords and Co-citation analysis) of all publications related to the topic of interest (Hazaea et al., 2023). The bibliometric approach was adopted because it is a common and rigorous method for exploring and analyzing a large amount of data enables researchers to create high-impact research for the review (Donthu et al., 2021). Next, a comprehensive systematic review was conducted on the sampled literature. This combination of SLR and bibliometric helps structure the research area's knowledge, which identifies gaps and links for future research directions (Kumar et al., 2020). Moreover, integrating bibliometric methods with a systematic review of the literature offers a more coherent review and provides more comprehensive results for review (Rialti et al., 2019; Linnenluecke et al., 2020). To extract the papers for our collection, four steps have been followed to complete the analysis in this study: identifying the main keywords, searching the literature for relevant studies, screening the initial sample to identify studies that explicitly address the topic of interest (the result was used in the descriptive and bibliometric analysis), and quality assessment of the published articles to identify quality articles for the systematic literature review.

As explained earlier, the literature is not about the clear definition or measurement of small and medium enterprises. Hence, several keywords related to small firms were utilized in searching the literature. Indeed, two different areas should be covered in the search process, including SMEs and ownership structure. The search string employed consists of several keywords related to each area. These keywords have been identified after reviewing similar studies and definitions in the literature. For SMEs, we followed Kumar et al. (2019) and Khatib et al. (2022) and used terms including 'Small and medium enterprise*', 'Medium firm*', 'SME*', 'Small business*', 'Small firm*', and 'Small compan*'. At the same time, the second one involved all the possible ownership structure-related keywords such as ownership* (Solarino & Boyd, 2020; Tihanyi et al., 2019). Table 1 presents the search string applied in this study.

Table 1. The searching string applied in the study

Topic	Related keywords
Ownership structure	"Ownership" or "Ownership structure" or "Family ownership" or "Ownership concentration" or "Foreign ownership" or "Institutional ownership" or "State ownership" or "Government ownership" or "Director* ownership" or "Managerial ownership" or "Bounder ownership" or "Political ownership" or "Business group ownership" or "Block*holder*"
and	
SMEs	"Small and medium enterprise*", "Medium firm", "SMEs", "Small business", "Small firm*", "startup", and "SME"

Two main databases, namely Scopus and Web of Science databases, have been utilised to search for the relevant literature in this study. In July 2023, the defined search string results in a sample of 2930 published research from the two databases. We then limited the result to the English language and source type of journal, which resulted in 2268 publications Block et al. (2019) and Khatib et al. (2021, 2022). This number of sampled studies was reduced to 1255 after the duplication check. Next, we manually evaluated the abstracts and titles of the remaining 281 studies to ensure that the articles explicitly address the ownership of SMEs. For a better understanding, the inclusion and exclusion method used in this paper is presented in Figure 1.

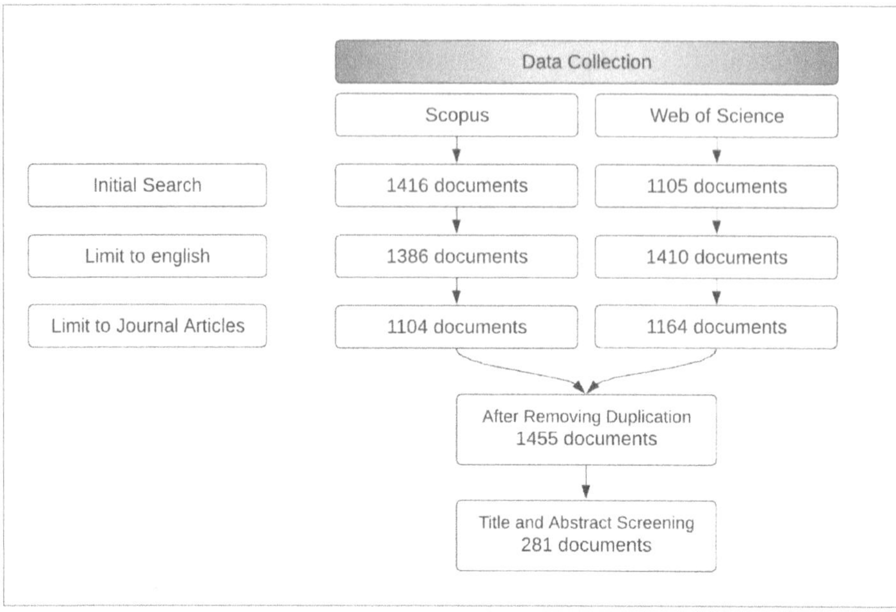

3. RESULTS AND DISCUSSION

A descriptive analysis of 237 articles was carried out to determine the primary ongoing trend of publication on this topic. Also, the same number of articles has been used for the bibliometric analysis (keywords and co-citation analysis). Figure 2 presents the publication trend on the ownership structure of SMEs. It displays a rising trend in the number of publications per year since 1984. For a period of 40 years, a total of 237 research articles were published. The year of 2016 shows the maximum number of publications, with over 21 research papers. The oldest publication dates to 1984 conducted by Geeraerts (1984) who focused on the organization size and its effect on the structure. The average number of articles published per year was less than five studies each year until 2004. Since then, annual publications have increased steadily, rapidly increasing the cumulative total publications. The growing interest in this research area might have been sparked by the international economic crisis of 2008. The literature provides ample evidence of how the financial crisis affects SMEs' profiles. La Rocca et al. (2019) suggested that, during the financial crisis, SMEs sought to keep the same cash stock, while it became more valuable to have a cash buffer in supporting the business. As this crisis increased, the prominence of systemic risk (Doan et al., 2020). More research is also expected to evaluate the impact of the current crisis (Covid-19) on SMEs' organizational behaviour and outcomes, as the Coronavirus pandemic is suggested to have a severe impact on all economies and sectors.

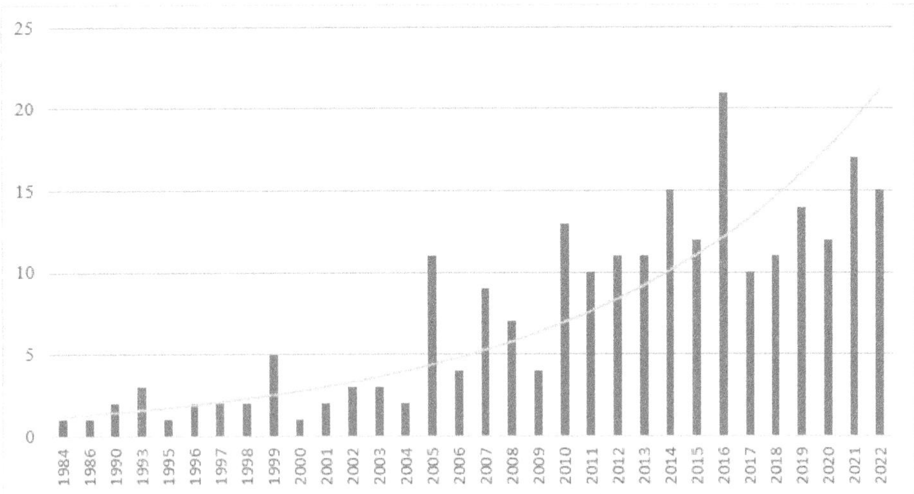

3.1. Theories

Numerous ideas have been used to analyse the ownership of SMEs in both philosophical and empirical articles. In total, 36 different theories were used in the selected literature, with 24 theoretical perspectives, each used in only one paper, while 16 studies did not apply any theory directly. The most common theoretical viewpoint, as seen in Table 2, is agency theory (34 papers), followed by stewardship theory (12 papers), Pecking order theory (10 papers), and trade-off theory (7 papers). Our results are consistent with previous analyses that illustrate the prevalence of agency theory, stewardship theory, pecking order theory, trade-off theory, institutional theory, stewardship theory, and pecking order theory (Kumar et al., 2020; Li et al., 2020). The review of the literature demonstrates frequent cases in which a single theoretical lens was applied (Ragab & Saleh, 2022). These studies generally focus on the agency problems that result from ownership separation. However, scholars should note that SMEs are significantly different compared to large firms, so the agency theory argument might not explicitly address the agency conflict that influences all business activities. For instance, family and concentration ownership are the sources of agency conflict; unlike large firms, it has been found to enhance the performance of SMEs (Caselli & Di Giuli, 2010; Chu, 2009).

We believe that the pecking order theory could provide a better explanation of the SMEs organizational behaviour than the common theoretical lenses that are applied in the literature (agency theory and Stewardship theory). Based on the agency and free cash flow hypothesis, cash holdings could generate agency problems associated with managerial discretion (Jensen & Meckling, 1976). Nevertheless, La Rocca et al. (2019) reported empirical evidence that cash holdings positively affect operating performance even in poorer institutional contexts. Burgstaller (2013) also investigated three theories, trade-off, pecking order, and agency theory, and found evidence supporting the pecking order theory in explaining the capital structure of SMEs. In line with this argument, Faulkender (2002) suggested that small firms' ownership is more varied than large firms, providing a better platform to examine the agency cost elements associated with cash holdings. The applicability of the pecking order theory and in which compatibility is enforced is important and will be explored in a later section.

Table 2. **List of the common theories in the literature**

Theories	Pre-1999	2000-2004	2005-2009	2010-2014	2015-present	Total
Agency theory	1	3	9	11	10	34
Stewardship theory			2	4	6	12
Pecking order theory		1	1	4	4	10
Trade-off theory		1	1	2	3	7
Resource-based view theory			3	1	3	7
Institutional theory			2	1	1	4
Socio-emotional wealth theory				1	3	4
Upper echelons theory			1		2	3
Behavioural theory			1		2	3
Eclectic theory			3			3
Stakeholder theory			1		1	2
Signalling theory			1	1		2
Other theories	3	3	9	3	6	24
No theory	1		3	7	5	16

Other theories include learning-by-doing theory, managerial efficiency theory, managerial hegemony theory, diffusion of innovation theory, stage theory, theory of planned behaviour, organisational theory, Jovanovic's learning theory, Gibrat's law, expense preference theory, international new venture theory, teleological theory, dialectic theory, contemporary theory, transaction cost theories, management control theory, organisational control theory, social network theory, social capital theory, free cash flow hypothesis, modern financial theory, the real options theory, and growth cycle theory.

3.1.1. Agency theory

Most studies (34/78) in our sampled literature employ agency theory as their main theoretical view. The fundamental concept of this theoretical view is that executives behave out of personal interests and, therefore, the interests of shareholders are not always protected. Often associated with the separation of ownership and control, literature explores topics such as ownership structure, various incentives to monitor management and protect the interest of shareholders (Jensen & Meckling, 1976), how corporate governance and ownership structure affect corporate performance-reflected agency issues (Abor & Biekpe, 2007; Lappalainen & Niskanen, 2013; Ragab & Saleh, 2022). Incomplete separation of ownership and control does not inherently eradicate agency issues. Specifically, agency theory helps clarify the monitoring and control functions, while various organisational aspects can be better understood with multiple theoretical grounds (Filatotchev & Boyd, 2009).

The entrenched reliance on agency theory warrants critical scrutiny, especially in light of contradictory empirical evidence and the unique characteristics of SMEs. The incongruence between agency theory and observed positive outcomes of family and concentration ownership in SMEs demands a re-evaluation of theoretical foundations. A critical stance necessitates questioning whether established theories, such as agency theory, are adequate in explaining the intricacies of SME organizational behavior. Future research must adopt a critical lens in exploring alternative theoretical frameworks that better align with the idiosyncrasies of SMEs, moving beyond traditional perspectives.

3.1.2. Pecking order theory (POT)

This theory suggests that because of unfavourable selection costs, companies have an order of choice in the use of their funding sources (Myers, 1984). The philosophy builds on asymmetric data issues between managers and outside investors. Since managers know more about the company's prospects than outside investors, managers may pass them on if external funding is necessary when facing new valuable investment opportunities. However, this theoretical perspective argues that a firm optimal capital structure varies over time depending on the needs for external funds, and small companies do not have a target debt-equity ratio (Romano et al., 2001). Lappalainen and Niskanen (2013) applied this theory to explain the financing preferences of family and non-family firms and found empirical evidence to support their argument that internal funds are preferred over external finance. Similarly, Bhaird and Lucey (2010) found that only firms with insufficient assets tend to secure business loans to finance their activities.

It should be noted that POT has been widely supported in small firms literature compared to the other theories (La Rocca et al., 2019). Romano et al. (2001) argued that the pecking order theoretical lens is particularly relevant to small businesses largely because the costs associated with external finance are higher for small businesses than they are for large firms. Furthermore, Burgstaller (2013) used three theories to explore the financial preference of SMEs, namely trade-off, pecking order, and agency theory, while the findings supported only the pecking order theory. This financing preference can explain other firms' behaviour, such as the expansion of small and medium (Zhang et al., 2012). Given that agency costs are a determinant of financial decision making including capital (or ownership) structure (Fleming et al., 2005), we believe that POT, in combination with other theories could provide a broad range of opportunities for a better understanding of the SMEs organizational behaviour, as these factors can create their own set of problems taking into account that SMEs follow different financing mechanisms as compared with larger firms.

3.1.3. Trade-off Theory

The trade-off theory implies that businesses are targeting an acceptable mix between equity and debt that maximises the gap between the gains and the expenses of debt issuance. Because of the effects of costs of financial distress, agency costs, and taxes, management needs to maintain a target debt-equity ratio (Romano et al., 2001). For example, an external source of funds like debts has the advantage of decreasing tax bill, but it increases business risk. Therefore, firms are supposed to choose the optimal debt level determined by a trade-off between the costs and benefits of borrowing (Bhaird & Lucey, 2010; Burgstaller, 2013).

3.1.4. Other theoretical perspectives

Other theories are only scarcely applied. For instance, in 3 quantitative studies, each behavioural and eclectic theory is applied. Similarly, in three research papers, the upper echelon hypothesis that discusses the relationship between top management team (TMT) features and organisational outcomes is used (see, Alayo et al., 2019; Brunninge et al., 2007; Dolz et al., 2019). In seven studies, the resource-based view hypothesis is used to describe an organisational dependency on external resources for their operations. According to this theory, access to vital resources must be developed by companies (Ahinful et al., 2021; Shapiro et al., 2015). Stakeholder theory, which normatively addresses how governance and ownership should be designed to represent various stakeholders' interests, is discussed in two research articles (Abor & Biekpe, 2007; Shapiro et al., 2015). Socio-emotional wealth theory is discussed in four studies. Colombo et al. (2014) applied this perspective to discuss the effect of family ownership on the positive correlation between employment changes and sales changes.

Our result suggests that new and other existing behavioural and cultural theories could lead future research in the right direction and address many complex issues of the ownership structure of SMEs. The behavioural theory was used by De Massis et al. (2015) to complement the agency argument in explaining the family ownership and family involvement influence upon TMT and firm performance, thus providing a more fine-grained understanding of the consequences of family involvement. However, behavioural and cultural aspects have largely been ignored by the research papers reviewed in this study. This may be because studies in this field have looked at ownership issues from a governance perspective, not the economic environment. Hence, we suggest future scholars consider the behavioural and cultural aspects when studying ownership of SMEs. Future scholars can also draw on a new theoretical lens to study this topic of interest (Chen et al., 2014). Finally, further work could focus more on the pecking order theory, which could provide a better explanation of the SMEs organizational behaviour than the common theoretical lenses that are applied in the literature (agency theory and Stewardship theory).

3.2. Research Methods Used

The sampled literature has been divided into five groups based on their methodology: quantitative research, qualitative research, mixed-method research, reviews, and non-empirical research. Table 3 shows that the field grew quickly in the early 2000s, and most of these studies are quantitative. Of 78 studies in our sample, 69 are quantitative studies, and a large number of these studies employ archival data, while others use survey data. The quantitative studies have covered several themes, including the performance of SMEs, financial policy (Burgstaller, 2013; Gebru, 2009), and internationalisation (Alayo et al., 2019; Eberhard & Craig, 2013) that will be discussed in the thematical section later. In our sampled literature, three studies are non-empirical and discuss general issues related to SMEs. The long-term persistence of family entrepreneurship in capital-intensive sectors in Europe was discussed by Pérez (2007).

One mixed process article only analyses interview data based on the energy efficiency of SMEs in China, both quantitatively and qualitatively (Kostka et al., 2013). Kostka et al. (2013) found that the position of family ownership systems, inadequate implementation of government regulations, the absence of government funding, and a shortage of skilled labour are the obstacles to energy-saving activities. Furthermore, two qualitative research papers have been identified. Based on three in-depth case studies, Aragón-Amonarriz et al. (2019) addressed how family ownership is transferred across generations. Moreover, there are three prior literature review articles providing insight into topics such as benefits and costs for lenders and borrowers (Duqi et al., 2018), determinants of franchising success (Nijmeijer et al., 2014), and internationalisation process (Morais & Ferreira, 2020). It should be noted that the lack of qualitative mixed-method research on the ownership structure of SMEs presents a major gap that provides academicians and researchers with a choice for exploring the issues in future (Bhaird & Lucey, 2010). These research methods could provide in-depth knowledge concerning certain topics, enable the collection of precise information that could not be measured using other sources of data, and add more explanation to the qualitative findings.

Table 3. Research method of the literature

Research methods	Pre-1999	2000-2004	2005-2009	2010-2014	2015-present	Total
Quantitative	4	3	17	23	22	69
Review				1	2	3
Qualitative				1	1	2
Non-empirical			3			3
Mixed method				1		1

3.3. Geographical Distribution

The findings of this study indicate that prior studies on the ownership of SMEs focused on the developed market. Table 4 indicates that of 73 empirical studies, 10 empirical research articles were based on evidence from Italy, Spain (8 articles), China (7 studies), Australia (5 studies), and The USA (5 studies). Moreover, only two research papers utilise evidence from multiple country, and there is a quality paucity. For instance, the rare cross-country papers do not have an adequate sample. Vos et al. (2007) investigated the financial behaviour of small businesses using a sample from the USA and the UK. Jinjarak and Wignaraja (2016) addressed the topic of financial constraint by utilising data from six countries: Chile, Israel, Korea, Mexico, Thailand, and Turkey. Also, Chandra et al. (2020) argued that different market conditions impact SMEs' abilities to achieve performance goals associated with internationalization. Surprisingly, few studies explore SMEs' ownership structure from developing markets or compare countries using cross-country samples (Abor

& Biekpe, 2007; Chen et al., 2014; D'Angelo et al., 2016; Roberts & Muralidharan, 2022). Several scholars (i.e., Colombo et al., 2014; De Cleyn & Braet, 2012) have suggested that more work is needed on less investigated markets to advance the knowledge on the ownership structure of SMEs in more than one market.

Table 4. Geographic distribution of studies on ownership structure of SMEs

Source title	Pre-1999	2000-2004	2005-2009	2010-2014	2015-present	Total
Italy				5	5	10
Spanish			3	2	3	8
China				3	4	7
Australia		2	2	1		5
United States	1		1	2	1	5
Sweden			2	1	1	4
Taiwan			1	2		3
Europe			1	1	1	3
Finland				3		3
The UK			2	1		3
Belgian	1			1		2
Austria					2	2
Cross-country			1		1	2
Other countries	2	1	5	3	5	16

Other countries include France, Ghana, Greece, Ireland, Japan, Kosovar, Malaysia, Mexico, Norway, Pakistan, Romania, Slovakia, Ethiopia, Canada, and Sri Lanka.

3.4. Modelling

Empirical studies on the ownership of the SMEs utilised survey samples include observations from at least 68 SMEs (Randøy & Goel, 2003) with a maximum of 43,728 firms (Deng et al., 2013). Table 5 provides a summary of the research modelling of prior empirical studies based on the themes addressed. It reveals that 12 of 69 quantitative research papers use moderating variables, and only one paper uses mediating variables. Family involvement and control is the most common moderating variable employ in these studies, indicating that the interaction of ownership structure with other organizational aspects should be considered to better evaluates the organizational outcomes like innovation, internationalization, performance, financial distress, and succession intention. Other studies used firm size (Fang et al., 2016), external managers (D'Angelo et al., 2016), and founder CEO (Yang et al., 2020). This means ownership cannot be separated from other organizational aspects that collectively influence SME outcomes.

One study has taken the analysis a step further and employed the mediating effect conducted by Zhang et al. (2012) to investigate the mediating impact of financial preferences on the relationship between firm ownership and business expansion. Indeed, the indirect relationship of ownership on firm outcomes like performance and internationalization has been investigated in several studies that considered large listed firms. This approach could be a promising technique for solving the inconsistency of prior studies' findings. Thus, it is possible to move forward in expanding the base of research through the mediating approach, as Ghobadian and O'Regan (2006) suggested that cultural factors are critical to the performance of SMEs. Also, this relationship can be tested through various dimensions such as sustainability, compliance with social responsibility, regulations, legislation, and others (Khatib, 2024a, 2024b, 2024d).

Furthermore, our analysis suggests that, while the majority of empirical studies focused on the linear relationship, a few papers used non-linear models to test non-monotonic relationships. Belghitar and Khan (2013) investigated the non-linear (U-shape) relationship between executive ownership and cash holdings. De Massis et al. (2013) found that family ownership dispersion has a non-linear effect on the performance of small-to-medium-size family firms. Also, Zhang et al. (2012) addressed the non-linear relationship between family ownership and the annual expansion rate. An additional examination may be needed to reveal further the inverted-U curve or indirect relationship relationships (Zhang et al., 2012).

The sampled literature employs a wide range of regression techniques, including OLS, probit, logit, 2SLS, GMM, and structural equations. Three quantitative studies use the structural equation model (SEM) (Alayo et al., 2019; Sanhokwe, 2022). On the other hand, SEM analysis has not been covered extensively, and this leaves a large analytical gap for future research. The properties of SEMs are expected to help researchers gain a more detailed understanding of the dynamic nature of the ownership of SMEs by investigating highly complex models. Similarly, in our study literature, only two studies used GMM (Huang et al., 2016; Martín-Ugedo & Minguez-Vera, 2014). This estimator is recommended for controlling for methodological issues such as serial autocorrelation and endogeneity (Khatib, 2024c). Consistent with our findings, academics have primarily used multiple regression to test hypotheses when conducting empirical studies. Other advanced methods that control for methodological issues, such as GMM and SEM, which are mostly absent in the current articles, are potential future research avenues.

Table 5. Analysis of methods in the empirical studies

Concepts under study	No. of papers	With mediator	With moderator	Avg. No. of hypotheses	Avg. No. of explanatory variables	Avg. No. of regression models	Avg. No. of sample
Performance	15	0	3	4.91	3.86	4.70	444.6
Financial policy	14	0	0	7.20	6.17	5.10	3216.5
Internationalization	8	0	4	4	2.13	3.75	904.71
Innovation	6	0	1	5.33	5	5	7682.5
Growth	5	1	0	6.8	6.40	6.25	6435
Others	21	0	4	4.9	3.31	4.07	1186.1

3.5. Concepts Under Study

Employing the same conditions in the earlier subsection, we recap the ideas considered in our sampled literature and present the associated results. All acknowledged concepts are classified into six categories: firm performance, financial policy, internationalisation, growth, innovation, and others (see Table 5). We incorporate a research article in the category if it explicitly addresses the theme of the group. For example, all research papers that address firm performance were included in the category of firm performance. The literature on these themes has been reviewed based on the pecking order theory complemented with other theoretical arguments. As shown in figure 3, the majority of research focuses on concepts related to firm performance, financial policy, and internationalization. In contrast, less attention is given to concepts related to growth and innovation. This may indicate that there is still room for further research in these areas. Interestingly, the figure also suggests that little attention is given to the external environment of the companies, such as the legal, economic, political, and social environment. This may be a significant research gap as these external factors may indirectly influence the various outcomes of SMEs. For example, the economic environment may impact the financial performance of an SME, while the political environment may impact its ability to expand internationally. Therefore, future research should consider external factors' role in understanding SMEs' outcomes.

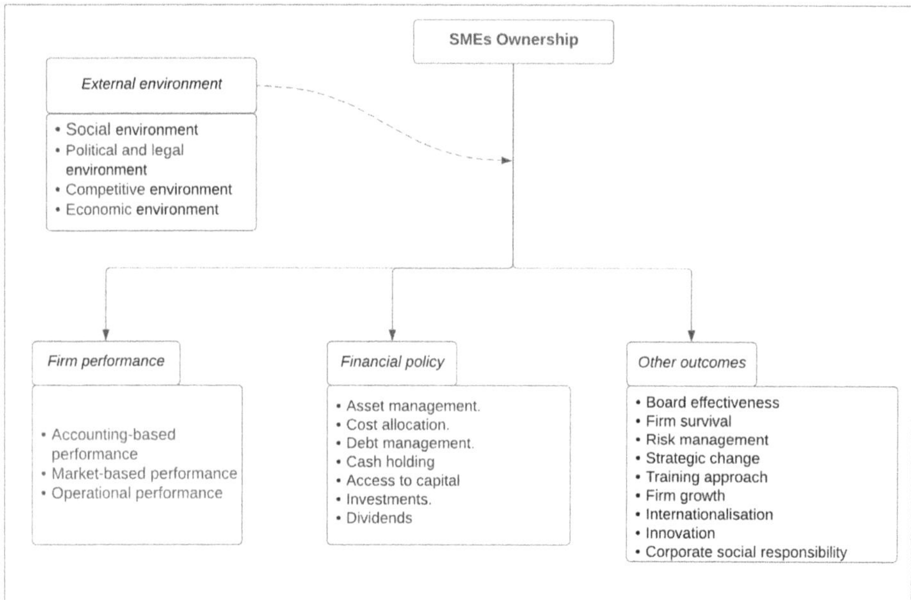

3.5.1. Financial performance

Firm financial performance is the most discussed theme in relation to the ownership structure of SMEs (15 studies). Based on various theoretical grounds, the literature has mixed findings about the relationship between ownership structure and SMEs performance. Family ownership, for instance, has been commonly found to positively impact performance. Yet, De Massis et al. (2015) and Ceptureanu et al. (2017) found that performance has an inverted U-shaped relationship with family ownership. Also, Singh and Rastogi (2022a) reported an insignificant association between financial performance ownership concentration. SMEs' strategies are significantly different from large firms, where small firms are highly concentrated and do not have a targeted capital structure compared to large firms. Also, family ownership has an inverse association with large firm performance (Klein et al., 2005). Whereas family ownership of a small firm is found to enhance its performance (Abor & Biekpe, 2007; Caselli & Di Giuli, 2010). Therefore, researchers might need to consider different theoretical lenses other than agency theory (the most common one in the literature) when explaining the association between ownership structure and firm performance. Based on the agency argument, cash holdings could generate agency problems associated with managerial discretion. Nevertheless, cash holdings positively affected small firms' operating performance even in poorer institutional contexts.

According to the pecking order theory, internal funds are preferred over external finance, and this theory has been commonly supported by many SMEs studies (i.e., Burgstaller, 2013; Gebru, 2009; La Rocca et al., 2019; Lappalainen & Niskanen, 2013). Meanwhile, larger firms have a target debt-equity ratio to achieve optimal performance (Romano et al., 2001). Lappalainen and Niskanen (2013) applied this theory to explain family and non-family firms' financing preferences and found empirical evidence supporting their argument that internal funds are preferred over external finance. Although this association is too complex to be explained by a single theory, studies could consider pecking order theory complemented by other theoretical grounds to better understand the nature of the ownership and performance association. In line with this argument, Ghobadian and O'Regan (2006) found that independent companies have better organisational outcomes but not all dimensions of performance.

The question that remained unanswered is whether ownership change affects SMEs' performance. The ownership of small firms is highly family-concentrated, and such ownership structure achieves high performance if it relies on internal funds (in line with pecking order theory). Evaluating the interrelation between ownership change and capital structure might help better explain this association's puzzle with regard to the financial preference change.

However, due to the inconsistent findings of prior literature, a limited number of studies have considered a complex theoretical framework in investigating this association (Abor & Biekpe, 2007; Massis et al., 2015). In the sampled literature, only four studies exploring financial performance consider firm-level factors' moderating role on organisational outcomes. These studies have used family involvement, while Chu (2011) examined the moderating impact of the firm size. Also, Randøy and Goel (2003) took the research a step further and provided empirical evidence that family leadership moderates the relationship between ownership structure and firm performance in Norway. Opposing the agency argument, Chu (2011) reported that a positive association is strong particularly when family members serve as CEOs, top managers, chairpersons, or directors of the firms; however, the association becomes weak when family members are not involved in firm management or control. It is worth mentioning that few studies have empirically explored the interaction between governance and ownership attributes such as family involvement and board characteristics (Chu, 2011; De Massis et al., 2013).

3.5.2. Firm growth

For non-financial performance, growth, innovation, and internationalisation are crucial outcomes of the ownership of SMEs (see, Fernández & Nieto, 2006; Hamelin, 2013; Lee & Ging, 2007; Sciascia et al., 2015; Zhang et al., 2012). Firm growth was explored in five research papers. These studies used employee growth as the single primary measure of business expansion (Bjuggren et al., 2013; Krasniqi & Mustafa, 2016; Variyam & Kraybill, 1994; Zhang et al., 2012). Although most of the prior work results are consistent, some studies reported a non- monotonic influence of ownership structure on growth (Hamelin, 2013). Apart from ownership structure, SMEs are smaller in scale, with correspondingly fewer resources, and to achieve a high growth rate; they might need an external source of finance. Small- and medium-sized family businesses' preference for internal financing usually negatively influences growth and expansion. Hence, the influence of ownership on small firms' growth should be evaluated indirectly, considering the policy changes within firms, including financial policy and preference. Although family resources may play a critical role during the very early stages of the business, external sources become increasingly important as the business grows and matures. If these small businesses cannot use external funds well, their growth and expansion will be restricted.

Also, further research may be required to further uncover the inverted-U curve or the indirect relationships (Zhang et al., 2012) by focusing on the explanatory factors behind conservative growth behaviour (Hamelin, 2013) and address methodological issues like endogeneity (Krasniqi & Mustafa, 2016).

3.5.3. Innovation

Innovation is discussed in six studies and is measured by new product sales, questionnaire and survey items (Lee & Ging, 2007), or R&D intensity. The findings of prior studies are inconclusive. Innovation has been found to be not determined by the ownership structure of SMEs, while Sciascia et al. (2015) and Xiang et al. (2019) concluded that it is inversely influenced by family ownership. Moreover, Lee and Ging (2007) focused on manufacturing firms and reported that public limited companies are less likely to innovate compared to sole-proprietorship medium-sized firms. In comparison, Shapiro et al. (2015) suggested that the impact depends on the measure of innovation.

Although the existing studies have significantly enhanced our understanding of the ownership and innovation topic of SMEs (Bagno et al., 2017; Cho et al., 2016; Guo et al., 2017; Holgersson, 2013; Huber et al., 2020; Marcelino Sádaba et al., 2016; Schiederig et al., 2012; Teirlinck, 2018; Zhang & Walton, 2017), there is a need for more work to examine the time-series effects of ownership structure on innovation (Xiang et al., 2019), use a larger sample, and cover more sectors in different countries. These studies need to count for the financing preferences of SMEs in comparison to large firms. Deng et al. (2013) reported that the antecedents of innovation and the innovation level are significantly moderated by firm characterises like ownership structure.

3.5.4. Internationalisation

Internationalisation is another organisational outcome investigated in eight studies and captured primarily by export sales and the number of foreign countries in which firms are operating. The findings of studies on the internationalisation of SMEs are mixed, pointing to the need for more work on ownership and internationalisation association (D'Angelo et al., 2016). An inverse association between family ownership and internationalisation has been reported by Yang et al. (2020). Unlike large firms, this could be a result of the stagnation strategies and financial preferences of family ownership (Zhang et al., 2012). Similarly, management with more family involvement was found to exert an inverse impact on export propensity (Cerrato & Piva, 2012). However, a study conducted by Chen et al. (2014) reported that internationalisation is enhanced by family shareholders as well as its interaction with institutional shareholders. Furthermore, a recent study conducted by Yang et al. (2020) reported that each family succession intention and the presence of founder CEOs interaction with ownership structure significantly explain the internationalisation level of small firms. Also, as explained earlier, the financial preferences of SMEs could be a significant factor that needs to be considered in future research in evaluating the complex nature of ownership and internationalisation correlation.

Also, in-depth work using longitudinal context through a panel-data analysis of ownership structure would be necessary. Future research might also incorporate other dimensions of internationalisation, such as the use of alliances and foreign direct investments, external borrowing and managers recruited from countries that are targets for internationalisation (Cerrato & Piva, 2012; D'Angelo et al., 2016).

3.5.5. Financial policy

In our sampled literature, 14 research papers have explored different financial policies in relation to the ownership structure of SMEs. Romano et al. (2001), Bhaird and Lucey (2010), Huang et al. (2016), and Burgstaller (2013) have investigated the capital structure of SMEs and concluded inconclusive results. For example, Romano et al. (2001) found that firm size, family control, business planning, and business objectives are significantly associated with debt, while the capital and retained profits are likely to be higher in family businesses, that planning to achieve growth through an increase in sales, but less is likely for family businesses in the manufacturing sector and lifestyle firms. On the other hand, Bhaird and Lucey (2010) found that the influence of age, size, ownership structure, and provision of collateral is similar across industry sectors. Belghitar and Khan (2013) concentrated on the cash holding of SMEs and concluded that cash holdings are high in firms with greater cash flow volatility and institutional investors, whereas leveraged and dividend-paying SMEs with non-executive owners keep less cash. They also found that ownership structure is substantial only in clarifying the cash holdings for firms with notable growth investment opportunities.

Additionally, various studies address the link between ownership structure and financial constraints, agency costs, financial sophistication, and financial preferences. Niskanen and Niskanen (2010) suggested that an increase in managerial ownership decreases loan availability, while an increase in managerial ownership initially increases interest rates; the effect is reversed at higher levels of ownership.

3.5.6. Metaverse

The metaverse presents a significant opportunity for SMEs to build sustainable business models that align with global sustainability goals. By integrating metaverse technologies, SMEs can create virtual supply chains that reduce the need for physical resources, thereby minimizing environmental impact. For example, virtual product design and testing in the metaverse can significantly cut down on material waste and energy consumption. Additionally, the use of blockchain-based solutions within the metaverse can enhance transparency and traceability across supply chains, ensuring that sustainable practices are adhered to at every stage of production and distribution. Moreover, the decentralized nature of the metaverse allows SMEs to explore new business models that prioritize sustainability. For instance, SMEs can create decentralized marketplaces where products are traded in a transparent and secure environment, reducing the carbon footprint associated with traditional logistics and transportation. These innovative approaches not only support sustainable practices but also position SMEs as leaders in the shift toward a more sustainable and digital economy.

The metaverse offers SMEs unprecedented opportunities to enhance customer engagement through immersive and interactive experiences that also promote sustainability. By creating virtual storefronts, product showcases, and events within the metaverse, SMEs can engage customers in a more personalized and dynamic way, leading to stronger brand loyalty and increased sales. These virtual environments allow customers to experience products and services in a simulated setting, reducing the need for physical samples and in-person visits, which can lower the environmental impact of marketing and sales activities. Furthermore, the metaverse enables SMEs to foster a sense of community and shared values among their customers. For instance, SMEs can create virtual spaces where customers can learn about the company's sustainability initiatives, participate in discussions, and even contribute ideas for new sustainable products or services. This level of engagement not only strengthens customer relationships but also encourages a more sustainable consumer culture, where customers are more informed and involved in making environmentally conscious decisions.

As metaverse technologies continue to evolve, their potential impact on SMEs and sustainability is expected to grow. One of the key future trends is the integration of artificial intelligence (AI) and machine learning within the metaverse, enabling SMEs to automate and optimize their operations in ways that further reduce environmental impact. For example, AI-driven analytics can help SMEs identify inefficiencies in their virtual supply chains and suggest improvements that enhance sustainability. Another emerging trend is the development of virtual reality (VR) and augmented reality (AR) technologies within the metaverse, which can provide even more immersive and realistic experiences for customers. These advancements will allow SMEs to offer virtual tours of their sustainable manufacturing processes, showcase the environmental benefits of their products, and create engaging educational content that promotes sustainability. Policy recommendations for fostering sustainability within the metaverse should focus on encouraging the adoption of green technologies and practices by SMEs. Governments and industry bodies can support this by providing incentives for SMEs to invest in sustainable metaverse solutions, such as tax breaks or grants for the development of virtual supply chains or blockchain-based sustainability initiatives. Additionally, regulatory frameworks should be established to ensure that metaverse technologies are developed and used in ways that prioritize environmental responsibility, helping to guide SMEs toward a more sustainable and prosperous future.

4. CONCLUSION

This review highlights the growing interest in the ownership structures of small and medium enterprises, reflecting their critical role in global economies. Despite the increase in research, there remains a need for comprehensive reviews to summarize the diverse approaches and identify gaps in this field. By conducting a systematic literature review and bibliometric analysis of 255 research articles, we have provided insights into the theoretical and empirical foundations of SME ownership structures. Our analysis reveals the dominance of agency theory, though other lenses like stewardship, pecking order, and trade-off theories offer valuable perspectives, especially given the unique characteristics of SMEs. Our study contributes to the literature by offering a detailed examination of the theories and methodologies used in understanding SME ownership, identifying six key research clusters, and suggesting avenues for future research. This work serves as a valuable resource for academics, policymakers, and practitioners, enhancing the understanding of SME ownership dynamics and guiding future investigations in this evolving field.

REFERENCE

Abor, J., & Biekpe, N. (2007). Corporate governance, ownership structure and performance of SMEs in Ghana: Implications for financing opportunities. *Corporate Governance (Bradford)*, 7(3), 288–300. DOI: 10.1108/14720700710756562

Ahinful, G. S., Boakye, J. D., & Osei Bempah, N. D. (2021). Determinants of SMEs' financial performance: Evidence from an emerging economy. *Journal of Small Business and Entrepreneurship*, 0(0), 1–24. DOI: 10.1080/08276331.2021.1885247

Al Amosh, H., & Khatib, S. F. A. (2021). Corporate governance and voluntary disclosure of sustainability performance: The case of Jordan. *SN Business & Economics*, 1(12), 165. DOI: 10.1007/s43546-021-00167-1

Alayo, M., Maseda, A., Iturralde, T., & Arzubiaga, U. (2019). Internationalization and entrepreneurial orientation of family SMEs: The influence of the family character. *International Business Review*, 28(1), 48–59. DOI: 10.1016/j.ibusrev.2018.06.003

Aragón-Amonarriz, C., Arredondo, A. M., & Iturrioz-Landart, C. (2019). How Can Responsible Family Ownership be Sustained Across Generations? A Family Social Capital Approach. *Journal of Business Ethics*, 159(1), 161–185. DOI: 10.1007/s10551-017-3728-7

Beck, T., Demirgüç-Kunt, A., & Pería, M. S. M. (2011). Bank Financing for SMEs: Evidence Across Countries and Bank Ownership Types. *Journal of Financial Services Research*, 39(1–2), 35–54. DOI: 10.1007/s10693-010-0085-4

Belghitar, Y., & Khan, J. (2013). Governance mechanisms, investment opportunity set and SMEs cash holdings. *Small Business Economics*, 40(1), 59–72. DOI: 10.1007/s11187-011-9366-z

Bhaird, C. (2010). Determinants of capital structure in Irish SMEs. *Small Business Economics*, 35(3), 357–375. DOI: 10.1007/s11187-008-9162-6

Bjuggren, C. M., Daunfeldt, S. O., & Johansson, D. (2013). High-growth firms and family ownership. *Journal of Small Business and Entrepreneurship*, 26(4), 365–385. DOI: 10.1080/08276331.2013.821765

Block, J., Fisch, C., & Rehan, F. (2019). Religion and entrepreneurship: a map of the field and a bibliometric analysis. In *Management Review Quarterly* (Issue 0123456789). Springer International Publishing. DOI: 10.1007/s11301-019-00177-2

Borocki, J., Radišić, M., Sroka, W., Grėblikaitė, J., & Androniceanu, A. (2019). Methodology for strategic posture determination of SMEs. *The Engineering Economist*, 30(3), 265–277. DOI: 10.5755/j01.ee.30.3.21966

Boyd, B. K., & Solarino, A. M. (2016). Ownership of Corporations: A Review, Synthesis, and Research Agenda. *Journal of Management*, 42(5), 1282–1314. DOI: 10.1177/0149206316633746

Brunninge, O., Nordqvist, M., & Wiklund, J. (2007). Corporate governance and strategic change in SMEs: The effects of ownership, board composition and top management teams. *Small Business Economics*, 29(3), 295–308. DOI: 10.1007/s11187-006-9021-2

Burgstaller, W., & Wagner, E. (2013). How do family ownership and founder management affect capital structure decisions and adjustment of SMEs. *The Journal of Risk Finance*, 16(1), 73–101. https://doi.org/http://dx.doi.org/10.1108/MRR-09-2015-0216. DOI: 10.1108/JRF-06-2014-0091

Caselli, S., & Di Giuli, A. (2010). Does the CFO matter in family firms? Evidence from Italy. In *European Journal of Finance* (Vol. 16, Issue 5). DOI: 10.1080/13518470903211657

Ceptureanu, S. I., Ceptureanu, E. G., & Marin, I. (2017). Assessing the Role of Strategic Choice on Organizational Performance by Jacquemin–Berry Entropy Index. *Entropy (Basel, Switzerland)*, 19(9), 448. DOI: 10.3390/e19090448

Cerrato, D., & Piva, M. (2012). The internationalization of small and medium-sized enterprises: The effect of family management, human capital and foreign ownership. *The Journal of Management and Governance*, 16(4), 617–644. DOI: 10.1007/s10997-010-9166-x

Chandra, A., Paul, J., & Chavan, M. (2020). Internationalization barriers of SMEs from developing countries: A review and research agenda. *International Journal of Entrepreneurial Behaviour & Research*, 26(6), 1281–1310. DOI: 10.1108/IJEBR-03-2020-0167

Chen, H. L., Hsu, W. T., & Chang, C. Y. (2014). Family ownership, institutional ownership, and internationalization of SMEs. *Journal of Small Business Management*, 52(4), 771–789. DOI: 10.1111/jsbm.12031

Chu, W. (2009). The influence of family ownership on SME performance: Evidence from public firms in Taiwan. *Small Business Economics*, 33(3), 353–373. DOI: 10.1007/s11187-009-9178-6

Chu, W. (2011). Family ownership and firm performance: Influence of family management, family control, and firm size. *Asia Pacific Journal of Management*, 28(4), 833–851. DOI: 10.1007/s10490-009-9180-1

Colombo, M. G., De Massis, A., Piva, E., Rossi-Lamastra, C., & Wright, M. (2014). Sales and employment changes in entrepreneurial ventures with family ownership: Empirical evidence from high-tech industries. *Journal of Small Business Management*, 52(2), 226–245. DOI: 10.1111/jsbm.12100

D'Angelo, A., Majocchi, A., & Buck, T. (2016). External managers, family ownership and the scope of SME internationalization. *Journal of World Business*, 51(4), 534–547. DOI: 10.1016/j.jwb.2016.01.004

Da Cruz, A. F., Kimura, H., & Sobreiro, V. A. (2019). What Do We Know About Corporate Cash Holdings? A Systematic Analysis. *Journal of Corporate Accounting & Finance*, 30(1), 77–143. DOI: 10.1002/jcaf.22368

Dao, T. N., Le, H. T. T., Chu, P. T. M., Pham, N. H., Luong, T. T. D., & Tran, D. T. (2021). Determinants of the Competitiveness of Women-Owned Small- and Medium-Sized Enterprises: An Empirical Study from Vietnam. *Journal of Asian Finance Economics and Business*, 8(12), 345–352. DOI: 10.13106/jafeb.2021.vol8.no12.0345

De Cleyn, S. H., & Braet, J. (2012). Do board composition and investor type influence innovativeness in SMEs? *The International Entrepreneurship and Management Journal*, 8(3), 285–308. DOI: 10.1007/s11365-010-0168-6

De Massis, A., Kotlar, J., Campopiano, G., & Cassia, L. (2013). Dispersion of family ownership and the performance of small-to-medium size private family firms. *Journal of Family Business Strategy*, 4(3), 166–175. DOI: 10.1016/j.jfbs.2013.05.001

De Massis, A., Kotlar, J., Campopiano, G., & Cassia, L. (2015). The Impact of Family Involvement on SMEs' Performance: Theory and Evidence. *Journal of Small Business Management*, 53(4), 924–948. DOI: 10.1111/jsbm.12093

Deng, Z., Hofman, P. S., & Newman, A. (2013). Ownership concentration and product innovation in Chinese private SMEs. *Asia Pacific Journal of Management*, 30(3), 717–734. DOI: 10.1007/s10490-012-9301-0

Denis, D. (1999). Ownership and board structures in publicly traded corporations. *Journal of Financial Economics*, 52(2), 187–223. DOI: 10.1016/S0304-405X(99)00008-2

Doan, A. T., Le, A. T., & Tran, Q. (2020). Economic uncertainty, ownership structure and small and medium enterprises performance. *Australian Economic Papers*, 59(2), 102–137. DOI: 10.1111/1467-8454.12174

Dolz, C., Iborra, M., & Safón, V. (2019). Improving the likelihood of SME survival during financial and economic crises: The importance of TMTs and family ownership for ambidexterity. *Business Research Quarterly*, 22(2), 119–136. DOI: 10.1016/j.brq.2018.09.004

Duqi, A., Tomaselli, A., & Torluccio, G. (2018). Is Relationship Lending Still a Mixed Blessing? a Review of Advantages and Disadvantages for Lenders and Borrowers. In *Journal of Economic Surveys* (Vol. 32, Issue 5). DOI: 10.1111/joes.12251

Eberhard, M., & Craig, J. (2013). The evolving role of organisational and personal networks in international market venturing. *Journal of World Business*, 48(3), 385–397. DOI: 10.1016/j.jwb.2012.07.022

Fang, H., Randolph, R. V. D. G., Memili, E., & Chrisman, J. J. (2016). Does Size Matter? The Moderating Effects of Firm Size on the Employment of Nonfamily Managers in Privately Held Family SMEs. *Entrepreneurship Theory and Practice*, 40(5), 1017–1039. DOI: 10.1111/etap.12156

Faulkender, M. W. (2002). Cash Holdings Among Small Businesses. SSRN *Electronic Journal*. DOI: 10.2139/ssrn.305179

Fernández, Z., & Nieto, M. J. (2006). Impact of ownership on the international involvement of SMEs. *Journal of International Business Studies*, 37(3), 340–351. DOI: 10.1057/palgrave.jibs.8400196

Filatotchev, I., & Boyd, B. K. (2009). Taking stock of corporate governance research while looking to the future: Guest editorial. *Corporate Governance*, 17(3), 257–265. DOI: 10.1111/j.1467-8683.2009.00748.x

Gebru, G. H. (2009). Financing preferences of micro and small enterprise owners in Tigray: Does POH hold? *Journal of Small Business and Enterprise Development*, 16(2), 322–334. DOI: 10.1108/14626000910956083

Geeraerts, G. (1984). The Effect of Ownership on the Organization Structure in Small Firms. *Administrative Science Quarterly*, 29(2), 232. DOI: 10.2307/2393175

George, G., Wiklund, J., & Zahra, S. A. (2005). Ownership and the internationalization of small firms. *Journal of Management*, 31(2), 210–233. DOI: 10.1177/0149206304271760

Ghobadian, A., & O'Regan, N. (2006). The impact of ownership on small firm behaviour and performance. *International Small Business Journal*, 24(6), 555–586. DOI: 10.1177/0266242606069267

Hamelin, A. (2013). Influence of family ownership on small business growth. Evidence from French SMEs. *Small Business Economics*, 41(3), 563–579. DOI: 10.1007/s11187-012-9452-x

Hazaea, S. A., Zhu, J., Khatib, S. F. A., & Elamer, A. A. (2023). Mapping the literature of internal auditing in Europe: A systematic review and agenda for future research. *Meditari Accountancy Research*, 31(6), 1675–1706. DOI: 10.1108/MEDAR-01-2022-1584

Huang, W., Boateng, A., & Newman, A. (2016). Capital structure of Chinese listed SMEs: An agency theory perspective. *Small Business Economics*, 47(2), 535–550. DOI: 10.1007/s11187-016-9729-6

Jensen, M. C., & Meckling, W. H. (1976). Theory of the firm: Managerial behavior, agency costs and ownership structure. *Journal of Financial Economics*, 3(4), 305–360. DOI: 10.1016/0304-405X(76)90026-X

Jinjarak, Y., & Wignaraja, G. (2016). An Empirical Assessment of the Export-Financial Constraint Relationship: How Different are Small and Medium Enterprises? *World Development*, 79, 152–163. DOI: 10.1016/j.worlddev.2015.11.012

Khatib, S. F. A. (2024a). Sustainability Assurance and Corporate Environmental Accountability. *Social and Environmental Accountability Journal*, 1–2(2), 176–177. Advance online publication. DOI: 10.1080/0969160X.2024.2336721

Khatib, S. F. A. (2024b). Corrupt practice and sustainability reporting: Lifecycle perspective. *Business Strategy & Development*, 7(2), e396. Advance online publication. DOI: 10.1002/bsd2.396

Khatib, S. F. A. (2024c). An assessment of methods to deal with endogeneity in corporate governance and reporting research. *Corporate Governance: The International Journal of Business in Society*. DOI: 10.1108/CG-12-2023-0507

Khatib, S. F. A. (2024d). The role of share repurchases for firms' social and environmental sustainability. *Social and Environmental Accountability Journal*, 44(1), 82–84. DOI: 10.1080/0969160X.2023.2281904

Khatib, S. F. A., Abdullah, D. F., Al Amosh, H., Bazhair, A. H., & Kabara, A. S. (2022). Shariah auditing: Analyzing the past to prepare for the future. *Journal of Islamic Accounting and Business Research*, 13(5), 791–818. DOI: 10.1108/JIABR-11-2021-0291

Khatib, S. F. A., Abdullah, D. F., Elamer, A. A., & Abueid, R. (2021). Nudging toward diversity in the boardroom: A systematic literature review of board diversity of financial institutions. *Business Strategy and the Environment*, 30(2), 985–1002. DOI: 10.1002/bse.2665

Klein, P., Shapiro, D., & Young, J. (2005). Corporate governance, family ownership and firm value: The Canadian evidence. *Corporate Governance*, 13(6), 769–784. DOI: 10.1111/j.1467-8683.2005.00469.x

Kostka, G., Moslener, U., & Andreas, J. (2013). Barriers to increasing energy efficiency: Evidence from small-and medium-sized enterprises in China. *Journal of Cleaner Production*, 57, 59–68. DOI: 10.1016/j.jclepro.2013.06.025

Krasniqi, B. A., & Mustafa, M. (2016). Small firm growth in a post-conflict environment: The role of human capital, institutional quality, and managerial capacities. *The International Entrepreneurship and Management Journal*, 12(4), 1165–1207. DOI: 10.1007/s11365-016-0384-9

Kumar, S., Sureka, R., & Colombage, S. (2020). Capital structure of SMEs: a systematic literature review and bibliometric analysis. In *Management Review Quarterly* (Vol. 70, Issue 4). Springer International Publishing. DOI: 10.1007/s11301-019-00175-4

La Rocca, M., Staglianò, R., La Rocca, T., Cariola, A., & Skatova, E. (2019). Cash holdings and SME performance in Europe: The role of firm-specific and macroeconomic moderators. *Small Business Economics*, 53(4), 1051–1078. DOI: 10.1007/s11187-018-0100-y

Lappalainen, J., & Niskanen, M. (2012). Financial performance of SMEs: Impact of ownership structure and board composition. *Management Research Review*, 35(11), 1088–1108. DOI: 10.1108/01409171211276954

Lappalainen, J., & Niskanen, M. (2013). Behavior and attitudes of small family firms towards different funding sources. *Journal of Small Business and Entrepreneurship*, 26(6), 579–599. DOI: 10.1080/08276331.2014.892309

Lee, C., & Ging, L. C. (2007). SME innovation in the Malaysian manufacturing sector. *Economic Bulletin*, 12(30).

Li, H., Terjesen, S., & Umans, T. (2020). Corporate governance in entrepreneurial firms: A systematic review and research agenda. *Small Business Economics*, 54(1), 43–74. DOI: 10.1007/s11187-018-0118-1

Machold, S., Huse, M., Minichilli, A., & Nordqvist, M. (2011). Board Leadership and Strategy Involvement in Small Firms: A Team Production Approach. *Corporate Governance*, 19(4), 368–383. DOI: 10.1111/j.1467-8683.2011.00852.x

Mak, Y., & Li, Y. (2001). Determinants of corporate ownership and board structure: Evidence from Singapore. *Journal of Corporate Finance*, 7(3), 235–256. DOI: 10.1016/S0929-1199(01)00021-9

Martín-Ugedo, J. F., & Minguez-Vera, A. (2014). Firm Performance and Women on the Board: Evidence from Spanish Small and Medium-Sized Enterprises. *Feminist Economics*, 20(3), 136–162. DOI: 10.1080/13545701.2014.895404

Morais, F., & Ferreira, J. J. (2020). SME internationalisation process: Key issues and contributions, existing gaps and the future research agenda. *European Management Journal*, 38(1), 62–77. DOI: 10.1016/j.emj.2019.08.001

Myers, S. C. (1984). Capitl Structure Puzzle. *The Journal of Finance*, 39(April), 574–592. DOI: 10.1111/j.1540-6261.1984.tb03646.x

Nijmeijer, K. J., Fabbricotti, I. N., & Huijsman, R. (2014). Making Franchising Work: A Framework Based on a Systematic Review. *International Journal of Management Reviews*, 16(1), 62–83. DOI: 10.1111/ijmr.12009

Niskanen, J., & Niskanen, M. (2010). Small business borrowing and the owner-manager agency costs: Evidence on finnish data. *Journal of Small Business Management*, 48(1), 16–31. DOI: 10.1111/j.1540-627X.2009.00284.x

Pascucci, F., Domenichelli, O., Peruffo, E., & Gregori, G. L. (2022). Family ownership and the export performance of SMEs: The moderating role of financial constraints and flexibility. *Journal of Small Business and Enterprise Development*, 29(4), 602–626. DOI: 10.1108/JSBED-03-2021-0113

Pérez, P. F. (2007). Small firms and networks in capital intensive industries: The case of Spanish steel wire manufacturing. *Business History*, 49(5), 647–667. DOI: 10.1080/00076790701428646

Ragab, Y. M., & Saleh, M. A. (2022). Non-financial variables related to governance and financial distress prediction in SMEs–evidence from Egypt. *Journal of Applied Accounting Research*, 23(3), 604–627. DOI: 10.1108/JAAR-02-2021-0025

Randøy, T., & Goel, S. (2003). Ownership structure, founder leadership, and performance in Norwegian SMEs: Implications for financing entrepreneurial opportunities. *Journal of Business Venturing*, 18(5), 619–637. DOI: 10.1016/S0883-9026(03)00013-2

Rasel, M. A., & Win, S. (2020). Microfinance governance: A systematic review and future research directions. *Journal of Economic Studies (Glasgow, Scotland)*, 47(7), 1811–1847. DOI: 10.1108/JES-03-2019-0109

Roberts, M. J. D., & Muralidharan, E. (2022). Internationalization of Service SMEs: Perspectives from Canadian SMEs Internationalizing in Asia. *Global Business Review*, 23(4), 890–910. DOI: 10.1177/0972150919887250

Romano, C. A., Tanewski, G. A., & Smyrnios, K. X. (2001). Capital structure decision making: A model for family business. *Journal of Business Venturing*, 16(3), 285–310. DOI: 10.1016/S0883-9026(99)00053-1

Sanhokwe, H. (2022). Opportunity Recognition and Discontinuation of Ownership in SMEs: The Role of Innovation, Opportunity Exploitation, and Instrumental Risk-Taking. *Journal of Small Business Strategy*, 32(3), 98–112. DOI: 10.53703/001c.35771

Sciascia, S., Nordqvist, M., Mazzola, P., & De Massis, A. (2015). Family ownership and R&D intensity in small- and medium-sized firms. *Journal of Product Innovation Management*, 32(3), 349–360. DOI: 10.1111/jpim.12204

Shapiro, D., Tang, Y., Wang, M., & Zhang, W. (2015). The effects of corporate governance and ownership on the innovation performance of Chinese SMEs. *Journal of Chinese Economic and Business Studies*, 13(4), 311–335. DOI: 10.1080/14765284.2015.1090267

Shleifer, A., & Vishny, R. W. (1986). Large Shareholders and Corporate Control. *Journal of Political Economy*, 94(3, Part 1), 461–488. DOI: 10.1086/261385

Singh, K., & Rastogi, S. (2022). Corporate governance and financial performance: Evidence from listed SMEs in India. *Benchmarking*. Advance online publication. DOI: 10.1108/BIJ-09-2021-0570

Solarino, A. M., & Boyd, B. K. (2020). Are all forms of ownership prone to tunneling? A meta-analysis. *Corporate Governance: An International Review*, corg.12344. DOI: 10.1111/corg.12344

Tihanyi, L., Aguilera, R. V., Heugens, P., van Essen, M., Sauerwald, S., Duran, P., & Turturea, R. (2019). State Ownership and Political Connections. *Journal of Management*, 45(6), 2293–2321. DOI: 10.1177/0149206318822113

Variyam, J. N., & Kraybill, D. S. (1994). Managerial Inputs and the Growth of Rural Small Firms. *American Journal of Agricultural Economics*, 76(3), 568–575. DOI: 10.2307/1243667

Vos, E., Yeh, A. J. Y., Carter, S., & Tagg, S. (2007). The happy story of small business financing. *Journal of Banking & Finance*, 31(9), 2648–2672. DOI: 10.1016/j.jbankfin.2006.09.011

Xiang, D., Chen, J., Tripe, D., & Zhang, N. (2019). Family firms, sustainable innovation and financing cost: Evidence from Chinese hi-tech small and medium-sized enterprises. *Technological Forecasting and Social Change, 144*(November 2017), 499–511. DOI: 10.1016/j.techfore.2018.02.021

Yang, X., Li, J., Stanley, L. J., Kellermanns, F. W., & Li, X. (2020). How family firm characteristics affect internationalization of Chinese family SMEs. *Asia Pacific Journal of Management*, 37(2), 417–448. DOI: 10.1007/s10490-018-9579-7

Zhang, X., Venus, J., & Wang, Y. (2012). Family ownership and business expansion of small- and medium-sized Chinese family businesses: The mediating role of financing preference. *Journal of Family Business Strategy*, 3(2), 97–105. DOI: 10.1016/j.jfbs.2012.03.002

Chapter 11
Sourcing Metaverse for More Customer Engagement

Tareq Nael Hashem
https://orcid.org/0000-0001-9564-931X
Applied Science Private University, Jordan

Ahmad Albattat
https://orcid.org/0000-0002-3127-4405
Medan Academy of Tourism (Akpar Medan), Indonesia

Anuj Kumar
https://orcid.org/0000-0002-1205-2794
Marwadi University, India

Sadfa El-Taher
https://orcid.org/0009-0008-1032-0506
Al-Azhar University, Egypt

ABSTRACT

The Metaverse represents a growing field for organizations looking to redefine how they engage with customers in the digital age. Using this feature opens up many opportunities for deep integration and smart marketing. One of the most important forms of communication is creating a visual environment that allows consumers to connect with the brand on their favorite level. Leveraging technologies such as virtual reality (VR) and augmented reality (AR), organizations can create experiences that transcend traditional boundaries and allow customers to explore products, services, and brand messaging in inclusive and inclusive ways. These immersive brand experiences not only capture attention, but also foster emotional connections

DOI: 10.4018/979-8-3693-9005-4.ch011

and drive deeper engagement and brand loyalty.

1. INTRODUCTION

The integration of artificial intelligence and the appearance of the metaverse presents people with a new vision of the future where the actual and digital worlds are interwoven. On that idea, Shaik (2023) noted that AI finds itself in a critical position in shaping and growing the metaverse through advanced solutions that help facilitate sophisticated interfaces and relevant content generation and interaction models. Aspect of Artificial intelligence means that computers can be programmed to make their avatars copy actual people's actions making the situations more realistic and engaging. Specifically, natural language processing (NLP) features enhance user-appealing and unrestricted communication between the individuals and AI-based entities within the metaverse environment (Bilgihan et al., 2024). Moreover, using different machine learning techniques, the AI processes a substantial amount of user information to enhance the personalization of virtual spaces, as well as the forecasts users' preferences, and the relevance of content shared within a metaverse to maintain and increase user interactivity (Rathore, 2023; Hashem etal.,2023).

According to Ameen et al. (2023), as the concept of metaverse progresses, AI has further possibilities to transform the experience of subjects in the space. Virtual assistants that employ AI technologies can offer users timely support, help them to make the right choice within the metaverse or even give those individuals step-by-step instructions on actions and steps which should help them better interact with it (Lv, 2023). Also, AI generation means that virtual landscapes, objects, and experiences can be created automatically, growing the variety of the possibilities of what can be created in the metaverse. With the help of AI technologies, the metaverse can grow out from the limited opportunities of the HCI, creating a new environment of interactions where the advanced AI solutions are the basis for the new ways people interact, work, and play in the virtual world (Koo et al., 2023).

Chintalapati and Pandey (2022) argued that the notion of the metaverse as an interconnected virtual environment that combines both physical and digital worlds has moved from being an SF storyline to a business reality that redefines the relationship between the organization and its consumers, employees and shareholders. The metaverse has come into the business world because of application of virtual reality (VR), augmented reality (AR), artificial intelligence (AI), blockchain, and other technologies (Hindolia et al., 2024).

While Haleem et al. (2022) saw that organizations are turning to the metaverse for the purpose of gaining better ways to engage with users, in order to provide them more engaging brand experiences and to consider brand new monetization opportunities. Businesses in different industries such as fashion, movies, classes, hospitals, and telecommunication are using the metaverse to design virtual shops, host virtual events, provide learning from virtual classes, and avail virtual customer support.

Petrescu and Krishen (2023) supported the same idea adding that the metaverse gives companies a chance not only to develop their digital presence beyond the limitations which can be observed for the further growth within a company but also to reach audiences of numerous countries all around the world. The use of meetings, conferences as well as collaborations such as working or business in the metaverse is already having significant impact on what can be referred to as remote body and borders where teams are not close geographically yet are becoming more joined.

Mariani et al. (2022) came also to prove that when organizations enter the metaverse and develop products or services within it, the answers are also found in the field of business since they are also problems related with collection of data, protection of data, legal requirements and usability design in this context. On the contrary, the following opportunities to use metaverse for business issues as customer engagement, brand awareness and operations' optimization explain why many organizations consider metaverse as a competitive strategic trend to compete because of demands in digital economy (Zainurin et al., 2024).

2. UNDERSTANDING THE METAVERSE

According to Peltier et al. (2024) and Au et al., (2023) metaverse, derived from the science fictional genre and advocated by Neal Stephenson's Snow Crash, defines the social world that is as one integrated, continual virtual reality space that connects the physical and digital worlds. In language and terminology, metaverse is a concept that points at the multi-layered immersive environment of virtual shared space where people can meet other users as well as avatars, interact with each other in real time.

From terminological perspective, Fadhel et al. (2024) stated that the metaverse has a very broad definition that include various virtual worlds, objects, and events that reflect and can be an extension of the real world. Huynh-The et al., (2023) stated that the metaverse is an ever-growing, interconnecting environment that cuts across tangible barriers, allowing users to experiment, design, and perform numerous actions within spaces existing within the digital realm. Some of the characteristics of the metaverse include content creation by people, the social aspect, user-controlled economies and entertainment, and innovation all of which entail extensive use of virtual spaces.

Conceptually speaking, the term metaverse that has recently become so popular is a merger of two terms – 'meta' that translates as beyond or higher and 'universe,' which defines a complete space or system. This linguistic construction illustrates the concept and its ability to go beyond the physical properties and build and construct an unlimited world in the digital environment for people to communicate, to socialize and to engage themselves in virtual activities (Guo et al., 2022). The language surrounding the metaverse also tends to be one of interconnection, immersion, and agency because it represents a living, connected environment that is constantly rewriting how people experience virtual space and interact with it in the present day (Hwang and Chien, 2022).

2.1. The Concept of Metaverse: Meaning and Orientation

According to Zawish et al. (2024), metaverse refers to a virtual common world that combines physical and digital domains to provide a social and comprehensive tangible reality where people can effectively meet and perform socially acceptable functions. A concept originally created by Neal Stephenson in a 1992 science fiction novel 'Snow Crash,' the metaverse has brought a real-world concept and its implications into existence.

Chamola et al., (2024) stated that fundamentally, the metaverse is defined as a persisting shared environment that exists beyond the confines of individual boundaries and that offers people opportunities for created, manipulation, and navigation through concrete virtual spaces and objects, as well as interactions with other subjects in such environments. In metaverse, it can be possible to customize one's identity, work on projects, act within economic systems and socialize with people from various parts of the world.

Thakur et al., (2023) argued that the main physical characteristics of the metaverse are connection, presence, and active control, the set and expansion of which form an open, constantly developing virtual environment that reflects and expands the physical reality. As the transition of the world towards a digital one accelerates, virtual reality, augmented reality, artificial intelligence, and blockchain bring a fresh and innovative concept to life; the metaverse allows creations and thus, new forms of communication, exchange and functioning.

From perspective of Ng (2022), the metaverse' s definition and layout are conditioned based on the current trends in IT developments, technologies users engage in, and the trends that reflect altering social standards. Organizations, people and neighborhoods are starting to look at the metaverse as a space for entertainment, learning, trading, socializing and other activities that level up the understanding of virtual worlds in today's society.

2.2. Metaverse as a New Canvas for Marketing

Barrera and Shah (2023) confirmed that the integration of the metaverse into the contextualized marketing environment is a transitional process that is currently configuring the new approach to the ways how organizations address consumers and promote goods and services, as well as introduce brands in virtual reality. Several industries, including marketing, use newer technologies like metaverse technologies like VR, AR and AI to engage the audience.

Cheng et al., (2022) supported the above idea arguing that perhaps one of the most important things about applying the metaverse in marketing is the potential of delivering arresting and immersive advertising material. It allows marketers to create engaging mythological and narrative-based promotions and engaging product and brand experiences beyond conventional display media. Given the opportunities of the metaverse, marketers have a chance to deliver remarkable and meaningful campaigns that will have an impact on the target audience and brand.

Bordegoni and Ferrise (2023) stated that the metaverse is almost unique in supplying marketers with the chance to reach out, gather, dissect and then individualize from the newer generation of consumers. This way, marketers, as well as other users, understand the consumer better and can sell and promote their products more effectively according to a user's online behavior and likes. With AI algorithms, marketers can parse through the large amount of data to provide a targeted content, recommendations and even offers making the marketing strategies in metaverse more efficient.

Huynh-The et al., (2023) had the same stream of thinking when they said that today, companies are still experimenting with the use of the metaverse in promotion whereas conduct issues including privacy, security, online content filtering, and ethical issues were rife. This is a critical challenge that has to be met to generate consumer trust in a virtual marketing environment by balancing creativity and innovation in marketing alongside responsibly in increasing sales return. Marketers and business leaders must realize the metaverse as both an opportunity and a challenge to enhancing brand extension strategies and creating incremental revenue sources for their organizations in a digital world.

2.3. Components of Metaverse

Park and Kim (2022); Khang et al., (2023); Chamola et al., (2024); Ahuja et al., (2023) confirmed that metaverse incorporates several primary components within the" world" in which people are immersed and can engage in social and other activities. Some of the fundamental components of the metaverse include:

1. Virtual Worlds

Avatars interact in virtual worlds which are places within the metaverse that are also formed from computer code but can be explored, objects manipulated, and people communicate with each other in real time. They can be as close to the actual people's environment as possible or fictional to the extent that is practically imaginable.

2. Avatars

Thanks to avatars, users have their digital persona within the metaverse. Avatar can be created to look like a user, or indeed, the user can select one that suits their personalities and likes; this allows the user to move around the social and interact with others.

3. Social Interaction

Communication is an opposite sector of the metaverse ecosystem and describes how people interact using text chat, voice, gestures, and actions. Other interactions within the metaverse involve community formation that creates the social interactions of the users.

4. Economy and Commerce

Web economies are found in the metaverse where people are able to conduct real economic transactions of virtual commodities, services, and properties. E-currencies, e-market places, and digital transactions are essential in the performance of economic activities in virtual worlds.

5. Content Creation Tools

Content creation instruments enable users to build and design new content within the virtual world, objects, environments, and experiences. These instruments help the user to create and show the imagination, work on avatars and objects, and make the metaverse richer.

6. Augmented Reality (AR) and Virtual Reality (VR)

AR and VR technology added to the realism of the metaverse to increase the number of affected sensory perceptions in a way that is human-centric. AR adds digital information to our physical space while VR immerses them in digital environment space.

7. Artificial Intelligence (AI)

For the intelligent and sophisticated behaviors in the metaverse, AI comes handy in providing all the intelligent experiences and automating most processes. Artificial intelligence strategies can strengthen the relations with users, improve the layout and design of virtual spaces in the metaverse, and stimulate the generation of dynamic content.

8. Blockchain Technology

Due to the functionality of the blockchain technology in enabling appropriate transactions, making of contracts happen, and creating credibility for virtual properties. Blockchain helps to define ownership, veracity and rarity of avatars and objects in the process of using the metaverse.

3. CUSTOMER ENGAGEMENT CE

As was noted by Lim et al. (2022) in the evolving world of marketing and business, the recent market focus on customer engagement has become of critical importance as organizations are now trying to create real connections with their target audiences. Customer engagement goes beyond traditional marketing practices, focusing much on a relationship beyond the transaction that is built on long-term trust, goodwill, and mutual value. Equipped with new channels and platforms digital technologies and social media gave customers much of the power in brand perception and in turning into their buying decisions. Hence companies are forced to become customer-centric at all levels of awareness and throughout the customer lifecycle (Hollebeek et al., 2022).

Lim and Rasul (2022) argued that effective customer engagement strategies utilize a profound understanding of consumer behavior, preferences, and expectations to customize interactions that cut across personal and generic interests. By customer engagements based on contextual, relevant, and more personalized content, interactive experiences, and seamless omnichannel communications, businesses are able to establish equally immersive and memorable touchpoints that could ensure satisfaction and loyalty.

While Hampton et al., (2022) added that the rise of data analytics and artificial intelligence represents a paradigm breakthrough in how business mutates the way in which it interacts with customers through predictive engagement on a massive scale. This engagement itself is very much driven by the applicability of data-driven intelligence-enabled approaches to power such engagement across various customer propositions that organizations need to give (McDonald et al., 2022). The importance of customer engagement in marketing and business comes down to establishing brand advocacy, building retention, and driving sustainable growth in an extremely competitive world. As businesses seek to embrace a world post-digitation, connectivity through customer engagement will provide fast input for building a loyal customer base (Rather et al., 2022).

3.1. Defining Customer Engagement

Customer engagement was defined, in many studies like According to Ao et al., (2023), to be a multidimensional construct that expands beyond mere transactional interactions, routinely into behavioral, cognitive, and emotional aspects of the customer-brand relationship. It indicates the active participation and involvement of customers in various stages of the consumer journey-facet from pre-purchase, purchase to post-purchase phases.

Hamilton (2022) and According to Elf et al., (2022) argued that customer engagement generally address factors influencing general levels of engagement, such as customer satisfaction, trust, brand loyalty, perceived value, and emotional attachment. Scholars are analyzing how an organization can engage customers by employing personalized communication, tailored experiences, or customer-centric strategies intended to meet individual needs and preferences.

Sim et al., (2022) confirmed that some studies also investigate some issues regarding the measurement and management of engagement metrics that perform the task of evaluating the effectiveness of engagement initiatives and tracking customer perceptions over time. Researchers examine the effect engagement has on key business outcomes such as customer retention, advocacy, and profitability in order to understand the value of building strong relationships with customers.

NasarAmini et al., (2022) and Gligor et al., (2023) stated that from the academic scholarship perspective, customer engagement is deemed a strategic imperative for any business interested in gaining competitive advantage, cultivating customer loyalty, and achieving sustainable growth. Customer engagement and its related topic have been studied within the ambit of specific scholarly research efforts.

3.2. Components of Customer Engagement

Bozkurt et al., (2022) argued that customer engagement is a complex concept consisting of specific constituents that play a critical role in the customer-brand relationship. An important element of **Interaction** when addressing customer engagement is of extreme importance. It can be defined as the exchange that is taking place between customers and brands through dialogues, purchase and other forms of communication exchanges. By now, social media communication, client interactions, and other possible dialogues with the buyer can help brands speak to consumers, gather information, and offer solutions that might correspond to their needs.

Han and Anderson (2022) agreed on the same idea arguing that among the elements of customer engagement include (Emotion). Perplexing and obvious emotions have a crucial role as they influence customers' perception, attitude, and behavior concerning brands. Brands can develop successful emotional associations and make people remember them through positive associations such as joy, trust, and satisfaction which are activated within particular experiences. Emotional engagement takes into account further than self-ascertain analytic and rational behaviors and instead focuses on stimulating the inherent psychology which gives life to customers and their allegiance. If properly adopted, the emotional engagement strategies help firms to achieve high levels of emotional connection with customers and, therefore, long-term customer relationships.

Banik et al. (2024) said that (Personality) is also another measure used to achieve success in customer appeal. Personalization relates to adaptation of services or goods, communication, or any kind of experience for consumption and perception according to the customer wants or needs. Assimilating and accumulating a customer data base helps brands to develop a unique way of delivering the products to the market that will ease the customers. Some of the personalization strategies can involve using direct adverts, direct communications, and product evaluations that show someone a picture of what they want by showing them the kind of things they prefer in their consumption. Through involving and timely content delivery in accordance with customer needs, brands are able to improve customer attention, boost their sales, and increase the loyalty of the people that are interested in their products (Parray et al., 2024).

Ajiga et al. (2024) stated that (Consistency) is one of the cornerstone strategies in any customer relations. Coherence refers to the extent to which different elements such as brand communications, organizational beliefs and brand encounters with the customer are in harmony. Consistency in the communication and appearance of brands, as well as the quality and character of the services that they offer creates reliability and positive perception among consumers, which in turn reposes the strengths of their brand messages. Continuous engagement activities contribute to the continuity of unified organizational image, certainty and dependability in clients' interactions adding to customer delight and lasting patronage. If many channels provide a unified and coordinated brand image, customers' bonds would be strengthened and brands would stand out from the crowd.

3.3. Emerging Customer Engagement through the Metaverse

Ibrahim (2024) confirmed that customer engagement through opportunities in the metaverse is a new way of breaking customer relationships to a new level, which promotes the creation of meaningful and lasting relationships as well as improving consumer experience. Using VR and AR, and other technologies, companies have searched for new approaches to selling products and reaching consumers in areas such as virtual reality that are only partially distinct from actual reality (Zawish et al., 2024; Watson, 2022).

Valaskova et al. (2022) supported the same allegations adding that one of the biggest benefits of communicating with customers in the metaverse is the given opportunity to deliver and develop unique and engaging experiences that connect with people. Hamilton (2022) and Newell (2022) stated that the opportunities for the creative storytelling, for product boosting, and for general interaction that such an environment offers are unmatched by tradition media communication means. By embodying an organization, customers often experience engagement and gain a stake of the business hence creating brands out of organizations (Cheung et al., 2024).

Further, having its advantage in that it liberates business from the reality of conventional locations, the metaverse enables business to connect with diverse customers with ease in a scalable and inexpensive fashion. Virtual events, virtual showrooms and virtual experiences also provide for customers to interact with companies from different regions of the world, and offer companies an array of ways to engage their customers (Thakur et al., 2023).

However, the present metaverse in customer engagement also has benefits and a few concerns and factors to note. Security related issues specifically privacy and data security are significant impediments, as business has to protect the customers' data in virtual environments (Bathla and Ahuja, 2024). Moderation of content and the supervision of the community are critical input parameters to ensure customers enjoy and are safe when interacting inside an environment. Furthermore, the importance cannot be overstated to consider better and equal usage opportunities of all user groups of the metaverse regardless of their technical abilities as well as physical disabilities (Aloqaily et al., 2022).

4. SOURCING METAVERSE FOR MORE CUSTOMER ENGAGEMENT

The metaverse which is a digital and physical universe holds a unique chance for new approaches to customer engagement models for most organizations. In the current complex business world of digital marketing, sourcing of the metaverse for improvement of customer relations is now considered as one of the great trends for competition and diversification. Metaverse can be used in such a way that companies employ applications of immersive technologies, interactive experiences in form of games, and personalized people-robot interactions to design environments that create brand enthusiasm, efficacy, and engagement as well as deepen people's relationships with the company.

In the search for better ways to engage customers, marketing in the metaverse is an open sandbox of opportunities. This free-for-all marketing space is way beyond conventional marketing regimentation, offering brands the opportunity to tell gripping stories; deploy more engaging marketing initiatives; and consequently foster rich branded experiences that are suitable for modern young audiences. For instance, by using virtual reality (VR), augmented reality (AR) and other emerging technologies, it is possible for an organization to get customers into aesthetically appealing worlds, and engage with products, services and brand values in ways that are almost indistinguishable from the real world. The fact is that the metaverse aims at offering people new ways of experiencing personalized, interactive, and emotionally appealing interactions, with limitless potential for commercial organizations in search of a distinctive way to build relationships with their target audiences. Among the most apparent realms which are found in metaverse and can influence customer engagement are:

4.1. Virtual Brand Presence

The metaverse might have opened many doors for brands to engage with consumers, however, the digital marketing world is changing every day and brands are still looking for better ways to connect with their customers. By putting customers in a virtual environment designed exactly like the brand's identity, companies can create stronger bonds with their audience. Through virtual showrooms and stores, brands can offer interactive experiences where customers can ponder and purchase products, try out virtual samples, and make a dynamic and engaging setting with sounds and light. This level of immersion is far above the traditional online shopping experience and through it, consumers are able to have a more personalized and memorable interaction that resonates with modern consumers who want to engage with a brand in an innovative and interactive way (Bilgihan et al., 2024).

Besides that, creating a virtual brand presence in the metaverse can mean new ways of creative storytelling and experiential marketing. Brands now have the opportunity to organize virtual events, for example, product launches or interactive experiences, irrespective of the geographical location of their target audience. Incorporating gamification elements, data personalization, and social interaction into these virtual experiences helps brands to strengthen the community, promote customer loyalty and make noise about their product. This is a win-win on two fronts, customer engagement is improved and brands are able to use technological advancements as a way of standing out from the crowd and being bolder than competitors (Wongkitrungrueng and Suprawan, 2024).

4.2. Immersive Experiences

According to Florido-Benítez (2024), the metaverse to increase customer engagement through immersive experiences is creating a real change in the way brands communicate with their audience in the digital marketing sector. By developing captivating virtual realities and interactive environments that speak to the senses, companies can create powerful bonds with their customers. Jha (2023) added that immersive experiences that take place in the metaverse offer new opportunities when compared to traditional advertising methods, creating a level of engagement that has never been seen before which resonates with modern consumers who are looking for unique and memorable interactions with brands. Using virtual reality (VR) and augmented reality (AR) technologies, brands have the ability to create lifelike simulations where customers can explore products, take part in virtual events, and interact with content in ways that are almost indistinguishable from the physical and digital worlds.

According to Rane et al., (2023), immersive experiences in the metaverse can be a medium for brands to write stories that reveal the ideas underlying their products and services to consumers. Using storytelling methods in virtual environments, firms can thus generate memorable brand experiences that, in turn, evoke emotions, curiosity, etc. and imprint themselves in customers' memories. These immersive experiences may encompass virtual product demonstrations, interactive storytelling sessions, and virtual tours of brand facilities to name a few. They all aimed to immerse customers in a world where the brand is able to engage with them on a personal and emotional level. By using the metaverse as a source for immersive experiences, brands can stand out from the crowd in a saturated digital space, establish deeper connections with their audience, and increase customer involvement like never before (Cheung et al., 2024).

4.3. Personalization

Spajić et al. (2022) confirmed that in the fast-paced world of digital marketing, using the metaverse to increase customer interaction through unique experiences is a powerful move for brands. Mourtzis et al. (2022) added that through adjusting interactions to match individual tastes and actions, businesses can make customers feel special and understood. In the metaverse, brands can suggest personalized products, create custom virtual experiences, and send messages that directly address each customer's needs and wants. This kind of personalization not only boosts customer interaction but also builds a stronger bond and loyalty to the brand (Abrokwah-Larbi, 2024).

Dwivedi et al. (2023) stated that in the metaverse, personalization goes beyond typical marketing methods, enabling brands to design special and engaging experiences that match each customer's interests. By using data and AI, companies can build lively virtual spaces where customers feel recognized, understood, and appreciated. This can be done through personalized avatars, customized product displays, or interactive stories that fit each customer's tastes. By offering these personalized experiences in the metaverse, brands can create significant connections that boost customer involvement, encourage loyalty, and set new benchmarks for customer-focused marketing in the digital world (Khatri, 2022).

4.4. Virtual Customer Service

Gursoy et al. (2023) stated that new products are increasingly moving into the virtual world to transform customer engagement through customer service. By establishing a virtual presence, companies can provide personalized and interactive support that goes beyond customer interactions. Brands can improve the overall customer experience by providing instant customer service, product demonstrations, and problem solving in a positive environment with virtual customer service representatives (Dwivedi et al., 2023; Banat etal.,2024).

This approach not only increases support, but also allows customers to interact with the brand in a powerful and engaging way. Virtual customer service in a virtual world opens up new possibilities for brands to connect with their audiences on a deeper level. Using technologies like VR and AI, companies can create lifelike avatars or virtual assistants that guide customers through questions and provide solutions to problems. This personalized approach to customer service fosters attention and care for individual needs, strengthening customer relationships and loyalty. By finding the Metaverse for virtual customers, brands can stand out in the competitive marketplace, guide customers, and set new standards for responsive and interactive support (Rane et al., 2023).

4.5. Augmented Reality (AR) Integration

Chen et al. (2024) saw that in a rapidly evolving consumer experience, incorporating Augmented Reality (AR) into the metaverse offers a unique opportunity for brands to create immersive and interactive experiences that engage their audience. Rauschnabel et al., (2022) agreed on the same idea arguing that brands can use AR technology to give consumers the ability to view products in a physical environment through their devices, creating a more engaging and engaging shopping experience. Whether trying on virtual clothes, previewing items in the living room, or trying on jewelry up close, incorporating AR into the metaverse will enhance the customer journey by offering interaction and reliability that traditional methods cannot match.

Abrokwah-Larbi (2024) added that incorporating augmented reality into the metaverse offers brands the opportunity to animate experiences beyond the simple visual, engage consumers in interactive storytelling, and deliver educational programs through creative mediums. AR-based experiences allow brands to create memorable moments with customers, increase engagement, and increase brand loyalty. By looking to Metaverse for AR integration, businesses can enhance their shopping experience, differentiate themselves in the marketplace, and build stronger relationships with their customers through new technologies that enhance the customer journey (Chandratreya, 2023).

4.6. Gamification

Tayal and Rajagopal (2023) argued that in the digital world, leveraging the metaverse to improve customer engagement through marketing has emerged as a powerful strategy for brands looking to engage and connect with their target audience. Wanick and Stallwood (2023) added that through incorporating game elements such as challenges, rewards, and interactive storytelling into virtual experiences, brands can create fun and engaging interactions that inspire customer interest and loyalty. Gamification in the metaverse allows consumers to engage with brands in a fun and interactive way, fostering motivation and fun that fosters ongoing relationships.

Arya et al. (2024) noted that through marketing, brands could turn everyday interactions into powerful and interactive experiences with consumers on a deeper level. By offering challenges, quizzes, and interviews in a virtual environment, companies can encourage customers, encourage visitors, and improve relationships among employees. By exploring the metaverse for gamification strategies, brands can not only improve customer relationships but also differentiate themselves in competitive markets, build brand relationships, and create experiences that leave a lasting impression on consumers (Tayal et al., 2022).

5. METAVERSE FROM AROUND THE WORLD

It has been noticed that metaverse has been adopted by many well-known organization (Alshurideh et al., 2024). Goldberg et al. (2023) stated that this move came in order to improve customer relation and develop innovative marketing strategies. Some of the most famous organizations that have utilized the metaverse to connect with audiences in unique and immersive ways and support their customer engagement are:

Nike

Nike, the world's leading sportswear manufacturer, has entered the metaverse by designing experiential services for virtual shoes and clothing. Nike has embraced virtual showrooms and virtual experiences and has interacted with the customers in virtual spaces by providing them with different ways of interacting with the company's products (Longo and Canalichio, 2024; Mancuso et al., 2023; Sawhney and Goodman, 2023).

Figure 1. Nike Utilizing Metaverse in for Marketing

Gucci

The luxury fashion brand Gucci has engaged virtual worlds such as Roblox to design virtual Gucci Gardens that present the physical visit like digital experiences inspired by Gucci's design and aesthetics. With use of virtual reality, Gucci has been able to expand its reach and influence not only brand consciousness but also young people who are conversant with virtual reality (Mancuso et al., 2023; Liu, 2022).

Figure 2. Gucci's Town on Metaverse Gamification

Red Bull

A good example of brands taking advantage of metaverse is the energy drink firm Red Bull with concerts and virtual extreme sports. This has also influenced Red Bull's appeal to audiences through use of Virtual Reality in a way that fosters engagement with audience and provides a viable experience through products that represent Red Bull image, that of thrills (Longo and Canalichio, 2024; Hsieh et al., 2023; Burrows, 2022).

Figure 3. Red bull Entering Metaverse through Gamification

Samsung

Samsung has used VR and AR technologies in presenting its products and novelties in virtual presentation areas. In being able to navigate the various 'realities' and 'spaces' of the Samsung devices, the above fold allows for increased customer interaction and a fresh way of engaging with the various electronic technologies that are offered by the company (Hsieh et al., 2023; Mancuso et al., 2023).

Figure4. Samsung Logo Appearing explicitly in Metaverse Game

The New York Times

Currently, New York Times has tested the ability to create VR journalism to share the story in the first person perspective that takes the readers to different places and events in the world. Using VR in combination with conventional journalism as the strategy, The New York Times has successfully presented new approaches to attract audiences and reconceive the news (Hsieh et al., 2023).

These organizations provide some insights to how the metaverse, when strategically deployed and managed, can create more relevant stakeholder touchpoints, increase brand salience, as well as build exceptional experiences for their audiences in this age of the digital world (Cheng et al., 2022; Dawson, 2022).

6. ETHICAL IMPLICATIONS OF METAVERSE IN MARKETING SETTINGS

Kour (2024) pointed out that metaverse heralds an era in which possibilities abound for marketers to create specifically space for engagement. Now, more than ever, this immersive and interactive platform allows reaching audiences in never-before-seen ways. However, within all the innovation, unpacking the metaverse in marketing settings comes with a range of ethical implications: transparency, privacy, and responsible engagement must all be under careful consideration (Rosa, 2022).

Tan and Salo (2023) presented key facets of concern with the metaverse are in the area related to privacy and security. Consumers within these virtual settings can be monitored based on their online visits, preferences, and behavior. To provide a personalized marketing experience, marketers should comply with data protection policies and should receive the complete consent of users to collect and use their data therein.

Further ethical problems may arise concerning manipulation and exploitation of more vulnerable audiences in virtual spaces. Marketers must ensure their advertising strategies on the metaverse are truthful, transparent, and do not deceive or manipulate the audience, in particular, children and others generally viewed as more easily swayed by the technically privileged, who can manipulate immersive experiences (Anshari et al., 2022; Hashem,2024).

Moreover, Dwivedi et al., (2023) added other urgent and uncomfortable questions related to inclusion and diversity in the metaverse including the design of avatars, experiences, and how this might inadvertently perpetuate biases toward some and exclude others. Marketers are admonished to create inclusive spaces that celebrate diversity and reflect the voices of many in a way that prejudices toward stereotypes are avoided, and cornered communities are not disenfranchised. While Petr and Caudan (2024) said that as users participate in the metaverse, their boundaries of contact between virtual and real-world experiences will often be compromised by ethical problems concerning consent. Interactive marketing campaigns often create an environment in which the user is placed in the position of involvement or participation.

7. POTENTIAL SECURITY RISKS

Jaber (2022) argued that integrating the metaverse into customer engagement strategies offers tremendous immersive experiences and personalized interactions, while bringing in multiple security concerns for businesses to meet for protecting the customers' data and privacy. Among these concerns what was mentioned by

Chen et al., (2022) including data privacy is probably the most important one. As users navigate their way through virtual worlds, they are generating many data connected to their actions, preferences, and interactions. This kind of information can be intercepted and manipulated despite good intentions. Businesses must put clearer data security laws and procedures in place to ensure their customers' personal information is protected in the metaverse (Upadhyay et al., 2024).

According to Chaudhari et al., (2024) other types of criminal activity such as phishing and social engineering may expose yet another security threat. Those tending their gardens of virtual users might indulge in something fraudulent, that is, through deceitful means, by coaxing unfortunate users into parting with their sensitive information or upon tapping by accidents on unintended links of destruction. Because of this, an organization should educate customers on safe cyber practices and, more importantly, set up appropriate safeguards to mitigate such phishing frauds (Wang et al., 2022).

Liu (2023) describes another dimension: mutual interdependence of the metaverse and the prerogative extended to the users in terms of coming up with and sharing content. Therefore, it is of utmost importance that organizations support initiatives for content moderation now more than ever. Simply put, it should always be insured that nothing from the content shared threatens the security and well-being of the customers inside the virtual space itself (Zhao et al., 2023).

8. REQUIREMENT OF SUCCESSFUL METAVERSE IMPLEMENTATION IN MARKETING SCHEME

Designing an efficient metaverse in order to provide a rewarding experience to the customers' calls for the basic technical enablers to be solidly in place. On that idea, Haavisto (2024) pointed out the availability of very good internet connection is very paramount for efficient and effective communication and participation in the virtual environment. A stable internet connection is something equally important for delivering great experiences, real time communication, and ability to move around virtual environments without having to experience lagging. Furthermore, stability and expandability of the network structures is crucial for the networks growth and maintaining proper availability and performance on various devices and operating systems (Hasani et al., 2024).

Eggenschwiler et al. (2024) argued that is why the integration of more sophisticated technologies, for example, virtual reality (VR), augmented reality (AR), and spatial computing capabilities is indeed a basic necessity for improving a customer experience in the metaverse. Some of the techniques that have encompassed advancements of VR headset, AR gadgets, and spatial mapping comprise; Consumers are able to engage with virtual environments, digital content, and products and service solutions that are within tangible interactivity periods (Gupta et al., 2024). These previously mentioned technical tools not only enhance the use experience but also facilitate the organizations to provide the most engaging communications that would indeed find a positive correlation with the customers. In addition, incorporating AI and machine learning within the metaverse may improve customer satisfaction by allowing for personalized tailored product recommendations, probability comprehensions, and even virtual business insight that adapts to the client's conduct, therefore improving the client's bond within the metaverse (Sarkar et al., 2024; Banik et al., 2024).

9. CRITICS ON INVOLVING METAVERSE IN MARKETING FIELD

Ali et al. (2022) stated that introducing the metaverse into the field of marketing raises important concerns and challenges that deserve careful investigation. The key issue is the metric's power to promote inequality and exclusion in society. Metaverse technologies, such as virtual reality headsets and the Internet of Things, are not universally accessible, which can be a problem for those who do not have the means to access these spaces properly (Soliman et al., 2022). This digital divide can widen the gap in access to information, services and opportunities, widening the divide between those who can access the market and those who cannot. In addition, the immersion and private nature of meta-text raises legitimate concerns about data privacy and consumer fraud (Rather, 2023). As marketers collect large amounts of personal data to personalize experiences in virtual environments, questions arise about the legitimacy of data collection practices and their legitimacy.

The metaverse as Yang et al. (2022) argued blurs the lines between the physical and digital worlds, creating fertile ground for advertising and deceptive practices that violate consumers' privacy and confidentiality. Protect user data and ensure that shopping practices on the metaverse follow ethical principles to prevent mistrust and the exchange of personal information. Furthermore, meteorology emphasizes that the existence of virtual reality and the risk of theft are preventing consumers from engaging with reality and fostering a culture of authenticity. Therefore, as according to Awadallah et al. (2024), by immersing people in virtual experiences that focus on entertainment and shopping, there are concerns that the metaverse could disrupt global discourse and contribute to a shallow consumer culture. It will be a challenge to create a positive and meaningful relationship with customers in an interactive environment through avatars and algorithms, which can reduce the emotional impact and the trust investment that support an effective marketing strategy. Creating a balance between managing the creative potential of metrics and maintaining a business model that focuses on support and customer loyalty (Mozumder et al., 2022).

10. CONCLUSION

The Metaverse represents a growing field for organizations looking to redefine how they engage with customers in the digital age. Using this feature opens up many opportunities for deep integration and smart marketing. One of the most important forms of communication is creating a visual environment that allows consumers to connect with the brand on their favorite level. Leveraging technologies such as virtual reality (VR) and augmented reality (AR), organizations can create experiences that transcend traditional boundaries and allow customers to explore products, services, and brand messaging in inclusive and inclusive ways. These immersive brand experiences not only capture attention, but also foster emotional connections and drive deeper engagement and brand loyalty. In addition, Metaverse provides organizations with the opportunity to incorporate game elements into their customer service efforts, improve communication, and encourage engagement. Through immersive experiences, companies can create challenges, quizzes, and reward systems in virtual environments that turn customers into passive participants. By using games and contests as content, organizations can add excitement and fun to their products, encourage and facilitate social interaction among consumers. Movement within a virtual universe not only adds excitement to conversations, but also helps organizations gather customer needs and desires, target media, and personalize experiences based on their needs.

In conclusion, the opportunity to engage customers through the metaverse can be considered as creating a new effective model of business-to-customer relations, brand Building, and constructing valuable experiences. Exploring the potential of metaverse presents businesses with chances to strengthen connections with their audiences, and remain relevant in the globally connected digital economy. In addition to that, although the metaverse provides prominent methodologies for customer engagement enhancement, the enterprises should take preemptive measures for security risks to maintain trust, secure any sensitive data, and develop a safe space for their customers to regard the virtual world as theirs. Adopting cyber security approaches as a priority measure with keen vigilance toward emerging threats enables the organization to exploit the metaverse's opportunities while efficiently minimizing security loopholes.

REFERENCES

Abrokwah-Larbi, K. (2024). Transforming metaverse marketing into strategic agility in SMEs through mediating roles of IMT and CI: Theoretical framework and research propositions. *Journal of Contemporary Marketing Science*, 7(1), 56–83. DOI: 10.1108/JCMARS-08-2023-0034

Ahuja, A. S., Polascik, B. W., Doddapaneni, D., Byrnes, E. S., & Sridhar, J. (2023). The digital metaverse: Applications in artificial intelligence, medical education, and integrative health. *Integrative Medicine Research*, 12(1), 100917. DOI: 10.1016/j.imr.2022.100917 PMID: 36691642

Ajiga, D. I., Ndubuisi, N. L., Asuzu, O. F., Owolabi, O. R., Tubokirifuruar, T. S., & Adeleye, R. A.David Iyanuoluwa AjigaNdubuisi Leonard NdubuisiOnyeka Franca AsuzuOluwaseyi Rita OwolabiTula Sunday TubokirifuruarRhoda Adura Adeleye. (2024). AI-driven predictive analytics in retail: A review of emerging trends and customer engagement strategies. *International Journal of Management & Entrepreneurship Research*, 6(2), 307–321. DOI: 10.51594/ijmer.v6i2.772

Ali, S., Abdullah, , Armand, T. P. T., Athar, A., Hussain, A., Ali, M., Yaseen, M., Joo, M.-I., & Kim, H.-C. (2023). Metaverse in healthcare integrated with explainable AI and blockchain: Enabling immersiveness, ensuring trust, and providing patient data security. *Sensors (Basel)*, 23(2), 565. DOI: 10.3390/s23020565 PMID: 36679361

Aloqaily, M., Bouachir, O., Karray, F., Al Ridhawi, I., & El Saddik, A. (2022). Integrating digital twin and advanced intelligent technologies to realize the metaverse. *IEEE Consumer Electronics Magazine*, 12(6), 47–55. DOI: 10.1109/MCE.2022.3212570

Alshurideh, M., Kurdi, B., Al-Gasaymeh, A., Abuhashesh, M., Jdaitawi, A., Alzoubi, H., Hamadneh, S., & Alquqa, E. (2024). How metaverse can enhance customer awareness, interest, engagement and experience: A practical study. *International Journal of Data and Network Science*, 8(3), 1907–1914. DOI: 10.5267/j.ijdns.2024.1.022

Ameen, N., Sharma, G. D., Tarba, S., Rao, A., & Chopra, R. (2022). Toward advancing theory on creativity in marketing and artificial intelligence. *Psychology and Marketing*, 39(9), 1802–1825. DOI: 10.1002/mar.21699

Anshari, M., Syafrudin, M., Fitriyani, N. L., & Razzaq, A. (2022). Ethical responsibility and sustainability (ERS) development in a metaverse business model. *Sustainability (Basel)*, 14(23), 15805. DOI: 10.3390/su142315805

Ao, L., Bansal, R., Pruthi, N., & Khaskheli, M. B. (2023). Impact of social media influencers on customer engagement and purchase intention: A meta-analysis. *Sustainability (Basel)*, 15(3), 2744. DOI: 10.3390/su15032744

Arya, V., Sambyal, R., Sharma, A., & Dwivedi, Y. K. (2024). Brands are calling your AVATAR in Metaverse–A study to explore XR-based gamification marketing activities & consumer-based brand equity in virtual world. *Journal of Consumer Behaviour*, 23(2), 556–585. DOI: 10.1002/cb.2214

Au, W. J. (2023). *Making a Metaverse That Matters: From Snow Crash & Second Life to A Virtual World Worth Fighting For*. John Wiley & Sons.

Awadallah, A., Eledlebi, K., Zemerly, J., Puthal, D., Damiani, E., Taha, K., Kim, T.-Y., Yoo, P. D., Choo, K.-K. R., Yim, M.-S., & Yeun, C. Y. (2024). Artificial intelligence-based cybersecurity for the metaverse: Research challenges and opportunities. *IEEE Communications Surveys and Tutorials*, 1. DOI: 10.1109/COMST.2024.3442475

Banat, H. F. M., Alotoum, F. J., & Hashem, T. N. (2024, February). Smart Banking Services and Their Impact on the Customers' Intentions to Use Mobile Banking in Commercial Banks: Evidence from UAE. In *2024 2nd International Conference on Cyber Resilience (ICCR)* (pp. 1-7). IEEE.

Banik, B., Banik, S., & Annee, R. R. (2024). The role of AI in enhancing customer engagement and loyalty. *Revista de Inteligencia Artificial en Medicina*, 15(1), 537–561.

Barrera, K. G., & Shah, D. (2023). Marketing in the Metaverse: Conceptual understanding, framework, and research agenda. *Journal of Business Research*, 155, 113420. DOI: 10.1016/j.jbusres.2022.113420

Bathla, D., & Ahuja, R. (2024). Customer Engagement in Metaverse Using Big Data. In *Ethical Marketing Through Data Governance Standards and Effective Technology* (pp. 62–73). IGI Global. DOI: 10.4018/979-8-3693-2215-4.ch005

Bilgihan, A., Leong, A. M. W., Okumus, F., & Bai, J. (2024). Proposing a metaverse engagement model for brand development. *Journal of Retailing and Consumer Services*, 78, 103781. DOI: 10.1016/j.jretconser.2024.103781

Bordegoni, M., & Ferrise, F. (2023). Exploring the intersection of metaverse, digital twins, and artificial intelligence in training and maintenance. *Journal of Computing and Information Science in Engineering*, 23(6), 060806. DOI: 10.1115/1.4062455

Bozkurt, S., Gligor, D., & Gligor, N. (2022). Investigating the impact of psychological customer engagement on customer engagement behaviors: The moderating role of customer commitment. *Journal of Marketing Analytics*, 10(4), 408–424. DOI: 10.1057/s41270-021-00146-3

Burrows, G. (2022). Your Life. In *The Metaverse: Everything you need to know about the virtual internet of tomorrow*. Gideon Burrows.

Chamola, V., Bansal, G., Das, T. K., Hassija, V., Sai, S., Wang, J., Zeadally, S., Hussain, A., Yu, F. R., Guizani, M., & Niyato, D. (2024). Beyond reality: The pivotal role of generative ai in the metaverse. *IEEE Internet of Things Magazine*, 7(4), 126–135. DOI: 10.1109/IOTM.001.2300174

Chamola, V., Bansal, G., Das, T. K., Hassija, V., Sai, S., Wang, J., Zeadally, S., Hussain, A., Yu, F. R., Guizani, M., & Niyato, D. (2024). Beyond reality: The pivotal role of generative ai in the metaverse. *IEEE Internet of Things Magazine*, 7(4), 126–135. DOI: 10.1109/IOTM.001.2300174

Chandratreya, A. (2023). Transforming Digital Marketing Through Metaverse. *Journal of Namibian Studies: History Politics Culture*, 33, 2869–2881.

Chaudhari, A., Mali, Y. K., Kulkarni, A., Jain, D., Sharma, L., Mahajan, K., . . . Bhogle, A. (2024, April). Cyber security challenges in social meta-verse and mitigation techniques. In *2024 MIT Art, Design and Technology School of Computing International Conference (MITADTSoCiCon)* (pp. 1-7). IEEE. DOI: 10.1109/MITADTSoCiCon60330.2024.10575295

Chen, C., Zhang, K. Z., Chu, Z., & Lee, M. (2024). Augmented reality in the metaverse market: The role of multimodal sensory interaction. *Internet Research*, 34(1), 9–38. DOI: 10.1108/INTR-08-2022-0670

Chen, Z., Wu, J., Gan, W., & Qi, Z. (2022, December). Metaverse security and privacy: An overview. In *2022 IEEE International Conference on Big Data (Big Data)* (pp. 2950-2959). IEEE. DOI: 10.1109/BigData55660.2022.10021112

Cheng, S., Zhang, Y., Li, X., Yang, L., Yuan, X., & Li, S. Z. (2022). Roadmap toward the metaverse: An AI perspective. *Innovation (Cambridge (Mass.))*, 3(5), 100293. DOI: 10.1016/j.xinn.2022.100293 PMID: 36032197

Cheung, M. L., Leung, W. K., Chang, L. M. K., Aw, E. C. X., & Wong, R. Y. (2024). Immersive time in the metaverse and visits to the physical world: Why not both? A holistic customer engagement framework. *International Journal of Contemporary Hospitality Management*, 36(11), 3674–3703. DOI: 10.1108/IJCHM-07-2023-0999

Chintalapati, S., & Pandey, S. K. (2022). Artificial intelligence in marketing: A systematic literature review. *International Journal of Market Research*, 64(1), 38–68. DOI: 10.1177/14707853211018428

Dawson, A. (2022). Data-driven consumer engagement, virtual immersive shopping experiences, and blockchain-based digital assets in the retail metaverse. *Journal of Self-Governance and Management Economics*, 10(2), 52–66.

Dwivedi, Y. K., Hughes, L., Wang, Y., Alalwan, A. A., Ahn, S. J., Balakrishnan, J., Barta, S., Belk, R., Buhalis, D., Dutot, V., Felix, R., Filieri, R., Flavián, C., Gustafsson, A., Hinsch, C., Hollensen, S., Jain, V., Kim, J., Krishen, A. S., & Wirtz, J. (2023). Metaverse marketing: How the metaverse will shape the future of consumer research and practice. *Psychology and Marketing*, 40(4), 750–776. DOI: 10.1002/mar.21767

Eggenschwiler, M., Linzmajer, M., Roggeveen, A. L., & Rudolph, T. (2024). Retailing in the metaverse: A framework of managerial considerations for success. *Journal of Retailing and Consumer Services*, 79, 103791. DOI: 10.1016/j.jretconser.2024.103791

Elf, P., Werner, A., & Black, S. (2022). Advancing the circular economy through dynamic capabilities and extended customer engagement: Insights from small sustainable fashion enterprises in the UK. *Business Strategy and the Environment*, 31(6), 2682–2699. DOI: 10.1002/bse.2999

Fadhel, M. A., Duhaim, A. M., Albahri, A. S., Al-Qaysi, Z. T., Aktham, M. A., Chyad, M. A., Abd-Alaziz, W., Albahri, O. S., Alamoodi, A. H., Alzubaidi, L., Gupta, A., & Gu, Y. (2024). Navigating the metaverse: Unraveling the impact of artificial intelligence—a comprehensive review and gap analysis. *Artificial Intelligence Review*, 57(9), 264. DOI: 10.1007/s10462-024-10881-5

Florido-Benítez, L. (2024). Metaverse cannot be an extra marketing immersive tool to increase sales in tourism cities. *International Journal of Tourism Cities.*

Gligor, D., Bozkurt, S., Welch, E., & Gligor, N. (2023). An exploration of the impact of gender on customer engagement. *Journal of Marketing Communications*, 29(4), 379–402. DOI: 10.1080/13527266.2022.2030390

Goldberg, M., Schär, F., & Thürkauf, D. (2023). Retailing and customer engagement in the metaverse: An empirical analysis. *Available atSSRN* 4547100. DOI: 10.2139/ssrn.4547100

Guo, Y., Yu, T., Wu, J., Wang, Y., Wan, S., Zheng, J., ... & Dai, Q. (2022). Artificial intelligence for metaverse: a framework. *CAAI Artificial Intelligence Research, 1*(1).

Gupta, R., Rathore, B., Biswas, B., Jaiswal, M., & Singh, R. K. (2024). Are we ready for metaverse adoption in the service industry? Theoretically exploring the barriers to successful adoption. *Journal of Retailing and Consumer Services*, 79, 103882. DOI: 10.1016/j.jretconser.2024.103882

Gursoy, D., Lu, L., Nunkoo, R., & Deng, D. (2023). Metaverse in services marketing: An overview and future research directions. *Service Industries Journal*, 43(15-16), 1140–1172. DOI: 10.1080/02642069.2023.2252750

Haavisto, J. (2024). Designing implementable tools: the importance of easy and fast implementation in the metaverse era.

Haleem, A., Javaid, M., Qadri, M. A., Singh, R. P., & Suman, R. (2022). Artificial intelligence (AI) applications for marketing: A literature-based study. *International Journal of Intelligent Networks*, 3, 119–132. DOI: 10.1016/j.ijin.2022.08.005

Hamilton, S. (2022). Deep learning computer vision algorithms, customer engagement tools, and virtual marketplace dynamics data in the metaverse economy. *Journal of Self-Governance and Management Economics*, 10(2), 37–51.

Hampton, H., Foley, A., Del Rio, D. F., Smyth, B., Laverty, D., & Caulfield, B. (2022). Customer engagement strategies in retail electricity markets: A comprehensive and comparative review. *Energy Research & Social Science*, 90, 102611. DOI: 10.1016/j.erss.2022.102611

Han, S., & Anderson, C. K. (2022). The dynamic customer engagement behaviors in the customer satisfaction survey. *Decision Support Systems*, 154, 113708. DOI: 10.1016/j.dss.2021.113708

Hasani, T., Rezania, D., & Mohammadi, M. (2024). Towards a framework for successful metaverse adoption in Small and Medium-sized Enterprises: An exploratory study. *International Journal of Engineering Business Management*, 16, 18479790241257118. DOI: 10.1177/18479790241257118

Hashem, T. (2024). Digital Marketing and the Ethical Code for Behavioral Tracking: Issues of Privacy and Consumer Trust. *Journal of Electrical Systems*, 20(10), 2842–2854.

Hashem, T., Alotoum, F. J., Allan, M., & Ali, N. (2023). Employing metaverse marketing through gaming and its impact on customer experience: Evidence from multiple online gaming platforms. *Calitatea*, 24(196), 193–206.

Hindolia, A., Arya, J., Pathak, R., & Kazmi, A. (2024). Halal B2B marketing in the metaverse: Crafting a conceptual framework to pinpoint opportunities and challenges, outlining the agenda for future research. *Journal of Islamic Marketing*. Advance online publication. DOI: 10.1108/JIMA-02-2024-0054

Hollebeek, L. D., Sharma, T. G., Pandey, R., Sanyal, P., & Clark, M. K. (2022). Fifteen years of customer engagement research: A bibliometric and network analysis. *Journal of Product and Brand Management*, 31(2), 293–309. DOI: 10.1108/JPBM-01-2021-3301

Hsieh, T. T., Emerson, R. W., Foster, I. I., Larry, D., Link, B. A., Sherman, C. A., & Trautman, L. J. (2023). Intellectual Property In the Era of AI, Blockchain and Web 3.0. *Blockchain and Web, 3*.

Huynh-The, T., Pham, Q. V., Pham, X. Q., Nguyen, T. T., Han, Z., & Kim, D. S. (2023). Artificial intelligence for the metaverse: A survey. *Engineering Applications of Artificial Intelligence*, 117, 105581. DOI: 10.1016/j.engappai.2022.105581

Huynh-The, T., Pham, Q. V., Pham, X. Q., Nguyen, T. T., Han, Z., & Kim, D. S. (2023). Artificial intelligence for the metaverse: A survey. *Engineering Applications of Artificial Intelligence*, 117, 105581. DOI: 10.1016/j.engappai.2022.105581

Hwang, G. J., & Chien, S. Y. (2022). Definition, roles, and potential research issues of the metaverse in education: An artificial intelligence perspective. *Computers and Education: Artificial Intelligence*, 3, 100082. DOI: 10.1016/j.caeai.2022.100082

Ibrahim, A. (2024). The Role of Artificial Intelligence in the Metaverse. *Arts and Design Studies.Image*, 1, •••. https://frontofficesports.com/nike-trademark-hints-at-metaverse-sneakers/

Image 2. https://jingdaily.com/posts/gucci-head-of-metaverse

Image 3. https://streamhatchet.com/blog/setting-the-hype-for-elden-ring-shadow-of-the-erdtree-with-redbull/

Image 4. https://news.samsung.com/us/creation-of-samsung-837x/

Jaber, T. A. (2022). Security Risks of the Metaverse World. *Int. J. Interact. Mob. Technol.*, 16(13), 4–14. DOI: 10.3991/ijim.v16i13.33187

Jha, A. (2023). Immersive Marketing on Metaverse: Development of Metrics for Performance Analysis and Security-Related Challenges. In *Confronting Security and Privacy Challenges in Digital Marketing* (pp. 267-289). IGI Global.

Khang, A., Shah, V., & Rani, S. (Eds.). (2023). *Handbook of Research on AI-Based Technologies and Applications in the Era of the Metaverse*. IGI Global. DOI: 10.4018/978-1-6684-8851-5

Khatri, M. (2022). Revamping the marketing world with metaverse–The future of marketing. *International Journal of Computer Applications*, 184(29), 1–5. DOI: 10.5120/ijca2022922361

Koo, C., Kwon, J., Chung, N., & Kim, J. (2023). Metaverse tourism: Conceptual framework and research propositions. *Current Issues in Tourism*, 26(20), 3268–3274. DOI: 10.1080/13683500.2022.2122781

Kour, M. (2024). Ethical Considerations in the Metaverse and Augmented Retail Reality Era. In *Consumer Experience and Decision-Making in the Metaverse* (pp. 99–110). IGI Global. DOI: 10.4018/979-8-3693-4167-4.ch006

Lim, W. M., & Rasul, T. (2022). Customer engagement and social media: Revisiting the past to inform the future. *Journal of Business Research*, 148, 325–342. DOI: 10.1016/j.jbusres.2022.04.068

Lim, W. M., Rasul, T., Kumar, S., & Ala, M. (2022). Past, present, and future of customer engagement. *Journal of Business Research*, 140, 439–458. DOI: 10.1016/j.jbusres.2021.11.014

Liu, J. (2022, December). Metaverse and brand: a study of luxury brand digital marketing strategy-taking Gucci as an example. In *2022 4th International Conference on Economic Management and Cultural Industry (ICEMCI 2022)* (pp. 1907-1913). Atlantis Press.

Liu, S. (2023). The security challenges of the "Metaverse". *Security and Safety*, 2, 2023010. DOI: 10.1051/sands/2023010

Longo, M. C., & Canalichio, P. (2024). *Strategic Brand Licensing: Building Brand Value Through Enduring Partnerships*. Taylor & Francis. DOI: 10.4324/9781003364566

Lv, Z. (2023). Generative artificial intelligence in the metaverse era. *Cognitive Robotics*, 3, 208–217. DOI: 10.1016/j.cogr.2023.06.001

Mancuso, I., Petruzzelli, A. M., & Panniello, U. (2023). Digital business model innovation in metaverse: How to approach virtual economy opportunities. *Information Processing & Management*, 60(5), 103457. DOI: 10.1016/j.ipm.2023.103457

Mariani, M. M., Perez-Vega, R., & Wirtz, J. (2022). AI in marketing, consumer research and psychology: A systematic literature review and research agenda. *Psychology and Marketing*, 39(4), 755–776. DOI: 10.1002/mar.21619

McDonald, H., Biscaia, R., Yoshida, M., Conduit, J., & Doyle, J. P. (2022). Customer engagement in sport: An updated review and research agenda. *Journal of Sport Management*, 36(3), 289–304. DOI: 10.1123/jsm.2021-0233

Mourtzis, D., Panopoulos, N., Angelopoulos, J., Wang, B., & Wang, L. (2022). Human centric platforms for personalized value creation in metaverse. *Journal of Manufacturing Systems*, 65, 653–659. DOI: 10.1016/j.jmsy.2022.11.004

Mozumder, M. A. I., Sheeraz, M. M., Athar, A., Aich, S., & Kim, H. C. (2022, February). Overview: Technology roadmap of the future trend of metaverse based on IoT, blockchain, AI technique, and medical domain metaverse activity. In *2022 24th International Conference on Advanced Communication Technology (ICACT)* (pp. 256-261). IEEE.

NasarAmini Jeloudarlou, S., Aali, S., Faryabi, M., & Bafandeh Zendeh, A.Nasar-Amini Jeloudarlou. (2022). The effect of servicescape on customer engagement: The mediating role of customer experience. *Journal of Quality Assurance in Hospitality & Tourism*, 23(2), 318–344. DOI: 10.1080/1528008X.2020.1867696

Newell, M. (2022). Customer Engagement and Data Visualization Tools, Ambient Sound Recognition Software, and Deep Learning-based Sensing Technologies in the Metaverse Economy. *Economics, Management, and Financial Markets*, 17(3), 25–41. DOI: 10.22381/emfm17320222

Ng, D. T. K. (2022). What is the metaverse? Definitions, technologies and the community of inquiry. *Australasian Journal of Educational Technology*, 38(4), 190–205. DOI: 10.14742/ajet.7945

Park, S. M., & Kim, Y. G. (2022). A metaverse: Taxonomy, components, applications, and open challenges. *IEEE Access : Practical Innovations, Open Solutions*, 10, 4209–4251. DOI: 10.1109/ACCESS.2021.3140175

Parray, Z. A., Iqbal, J., & Mushtaq, R. (2024). Customer perception of corporate social responsibility and its impact on customer engagement: Critical significance of corporate reputation. *Corporate Communications*, 29(4), 592–606. DOI: 10.1108/CCIJ-05-2023-0063

Peltier, J. W., Dahl, A. J., & Schibrowsky, J. A. (2024). Artificial intelligence in interactive marketing: A conceptual framework and research agenda. *Journal of Research in Interactive Marketing*, 18(1), 54–90. DOI: 10.1108/JRIM-01-2023-0030

Petr, C., & Caudan, P. (2024). Ethical marketing framework for metaverse simulated experiences of tourism (SET): An exploration of consumers' aspirations and fears. *Journal of Retailing and Consumer Services*, 79, 103785. DOI: 10.1016/j.jretconser.2024.103785

Petrescu, M., & Krishen, A. S. (2023). Hybrid intelligence: human–AI collaboration in marketing analytics. *Journal of Marketing Analytics*, 11(3), 263–274. DOI: 10.1057/s41270-023-00245-3

Rane, N., Choudhary, S., & Rane, J. (2023). Metaverse marketing strategies: enhancing customer experience and analysing consumer behaviour through leading-edge Metaverse technologies, platforms, and models. *Platforms, and Models (November 3, 2023).*

Rane, N., Choudhary, S., & Rane, J. (2023). Metaverse marketing strategies: enhancing customer experience and analysing consumer behaviour through leading-edge Metaverse technologies, platforms, and models. *Platforms, and Models (November 3, 2023).*

Rather, R. A. (2023). Metaverse marketing and consumer research: Theoretical framework and future research agenda in tourism and hospitality industry. *Tourism Recreation Research*, •••, 1–9. DOI: 10.1080/02508281.2023.2216525

Rather, R. A., Hollebeek, L. D., & Rasoolimanesh, S. M. (2022). First-time versus repeat tourism customer engagement, experience, and value cocreation: An empirical investigation. *Journal of Travel Research*, 61(3), 549–564. DOI: 10.1177/0047287521997572

Rathore, B. (2023). Digital transformation 4.0: integration of artificial intelligence & metaverse in marketing. *Eduzone: International Peer Reviewed/Refereed Multidisciplinary Journal, 12*(1), 42-48.

Rauschnabel, P. A., Babin, B. J., tom Dieck, M. C., Krey, N., & Jung, T. (2022). What is augmented reality marketing? Its definition, complexity, and future. *Journal of Business Research*, 142, 1140–1150. DOI: 10.1016/j.jbusres.2021.12.084

Rosa, N. (2022). *Understanding the Metaverse: A Business and Ethical Guide*. John Wiley & Sons.

Sarkar, B. D., Shardeo, V., Mir, U. B., & Negi, H. (2024). Harvesting success: Metaverse adoption in agriculture sector as a sustainable business strategy. *Journal of Enterprise Information Management*, 37(6), 1858–1884. DOI: 10.1108/JEIM-10-2023-0536

Sawhney, M., & Goodman, P. (2023). *Nike: Tiptoeing Into the Metaverse*. Kellogg School of Management.

Shaik, M. (2023). Impact of artificial intelligence on marketing. *East Asian Journal of Multidisciplinary Research*, 2(3), 993–1004. DOI: 10.55927/eajmr.v2i3.3112

Sim, M., Conduit, J., Plewa, C., & Hentzen, J. K. (2022). Customer engagement with service providers: An empirical investigation of customer engagement dispositions. *European Journal of Marketing*, 56(7), 1926–1955. DOI: 10.1108/EJM-12-2020-0879

Soliman, M. M., Ahmed, E., Darwish, A., & Hassanien, A. E. (2024). Artificial intelligence powered Metaverse: Analysis, challenges and future perspectives. *Artificial Intelligence Review*, 57(2), 36. DOI: 10.1007/s10462-023-10641-x

Spajić, J., Mitrović, K., Lalić, D., Milić, B., & Bošković, D. (2022, September). Personalized brand experience in metaverse. In *10th International Conference on Mass Customization and Personalization–Community of Europe (MCP-CE 2022)* (pp. 21-23).

Tan, T. M., & Salo, J. (2023). Ethical marketing in the blockchain-based sharing economy: Theoretical integration and guiding insights. *Journal of Business Ethics*, 183(4), 1113–1140. DOI: 10.1007/s10551-021-05015-8

Tayal, S., & Rajagopal, K. (2023, May). Marketing gamification in metaverse web 3.0 with artificial intelligence (ai). In *2023 7th International Conference on Intelligent Computing and Control Systems (ICICCS)* (pp. 646-652). IEEE.

Tayal, S., Rajagopal, K., & Mahajan, V. (2022, March). Virtual reality based metaverse of gamification. In *2022 6th International Conference on Computing Methodologies and Communication (ICCMC)* (pp. 1597-1604). IEEE. DOI: 10.1109/ICCMC53470.2022.9753727

Thakur, S. S., Bandyopadhyay, S., & Datta, D. (2023). Artificial intelligence and the metaverse: Present and future aspects. In *The Future of Metaverse in the Virtual Era and Physical World* (pp. 169–184). Springer International Publishing. DOI: 10.1007/978-3-031-29132-6_10

Thakur, S. S., Bandyopadhyay, S., & Datta, D. (2023). Artificial intelligence and the metaverse: Present and future aspects. In *The Future of Metaverse in the Virtual Era and Physical World* (pp. 169–184). Springer International Publishing. DOI: 10.1007/978-3-031-29132-6_10

Upadhyay, U., Kumar, A., Sharma, G., Saini, A. K., Arya, V., Gaurav, A., & Chui, K. T. (2024). Mitigating Risks in the Cloud-Based Metaverse Access Control Strategies and Techniques. [IJCAC]. *International Journal of Cloud Applications and Computing*, 14(1), 1–30. DOI: 10.4018/IJCAC.334364

Valaskova, K., Machova, V., & Lewis, E. (2022). Virtual marketplace dynamics data, spatial analytics, and customer engagement tools in a real-time interoperable decentralized metaverse. *Linguistic and Philosophical Investigations*, 21(0), 105–120. DOI: 10.22381/lpi2120227

Wang, Y., Su, Z., Zhang, N., Xing, R., Liu, D., Luan, T. H., & Shen, X. (2022). A survey on metaverse: Fundamentals, security, and privacy. *IEEE Communications Surveys and Tutorials*, 25(1), 319–352. DOI: 10.1109/COMST.2022.3202047

Wanick, V., & Stallwood, J. (2023). Brand storytelling, gamification and social media marketing in the "metaverse": A case study of the Ralph Lauren winter escape. In *Reinventing fashion retailing: Digitalising, gamifying, entrepreneuring* (pp. 35–54). Springer International Publishing. DOI: 10.1007/978-3-031-11185-3_3

Watson, R. (2022). The virtual economy of the metaverse: Computer vision and deep learning algorithms, customer engagement tools, and behavioral predictive analytics. *Linguistic and Philosophical Investigations*, (21), 41–56.

Wongkitrungrueng, A., & Suprawan, L. (2024). Metaverse meets branding: Examining consumer responses to immersive brand experiences. *International Journal of Human-Computer Interaction*, 40(11), 2905–2924. DOI: 10.1080/10447318.2023.2175162

Yang, Q., Zhao, Y., Huang, H., Xiong, Z., Kang, J., & Zheng, Z. (2022). Fusing blockchain and AI with metaverse: A survey. *IEEE Open Journal of the Computer Society*, 3, 122–136. DOI: 10.1109/OJCS.2022.3188249

Zainurin, M. Z. L., Haji Masri, M., Besar, M. H. A., & Anshari, M. (2023). Towards an understanding of metaverse banking: A conceptual paper. *Journal of Financial Reporting and Accounting*, 21(1), 178–190. DOI: 10.1108/JFRA-12-2021-0487

Zawish, M., Dharejo, F. A., Khowaja, S. A., Raza, S., Davy, S., Dev, K., & Bellavista, P. (2024). AI and 6G into the metaverse: Fundamentals, challenges and future research trends. *IEEE Open Journal of the Communications Society*, 5, 730–778. DOI: 10.1109/OJCOMS.2024.3349465

Zhao, R., Zhang, Y., Zhu, Y., Lan, R., & Hua, Z. (2023). Metaverse: Security and privacy concerns. *Journal of Metaverse*, 3(2), 93–99. DOI: 10.57019/jmv.1286526

Chapter 12

The Effect of NFTs Metaverse Engagement and Digital Personalization on Brand Accessibility: The Mediating Role of Inclusive Brand Strategies

Sumaira Aslam
https://orcid.org/0000-0001-9730-4753
University of Management and Technology, Lahore, Pakistan

Muhammad Ussama Majeed
https://orcid.org/0000-0002-2676-0732
National University of Modern Languages, Pakistan

Zahid Hussain
https://orcid.org/0009-0006-2182-9303
Khadim Ali Shah Institute of Technology, Pakistan

ABSTRACT

Purpose: This paper investigates the impact of Non-fungible Tokens (NFTs), Metaverse Engagement (ME), and Digital Personalization (DP) on Brand Accessibility (BA) with a focus on the mediating role of Inclusive Brand Strategies (IBS). Methodology: A total of 256 participants from the Fashion retailing sector participated in the paper. Data analysis using SEM with the SMART-PLS tool using a purposive sampling

DOI: 10.4018/979-8-3693-9005-4.ch012

strategy. Findings: NFTs, Metaverse Engagement and Digital Personalization all Significantly enhance Brand Accessibility. Furthermore, it was discovered that inclusive brand strategies mediate this link highlighting the significance of inclusive strategies in improving brand accessibility. Originality/Value: This paper adds to the growing body of knowledge about brand accessibility in modern technology. It gives brands looking to promote accessibility and inclusion into their online presence beneficial knowledge by looking at the significance of novel technologies and Inclusive tactics.

1. INTRODUCTION

As the world grows more digitally connected, brands are looking for new and creative ways to enhance their inclusiveness and accessibility since they know how important these elements are to drawing in current customers (Zhou et al., 2024). NFTs(Non-fungible Tokens), ME(Metaverse Engagement), and DP(Digital Personalization) are a few of the cutting-edge online marketing techniques that have drawn a lot of attention due to their ability to shift the way that brands and customers engage (Periyasania et al., 2022). While these techniques offer distinctive features for businesses to create more meaningful connections with their customers, it is still unclear how they will affect brand awareness. According to Wang et al., (2023), NFTs-based advertising initiatives enhance customer's opinions of the brand's worth and memorability, which enhances customer engagement and brand awareness by creating immersive brand experiences. According to Nalbant et al., (2023), ME in brand narratives supports to creation of emotional ties among customers and enhances brand loyalty. The usefulness of DP techniques in strengthening brand-customer links is highlighted by the great impact that Personalized recommendations have on customer purchasing intentions and commitment to online shopping. According to Lee et al., (2022), IBS has a significant impact on customer confidence and brand devotion with customers being more engaged and advocating for businesses they perceive to be more diverse. When NFTs are included in brand marketing initiatives, there is a long-term consistent rise in customer interactions and exposure which strengthens their image (Kraust et al., 2024). According to Kilicaslan et al., (2022) by providing immersive digital experiences that align with their passions and goals, ME has a significant impact on their perceptions of the brand and their propensity for buying it. Brand memory and customer engagement are significantly enhanced by Personalized marketing campaigns in digital marketing, which enhances brand recognition and attention (Gupta et al., 2023). Deep emotional ties among brands and customers are created when they embrace diversity and inclusiveness in their campaigns. This leads to enhanced customer brand management and loyalty. According to Kemac et al., (2022), NFTs increase views on brand worth and attractiveness among rich customers in the luxury industry by improving brand distinction. In the hospitality industry, Personalized client experiences are found in greater brand loyalty and beneficial word-of-mouth suggestions enhancing the importance of DP in enhancing consumer confidence (Colicev et al., 2023). According to Hakkarainen et al., (2023), brands use VR to create immersive brand experiences in the metaverse, which enhances customer-centric brand bonds and enhances the image with the demographics. IBS enhancing credibility and cultural diversity strengthens links with diverse customers by enhancing trust and confidence throughout a range of socio-economic developments (Deventer et al., 2024). NFTs and blockchain systems enhance customer trust and brand value via transparency and traceability in supply chain management and brand management (Santos et al., 2023).

In the retail sector, Personalized product recommendations beat traditional recommendations in terms of enhancing customer satisfaction and profitability, which in turn leads to enhanced income and more ongoing development (Koo et al., 2022). According to Khan et al., (2023), IBS that utilize a variety of views and narrative devices connect with socially aware customers on a deep level, which enhances brand recognition and loyalty. Prior research has mostly concentrated on how NFTs, ME, and DP individually affect brand loyalty and commitment. On the other hand, little is known regarding how these developments work together to affect BA while IBS functions as a mediator in this procedure. By investigating the cumulative impact of NFTs, ME, and DP on BA and how IBS mediates these associations, this research seeks to close this gap. With the mediating role of IBS, this paper examines the link among NFTs, ME, DP, and BA. In all, 256 individuals working in the fashion retail sector took advantage of the research. Purposive sampling was used in the SEM and SMART-PLS software evaluation process. The paper provides sophisticated views on how Brands use these innovations and inclusive tactics to enhance accessibility with digital spaces by exploring these links. Furthermore, it was clear that the key variable impacting BA was IBS's mediating role. Implementing these initiatives enhances inclusion and brand reputation among customers. This study provides new advanced insights related to these associations and practical implications for several stakeholders.

2. THEORETICAL FOUNDATIONS AND HYPOTHESIS DEVELOPMENT

2.1 Theoretical Foundations

There are several theories regarding the impact of DP, ME, and NFTs on BA and the mediating role of IBS. According to the View based on resources (RBV) theory, brands can get a competitive edge by utilizing NFTs, ME, and DP as important resources, ME and DP help brands to use technologies to fulfill the customer needs and wants, NFTs create more advanced features, which enhance customer satisfaction (Wang eta al., 2023). Similarly, social exchange theory (SET) shows that NFTs and ME enhance customer-brand engagements and create trust and loyalty to provide advanced digital features and a completely immersive experience (Nalbant et al., 2023). Same as Technology Acceptance Model (TAM) can utilized to change customer perceptions and clarify why they adopt advanced technologies. By making online relationships more pertinent and intuitive, DP improves consumer happiness and planned purchases, hence improving BA (Gupta et al., 2023). The enduring worth of interactions with clients is emphasized by the client capital it. IBS promotes multiculturalism and inclusivity, which fortifies client support and devotion and improves consumer equality (Lee et al., 2022). The notion of Diffusion of Innovations (DOI) describes how new ideas are embraced by an industry. As cutting-edge marketing strategies, NFTs and ME spread among early users and impact greater consumer interaction and perceived value (Kraust et al., 2024). The notion of Brand reputation emphasizes the significance of brand connections, perceived value, and popularity. By strengthening the uniqueness of the brand and retention, NFTs and tailored online interactions raise reputation value (Kemac et al., 2022). Service-dominant logic (SDL) emphasizes the sharing of values via service-to-service interactions. By including consumers in realistic brand stories and situations, ME helps businesses generate mutually beneficial possibilities (Kilicaslan et al., 2022). According to the Expectancy-Value Theory (EVT), an action's anticipated effects determine its conduct. By offering individualized situations, DP meets the requirements of its clients, boosting their loyalty and sense of happiness within the company (Gupta et al., 2023). According to stakeholder theory, it's critical to attend to the demands of all parties involved. IBS increases confidence and reputation values by encouraging broad acceptance and ensuring that companies live up to the requirements set by a variety of interested parties (Deventer et al., 2024). Self-Determination Theory (SDT) emphasizes the underlying incentives that propel action. By matching consumers' passions and tastes, personalized marketing strategies strengthen their fundamental drives, fostering greater psychological connections and increasing company loyalty (Khan et al., 2023). Research shows that NFTs-based marketing campaigns enhance consumers' impressions of a company's worth and recall value, which raises reputation and improves client retention via complete immersion (Wang et al., 2023). NFTs improve brand differentiation in the luxury sectors, which raises their value and appeal amongst wealthy consumers (Kemac et al., 2022). Virtual reality in the metaverse strengthens brand ties with customers and boosts brand perception across all demographics (Hakkarainen et al., 2023). By offering tailored recommendations that improve client happiness and revenue, DP approaches have significant effects on client dedication to and planned purchases (Gupta et al., 2023; Koo et al., 2022). In the tourism sector, they create customer engagements, which enhances significant referrals and enhances trust in brands (Colicev et al., 2023). IBS is important for enhancing brand loyalty and trust among customers, brands use them to enhance experience and engagement (Lee et al., 2022).

2.2 Non-fungible Tokens (NFTs)

Integrating blockchain, NFTs refer to the collection of digital assets, artwork and antiquities (Radanliev et al., 2023). NFTs provide online platforms, which show ownership of digital assets enabling effective payments and advanced sources of income (Schauman et al., 2023). NFTs improve the accessibility and innovation of online connections and provide open and unforgettable ownership information (Sung et al., 2023). Integrating NFTs in marketing improves customer perceptions related to brand value and memorability, which improves customer loyalty and brand awareness (Zadorozhnyi et al., 2022). When NFTs are involved in brand marketing initiatives, there is a long-lasting, constant increase in customer engagement and perceived value, which is an enhanced image (Yoo et al., 2023). NFTs provide access of data and tracking in supply chain management and brand management, which enhances customer trust and brand Responsibilities (Nalbant et al., 2023). Customers are more interested in demanding branded NFTs as a digital asset when brands utilize them to create scarcity and uniqueness in digital artifacts and online connections (Koo et al., 2022). According to Lee et al., (2023), NFTs provide tokenized assets for brand Interactions and decisions which enhance customer engagement, brand commitment, and retention. Brands and artists work together to create digital artwork with NFTs to generate income and brand cooperation options, which enhance brand awareness and impact in the digital artwork environment (Hakkarainen et al., 2023). Brands have high authority around intellectual property rights and brand licensing agreements, and NFTs provide decentralized venues for tokenization and trading of digital assets. They also enhance customer trust and transparency (Christodoulou et al., 2022).

2.3 Metaverse Engagement

Immersive experience and brand narratives are made possible by ME, which refers to immersive experiences in a digital format wherein customers engage with digital representations of themselves, other individuals, and brand sources (Lee et al., 2024). ME involves the usage of VR to create dynamic brand ecosystems and realistic user experiences, which allows brands to engage with customers in novel and meaningful ways while fostering emotional ties (Khan et al., 2023). ME integrates AR, VR and Social sites to enhance immersive brand experiences that transcend the limitations among actual and digital locations and enhance customer engagement and perceived value (Leahy et al., 2022). ME in corporate storytelling supports to creation of emotional ties with customers and enhances brand loyalty by providing realistic brand experiences and enhancing customer perceptions that align with their interests and aspirations (Kraust et al., 2024). Brands utilize VR to create immersive brand environments in the metaverse, which enhances customer-brand bonds and their resonance with their customers (Joy et al., 2022). VR-based brand experiences that replicate Personal connections and product demos within immersive environments enhance customer intention and loyalty resulting in high conversion rates and promoting a brand's virtual meetings and gatherings centered in the metaverse (Duggal et al., 2023). Metaverse helps advertisers the possibility to interact with customers around the world in an advanced digital way creating effective links and connections with brands in the current period (Colicev et al., 2023). AR marketing initiatives enhance brand experiences and customer engagement by adopting interpersonal links and significant experiences through stimulated brand communities in multiplayer digital games and simulated ways (Arya et al., 2024). Metaverse connects active customers supports brand devotion and develops new advanced awareness patterns (Leahy et al., 2022).

2.4 Digital Personalization

DP utlize to enhance customer relevancy and engagement through providing information and algorithms to customize user interfaces recommend products and marketing initiatives to each person's interests and actions (Multazam et al., 2022). DP entails the diversification of Personalized data to create links and enhance transformation which will improve experiences via online sites by fulfilling customer needs, population demographics, and previous interactions (Rosario et al., 2023). DP uses ML to forecast and satisfy the wants and needs of customers offering individualized experiences that speak to Each person personally (Zhou et al., 2024). The usefulness of DP techniques in enhancing brand-customer links is explored by the diverse impacts that Personalized recommendations have on customer purchasing intentions and commitment in e-commerce (Kim et al., 2024). In the hospitality industry, Personalized client experiences show high brand devotion and significant word-of-mouth suggestions enhancing the importance of online Personalization in return customers (Murtas et al., 2024). Brand memory and customer engagement are significantly enhanced by DP in Online marketing, which enhances brand recognition and attention (Santos et al., 2023). In e-commerce, Personalized recommended goods dramatically enhance sales conversions and customer satisfaction and impact customer choices (Yencha et al., 2023). According to Lee et al., (2022), Personalized marketing emails based on particular preferences and elements have high open and clicking rates enhancing the importance of DP in increasing marketing efficiency. Price charge tools modify prices in reaction to current market situations and customer behavior pricing sensitivity and transparency enhance customer trust and loyalty (Nalbant et al., 2023). A high amount of engagement and brand loyalty is achieved via customized content experiences that use ML and AI to create Personalized content recommendations via digital sites (Kilicaslan et al., 2022).

2.5 Brand Accessibility

The term " Brand Accessibility" refers to how simple customers engage with themselves, are accessible and get an advantage via the brand's products, services, and online sources via verification of interfaces and pathways to enhance simplicity and inclusiveness for diverse customers (Yang et al., 2024). BA overcomes the challenges and enhances the easy-to-use accessibility enhancements and Inclusive design guidelines for every socio-economic status with equal access to brand experiences (Periyasania et al., 2022). According to Mancuso et al., (2023), BA enables brands to develop Inclusive experiences, hospitable and pertinent to different customer elements with specific requirements. According to Payal et al., (2024), IBS has a significant impact on customer trust and brand image where customers engage and advocate for businesses they perceive differently. According to Kemac et al., (2022), socially aware customers are more receptive to diverse brand narratives that integrate different views and storyline elements, which enhances brand image and trust. Website visitors and conversation rates among customers with impairments are high for businesses that employ inclusive components like subtitles for videos and adaptive web designs (Khan et al., 2023). High engagement and lower abandonment rates on website pages are outcomes of high enhancement in user interface and BA origin about mobile-friendly layout and simple access (Deventer et al., 2024). According to Hakkarainen et al., (2023) facilitating access to customers via different languages and translation abilities in digital sites supports brands encompasses visibility, and penetrates novel markets. According to Duggal et al., (2023) offering reductions to peers and youngsters was a manifestation of a reasonable Inclusive pricing strategy, which enhances BA appeals to price-conscious customers elements and enhances satisfaction rates and sales rates.

2.6 Inclusive Brand Strategies

IBS is a meaningful contribution of equal chance and inclusion concepts into marketing strategies, brand culture, and brand message to provide participation feeling of belonging for disadvantaged and marginalized customers (Yoo et al., 2023). IBS initiatives like embracing variety, social accountability, and availability support brands to represent themselves as the main leader of justice and fairness simultaneously appealing to customers who are eco-friendly and search for credibility and moral standards (Radanliev et al., 2023). According to Ahn et al., (2024), IBS creates accessible brand experiences that transcend beyond a variety of demographic information and create deep connections with ethnic customers, which enhances cultural awareness, Interactions, and strength. According to Duggal et al., (2023), good connections with brands and customers are established when they embrace diversity and inclusiveness in their campaigns, which enhances customer brand engagement rates and loyalty. IBS shows the genuineness and cultural diversity among different customers by enhancing their trust and loyalty through a wide range of demographic figures (Joy et al., 2022). Brands must enhance their image and create connections with responsible customers by connecting with diversity-based institutions and get a competitive advantage of social initiatives that enhance Inclusion and responsible behavior (Kim et al., 2024). According to Lee et al., (2023), minority groups are more likely to comprehensive marketing campaigns where they use diverse elements and Actual narratives, which enhances brand loyalty and beneficial word-of-mouth suggestions. According to Murtas et al., (2024) adding accessible enhancements like closed captioning and audio explanations into campaigns shows a brand's trust in diversity and enhances customer trust and loyalty among people with impairments. According to Wang et al., (2023), the brand may connect meaningfully with different customer elements via inclusive initiatives and sponsorships that enhance different cultures and advance social issues, which enhance customer support and trust.

3. HYPOTHESIS DEVELOPMENT

H1:*NFTs has a positive impact on Inclusive Brand Strategies.*

Rosario et al., (2023) found that brands using NFTs-based advertising strategies enhanced customer views regarding brand value and image, suggesting that NFTs can enhance brand awareness. Schauman et al., (2023) found that adopting NFTs helps to enhance long-term relationships and enhance customer engagement and brand value showing a significant connection among NFTs and Brand Strategies.

H2: Metaverse Engagement has a positive impact on Inclusive Brand Strategies.

Santos et al., (2023) found that ME can create emotional bonds with customers and enhance immersive experience showing that ME has the capacity to affect brand strategis. Zho et al., (2024) found that ME had a significant impact on customers' Perceptions regarding brands and enhanced purchasing intentions showing a significant connection between brand strategy and ME.

H3:*Digital Personalization has a positive impact on Inclusive Brand Strategies.*

San Miguel et al., (2024) analyzed that Customer loyalty and purchase intentions were significantly impacted by Personalized suggestions indicating that DP enhances brand strategy. Zadorozhnyi et al., (2022) found that individualized customer experiences enhance customer trust and encourage beneficial word-of-mouth suggestions showing that DP has a significant impact on brand Strategies.

H4:*NFTs has a positive impact on brand accessibility.*

Joy et al., (2022) found that customers' perspectives regarding a brand's value and visibility are enhanced by NFTs-based advertising strategies showing a strong connection among NFTs and BA. Gupta et al., (2023) show that brands using NFTs-based advertising strategies for enhancing their customer's engagement and brand value shows that NFTs enhance BA.

H5:*Metaverse Engagement has a positive impact on Brand Accessibility.*

Koo et al., (2022) found that ME creates emotional ties with customers and enhances immersive experiences showing a significant connection between ME and BA. Belk et al., (2022) show that ME positively impacts customer perceptions and purchasing intentions in benefiting way suggesting that ME positively affects on BA.

H6:*Digital Personalization has a positive impact on Brand Accessibility.*

Leahy et al., (2022) found that customers' trust and purchasing intentions are significantly impacted by Personalized recommendations showing that DP enhances BA. Christodoulou et al., (2022) found that tailored customer experience outcomes in higher brand loyalty and significant word-of-mouth suggestions show that DP impacts BA.

H7:*Inclusive Brand Strategies has a positive impact on Brand Accessibility.*

Arya et al., (2024) found that IBS had a significant impact on customer choices and trust indicating that Inclusive tactics can enhance BA. Lee et al., (2024) found that brands should embrace diversity and inclusiveness in their campaigns to create deeper emotional ties through their customers suggesting that inclusive tactics significantly impact on BA.

H8:*Inclusive Brand strategies mediate the relationship between NFTs and brand accessibility.*

Multazam et al. (2022) Found that IBS effectively impacts on customer trust and loyalty showing that IBS has a mediating role in the link between NFTs and BA. Same as Olaleye et al., (2022) IBS, can create a buffering among NFTs and BA. They show that brands that value diversity and inclusion have more significant links with their target customers.

H9:*Inclusive Brand strategies mediate the relationship between Metaverse engagement and brand accessibility.*

According to Zhou et al., (2024), IBS significantly impacts customer retention and trust, showing that IBS can mediate variables between me and BA. Same as Sung et al., (2023) show that brands prioritize diversity and inclusion among significant links with customers. This shows that an argument between ME and BA should be IBS measures.

H10: Inclusive Brand strategies mediate the relationship between digital personalization and brand accessibility.

Rosario et al., (2023) found that IBS significantly impacts customer trust and brand commitment shows that IBS should make a mediator among DP and BA. Same as Wang et al., (2023) shows that brands prioritise diversity and inclusion enhance significant link among customers, shows that DP and BA should be informed by using inclusive methods.

Figure 1.Conceptual Framework of the study

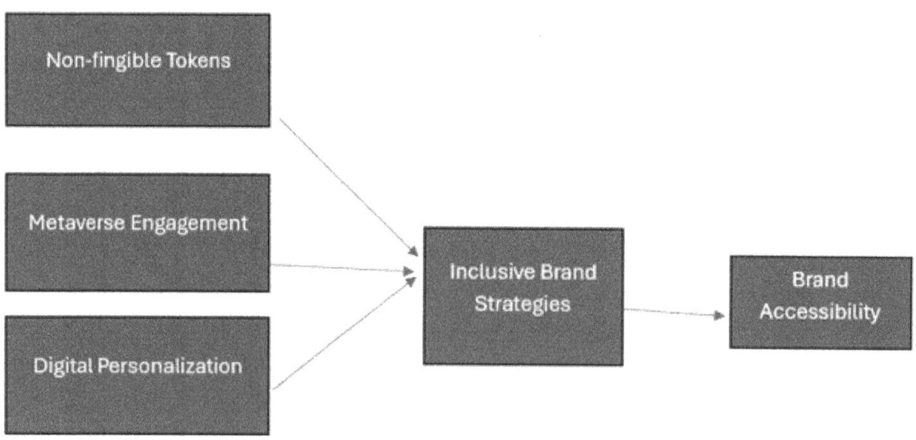

4. METHODOLOGY

4.1 Population and Research Sampling

All the individuals, objects, or events the study seeks to investigate are collectively referred to as the "population." It encompasses the whole that sparks the investigator's interest and provides the basis for deductions. The sample data used in this article includes predetermined periods, demographic restrictions, and certain characteristics. Sampling is a technique used to pick a subset of an audience that represents the complete population, which helps facilitate data gathering and evaluation.

4.2 Sample Data and Data Collection

The sample data for this investigation was gathered through the fashion retailing sector, with an emphasis on the behaviors and viewpoints of the consumers. To determine the research's appropriate geographic boundaries, characteristics, and events, demographics were gathered. The survey consisted of 32 assertion questions in entirety, and variables from 5 to 10 were used to assess the subject matter samples. Information was acquired from 256 participants. Purposive sampling was used in the research to guarantee that the sample fairly represents the relevant population and to promote equal opportunities for selection. Addressing different categories inside a wider population constitutes a particularly advantageous application of this strategy.

5. RESULTS AND ANALYSIS

The participants were consumers of retailing fashion. There were 256 respondents to the questionnaire, which yielded insightful responses for evaluation. Important demographic discoveries consist of different ways like gender differences, the sample consisted primarily of female clients, as indicated by the 70.38% female respondents. In the age group, 21–30-year-olds make up 77.68% of the participants, indicating that younger consumers are especially drawn to the technological industry. The curiosity of these individuals has a big influence on the development of goods and services that are suited to the needs of consumers. In Educational Background, the client population was highly educated and possessed substantial experience in technologically driven areas, as seen by the 58.15% of participants who had bachelor's degrees. The aforementioned demographics offer valuable insights into the tastes and behaviors of fashion retailing consumers, particularly about the acceptance of emerging technologies such as NFTs, ME, and DP.

Table 1. The convergent validity test ouctomes

Variable	Indicator	Outer Loading	Condition	Information
Brand Accessibility	BA2	0.548	<0.7	Accepted
	BA3	0.763	<0.7	Accepted
	BA4	0.738	<0.7	Accepted
	BA5	0.709	<0.7	Accepted
	BA6	0.778	<0.7	Accepted
	BA7	0.796	<0.7	Accepted
	BA8	0.757	<0.7	Accepted
Inclusive Brand Strategies	IBS1	0.763	<0.7	Accepted
	IBS2	0.848	<0.7	Accepted
	IBS3	0.828	<0.7	Accepted
	IBS4	0.843	<0.7	Accepted
	IBS5	0.868	<0.7	Accepted
NFTs	NFT1	0.742	<0.7	Accepted
	NFT2	0.814	<0.7	Accepted
	NFT3	0.809	<0.7	Accepted
	NFT4	0.723	<0.7	Accepted
	NFT5	0.858	<0.7	Accepted
	NFT6	0.785	<0.7	Accepted
	NFT7	0.769	<0.7	Accepted
Metaverse Engagement	ME1	0.802	<0.7	Accepted
	ME2	0.732	<0.7	Accepted
	ME3	0.752	<0.7	Accepted
	ME4	0.794	<0.7	Accepted
	ME5	0.818	<0.7	Accepted
Digital Personalization	DP3	0.769	<0.7	Accepted
	DP4	0.768	<0.7	Accepted
	DP5	0.824	<0.7	Accepted
	DP6	0.802	<0.7	Accepted
	DP7	0.755	<0.7	Accepted

The results of this convergence validity show that the factors across all variables BA, IBS, NFTs, ME, and DP mostly surpass the 0.7 outer loadings criterion. This fact shows that the majority of factors possess robust loadings that assess the corresponding structures accurately. Factors like IBS, NFTs, ME, and DP had outer loadings surpassing the 0.7 showing excellent convergence validity. Despite being under the cutoff of 0.548, BA2 is nothing allowed showing the value does not have much impact on the general model. Acceptance across all factors even those Belo the cutoff points to a comprehensive strategy for preserving factor validity in the model. Lastly, the results support the validity of the paper's paradigm by enhancing that the factors used in this paper offer accurate and valid examination regarding their particular elements.

Table 2. Average Variance Extracted

Variable	Condition	AVE
BA	<0.5	0.602
IBS	<0.5	0.691
NFTS	<0.5	0.619
ME	<0.5	0.609
DP	<0.5	0.613

All factors have AVE values that are more than the 0.5 cut-off. This shows that all the factors have good convergence validity with every one explaining a sizable amount of variation among its indications. The reliability and validity of the evaluation methodology employed in the paper are supported using the fact that the factors are successfully assessed using their corresponding indications.

Table 3. The discriminant validity (Fornell-Lacker Criterion)

Variable	IBS	NFTs	ME	BA	DP
IBS	0.832				
NFTs	0.819	0.847			
ME	0.781	0.808	0.888		
BA	0.758	0.788	0.808	0.816	
DP	0.714	0.746	0.802	0.812	0.852

The table demonstrates that every element (IBS, NFTs, ME, BA, and DP) satisfies the discriminating validity requirement set forth by Fornell-Larcker. For IBS, the square base of AVE is 0.832. Excellent discriminating reliability for IBS is shown by this result, which is greater than its associations with NFTs (0.819), ME (0.781), BA (0.758), and DP (0.714). For NFTs, the square root of AVE is 0.847. The fact that this number is higher than the associations with ME (0.808), BA (0.788), and DP (0.746) indicates that NFTs have discriminating validity. For ME, the square root of AVE is 0.888. This value shows that ME has discriminating reliability because it is higher than its associations with BA (0.808) and DP (0.802). For BA, the square root of AVE is 0.816. The fact that this number is greater than the relationship with DP (0.812) suggests that BA has a discriminatory validity. For DP, AVE has a square root of 0.852. This number validates the discriminating reliability of DP, outperforming all of its relationships with additional factors.

Table 4. Cronbach's Alpha (CA) and Composite Reliability(CR)

Variable	Cronbach's Alpha (CA)	Composite Reliability (CR)	Remarks
BA	0.884	0.909	Reliable
IBS	0.886	0.917	Reliable
NFTs	0.895	0.918	Reliable
ME	0.837	0.889	Reliable
DP	0.842	0.889	Reliable

In this table, CR and CA shows the reliability and validity of elements, with CA values above 0.80 for every element. High internal coherence and reliability are shown. High reliability is confirmed by CR scores over 0.80 for every build. Excellent reliability across the board denotes the consistency and dependability of the components employed for assessing every element. This dependability guarantees that the constructions appropriately represent the factors under investigation, offering a strong basis for the examination and understanding of the connections inside the study's paradigm.

Table 5. R-Square test outcome

Variable	R-Square
BA	0.883
IBS	0.836

The model's capability to explain phenomena is indicated by the R-Square scores. BA: R2 = 0.883 indicates that NFTs, DP, ME, and IBS account for 88.3% of the variance in BA. IBS: R2 = 0.836 indicates that NFTs, ME, and DP account for 83.6% of the variation in IBS. These strong R2 values show how well the framework can describe the connections between the various factors.

Table 6. The R-Square test outcome

Variable	R-Square	Remarks
IBS > BA	0.080	Weak
NFTs> BA	0.065	Weak
NFTs > IBS	0.097	Weak
ME > BA	0.136	Weak
ME > IBS	0.139	Weak
DP > BA	0.018	Weak
DP > IBS	0.039	Weak

The strength of each connection between the parameters is shown by the R-Square figures in Table 6. IBS, NFTs, ME, and DP → BA: All of these correlations exhibit low explanation capacity, with ME > BA having the greatest R^2 at 0.136. NFTs, ME, DP → IBS: In the same way, all correlations show limited explanatory ability; ME > IBS has the greatest R^2, at 0.139. These low R2 values imply that although those parameters influence BA and IBS, there may be additional noteworthy variables impacting these results that are not taken into account by our equation.

Table 7. Hypothesis Testing and outcomes

No	Hypothesis	Original sample	Std. deviation	T-statistics	P-value	Description	Outcomes
1	NFTs>IBS	0.310	0.084	3.588	0.000	Significant	Accepted
2	ME> IBS	0.481	0.073	6.943	0.000	Significant	Accepted
3	DP>IBS	0.174	0.056	3.147	0.001	Significant	Accepted
4	NFTs >BA	0.214	0.068	3.216	0.001	Significant	Accepted
5	ME>BA	0.308	0.068	4.612	0.000	Significant	Accepted
6	DP> BA	0.256	0.049	5.277	0.000	Significant	Accepted
7	IBS> BA	0.228	0.071	3.204	0.001	Significant	Accepted
8	IBS>NFTs>BA	0.071	0.036	2.004	0.045	Significant	Accepted
9	IBS>ME>BA	0.110	0.033	3.481	0.001	Significant	Accepted
10	IBS>DP>BA	0.042	0.021	2.326	0.025	Significant	Accepted

The findings of the hypotheses analysis for correlations between the research's parameters are shown in Table 7. Using T-statistics and P-values, every assumption evaluates the statistical significance of the association among the IV (NFTs, ME, DP) and the DV (IBS, BA). With lower P-values (all < 0.05) and substantial findings for all ten hypotheses, there is compelling evidence for rejecting the null hypothesis. Acceptance among all hypotheses equally important indicates that NFTs, ME, and DP are beneficial for BA and IBS. The results demonstrate how novel online approaches (NFTs, ME, DP) have a significant impact on improving IBS and BA. The hypotheses put forward are supported by the findings, which validate the theoretical basis by showing how utilizing NFTs, ME, and DP significantly improves IBS and BA in online contexts.

Table 8. The construct cross-validation redundancy test ouctomes

Variable	S	SSE	Q2 (=SSE/SS0)
BA	1.788.000	861.795	0.525
IBS	1.285.000	561.845	0.565

Findings of the developed cross-validations redundant testing are shown in Table 8. In Q2, BA accounts for 52.5% of the variation, suggesting a modest level of predictive significance. IBS demonstrates excellent predictive significance by accounting for 56.5% of the variation with Q2. These results highlight how well the simulation explains BA and IBS in the circumstances of the investigation. Measurements like SSO and SSE show how well the framework takes residual mistakes and volatility into consideration. Overall, the findings support the research's theoretical basis by validating the model's capacity to forecast results about IBS and BA.

6. DISCUSSIONS

The findings show that NFTs have a significant impact on IBS. Previous investigations show that brands adopting NFTs-based advertising initiatives enhance their worth and brand value among clients. The findings of this paper support previous investigations that NFTs have a significant impact on IBS (Original Sample: 0.310, T-statistics: 3.588, p-value: 0.000). This connection is confirmed by the beneficial CR 0.918 and the outer loadings show in NFTs varying from 0.723 to 0.858. High convergence validity confirmed via AVE 0.619 shows that NFTS improves brand strategies memorably and more recognizably. The findings show that I have a significant impact on IBS. The figures (original sample: 0.481, T-statistics:6.943, p-value: 0.000) show that ME is an effective way of creating passionate and engaged brand experiences. A high convergence validity of 0.889 and high outer loadings connected with ME measures ranging from 0.732 to 0.818 support them. The findings show that ME enhances brand strategies by providing customers with vibrant, memorable, and enjoyable experiences and achieving an AVE of 0.609. The outcomes of this hypothesis show that DP has a significant impact on IBS. DP experiences enhance client engagement and devotion. According to table data, which reveals a significant impact (original sample: 0.174, t-statistics: 3.147, p-value: 0.001). This supports the impact of DP, which has significant outer loadings from 0.755 to 0.824 and CR 0.889. High convergence validity is shown via an AVE score of 0.613, which shows the contribution of DP to enhance brand strategies through customer experiences and customer needs. The findings show that NFTs significantly enhance BA (original sample: 0.214, T-statistics: 3.216, p-value: 0.001). This shows that NFTs enhance customer participation and brand awareness. These results are supported by strong outer loadings for NFTs and CR of 0.918. The convergence validity is supported by an AVE of 0.619, which implies that NFTs enhance BA and brand strategy. This 5th hypothesis shows that ME's significant impact on BA is significantly supported by the figures (original sample: 0.308, T-statistics: 4.612, p-value: 0.000). The high outer loadings of ME with CR of 0.889 serve as proof of them. The significant impact is more support via an AVE of 0.609, which shows that ME enhances BA via unforgettable moments and immersive brand experiences. The 6th hypothesis shows that DP enhances BA with the figures (original sample: 0.256, T-statistics: 5.277, p-value: 0.000). The DP has CR of 0.889 shows significant outer loadings. ABA significantly enhanced via Personalized online interactions as shown by the AVE of 0.613, which shows strong convergence validity. The 7th hypothesis shows that IBS has a significant impact on BA (original sample: 0.228, T-statistics: 3.204, p-value: 0.001). As shown by significant outer loadings and an elevated CR of 0.917. Inclusive ways enhance customer trust and commitment. Convergence validity is supported by the AVE of 0.691, which demonstrates that significant inclusiveness enhances BA. The findings show that IBS mediates the connection among NFTs and BA, (original sample: 0.071, T-statistics: 2.004, p-value: 0.045). This implies that NFTs enhance BA outright, their impact is amplified when paired with IBS. This mediation impact shows significant outer loadings and elevated CR across both components through the AVE of 0.691 for IBS and 0.629 for NFTs. The findings show that IBS mediates the connection between ME and BA (original sample: 0.110, T-statistics: 3.481, p-value: 0.001). This shows that when combined with Inclusive approaches, the immersive experiences provided by ME have a significant potential to enhance BA. The strength of mediation impact is confirmed by significant outer loadings, significant AVE figures, and significant CR. The findings show that IBS mediates the connection (original sample: 0.042, T-statistics: 2.326, p-value:0.025) among DP and BA. This implies that the benefits of DP on BA are enhanced with the utilization of IBS. This mediation effect is validated by the significant outer loadings, significant CR among the factors, and AVE figures. The findings show that NFTs, ME, and DP have a significant impact on IBS and BA. IBS plays a significant mediating role in the connection between technological advancements and BA. The model's empirical evidence shows that its elevated combined reliability and AVE evaluations provide compelling proof for the recommended hypotheses.

To optimize their impact, brands aiming to increase openness and participation in modern times should prioritize incorporating NFTs involved in the metaverse and customized digital connections.

7. CONCLUSION

This paper shows the mediating role of IBS as it assesses the impacts of NFTs, ME, and DP on BA. This paper shows that wide variety of significant outcomes including the fact that NFTs significantly impact IBS and BA. The information was collected from 256 participants in the fashion retailing sector and analyzed by using SEM, utilizing SMART-PLS. BA, perceived value, and retention are all enhanced by NFTs-based advertising. I Significantly enhanced my BA and IBS. Customer brand impressions and buying intention are improved by emotionally compelling and engaging brand experiences within the metaverse. DP enhances BA and IBS. Buying motives, brand devotion, and significant word-of-mouth suggestions are appreciated by Personalized recommendations and customer experiences. The links among NFTs, ME, DP, and BA are significantly mediated by IBS. This recommends that utilizing Inclusive approaches might enhance these digital innovations' efficacy in improving BA. Greater attachments with diverse customers are fostered by Inclusive approaches, which enhance customer trust and brand loyalty. High convergence validity shows that every element has the majority of outer loadings surpassing the 0.7 criterion. The AVE evaluations of all elements are more than 0.5 and show high convergence validity. Every element has significant discriminant validity according to the Fornell-Larcket criterion with every element's squared root of Ave having better than its links with different elements. There were significant associations among NFTs, ME, DP, IBS, and BA as shown by backing for all hypotheses. By IBS's mediating role, the paper demonstrates the long-lasting impacts of NFTs, ME, and DP in enhancing IBA. These outcomes must be used by brands in the fashion industry and other sectors to create greater marketing strategies that cooperate with Inclusion and novel technology. These results not only enhance customer interactions and brand awareness but also create trust and loyalty across a wide range of customers. The paper adds to the body of knowledge and provides further research directions related to this area.

8. THEORETICAL AND PRACTICAL IMPLICATIONS

8.1 Practical Implications

To reinvent their advertising tactics, brands can carefully execute DP, ME, and Non-Fungible Tokens NFTs. Personalized advertising efforts according to client preferences, the development of realistic Metaverse situations, and the creation of NFT-based digital content are examples of real-world applications. The findings show that brands improving their visibility and engagement must implement them practically to enhance BA. Brands can utilize ME to create immersive experiences or digital exhibits to enhance customer engagement and perceived value. Brands can integrate inclusiveness and diversity into their marketing strategies to link them to different customers' demography, which enhances brand loyalty. Integrating tools like SEM with SMART-PLS shows that brands assess and refine their strategies by using empirical evidence. This approach supports significant decision-making and guarantees that resources are distributed to strategies that have significant influences on BA and IBS. Brands must use online platforms, IBS and BA with customized analytics, which provide tailored recommendations to customers during their buying online, which creates a competitive edge in the market. Brands enhance their brand engagement by adopting these techniques, which creates a competitive edge in the marketplace. Practical implications enhance innovation and technological shift with an eye on a sustainable future. Brands that link in IBS and BA strategies to enhance reputation, close connections with customers and maintain growth with shifted customer choices and Market situations. This paper recommends brands use online tools to predict ethical standards, which enhances good impressions regarding brand and CSR by supporting to protection of customer information, enhancing cultural contexts in marketing, and maintaining inclusive standards. Finally, these practical implications provide brands with significant information on how these technologies integrate inclusive strategies and future tools. Brands can create a long-term competitive advantage, enhance their customer service, and augment their digital visibility by putting these findings into practice.

8.2 Theoretical Implications

The Study suggested that brands involve DP, ME, and NFTs in their advertising strategies in a significant manner, by enhancing their customer's engagements and their digital visibility, which will enhance BA. The paper shows that brands give inclusiveness as a priority when it comes to branding and advertising strategies. This strategy not only connects more customer segments but also enhances market penetration, customer trust, and loyalty. Especially in the fashion industry, this paper shows that by using digital, IBS, and BA tools, brands can create streamlined marketing initiatives and maintain a competitive advantage in the market. Integrating reliable tools such as SEM and SMART-PLS shows significant facts. Brands can clarify their strategy and allocate resources with a significant effect. Brands may secure their marketing strategies by comprehending the theoretical foundations of advanced technologies and significant initiatives. Brands adopt technologies to predict patterns, shift digital landscape patterns, and advance their strategies. These recommendations help marketers focus on enhancing accessibility and customer engagement utilizing advanced technologies such as NFTs, BA, ME, and others to enhance their reputation and create links with customers which will support them in future development and long-lasting constancy in the market. Especially, brands' Organizational culture uses these techniques and inclusive strategies to enhance trust and loyalty among their employees. Brands can confidently traverse digital change and accomplish their targets in improving BA and client engagement by combining these findings with real-world execution.

9. FUTURE RESEARCH DIRECTIONS

Further undertake longitudinal research to monitor and extend the impacts of NFTs ME and DP on BA and customer behavior continuously, which will provide long-lasting and sustainable connections in these variables. Examining these studies in different other business sectors. Also utilizing the efficacy of NFTs, ME, and DP in medical, technology, or entertainment industries. Examining the cultural distinctions affect both IBS and digital innovations affect BA through Cross-cultural research. This will provide significant information regarding how to adopt marketing techniques in different cultural contexts. Find out the customer demographic to how they feel about NFTs, ME, DP, and IBS. Examining the different group's perceptions regarding BA initiatives and pinpointing the primary customers for particular techniques. To look at the relationship among these factors using experimental designs. To find out how these factors affect BA and customer perceptions directly utilizing random sampling. To look at a more comprehensive review of customer perceptions and experience with NFTs, ME, DP, and IBS using qualitative approaches including focus groups and comprehensive interviews alongside quantitative methods. Examining the ethical ramifications of using DP, ME, and NFTs in brand advertising. Consider possible ethical issues with privacy, and managing the digital rights of customers. Then investigate approaches to these issues. To look at the new developments in technology and fashion that might affect BA and customer behavior. Examining the advanced technologies like VR, Blockchain, AR, and AI impacts on customer loyalty and enhance diversity. Scholars must explore the possible relationships among these digital innovations IBS and BA initiatives advertising strategies and customer experiences.

CONFLICT OF INTEREST:

There is no Conflict of interest.

REFERENCES

Ahn, S., Jin, B. E., & Seo, H. (2024). Why do people interact and buy in the Metaverse? Self-Expansion perspectives and the impact of hedonic adaptation. *Journal of Business Research*, 175, 114557. DOI: 10.1016/j.jbusres.2024.114557

Arya, V., Sambyal, R., Sharma, A., & Dwivedi, Y. K. (2024). Brands are calling your AVATAR in Metaverse–A study to explore XR-based gamification marketing activities & consumer-based brand equity in virtual world. *Journal of Consumer Behaviour*, 23(2), 556–585. DOI: 10.1002/cb.2214

Belk, R., Humayun, M., & Brouard, M. (2022). Money, possessions, and ownership in the Metaverse: NFTs, cryptocurrencies, Web3 and Wild Markets. *Journal of Business Research*, 153, 198–205. DOI: 10.1016/j.jbusres.2022.08.031

Christodoulou, K., Katelaris, L., Themistocleous, M., Christodoulou, P., & Iosif, E. (2022). NFTs and the metaverse revolution: Research perspectives and open challenges. Blockchains and the Token Economy. *Theory into Practice*, •••, 139–178.

Colicev, A. (2023). How can non-fungible tokens bring value to brands. *International Journal of Research in Marketing*, 40(1), 30–37. DOI: 10.1016/j.ijresmar.2022.07.003

Deventer, C., de Sousa, V. A., & Pirnay, L. (2024). NFTByBrands: Value Identification Framework for Analysis and Design of NFT Initiatives. *International Journal of Electronic Commerce*, 28(1), 1–30. DOI: 10.1080/10864415.2023.2295070

Duggal, A., Gupta, M., & Gupta, D. (2023). Significance of NFT Avtaars in Metaverse and their Promotion: Case Study. *Scientific Journal of Metaverse and Blockchain Technologies*, 1(1), 28–36. DOI: 10.36676/sjmbt.v1i1.04

Gupta, M., Gupta, D., & Duggal, A. (2023). NFT Culture: A New Era. *Scientific Journal of Metaverse and Blockchain Technologies*, 1(1), 57–62. DOI: 10.36676/sjmbt.v1i1.08

Hakkarainen, T., & Colicev, A. (2023). Blockchain-enabled advances (BEAs): Implications for consumers and brands. *Journal of Business Research*, 160, 113763. DOI: 10.1016/j.jbusres.2023.113763

Joy, A., Zhu, Y., Peña, C., & Brouard, M. (2022). Digital future of luxury brands: Metaverse, digital fashion, and non-fungible tokens. *Strategic Change*, 31(3), 337–343. DOI: 10.1002/jsc.2502

Kemec, A. (2022). From reality to virtuality: Re-discussing cities with the concept of the metaverse. *International Journal of Management Accounting*, 4(1), 12–20.

Khan, M. N., & uddin Qadri, S. M. (2023). Exploring the Influence of Advertising within the Metaverse and its Synergy with Non-Fungible Tokens (NFTs). *International Journal of Management Perspective and Social Research*, 2(1), 22–43.

Kılıçaslan, F., & Ekizler, H. (2022). Factors effecting purchase intention in blockchain and NFT (non-fungible token) technologies. *Journal of Research in Business*, 7(2), 604–623. DOI: 10.54452/jrb.1177600

Kim, Y., & Lee, H. (2024). Consumers' responses to metaverse ads: The roles of hedonic versus utilitarian appeal and the moderating role of need for touch. *Journal of Business Research*, 179, 114677. DOI: 10.1016/j.jbusres.2024.114677

Koo, H., & Kwon, K. H. (2022). The applicability of scarcity, originality, and transaction tracking characteristics of the dermatological industry and non-fungible token. *Journal of Cosmetic Dermatology*, 21(12), 6628–6635. DOI: 10.1111/jocd.15406 PMID: 36152011

Kräussl, R., & Tugnetti, A. (2024). Non-fungible tokens (NFTs): A review of pricing determinants, applications and opportunities. *Journal of Economic Surveys*, 38(2), 555–574. DOI: 10.1111/joes.12597

Leahy, B., & Delehanty, C. (2022). Brands In the Metaverse: Opportunities, Risks and Strategies. *The Intellectual Strategist Journal, 28(6).*

Lee, C. T., Ho, T. Y., & Xie, H. H. (2023). Building brand engagement in metaverse commerce: The role of branded non-fungible toekns (BNFTs). *Electronic Commerce Research and Applications*, 58, 101248. DOI: 10.1016/j.elerap.2023.101248

Lee, C. T., Shen, Y. C., Li, Z., & Xie, H. H. (2024). The *e*ffects of non-fungible token platform affordances on customer loyalty: A Buyer–Creator duality perspective. *Computers in Human Behavior*, 151, 108013. DOI: 10.1016/j.chb.2023.108013

Lee, J., & Kwon, K. H. (2022). Novel pathway regarding good cosmetics brands by NFT in the metaverse world. *Journal of Cosmetic Dermatology*, 21(12), 6584–6593. DOI: 10.1111/jocd.15277 PMID: 35894837

Mancuso, I., Petruzzelli, A. M., & Panniello, U. (2023). Digital business model innovation in metaverse: How to approach virtual economy opportunities. *Information Processing & Management*, 60(5), 103457. DOI: 10.1016/j.ipm.2023.103457

Multazam, M. T. (2022). Exploring the Legal and Policy Implications of Non-Fungible Tokens. *Jurnal Politik dan Pemerintahan Daerah, 4(2), 293-303.*

Murtas, G., Pedeliento, G., & Mangiò, F. (2024). Luxury fashion brands at the gates of the Web 3.0: An analysis of early experimentations with NFTs and the metaverse. *Journal of Global Fashion Marketing*, 15(1), 90–114. DOI: 10.1080/20932685.2023.2249476

Nalbant, K. G., & Aydın, S. (2023). Development and transformation in digital marketing and branding with artificial intelligence and digital technologies dynamics in the Metaverse universe. *Journal of Metaverse*, 3(1), 9–18. DOI: 10.57019/jmv.1148015

Olaleye, S. A., Kwafo, D., Atobatele, A. J., & Olaoye, O. P. (2022, December). The Bibliometric Commingling of Metaverse and Non-fungible Tokens in Marketing. *InInternational Conference on Marketing and Technologies(pp.387-399).Singapore: Springer Nature Singapore.*

Payal, R., Sharma, N., & Dwivedi, Y. K. (2024). Unlocking the impact of brand engagement in the metaverse on Real-World purchase intentions: Analyzing Pre-Adoption behavior in a futuristic technology platform. *Electronic Commerce Research and Applications*, 65, 101381. DOI: 10.1016/j.elerap.2024.101381

Periyasami, S., & Periyasamy, A. P. (2022). Metaverse as future promising platform business model: Case study on fashion value chain. *Businesses*, 2(4), 527–545. DOI: 10.3390/businesses2040033

Radanliev, P., De Roure, D., Novitzky, P., & Sluganovic, I. (2023). Accessibility and inclusiveness of new information and communication technologies for disabled users and content creators in the Metaverse. *Disability and Rehabilitation. Assistive Technology*, •••, 1–15. PMID: 37585705

Rosário, A. T., Lopes, P. R., & Rosário, F. S. (2023). Metaverse in Marketing: Challenges and Opportunities. *Handbook of Research on AI-Based Technologies and Applications in the Era of the Metaverse, 204-227.*

SanMiguel, P., Sádaba, T., & Sayeed, N. (2024). Fashion brands in the metaverse: Achievements from a marketing perspective. *Journal of Global Fashion Marketing, 1-21.*

Santos, V., & Sousa, B. (2023, November). Technology Towards Luxury Brands: Preliminary Insights on Fashion Tourism, Metaverse and Non-fungible Token (NFT). *InInternational Conference on Tourism, Technology and Systems(pp.269-277).Singapore: Springer Nature Singapore.*

Schauman, S., Greene, S., & Korkman, O. (2023). Sufficiency and the dematerialization of fashion: How digital substitutes are creating new market opportunities. *Business Horizons*, 66(6), 741–751. DOI: 10.1016/j.bushor.2023.03.003

Sung, E., Kwon, O., & Sohn, K. (2023). NFT luxury brand marketing in the metaverse: Leveraging blockchain-certified NFTs to drive consumer behavior. *Psychology and Marketing*, 40(11), 2306–2325. DOI: 10.1002/mar.21854

Wang, M., & Lau, N. (2023). NFT digital twins: A digitalization strategy to preserve and sustain Miao silver craftsmanship in the metaverse era. *Heritage*, 6(2), 1921–1941. DOI: 10.3390/heritage6020103

Yang, H. (2024). The Genesis Effect: Digital Goods in the Metaverse. *The Journal of Consumer Research*, 51(1), 129–139. DOI: 10.1093/jcr/ucad072

Yencha, C. (2023). Spatial heterogeneity and non-fungible token sales: Evidence from Decentraland LAND sales. *Finance Research Letters*, 58, 103628. DOI: 10.1016/j.frl.2023.103628

Yoo, K., Welden, R., Hewett, K., & Haenlein, M. (2023). The merchants of meta: A research agenda to understand the future of retailing in the metaverse. *Journal of Retailing*, 99(2), 173–192. DOI: 10.1016/j.jretai.2023.02.002

Zadorozhnyi, Z. M., Muravskyi, V., Humenna-Derij, M., & Zarudna, N. (2022). Innovative accounting and audit of the metaverse resources. *Marketing i menedžment innovacij, 13(4), 10-19.*

Zhao, Y., & Zhan, Y. (2024, May). Investigating the Impact of Cultural Tourism NFTs' Perceived Value and Experiential Evaluation on WOM of a Tourism Destination: A Generational Difference Moderation Approach. *InWuhan International Conference on E-business(pp.25-36).Cham: Springer Nature Switzerland.* DOI: 10.1007/978-3-031-60260-3_3

Zhou, M., & Liu, C. (2024, January). How The Existence Of Luxury Brands' Digital Fashion In A Metaverse Influence Consumers' Perception Of Luxury Brands. *InInternational Textile and Apparel Association Annual Conference Proceedings(*Vol. 80, *No. 1). Iowa State University Digital Press.* DOI: 10.31274/itaa.17392

Chapter 13
The Impact of Service Automation and Robotics on Hospitality Business Models

Madhu Kumari
https://orcid.org/0009-0006-7300-3597
Chandigarh University, India

Suneel Kumar
Shaheed Bhagat Singh College, University of Delhi, India

Nisha Devi
Shri Ram College of commerce, University of Delhi, India

ABSTRACT

This study aims to comprehensively evaluate research on the role of service automation and robots in changing business models in the hospitality industry as well as identifying research gaps and future research initiatives. To investigate how automatic services and robotics have an effect on hospitality business models and provider enterprise models, this examination uses bibliometric analysis. The findings show that service automation enhances operational reduces labor costs, improves consumer experience, and increases operational consistency and efficiency. However, challenges include initial investment costs, technological maintenance, and potential reductions in the human touch that some customer's value. This study emphasizes the use of service robots in hospitality while noting limitations and making recommendations for further research.

DOI: 10.4018/979-8-3693-9005-4.ch013

1. INTRODUCTION

The hospitality service has experienced an exquisite increase and continuous growth of motel manufacturers within the international marketplace. In addition to this increase, customer expectancies have additionally developed. They need a quicker and more correct provider. To meet these growing expectancies and overcome the demanding situations that stand up, the hospitality quarter is increasingly using advanced technology and automation to offer exquisite service that exceeds customer wishes. The rise of robots and artificial intelligence (AI) technology has had a huge impact on the global economy. According to the International Robotics Society (2020), sales of professional service robots increased 32% to $11.2 billion worldwide from 2018 to 2019. Impact of the COVID-19 pandemic. We expect this market to grow even faster, due to advanced digital technology, AI, which has largely replaced human workers, has enabled contactless services (Chiang & Trimi, 2020). Two characteristics of AI that are both promising and challenging have had a significant impact on the service industry (Ruel & Njoku, 2020). Although AI can potentially disrupt service operations by replacing human capabilities with technology (Huang & Rust, 2018), it also provides many benefits. AI and robots in the service sector have become important drivers of innovation, efficiency, and profitability (Ivanov & Webster, 2019). AI also helps increase productivity in the workplace by enabling smarter operations. Promote better business results and hone new skills and capabilities (Ruel & Njoku, 2020) of technology. Understanding consumer adoption is important for marketers and hospitality businesses. This is because it will affect the acceptance and use of such innovations (Ukpabi & Karjaluoto, 2017). This study examines the impact of robots on services provided by hotels (satisfaction vs. utility objectives) and travel objectives (business vs. leisure) to understand how robotic services affect the customer experience. Existing research on consumer responses to robot services in hotels. Some studies reveal positive responses from hotels using robots (Ivanov et al., 2018; Qiu et al., 2020), while other studies show mixed findings. It addresses skepticism and challenges related to customer adoption (Io & Lee, 2020; Mori et al., 2012). Issues such as lack of human interaction and customer effort to engage with new technology may affect the overall customer experience (Ameen et al., 2021, 2019). Despite extensive research on AI, little attention has been paid to the potential of AI-powered experiences to change perceptions of service quality customer engagement with service providers and evaluating the overall AI-powered experience (Ameen et al., 2021) from an enterprise perspective. Its focus is on AI (Jarrahi, 2018), leaving a gap in understanding customer perceptions of robots and other AI technologies, which are considered an essential part of the service experience. This end includes the ability to increase satisfaction and strengthen brand relationships (Shank et al., 2019; Wang et al., 2020). In addition, important aspects of customer experience transformation, such as value categories (elevation and satisfaction vs. utility) (Klaus & Maklan, 2013) and travel objectives,(Business vs., 2009).

1.1 Service Automation in Hospitality

The hospitality service has visibly revolutionized service automation, which is changing the way offerings are provided to meet changing purchaser expectancies. Self-service kiosks and chatbots are driven through artificial intelligence, and robotic concierges are examples of automation technology that contribute quicker, extra specific and custom-designed services, that the finest client needs for consolation and overall performance. For instance, self-providers take a look at ins and test-outs have reduced wait times, permitting hotels to provide seamless and contactless guest reviews (Ivanov & Webster, 2019). Similarly, AI chatbots are being leveraged to deal with patron inquiries, deliver personalized recommendations, and help with bookings, improving carrier accessibility and visitor delight (Chiang & Trimi, 2020). The COVID-19 pandemic, in addition, multiplied the adoption of service automation, as hospitality organizations sought to ensure hygiene and protection while maintaining operational continuity. Robotic offerings, consisting of cleansing robots and automatic food delivery systems, not only minimized human interplay but also superior operational efficiency (Qiu et al., 2020).

Service automation in the hospitality sector has many advantages and poses challenges including reduced human interaction. This is important for many customers (Ameen et al., 2021). Automation improves the quality and efficiency of services but there must be a balance between technological innovation and the human touch that is critical to guest satisfaction. The development of automated services has its roots in the industrial revolution (Collier, 1983), making amazing progress through information and communications technology (ICT), which increases service efficiency and improves customer experience (Law, Buhalis, & Cobanoglu, 2014), entry/Exit Keyless room access, facial care and certification, and robot concierge. These innovations are improving service delivery. Increase operational efficiency and revolutionize the guest experience. Self-service kiosks, widely used in hotel lobbies, help guests freely arrange check-in and receive room keys. Modern lodgings incorporate systems for fully automated evaluations, offering services like baggage delivery and room service through applications. For example, Japan's Henn-na hotel uses multilingual humanoid robots for check-ins, cleaning, and luggage handling, demonstrating automation's ability to efficiently meet guest expectations (Chen & Hu, 2013; Murphy et al., 2017). Provider shipping is made even more beautiful by emerging technologies like AI and IoT. AI applications, along with natural language processing and video reputation, optimize operations and guest interactions.

IoT-powered devices enable voice-managed room functions, exemplified by the assistance of Marriott's virtual assistants. These improvements display how the hospitality enterprise leverages automation even as it maintains personalized care to fulfill dynamic client expectancies (IFR, 2016a; IFR, 2016b).

1.2 Advancements in Robotic Technologies

One of the best sizeable repercussion of the Fourth Industrial rebellion, first brought at the Hannover Fair in Germany in 2011 (Schwab, 2016), is the renewal of synthetic intelligence (AI) and robot technologies from technological know-how fiction into realistic gear often used in everyday existence. AI has emerged as a subfield of laptop engineering targeted at enabling machines to perform duties that require intelligence (Tussyadiah, 2020). According to Gil et al. (2020), synthetic intelligence entails designing structures capable of acting intelligently, encompassing talents like problem-fixing, reminiscence retention, and understanding human language. Wang (2004) defines AI as a system with features consisting of storing statistics, fixing issues, and decoding human conversation. Similarly, Kaplan and Haenlein (2019) describe AI as "the potential of a device to interpret external information efficaciously, research from it, and use those learning's to acquire unique desires and duties through bendy edition." Service robots, on the other hand, are designed to carry out beneficial obligations for people or devices outside of business automation programs (ISO, 2012). Murphy et al. (2017) in addition provide an explanation for the characteristics of industrial robots and provider robots. It states that commercial robots have much less mobility and restricted social interplay. Meanwhile, service robots are becoming more independent and socially interactive. Recent advances highlight the growing prominence of service robots, which show more agility than their industrial counterparts in social interactions, for example, personal service robots that have a high degree of autonomy. It is designed not only to perform tasks but also to attract and entertain users. Promoting high levels of social interaction (Murphy et al., 2017), current estimates indicate that service robots will see significant use in the coming years, driven by their ability to integrate movement, social interaction, and adaptability to various applications (Tussyadiah, 2023; Gil et al., 2024).

1.3 Evolution and Advancements in Artificial Intelligence Technology

By the late 1980s, AI transitioned into industrialization, underscored by using extended investments in the United States, Japan, and Germany, along with the established order of the German AI Research Center in 1988 (CAICT, 2018). AI won public interest while applications like HiTech and IBM's Deep Blue performed milestones in chess, defeating international champions in 1988 and 1997, respectively (Chen, 2019). From the 2000s onward, AI entered an explosive increase segment fueled using massive data, machine-gaining knowledge of, and deep studying technologies. Machine learning, a subset of AI since the 1950s, focuses on optimizing machine overall performance through the use of ancient statistics, at the same time deep learning, an offshoot of machine learning, emerged in 2006, driving advancements in vision, speech recognition, and robotics (Alpaydin, 2014; Alom et al., 2019). The transition from automation structures in advanced commercial revolutions to smart structures in the Fourth Industrial Revolution highlights AI's integration into day-to-day existence and its developing presence throughout sectors (Schwab, 2016). Today, AI-powered devices and programs are redefining business and societal paradigms.

2. LITERATURE REVIEW

2.1 Automation and Robotics in Hospitality Operations

In the past few years, the hospitality enterprise has adopted automation and robotics to improve operations and reduce charges. Automation includes the check-in/check-out manner. Room provider transport and guest help gadgets today; robots increase concierge offerings, cleansing, and baggage managing. According to Ivanov & Webster (2024), computerized technologies such as self-carrier kiosks and cellular packages, it has emerged as not unusual in accommodations. There are several offerings available, wherein guests can take a look into their rooms and request services with nearly no need to have interaction with human beings. This trend is becoming more evident in luxury hotels that combine high-tech services with privacy aimed at increasing guest comfort and satisfaction. The rise of robots in the service industry performs tasks previously performed by human workers. Change is taking place where robots deliver food to hotels by providing automated baggage assistance (Buhalis et al., 2023). The role of robotics in increasing operational efficiency and reducing costs has been a key topic in recent studies (Jiang & Zhao, 2023); robotic concierge services are also being introduced to help guests more efficiently. This is especially true for hotels located in technologically advanced cities (Lee, 2023).

2.2 The Role of Robotic Technologies in Shaping the Future of Hospitality Business

The introduction of robotics technology is revolutionizing the travel and hospitality industry. These technologies are an essential part of many departments especially reception and food and beverage operations along with expanding its use in housekeeping and other back-end functions. Current advancements include robotic receptionists. Self-service kiosks, robot chefs, and automated food delivery systems via drones or conveyor belts (Yang et al., 2020) AI-powered smart rooms of the future Guests control room settings through a voice-sensitive virtual assistant. The AI system can adjust the environment according to the guest's mood; adjustments in Personalization will extend to mobile applications that capture guest preferences. Meeting and event management leverages AI for a seamless attendee experience. It uses remote identification robots and QR code recognition systems to increase efficiency and reduce logistics costs robotic drones in golf and tourism Accept tasks such as mowing the grass and collecting balls. This is expected to happen when the automatic dune buggy improves guest comfort, and facial recognition systems at airports will improve passport control save travelers time, and increase safety. Travel companies are expected to use AI to predict demand, chat-bots, and robot guides that can offer multilingual tours and personalized assistance. These technological innovations aim to improve operational efficiency, reduce costs, and improve the guest experience putting them at the center of the industry's future evolution (Yang et al. 2020).

2.3 Robotic Technologies in Tourism: Opportunities and Challenges

The integration of robot technologies in tourism is reshaping the industry with the aid of improving operations, visitor reports, and enterprise performance. These technologies are already in use for warm air balloon protection through IoT systems, robotic courses in museums, automation in the front workplace, housekeeping, and meals and beverage offerings. Future improvements embody robots for responsibilities like cleansing, shipping, and nighttime shifts, and clever structures for personalized guest research (Özen, 2020). AI and robotics positively affect worker performance, addressing problems like high work turnover and nighttime time-shift availability while those technologies can further improve certain roles as well. It also creates opportunities for new businesses to slap on logos and increase collaboration between humans and robots. AI-powered services for traffic boast speed, accuracy, and interactivity, while tech-savvy customers appreciate the rates. By such assessments, in practice, such generations would increase production capacity, reduce tax rates, and improve overall financial performance. However, uneven startup fees infrastructure needs, and criminal investigations can prevent adoption. Businesses should educate employees, and frame, and prepare ecosystems for integrating robots to gain a competitive advantage (Ivanov & Webster, 2020). But challenging cultural differences Personnel resistance and cyber security risks may hinder adoption. Ethical issues and record confidentiality must also be addressed to ensure the stable and effective use of those technologies.

2.4 Impact on Service Quality and Customer Experience

The impact of service automation and robotics on service quality and customer experience is widely discussed in recent literature. According to Tan, Mohan, & Watanabe (2022), service automation can lead to a better guest experience by enhancing operational efficiency, reducing waiting times, and offering personalized services through AI. However, while automation and robotics enhance convenience, they must be integrated in a way that does not compromise the quality of personal interactions, which remain vital in hospitality (Buhalis et al., 2022).Several studies emphasize that guest satisfaction is enhanced when automation and robotics are used to handle routine tasks, allowing staff to focus on personalized service (Gretzel et al., 2023). However, challenges remain regarding customer acceptance of robots in hospitality settings. Research by Kuo & Wu (2022), shows that older customers and those less familiar with technology often feel uncomfortable with robotic interactions, thus highlighting the importance of a balanced approach between technology and human engagement.

2.5 Implementing Automation and Robotics in Hospitality Business

The successful implementation of automation and robotics in hospitality calls for overcoming several demanding situations, both from a technical and purchaser perspective. According to Lee (2021), the number one mission lies in ensuring seamless integration among automated structures and the human team of workers. Robots, on the other hand, can perform repetitive responsibilities, including cleaning and transportation. Human workers must manage complex interactions that require empathy and judgment. This balance is important to maintain customer happiness (Kandampully et al., 2021), Ivanov & Webster (2021) note that while big hotel chains have the financial potential to spend money on robot systems, the initial investment for smaller residences remains a barrier. Moreover, schooling the workforce to paint alongside robots and coping with the hybrid body of workers model is an ongoing project (Murphy et al., 2021).

2.6 The Impact of Automation and Robotics on Hospitality Operations

From a commercial enterprise model angle, the adoption of carrier automation and robotics requires extensive shifts in methods. A key fashion identified by Gretzel et al. (2020) is the transition towards a "tech-centric" hospitality version, which relies more and more depend upon digital systems, robots, and AI-driven systems to supply offerings. These technologies permit motels to supply personalized experiences at scale, improving operational efficiency and customer loyalty. Research using Chathoth et al. (2021) indicates that the integration of AI and robotics now not only reduces operational fees but additionally complements revenue streams via offering new offerings, inclusive of robotic-led excursions or automatic room customization. To provide better guest cost propositions, commercial agency-style inns are progressively working to modernize unreliable provider carriers through a set of human skills and decades. The literature does, however, also emphasize how challenging it is to challenge the capabilities of conventional commercial business firm styles. According to Ivanov & Webster (2020), the fast adoption of generation can also result in activity displacement, growing resistance from the inner body of workers, and exertions from unions. This task necessitates the development of new hard work fashions that integrate generation and human resources efficaciously.

2.7 The Future of Automation and Robotics in Hospitality

The future of service automation and robots in the service sector is also promising. With opportunities to create additional innovations According to Buhalis and colleagues (2023), AI includes voice assistants for room customization and AI-powered recommendations, which increases guest satisfaction. Moreover, the use of the Internet of Things (IoT) together with AI and robots has revolutionized hotel operations (Tan, Mohan, and Watanabe, 2024), IoT-enabled devices such as smart thermostats, lighting, and systems. Entertainment allows guests to control their environment through a mobile app. This results in a more seamless and integrated experience COVID-19 outbreak in the service sector of automation, robots, and acceleration, adoption due to guest safety, contactless technology has become essential in maintenance (Ivanov & Webster, 2020). The future of service automation and robots in the service sector is also promising. With opportunities to create additional innovations According to Buhalis and colleagues (2023), AI includes voice assistants for room customization and AI-powered recommendations, which increases guest satisfaction. Moreover, handling the Internet of Things (IoT) with AI and robots has revolutionized hotel operations (Tan, Mohan, and Watanabe, 2024), IoT-enabled devices such as smart thermostats, lighting, and systems. Entertainment allows guests to control their environment through a mobile app. This results in a more seamless and integrated experience, COVID-19 outbreak in the service sector of automation, robots, and acceleration, adoption due to guest safety, contactless technology has become essential in maintenance (Ivanov & Webster, 2020).

3. RESEARCH METHODOLOGY

This study focuses on peer-reviewed academic publications to analyze the evolution and advancement of research on the influence of service automation and robotics on service business models on September 19, 2024. We gathered information from the Web of Science (WoS) database, which has more extensive bibliographic data for citation analysis than other databases such as Scopus, Google Scholar, Science Direct, Research Gate, and SCI (Falagas et al. 2008). WoS was chosen because of its reputation as a reliable source of research published in leading journals, (Merigó et al., 2015) service technology" with related conditions. This search initially returned 170 results. We selected papers to deal specifically with robot applications within hospitality. Finally, 73 papers published between 2010 and 2024 were included in the analysis. It consists mainly of research articles and reviews, as well as a small number of book reviews, editorials, and symposiums. Research into service automation and robots in service business models is still emerging. To provide a comprehensive view, we include all document types in our analysis.

Figure 1. Map of the top countries focusing on robotics automation in hospitality

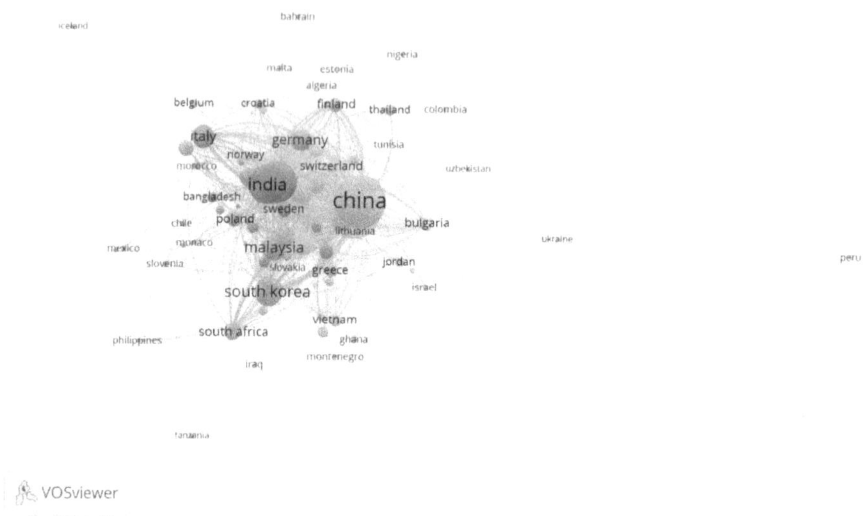

3.1 Bibliometric Data Analyses

This study employed bibliometric analysis evaluation to assess article metadata retrieved from a citation database. As a statistical technique, bibliometric analysis measures research overall performance and its impact, imparting "quantitative rigor into the subjective evaluation of literature" (Zupic & Čater, 2015). Bibliometrics serves primary functions: performance assessment and mapping analysis. Performance evaluation assesses the contributions of researchers, establishments, or international locations, while mapping evaluation examines bibliometric records, including key phrases, authors, and citations, to perceive patterns and relationships. This has to investigate the overall performance of nations and journals in studies on automation service and robotics in the hospitality enterprise discipline. For mapping analysis, writer-supplied key phrases, instead of system-generated ones, have been decided on for the number one analysis. The Vosviewer turned into used-to behavior, both performance assessment and mapping evaluation. This tool enabled the identification of the countries and journals with the most sizeable contributions to robotics-related research.

Figure 2.Co-word map for articles on automation service and robotics published from 2010 to 2024.

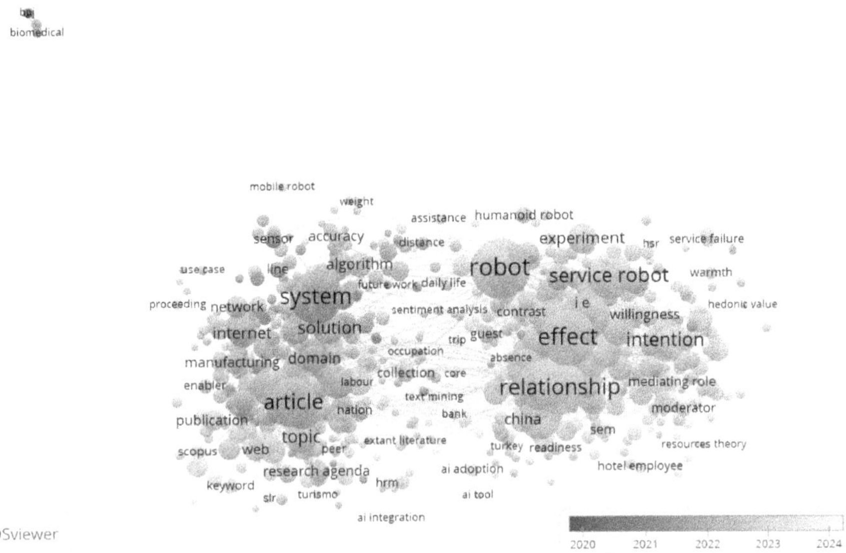

Figure 3. Co-citation analysis map for automation service and robotics in hospitality.

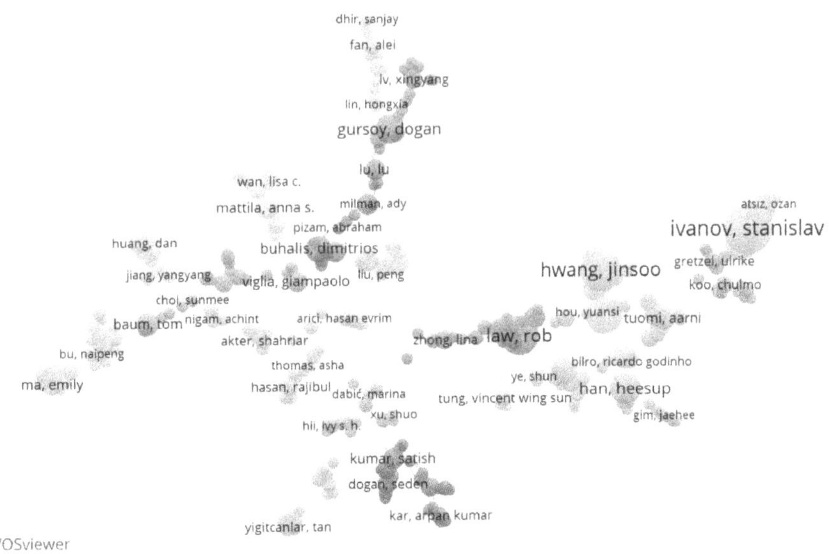

3.2 Keyword Network Analysis

The Vosviewer function was used to create a keyword network based on keyword co-occurrence. This approach is based on Callon et al.'s (1983) co-word analysis methodology, which is intended to highlight relevant study topics and trends by grouping closely related terms. According to Callon et al. (1991), co-word analysis captures research dynamics by detecting interrelated phrases. Each map in the generated keyword network represents a keyword, and linkages between vertices indicate that the keywords existed in the same document.

Figure 4. Map of the top universities focusing on automation service and robotics in hospitality industry.

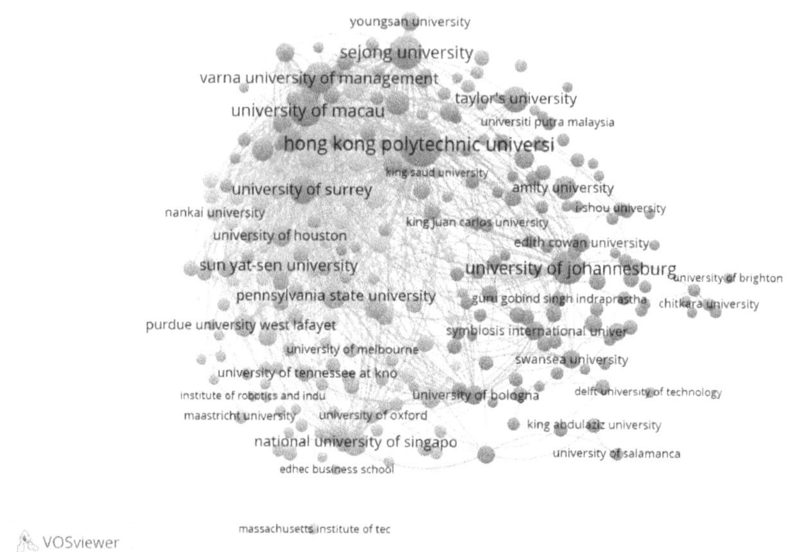

4. DISCUSSION

Service automation and robots are revolutionizing the provider industry transforming traditional commercial enterprise fashions to deliver revolutionary procedures to client interaction and operational efficiency although these technologies provide many advantages; they additionally offer important demanding situations that ought to be cautiously taken into consideration. Hospitality companies are investing in these technologies to obtain a competitive advantage and boost efficiency. Artificial intelligence has rapidly being used in various organizations, particularly through the deployment of service robots. As a result, this section investigates the use of artificial intelligence in service firms. Concrete instances of the employment of such applications in the field, and the relevance of applications In this context, this study refers to Samala et al.'s (2020) classification of artificial intelligence technology, which includes robotic technology, facial recognition technology, chat-bots, language translation programs, customization services, and other artificial intelligence applications.

4.1 Robotic Technologies and Their Application in Reception

Robotic technology represents the most everyday utility of synthetic intelligence within the tourism and hospitality enterprise. As current, piloted innovations, robots are gaining big traction, with their utilization becoming increasingly considerable. They are diagnosed as key rising technologies in this area. Below, unique examples of robot technology packages in tourism and hospitality are highlighted. The Henn-na Hotel in Japan, diagnosed as the arena's first robot lodge, employs humanoid robots to greet visitors and take care of check-in processes (Tung & Au, 2018, p. 2685). Additionally, the motel makes use of notably functional delivery robots within its front office operations. These robots assist guests by wearing baggage, offering reception offerings, and accompanying them to their rooms (Lewis-Kraus, 2016).

4.2 Robot Bellboy and Robot Concierge

The service robot “Sacarino” serves as a robotic bellboy, providing visitors with numerous services (Zalama et al., 2014). Sacarino offers information about hotel amenities, neighborhood activities, restaurant hours, menus, and video conferencing services. It may summon cabs, accompany visitors to hotel restaurants or rooms, and search for information online as guests want. It also has self-charging capabilities, connecting to a charging station in the hotel lobby on a regular basis (Park, 2020; Pinillos et al., 2016; Zalama et al., 2014). Another splendid innovation is YOBOT, the world's first robotic arm-shaped suitcase provider, operational at Yotel New York, 2020. Hilton partnered with IBM to create “Connie,” a humanoid robotic concierge powered with the aid of the Watson AI platform. Connie gives guests data approximately the resort and its environment, answering questions about hotel offerings and recommending close by attractions (Davis, 2016; Hilton Worldwide, 2016; Park, 2020).Supported with the aid of artificial intelligence, Connie learns and improves with each interplay, adapting to capability destiny queries (Ivanov et al.in 2017). Italy introduced its first robotic concierge in 2018, “Robby Pepper,” developed through Soft Bank Robotics. Robby Pepper serves in Italian, English, and German and is used in a inn on the shores of Lake Garda, offering facts approximately nearby attractions, sports, and resort info based on climate and guests' test-out dates (Barry and Pele, 2018; CRM Medya Turizm, 2020). Another first-rate robotic concierge, "Mario," is employed at the Ghent Marriott Hotel in Belgium (Chestler, 2016 and Review Pro, 2016).

4.3 Robot Bartender and Robotic Butler

Robot bartenders, which can be designed as robotic fingers or humanoid figures, are an innovative utility of automation in hospitality (Tussyadiah et al., 2020). Typically, they feature two robot fingers located beneath the bar's bottles, enabling them to perceive visitors as human beings, take beverage orders, and serve liquids (Berezina et al., 2019, p. 205; Giuliani et al., 2013, p. 263).A high-quality example is the robotic bartender aboard Royal Caribbean's Quantum of the Seas, the first of its kind in cruise tourism. Guests locate their orders through capsules on the bar, and the robotic arm prepares the liquids in full view. Pre-programmed with particular mixture ratios, the robot selects the desired ingredients, prepares the drinks, and serves them garnished with ice and lemon (Sloan, 2014). Robotic butlers and shipping robots are increasingly applied inside the hospitality industry to enhance visitor reports. At Aloft Hotels, a Starwood brand, a robotic butler delivers orders to visitor rooms, replacing the need for a human workforce (Crook, 2014; Markoff, 2014; Park, 2020). Similarly, the Residence Inn Marriott LAX Hotel employs a shipping robot named "Wally" for room service (Tung & Au, 2018).Hotel Jen in Tanglin features shipping robots, "Jeno" and "Jena," stationed within the foyer and wearing uniforms. These robots tour at a mean pace of 2.5 km/h, slower than on-foot speed, to deliver orders. They navigate the hotel independently, function the elevators, name the visitor's room upon arrival, and hand over the orders (Lin, 2017; Ivanov et al., 2017). For additional requests like toothbrushes or towels, the body of workers loads the gadgets into the robot, which then grants them directly to the guest's room, Crook,in 2014.

4.4 Robot Chef and Robot Waiter

In 2017, M Social Singapore Hotel brought the robotic chef "Ausca," able to cook sunny-side-up eggs and omelets, with the ability to analyze and enhance its egg-cooking techniques over the years (Lin, in 2017). Additionally, different robotic cooks are rising inside the culinary world, inclusive of the ones designed to prepare sushi (Sushirobo.Com, 2020), noodles just like the "Foxbot" (Elkins in 2015), sausages via the "BratWurst Bot", Filloon in 2016, and burgers (Troitino, 2018).

These advancements showcase the growing role of robotics in food coaching in the hospitality industry. The use of robots as waiters in the carrier industry is turning into increasingly tremendous. Restaurant owners regularly flip to robot waiters to help when staff is unable to keep up with orders or while there are insufficient waiters (Cheong et al., 2016). Robot waiters and bussers can assist in manipulating high volumes of customers, but there are issues that immoderate reliance on robots may want to lead to process displacement for a few personnel (Ivanov and Webster, 2020). In Singapore, at a seafood restaurant named Rong Heng, robot waiters "Lucy" and "Mary," dressed in stylish scarves and purple aprons, supply guests' orders on trays, improving the dining experience (Ang, 2016).

4.5 Robot Housekeeper and Robot Host/Hostess

The Park Avenue Rochester Hotel in Singapore has become the first business hotel in the city to use robots in its operations and bulk products between layers With its efficient performance, Roby manages the work of 3.5 full-time employees, which leads to significant cost savings for the hotel (Lin, 2017). Robots are also being used to drive sales in the hospitality industry. For example, Tanooki Restaurant in Dubai employs robot hosts to attract customers. This robot doesn't just communicate with guests, but it also gives them discount coupons and encourages them to eat at restaurants (Ivanov & Webster, 2020). Robotic hosts act as an alternative to human hosts. This is especially true in tech-savvy restaurants or those catering to a younger, tech-focused audience. Interacting with such robots provides a state-of-the-art experience to these customers increasing the fun and excitement of their visit (Berezina et al., 2019).

4.6 Chat bots and Facial Recognition

A chatbot is a software program that allows users to interact with a system in their own language (Abu Shawar & Atwell, 2007). Often referred to as a "virtual agent" or "chatbot," chatbots are a prime example of technology self-service. They are typically found on professional websites or mobile applications (Melián-González et al., 2019). According to a study by Melián-González et al. (2019), guests of hotels, restaurants, transportation, and entertainment centers often use chatbots as can be seen from reviews on platforms like Tripadvisor, for example, at Marriott International. Guests can book any of over 4,700 hotels via a chatbot on Facebook Messenger. (Phaneuf, 2020) Biometric technology, which uses physical characteristics such as eyes, fingerprints, face, or voice, aims to make this easier. Individuals make use of biometric data for the daily tasks they do. Facial recognition is a prime example in this category. It is most commonly used in the travel industry. For example, passengers at Gatwick Airport in the UK used facial recognition to control their service passports (Ivanov and Webster). At Ufood Grill in Maryland, customers can order and pay within 10 seconds using facial recognition technology (Marston, 2017). A KFC kiosk in Beijing also uses facial recognition to serve food based on the customer's gender, age, and mood (Wu, 2017) many hotels, e.g., Fairmont Singapore and Swissotel. The Stamford enables faster check-in and check-out through facial recognition (Rajagopal, 2019). China's Alibaba Flyzoo hotel has further enhanced the experience with room selection and booking through technology (Wolfe, 2019). The global facial recognition market, which was valued at US$4.05 billion in 2017, is expected to reach US$7.76 billion by 2022, highlighting the increasing spread of these technologies in the travel sector. and services (Hristova, 2019).

4.7 Self-Service Check-In and Check-Out Kiosks

Self-service check-in and check-out kiosks are a new technology in the hospitality industry. This allows guests to check in and out freely without needing to go to the front desk (Kim & Qu, 2014, 2015). Yotel New York, for example, provides a seamless experience with self-service kiosks. Help guests check in quickly and easily. Similar to the process at airports (Yotel New York, 2020), these kiosks are not limited to hotels. It is also widely used in airports. By allowing passengers to check in, print your boarding pass, Future Travel Experience in 2013, and check in your baggage (Nicas and Michaels in 2012), all without human intervention.

4.8 Virtual Assistant

Wynn Las Vegas made news (2016), when every room was equipped with Echo, a voice-activated speaker that can be controlled by Amazon's Alexa. This is the main function of this period. This enables voice commands for virtual assistants to control the operation of different rooms.(Hotelmanagement.Net, 2016). Virtual assistants additionally provide broader capabilities, which include connecting to journey agencies' websites to assist guests with vacation spot activities, flight bookings, and lodging reservations (Ivanov et al., 2017). In collaboration with Arçelik, Divan Istanbul added the clever virtual assistant “Assista,” permitting visitors to control room features like lights, curtains, and air conditioning, in addition to getting right of entry to records on local climate, trade costs, news, and activities (CHIP Online, 2018). Additionally, in Singapore, the virtual assistant SARA gives traveler facts, guiding traffic via the metropolis with voice, text, or QR code interplay (Niculescu et al., 2014).

5. MANAGERIAL IMPLICATION

Adopting robots in the service industry presents an important opportunity to increase efficiency. Profitability and customer experience Robots are becoming more adept at performing more complex physical and cognitive tasks. This makes robots a valuable asset for hotel operations. Many hotels have already started using social robots to help guests and improve their experience (Lu et al., 2020). However, for these innovations to succeed, customer acceptance is important in the short and long term. Research suggests that service robots can improve the overall guest experience. This is especially true for technology-focused customers who are looking for innovation and innovation. Promoting robots as an interactive and fun service element can increase customer satisfaction and referrals (Ivanov & Webster, 2019). However, managers must address the discomfort this may cause guests. Elderly people and women may feel uncomfortable interacting with robots. Providing support and clear guidance can help reduce this hesitation. The concept of robot service adoption to optimize robot integration provides a framework for evaluating customer adoption potential. This approach allows businesses. They customize their robot services through a process of trial and error. This increases the efficiency of the robot solution and reduces costs. Finally, careful planning and a customer-focused strategy are essential for the strong application of robots in a service facility.

6. LIMITATIONS AND DIRECTIONS FOR FUTURE RESEARCH

This study emphasizes the use of service robots in hospitality while noting limitations and making recommendations for further research. For example, study focusing on various robot and AI technologies to better understand their overall impact on consumer surveys. Furthermore, 28.6% of donors had prior technology experience, which likely skewed the findings. Future studies need to consider more technologically adapted members to capture nuanced views (Park, 2020; Fan et al., 2019). Service robots are reshaping the hospitality quarter through the way of enhancing performance and lowering prices. However, the degree of automation in carrier delivery must be context-sensitive. Hospitality leaders are encouraged to strategically determine where automation can be best even as they make sure they are prepared for technological challenges. Developing contingency plans to address technical problems is critical for seamless integration (Park, 2020).

Additionally, carrier robots are an appealing street for market differentiation in line with branding techniques. By integrating robots into advertising communications It goals a digitally engaged demographic. Especially for young experts, groups can increase customer engagement and emblem appeal (Fan et al., 2019). Service robots are redefining the position of employees in a team of workers management. Frontline personnel may additionally transition into specialized roles, inclusive of product ambassadors or skilled guides. Meanwhile, lower back-stop roles might also evolve into innovative responsibilities including meal presentation and recipe innovation. These changes highlight the changing impact of technology on work structures (Park, 2020). Ultimately, this study contributes to the discourse on automation in the hospitality industry. It provides strategic guidance for managing technology integration and responding to changing customer expectations.

7. CONCLUSION

This article highlights the management challenges associated with automation and service robots in frontline roles in hospitality and tourism. As the industry embraces digital transformation important regulatory, legal, and ethical issues arise. By requiring the active participation of stakeholders (Giuliano et al., 2017), innovations that enhance the service experience must prioritize principles such as responsibility, inclusiveness, and co-design. Co-design involves creating humanoid robots that work together. Enhance the potential of stakeholders. Both resident's visitors and consumers determine the type of service they want. The democratization of this disruptive technology promotes public participation in policymaking and action that ensures corporate digital responsibility and social well-being. Achieving this goal requires digital literacy and equal access to ICT. Facilitating "smart democracy" goes hand in hand with "digital democracy" (Hacker et al., 2020) as human-machine interactions evolve. Society should be led responsibly by technology. A system in which traditional humanist values are challenged by post humanists and Tran's humanists, anthropology, and animal forms creative change is redefining "personality," and new ways of analyzing these changes are needed. Post humanist approaches such as actor-network theory and Deleuzian ethics provide an important framework for exploring service robot innovation alongside relational and non-dualist epistemologies (Forlano et al., 2017). Additionally, as Robotic and Artificial Intelligence Service Automation (RAISA) accelerates, attention to robot-ethics is increasingly important. Current research on the ethics of robots in tourism is limited. Therefore, the legal and ethical dimensions need to be seriously explored.

REFERENCES:

Ameen, N., Tarhini, A., Reppel, A., & Anand, A. (2021). Customer experiences in the age of artificial intelligence. *Computers in Human Behavior*, 114, 106548. DOI: 10.1016/j.chb.2020.106548 PMID: 32905175

Belanche, D., Casaló, L. V., Flavián, C., & Schepers, J. (2020). Robots or frontline employees? Exploring customers' attributions of responsibility and stability after service failure or success. *Journal of Service Management*, 31(2), 267–289. DOI: 10.1108/JOSM-05-2019-0156

Blut, M., Wang, C., Wünderlich, N. V., & Brock, C. (2021). Understanding anthropomorphism in service provision: A meta-analysis of physical robots, chatbots, and other AI. *Journal of the Academy of Marketing Science*, 49(4), 1–27. DOI: 10.1007/s11747-020-00762-y

Bowen, J., & Morosan, C. (2018). Beware hospitality industry: The robots are coming. *Worldwide Hospitality and Tourism Themes*, 10(6), 726–733. DOI: 10.1108/WHATT-07-2018-0045

Bowen, J., & Morosan, C. (2018). Beware hospitality industry: The robots are coming. *Worldwide Hospitality and Tourism Themes*, 10(6), 726–733. DOI: 10.1108/WHATT-07-2018-0045

Broadbent, E., Stafford, R., & MacDonald, B. (2009). Acceptance of healthcare robots for the older population: Review and future directions. *International Journal of Social Robotics*, 1(4), 319–330. DOI: 10.1007/s12369-009-0030-6

Buhalis, D., Law, R., & Sigala, M. (2023). The impact of robotics and AI on the hospitality industry: Trends and future directions. *Journal of Hospitality and Tourism Technology*, 14(2), 217–232.

Chathoth, P. K., & Ungson, G. R. (2023). Service agents' risk behavior and implications for co-creation. *International Journal of Contemporary Hospitality Management*, 35(9), 3344–3359. DOI: 10.1108/IJCHM-06-2022-0730

Chen, H., Chiang, R. H., & Storey, V. C. (2012). Business intelligence and analytics: From big data to big impact. *Management Information Systems Quarterly*, 36(4), 1165–1188. DOI: 10.2307/41703503

Chiang, A. H., & Trimi, S. (2020). Impacts of service robots on service quality. *Service Business*, 14(3), 439–459. DOI: 10.1007/s11628-020-00423-8

Fan, A., Wu, L., Miao, L., & Mattila, A. S. (2020). When does technology anthropomorphism help alleviate customer dissatisfaction after a service failure?–The moderating role of consumer technology self-efficacy and interdependent self-construal. *Journal of Hospitality Marketing & Management*, 29(3), 269–290. DOI: 10.1080/19368623.2019.1639095

Forlano, L. (2017). Posthumanism and design. *She Ji: The Journal of Design, Economics, and Innovation*, 3(1), 16–29.

Giuliano, L., Lupetti, M. L., Khan, S., & Germak, C. (2017). Ethic reflections about service robotics, from human protection to enhancement: Case study on cultural heritage. In *Robotics-Legal, Ethical and Socioeconomic Impacts*. IntechOpen.

Guia, J., & Jamal, T. (2020). A (Deleuzian) posthumanist paradigm for tourism research. *Annals of Tourism Research*, 84, 102982. DOI: 10.1016/j.annals.2020.102982 PMID: 32834223

Hacker, K. L., & Van Dijk, J. (2000). *Digital Democracy: Issues of Theory and Practice*. Sage. DOI: 10.4135/9781446218891

Haenlein, M., & Kaplan, A. (2019). A Brief History of Artificial Intelligence: On the Past, Present, and Future of Artificial Intelligence. *California Management Review*, 61(4), 5–14. DOI: 10.1177/0008125619864925

Huang, M. H., & Rust, R. T. (2018). Artificial Intelligence in Service. *Journal of Service Research*, 21(2), 155–172. DOI: 10.1177/1094670517752459

International Federation of Robotics. (2020). *IFR International Federation of Robotics*. https://ifr.org/

International Federation of Robotics (IFR). (2022). World [IFR.]. *Robotics Reports*, •••, 2022.

Io, H. N., & Lee, C. B. (2020). Social Media Comments about Hotel Robots. *Journal of China Tourism Research*, 16(4), 606–625. DOI: 10.1080/19388160.2020.1769785

Ivanov, S., & Webster, C. (2019). Conceptual framework of the use of robots, artificial intelligence and service automation in travel, tourism, and hospitality companies. Ivanov, S., Webster, C. (Eds.), Robots, Artificial Intelligence and Service Automation in Travel, *Tourism and Hospitality. Emerald Publishing,* 7-37 DOI: 10.1108/978-1-78756-687-320191001

Ivanov, S., & Webster, C. (2021). Robotics and artificial intelligence in hospitality: The future of service automation. *Tourism Management Perspectives*, 37, 100771.

Ivanov, S., Webster, C., & Berezina, K. (2019). Robotics in tourism and hospitality. *Current Issues in Tourism*, 22(9), 1007–1025.

Ivanov, S., Webster, C., & Berezina, K. (2019). Robotics in tourism and hospitality. *Current Issues in Tourism*, 22(9), 1007–1025.

Jiang, Y., & Zhao, Y. (2023). Automation in hotel operations: Technological advancements and managerial implications. *Journal of Hospitality Marketing & Management*, 32(4), 432–446.

Kandampully, J., Zhang, T., & Bilgihan, A. (2021). Exploring the challenges of robotics and automation in hospitality. *International Journal of Hospitality Management*, 97, 103049.

Kaplan, A., & Haenlein, M. (2019). Rethinking AI: Interpreting Data for Strategic Goals. *Journal of Marketing*, 83(1), 15–22.

Kuo, C., & Wu, C. (2022). Guest acceptance of service robots in hotels: A generational perspective. *Journal of Hospitality & Tourism Research (Washington, D.C.)*, 46(2), 252–271.

Lee, S. (2023). Service quality and customer satisfaction in the era of robotics: A hospitality perspective. *International Journal of Hospitality & Tourism Administration*, 24(1), 65–80.

Liu, J., Hall, C. M., Zhu, C., & Ting Pong Cheng, V. (2024). Redefining the concept of smart tourism in tourism and hospitality. *Anatolia*, 35(3), 566–578. DOI: 10.1080/13032917.2023.2282712

Murphy, J.. (2017). Robotics in the Digital Age: Understanding Their Role and Future. *AI Magazine*, 38(1), 106–108.

Murphy, J., Gretzel, U., & Pesonen, J. (2019). Marketing robot services in hospitality and tourism: The role of anthropomorphism. *Journal of Travel & Tourism Marketing*, 36(7), 784–795. DOI: 10.1080/10548408.2019.1571983

Murphy, J., Tan, W., & Watanabe, T. (2021). The future of service robots in hospitality: Opportunities and challenges. *Journal of Hospitality and Tourism Technology*, 12(4), 535–548.

Pine, B. J., & Gilmore, J. H. (2011). *The Experience Economy: Work Is Theater and Every Business a Stage*. Harvard Business Review Press.

Russell, S., & Norvig, P. (2016). *Artificial Intelligence: A Modern Approach* (3rd ed.). Pearson.

Schwab, K. (2016). The Fourth Industrial Revolution. *World Economic Forum.*

Tan, M., Mohan, A., & Watanabe, T. (2024). The integration of IoT and robotics in hospitality: Transforming guest experiences. *Journal of Service Research*, 27(1), 50–68.

Tussyadiah, I. (2023). Exploring AI in Hospitality and Tourism: Trends and Applications. *Tourism Management Perspectives*, 37, 100813.

Wirtz, P., Patterson, P. G., Kunz, W. H., Gruber, T., Lu, V. N., Paluch, S., & Martins, A. (2018). Brave new world: Service robots in the frontline. *Journal of Service Management*, 29(5), 907–931. DOI: 10.1108/JOSM-04-2018-0119

Chapter 14
The Role of the Metaverse in Transforming Financial Management Practices for SMEs

Abdul Qadeer
https://orcid.org/0009-0004-4157-2387
Shaheed Benazir Bhutto University, Nawabshah, Pakistan

Raja Sultan
Shaheed Benazir Bhutto University, Nawabshah, Pakistan

Mukhtiar Ali Erri
Shaheed Benazir Bhutto University, Nawabshah, Pakistan

Abdul Waheed
Shaheed Benazir Bhutto University, Nawabshah, Pakistan

ABSTRACT

The rapid advancement of technologies such as Virtual Reality (VR), Artificial Intelligence (AI), Augmented Reality (AR), and Big Data has introduced transformative possibilities for financial management. Among these innovations, the Metaverse is emerging as a disruptive platform, offering unique opportunities to reshape financial practices, particularly for Small and Medium Enterprises (SMEs). The integration of mobile-based, always-on accessibility and virtual currency systems, coupled with the rise of Non-Fungible Tokens (NFTs), has elevated the Metaverse into a powerful

DOI: 10.4018/979-8-3693-9005-4.ch014

tool for financial innovation and operational improvement. This study explores the attributes, applications, and potential benefits of the Metaverse in revolutionizing SME financial management

1. INTRODUCTION

The global metaverse market is projected to grow from $40 billion in 2021 to over $1,607 billion by 2030, reflecting a compound annual growth rate (CAGR) of 37.73%. This growth is fueled by advancements in virtual currencies, blockchain, and decentralized technologies (Iqbal et al., 2024). Blockchain underpins the metaverse, enabling decentralized ownership of digital assets, such as cryptocurrencies and NFTs, which are critical for secure, transparent financial transactions (Alvarez et al., 2024). Decentralized finance (DeFi) within the metaverse allows SMEs to access alternative financial systems, bypassing traditional intermediaries. This increases financial inclusion for businesses with limited access to banking services (Wang, 2024). Integration of stablecoins and Central Bank Digital Currencies (CBDCs) within the metaverse provides secure, real-time cross-border transactions, enabling SMEs to engage in global trade more efficiently (Xu et al., 2024). SMEs are leveraging tokenized virtual real estate in the metaverse to establish a digital presence, creating new revenue streams and marketing opportunities through immersive customer engagement (Srinivasan & Wahyuningsih, 2024). The metaverse enables cost reductions in financial operations through automated smart contracts and AI-driven financial advisory systems, eliminating manual processes (Spinner, 2024). SMEs use the metaverse to deliver personalized financial services through AI-driven avatars and virtual reality interfaces, increasing customer satisfaction and retention rates (Truong & Niyato, 2023). Blockchain's immutable ledger enhances transparency in financial management, reducing the risks of fraud and improving trust among stakeholders. SMEs are adopting metaverse technologies to streamline supply chain financing, ensuring better liquidity management and reducing delays in payment cycles (Vidal-Tomas, 2023). According to Saivasan & Lokhande (2023), blockchain's decentralized ledger technology enhances financial transparency, providing SMEs with immutable transaction records and reducing fraud risks. Randan Live (2024) identified that stablecoins are pivotal in the metaverse economy, enabling secure and seamless peer-to-peer payments for SMEs conducting global transactions. Alvarez et al., (2024) highlighted the use of Ethereum-based smart contracts to automate financial processes, reducing administrative costs for SMEs in the metaverse. Hutson et al., (2023) demonstrated how SMEs utilize VR-based customer service in the metaverse to increase customer loyalty and engagement through immersive interactions. According to Ariza et al., (2024), SMEs can tokenize assets in the metaverse to secure financing through decentralized fundraising platforms, bypassing traditional banking systems. Katterbauer et al., (2024) showed SMEs buying virtual land in platforms like Decentraland to establish their digital brand presence, leading to higher visibility and customer outreach. Chu (2023) explored AI-powered tools in the metaverse that provide SMEs with predictive financial analytics, enabling better budget allocation and revenue forecasting. Bisht et al., (2022) highlighted the integration of metaverse technologies in supply chain financing, helping SMEs optimize cash flows and enhance supplier relationships. Aysan et al., (2024) showed that SMEs leverage VR-based financial education programs to upskill employees and improve financial literacy. Aysan et al., (2024) discussed the evolving metaverse regulations, emphasizing the need for SMEs to adapt to compliance requirements while gaining from early adoption. Cano et al., (2023) found that virtual banks in the metaverse provide SMEs with access to low-interest loans and financial services, reducing barriers faced in traditional banking. Brahmi et al., (1988) explored the integration of sustainability metrics in metaverse-based financial tools, enabling SMEs to track and report their ESG (Environmental, Social, Governance) performance for green financing.These findings shows the metaverse's extensive potential in reshaping financial management for SMEs, offering cost-efficient, transparent, and innovative financial tools while addressing global regulatory and operational challenges. SMEs utilize immersive training modules in the metaverse to enhance employees' financial literacy and decision-making capabilities, creating a more informed workforce.

2. LITERATURE REVIEW

2.1 Metaverse and it's role in SMEs Financial Management

The metaverse facilitates virtual trade fairs and financial summits, allowing SMEs to network globally without incurring significant travel costs, broadening their market reach. Fathi (2024) indicates that regulatory frameworks for digital transactions in the metaverse are still evolving, offering opportunities for SMEs to shape standards but also posing compliance challenges. These findings highlight the transformative potential of the metaverse in redefining financial management practices for SMEs, offering innovative solutions while posing new challenges. Blockchain technology within the metaverse enables immutable and transparent records, reducing fraud and improving trust in financial dealings (Koi & Dinner, 2023). SMEs benefit from metaverse-enabled banking platforms offering easier access to services like loans and account management (Firmanyah & Umar, 2023). Smart contracts and decentralized exchanges within the metaverse allow SMEs to bypass intermediaries, saving costs and time (Frank & Rudolf, 2024). Integration of cryptocurrencies like stablecoins ensures low-cost, real-time international transactions, crucial for SMEs (Ghaffar & Setiawan, 2024). AI-driven credit analysis tools in the metaverse provide accurate and timely creditworthiness assessments for SMEs (Ho & Song, 2023). Metaverse-based crowdfunding platforms enable SMEs to connect with a global audience, enhancing fundraising capabilities. Automation of financial processes in the metaverse significantly reduces administrative overheads (Gholjash et al., 2024). Real-time analytics and blockchain solutions optimize liquidity management for SMEs in the metaverse (Far et al ., 2023). Adoption of secure digital wallets simplifies financial management and virtual currency handling for SMEs. Tokenization and virtual asset trading in the metaverse provide new avenues for capital generation (Hussain et al., 2023). VR-based financial training programs within the metaverse boost SME owners' and employees' financial knowledge. Blockchain applications in trade finance streamline operations like invoicing and payment reconciliation (Hutson et al., 2023). Advanced fraud detection mechanisms leveraging AI and blockchain enhance financial security. SMEs use metaverse tools to deliver personalized financial wellness and benefits to employees (Hussain, 1988). Personalized financial products developed through AI algorithms increase customer satisfaction. Blockchain-led systems in the metaverse facilitate accurate and transparent reporting on environmental, social, and governance metrics (Hussain, 2024). SMEs leverage metaverse platforms to connect with investors and venture capitalists worldwide. Virtual advisory services enable SMEs to receive expert consultation from anywhere (Hussain et al., 2022). Automated tax compliance tools reduce complexity and enhance accuracy for SMEs operating in the metaverse. Interactive tools enhance engagement and simplify complex financial decision-making processes (Kumar et al., 2024). SMEs optimize cash flow through blockchain-backed supply chain financial solutions in the metaverse. Virtual platforms provide SMEs with easier access to sustainability-linked loans and grants (Kadhim & Al Ani, 2023). SMEs raise capital through tokenized equity offerings in metaverse-enabled stock exchanges. Analytics tools offer SMEs actionable insights for better financial planning and execution (Lazaroiu et al., 2024). SMEs leverage blockchain for transparent and error-free audits (Liu et al., 2024). Digital platforms in the metaverse help SMEs showcase their financial capabilities and offerings to stakeholders. SMEs use tokenized assets for secure collateralization and loan applications (Malekolkalami, 2024). SMEs engage in metaverse commerce, driving financial innovations and new revenue streams. Predictive analytics identify financial risks, allowing proactive management. SMEs benefit from participating in growing metaverse ecosystems that include decentralized markets (Pandey & Gilmour, 2024). Blockchain ensures secure and efficient payroll processing for globally distributed teams (Pinciro-Chousa et al., 2024). AI-powered forecasting tools support strategic decision-making.. SMEs leverage metaverse-based microfinance platforms for capital in underserved markets. Intelligent systems prevent financial fraud by identifying anomalies in transaction patterns (Mozunder et al., 2023). Metaverse tools enable real-time client interactions, boosting satisfaction and retention. SMEs gain equal access to global financial systems through metaverse-enabled solutions (Musleh Alsartawi & Hussainey, 2024). SMEs attract funding for green initiatives through transparent and innovative virtual platforms. Participation in metaverse-hosted summits facilitates networking with global financial experts (Hussain, 2024). SMEs explore and benefit from trading tokenized assets and NFTs as part of diversified portfolios. Virtual collaboration tools streamline financial planning and execution for SME teams (Mbaye, 2023). These underscores the transformative potential of the metaverse in reshaping financial management for SMEs.

3. METHODOLOGY

This study employs an exploratory approach, synthesizing accessible applications, practices, and literature on the role of the metaverse in financial management for SMEs. The study incorporates information gathered from a comprehensive literature review on the topic. It examines the existing body of research on the metaverse, virtual reality, and its applications in financial management for SMEs, including peer-reviewed journal articles, unpublished/accepted studies, reports, and policies. A systematic search was conducted using terms such as "metaverse in financial management," "virtual reality in finance," "metaverse in SME finance," "blockchain in financial operations," and "digital finance in SMEs." Various research databases, including Scopus, Google Scholar, ResearchGate, and industry-specific resources such as ScienceDirect, Emerald, and IGI Global, were utilized to gather relevant papers. The study drew on publications from top international journals, primarily those indexed in Scopus, including the Journal of Small Business Management, International Journal of Financial Management, Journal of Business Research, Technovation, and Journal of Business Venturing*, among others. The paper identifies existing practices and measures taken to integrate the metaverse into financial management in SMEs, focusing on improving financial performance, profitability, and operational efficiency. This integration is expected to enhance customer service, streamline financial operations, and ultimately boost overall satisfaction for both businesses and clients. Additionally, the study seeks to analyze and combine insights from various metaverse-related financial investigations, identifying emerging trends and highlighting areas that require further exploration. The desk research approach used in this paper expands the scope of data, providing a clearer understanding of the application of the metaverse in financial management for SMEs. The findings of this research aim to address knowledge gaps in the current literature, offering valuable insights and suggesting new avenues for future research in the field.

Table 1. Applications of Metaverse in Financial Management for SMEs and Its Benefits

Application	Description	Benefits
Virtual Financial Meetings and Consultations	Use of virtual meeting spaces in the metaverse for financial consultations and collaboration.	Enhanced communication, reduced travel costs, and global access to expert advice.
Financial Reporting and Analytics	Metaverse-enabled platforms provide immersive data visualizations for financial reporting.	Improved decision-making through interactive data analysis and easy-to-understand financial insights.
Training and Education for Financial Professionals	Virtual training environments for financial staff on using digital tools and systems.	Reduced training costs, enhanced learning experiences, and better employee skill development.
Digital Twin for Financial Management Systems	Creating virtual models of financial operations and systems for better analysis and forecasting.	Accurate forecasting, risk assessment, and enhanced financial strategy development.
Client Financial Management Interaction	Virtual spaces for direct interaction between clients and financial managers, enhancing client service.	Improved client engagement and personalized financial solutions.
Blockchain and Cryptocurrency Integration	Facilitating the use of blockchain and virtual currencies for real-time financial transactions.	Secure, transparent transactions and the possibility of new revenue streams through virtual currencies.
Metaverse-Driven Business Simulations	Simulating financial scenarios in a virtual environment to test decision-making strategies.	Lower risk in decision-making and the ability to test multiple strategies without real-world consequences.
Automated Smart Contracts	Using virtual contracts and smart agreements for financial transactions and agreements.	Increased efficiency, cost reduction, and transparency in contract management.
Crowdfunding in Virtual Environments	Using virtual reality to host immersive fundraising and crowdfunding campaigns.	Access to global investors, increased engagement, and higher potential for funding.
Metaverse-Based Investment Platforms	Providing virtual platforms for investors to explore, track, and invest in businesses.	Streamlined investment processes, enhanced user experience, and broader market access.
Peer-to-Peer Lending	Offering decentralized lending options in virtual environments using cryptocurrencies.	Lower interest rates, faster lending processes, and greater financial inclusion.
Virtual Financial Markets	Trading financial instruments like stocks, bonds, and cryptocurrencies in the metaverse.	Increased market access, 24/7 trading, and more diverse investment opportunities.
Decentralized Finance (DeFi)	Implementing decentralized financial services within the metaverse using blockchain.	Removal of intermediaries, lower costs, and increased financial autonomy.
Digital Asset Management	Managing digital assets such as NFTs, cryptocurrencies, and virtual real estate in the metaverse.	Enhanced asset liquidity, easy tracking, and opportunities for virtual real estate investment.

The following graph visually represents the relationship between different metaverse applications and the benefits they bring to financial management in SMEs.

Figure 1. Applications of Metaverse in Financial Management vs. Benefits

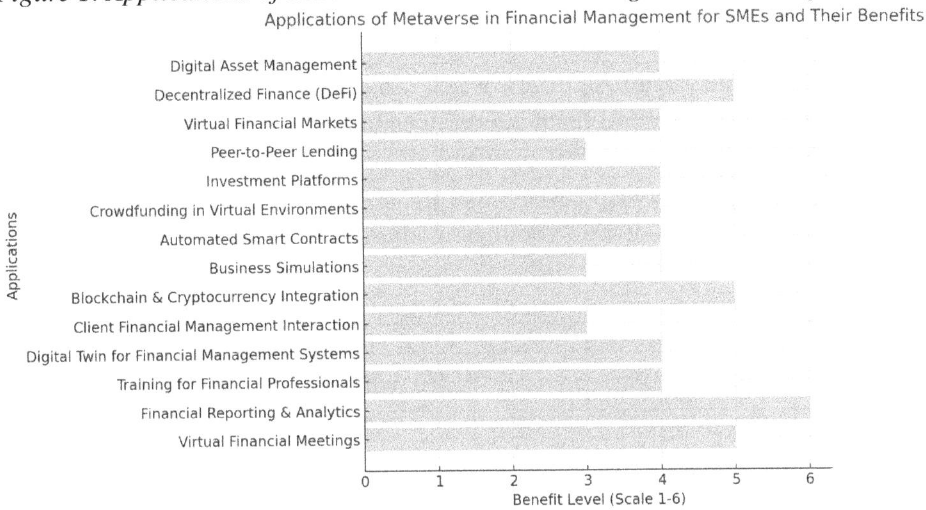

This chart highlights how different applications in the metaverse contribute to enhancing various financial management practices for SMEs, emphasizing benefits like decision-making improvement, cost reduction, financial inclusion, and better market access.

Results

The findings of this study reveal several significant insights into the potential role of the metaverse in enhancing financial management practices for SMEs. A detailed analysis of the existing literature shows that the metaverse, as an immersive digital space, offers unique capabilities that can fundamentally reshape how SMEs handle various financial operations. These insights were gathered through an extensive review of peer-reviewed journal articles, reports, case studies, and other relevant literature. The integration of metaverse technologies in SMEs has the potential to optimize several aspects of financial management, including budgeting, financial forecasting, and financial reporting. Virtual environments in the metaverse can enable real-time collaboration and more accurate financial analysis, helping SMEs make better-informed decisions by leveraging virtual financial models and simulations. These applications can be particularly beneficial for businesses operating with limited resources, enabling more effective financial planning and risk management. Blockchain technologies, often linked with the metaverse, play a crucial role in improving the transparency, security, and traceability of financial transactions. SMEs can utilize blockchain-based applications in the metaverse to securely manage financial records, reduce fraud risks, and increase trust with stakeholders. The decentralized nature of blockchain allows for secure peer-to-peer transactions without relying on intermediaries, reducing costs for SMEs and increasing the speed of transactions. The metaverse offers a new dimension in financial management by improving accessibility to financial services for SMEs, especially those in developing regions. Through virtual financial institutions and decentralized finance (DeFi) systems, SMEs can gain access to a wider range of financial products, such as micro-loans, investment opportunities, and capital-raising methods that were previously unavailable. The metaverse also makes it easier for businesses to tap into global financial markets, enhancing cross-border trade and international investment opportunities. Virtual advisors, powered by artificial intelligence and augmented reality within the metaverse, can assist SMEs with day-to-day financial management tasks. These virtual advisors can analyze financial data in real-time and offer tailored advice on investment strategies, cash flow management, and tax planning. By using VR-based simulations, these advisors can create immersive scenarios for SMEs to better understand the financial impact of their decisions before implementation. The metaverse supports the automation of various financial operations through smart contracts and AI-driven systems. These technologies enable SMEs to automate payments, manage accounts payable and receivable, and streamline their accounting processes without human intervention. This automation reduces the time spent on manual processes and lowers the chances of human error, making the financial management process more efficient and cost-effective. The integration of metaverse technologies into financial management has a direct correlation with improving profitability. By enhancing financial efficiency, reducing operational costs, and expanding access to new financial opportunities, SMEs can expect an overall improvement in their profitability. The metaverse also allows businesses to create new revenue streams through virtual products, digital marketing, and online retail, which could further boost their income potential. In the metaverse, SMEs can create virtual experiences that enhance customer engagement with their financial services. Virtual stores, interactive financial simulations, and personalized experiences in the metaverse can improve customer loyalty and satisfaction. Additionally, metaverse-driven marketing strategies, such as virtual events and experiences, can help SMEs attract new clients and expand their customer base. Through the synthesis of current literature and data, this study identifies several knowledge gaps in understanding the full impact of the metaverse on financial management for SMEs. There is a need for further research on the practical challenges SMEs face when adopting metaverse technologies, including the financial investment required, technological barriers, and the skillsets needed to operate in this new digital space. Future studies should explore the integration of the metaverse with traditional financial systems and assess the scalability of such solutions for SMEs across various industries. While the benefits are substantial, the study also highlights key challenges that SMEs face in implementing metaverse technologies for financial management. These include a lack of technical expertise, high initial investment costs, and limited awareness of the available metaverse tools. SMEs need to overcome these barriers through strategic partnerships, training, and the development of user-friendly platforms tailored to their specific needs. The role of regulatory bodies in ensuring the ethical use of the metaverse in financial management is critical. The study discusses the importance of establishing clear regulations to prevent misuse of virtual financial services, protect user data, and ensure fair access to financial opportunities. Ethical concerns surrounding privacy, data security, and the digital divide must be addressed to ensure equitable access to the metaverse for SMEs. These findings underscore the transformative potential of the metaverse in revolutionizing financial management for SMEs. By providing insights into operational efficiencies, financial accessibility, and customer engagement, the study highlights the metaverse's ability to reshape SME financial landscapes. However, addressing the challenges of implementation, regulation, and scalability will be crucial in ensuring its successful integration into financial management practices for SMEs.

CONCLUSION

This study provides an in-depth exploration of the role of the metaverse in transforming financial management practices for Small and Medium-sized Enterprises (SMEs). The metaverse has the potential to significantly revolutionize financial management for SMEs by optimizing operational processes such as budgeting, financial forecasting, reporting, and cash flow management. By incorporating virtual environments and immersive technologies, SMEs can gain deeper insights into financial data and enhance decision-making, which can lead to more accurate financial planning. Moreover, the metaverse facilitates real-time collaboration, enabling SME stakeholders to engage in dynamic financial planning discussions regardless of geographical barriers. Blockchain and decentralized technologies within the metaverse contribute to enhanced transparency and security in financial transactions. By leveraging blockchain's immutability and secure nature, SMEs can ensure that their financial records are tamper-proof and easily auditable, thereby increasing trust with clients, investors, and regulatory bodies. This not only mitigates the risk of fraud but also reduces reliance on intermediaries, thus decreasing transaction costs. One of the most promising benefits of the metaverse for SMEs is the improvement in financial accessibility. SMEs, particularly those in emerging markets or regions with limited access to traditional banking, can leverage decentralized finance (DeFi) platforms within the metaverse to access loans, investment opportunities, and other financial products. The ability to conduct financial transactions in a virtual environment, without geographical constraints, opens up global financial markets to SMEs that were previously excluded due to barriers such as high fees, lengthy approval processes, and limited access to capital. Automation is a key benefit of the metaverse for SMEs, with the introduction of AI-driven financial systems and smart contracts that automate routine financial tasks such as invoicing, payments, payroll processing, and accounting. By reducing human intervention, these technologies not only save time but also minimize the risk of human errors and operational inefficiencies. As a result, SMEs can focus on more strategic financial decisions, knowing that day-to-day tasks are handled automatically and accurately. Virtual financial advisors powered by AI and virtual reality (VR) are another area where the metaverse can have a profound impact on SMEs. These virtual advisors can analyze a business's financial health in real-time, offering customized advice and simulating various financial scenarios. This helps SMEs make better-informed decisions, whether it's for cash flow management, investment strategies, or financial risk assessments, leading to enhanced business growth and sustainability. The metaverse also presents new opportunities for SMEs to enhance customer engagement and improve the customer experience through virtual storefronts, financial services, and interactive events. By providing immersive virtual experiences, SMEs can create more personalized and memorable interactions with customers, which can drive loyalty, increase brand awareness, and attract a wider audience. Furthermore, through VR-based product demos and financial simulations, SMEs can engage customers in innovative ways, fostering deeper relationships and improving customer satisfaction. While the metaverse offers numerous advantages for SMEs, this study identifies significant knowledge gaps in understanding the full extent of its impact on financial management practices. Many of the existing studies focus on the theoretical potential of the metaverse, with limited empirical research on its practical applications in real-world SME financial operations. Future research should explore the challenges SMEs face when adopting metaverse technologies, such as the costs, technical expertise required, and the scalability of these tools for businesses of different sizes. Additionally, the integration of the metaverse with traditional financial systems and the regulatory landscape needs further investigation to ensure a smooth and secure transition for SMEs. The implementation of metaverse technologies in SMEs is not without its challenges. High initial investment costs, a lack of technical skills, and the complexity of integrating metaverse platforms with existing financial systems are some of the barriers that SMEs may encounter. Additionally, SMEs may face resistance to change due to the unfamiliarity of the metaverse and its technologies. Overcoming these barriers requires careful planning, strategic partnerships, and investment in training and development for SME stakeholders. The study emphasizes the importance of establishing clear and comprehensive regulations to guide the ethical use of the metaverse in financial management. Issues related to data privacy, cybersecurity, and fair access to financial services must be addressed to ensure that the metaverse remains a safe and equitable space for all SMEs. Regulatory bodies must ensure that metaverse financial services are compliant with existing financial regulations and that adequate safeguards are in place to protect users from potential risks. In conclusion, the metaverse offers a transformative opportunity for SMEs to enhance their financial management practices, improve operational efficiency, and expand access to financial services. The potential benefits—such as increased transparency, improved customer engagement, automation, and enhanced security—make the metaverse a valuable tool for SMEs. However, for the full potential of the metaverse to be realized, SMEs must overcome significant barriers such as high costs, technical challenges, and the need for regulatory frameworks. Future research will play a critical role in bridging the gaps in knowledge and understanding, paving the way for successful integration of the metaverse into SME financial management. As the metaverse continues to evolve, it will be essential for SMEs to stay informed about new developments and adapt their strategies accordingly to remain competitive in an increasingly digital financial landscape.

Future Research Directions

The study provides a comprehensive overview of the role of the metaverse in transforming financial management for Small and Medium-sized Enterprises (SMEs). Based on the findings and existing gaps in the literature, several future research directions can be pursued to deepen the understanding of the metaverse's impact on SME financial practices. Future research should focus on empirical studies that examine the practical implementation and adoption of metaverse technologies within SMEs. While existing literature provides theoretical frameworks, there is limited real-world data on how SMEs are integrating these technologies into their financial operations. Researchers could conduct case studies and surveys to gather data on the challenges, benefits, and barriers SMEs face when adopting the metaverse for financial management. This could help identify best practices and provide insights into how SMEs can effectively leverage these technologies. Blockchain and decentralized finance (DeFi) are central components of the metaverse that can significantly enhance the transparency and security of financial transactions for SMEs. Future research could investigate how SMEs can integrate blockchain and DeFi solutions into their financial systems, with a focus on areas such as secure transactions, real-time payments, and supply chain traceability. Additionally, research could explore the potential of smart contracts to automate financial processes like payments, invoicing, and tax reporting, and how these technologies can reduce transaction costs and enhance operational efficiency for SMEs. A critical area for future research is conducting cost-benefit analyses for SMEs considering the adoption of metaverse technologies. Given the high initial investment costs associated with implementing metaverse tools and technologies, research could explore the long-term financial benefits, such as cost reductions, productivity gains, and improved decision-making, that outweigh the initial costs. Such studies could provide SMEs with evidence-based insights on the financial viability and sustainability of adopting metaverse technologies in their financial management practices. As the metaverse evolves, regulatory and legal frameworks will need to be developed to ensure its safe and ethical use in financial management. Research should focus on understanding the legal challenges SMEs might face when adopting metaverse technologies, such as data privacy, cybersecurity risks, taxation, and intellectual property issues. Additionally, studies could explore how existing financial regulations (e.g., anti-money laundering laws, financial reporting standards) can be adapted to account for virtual financial transactions and activities in the metaverse. Collaboration between researchers, policymakers, and legal experts will be necessary to establish clear and comprehensive guidelines for SMEs. Another promising research direction is the study of how SMEs can integrate metaverse technologies with their existing financial systems and software. Many SMEs already use enterprise resource planning (ERP) systems and financial management tools, and research could explore the compatibility of these systems with metaverse platforms. This would include examining how virtual tools like virtual reality (VR) and augmented reality (AR) can be used alongside traditional financial software to enhance user experience and improve financial decision-making. Research could also investigate the technical challenges of system integration, data synchronization, and the seamless flow of financial information between traditional and metaverse-based platforms. The use of AI-powered virtual financial advisors in the metaverse presents an exciting area for future research. Researchers could explore how AI and machine learning algorithms can assist SMEs in financial decision-making, offering customized advice on investments, cash flow management, and financial risk mitigation. This research could involve designing models for AI-driven financial advisors that analyze real-time data and provide actionable insights to SME owners and managers. Furthermore, the ethical considerations of relying on AI for financial decision-making, including biases in algorithms and the need for transparency, should also be examined. As the metaverse allows for the creation of immersive virtual environments, future research could focus on how SMEs can use these environments to enhance customer experience and engagement in financial services. Studies could explore how virtual financial services, such as virtual banks, investment platforms, or financial advisory sessions, can provide a more personalized and interactive experience for customers. Research could also investigate how customer behaviors and expectations are evolving in virtual spaces and how SMEs can adapt their strategies to meet these new demands, leading to higher customer satisfaction and loyalty. A significant challenge for SMEs in adopting metaverse technologies is the lack of digital literacy and technical skills among key stakeholders, including business owners, financial managers, and employees. Future research could explore the importance of digital literacy training and the development of specialized skills for navigating the metaverse. Studies could examine the types of skills needed for SME employees to work effectively in a metaverse-driven financial environment and the best approaches for skill development, including online training programs, workshops, and partnerships with technology providers. The metaverse offers an opportunity to promote financial inclusion in emerging markets, where traditional financial services may be inaccessible or inefficient. Research could explore how the metaverse can provide SMEs in these regions with access to financial products and services, such as microloans, crowdfunding, or insurance, through decentralized platforms. Studies could also investigate the potential of the metaverse to overcome challenges such as high transaction fees, limited banking infrastructure, and geographical barriers, thus enabling SMEs to participate in global financial markets. As sustainability becomes an increasingly important consideration for businesses, research could examine the environmental impact of metaverse technologies on financial management. Virtual environments and blockchain platforms consume significant amounts of energy, and future studies could investigate the sustainability of using the metaverse in financial services. Researchers could explore energy-efficient practices, such as utilizing renewable energy sources for metaverse platforms or adopting carbon-offset strategies, to reduce the ecological footprint of metaverse-based financial operations. Finally, future research could investigate the long-term impact of metaverse adoption on the growth and financial performance of SMEs. This research could involve longitudinal studies that track the financial performance of SMEs before and after integrating metaverse technologies into their financial management processes. Key performance indicators (KPIs), such as revenue growth, profitability, operational efficiency, and market share, could be assessed to determine the tangible benefits SMEs experience from adopting the metaverse.These future research directions aim to fill the gaps identified in the existing literature and further advance the understanding of how the metaverse can reshape financial management for SMEs. By exploring these areas, researchers can contribute to a more comprehensive and practical understanding of the metaverse's role in the financial sector and provide SMEs with valuable insights to navigate this emerging technology.

REFERENCES

Alvarez, J., Segura-Dominguez, C., Tobias, R. G., & Navarrete-Bear, M. (2024, October). Comparative Analysis of Traditional and Metaverse-Based Learning on Financial Decision-Making Skills in Mathematics Students. In *2024 IEEE International Conference on Engineering Veracruz (ICEV)* (pp. 1-6). IEEE. DOI: 10.1109/ICEV63254.2024.10765998

Ariza, A. M. V., Marín, M. C., & Duran, M. L. D. (2024). The Metaverse: Financial Assurance Procedures in Smart Contracts and NFTs. *International Journal of Religion*, 5(11), 223–232. DOI: 10.61707/cd824339

Aysan, A. F., Batten, J., Gozgor, G., Khalfaoui, R., & Nanaeva, Z. (2024). Metaverse and financial markets: A quantile-time-frequency connectedness analysis. *Research in International Business and Finance*, 72, 102527. DOI: 10.1016/j.ribaf.2024.102527

Aysan, A. F., Gozgor, G., & Nanaeva, Z. (2024). Technological perspectives of Metaverse for financial service providers. *Technological Forecasting and Social Change*, 202, 123323. DOI: 10.1016/j.techfore.2024.123323

Bisht, D., Singh, R., Gehlot, A., Akram, S. V., Singh, A., Montero, E. C., Priyadarshi, N., & Twala, B. (2022). Imperative role of integrating digitalization in the firms finance: A technological perspective. *Electronics (Basel)*, 11(19), 3252. DOI: 10.3390/electronics11193252

Brahmi, M., Hussain, Z., & Khan, A. (1988, May). Driving Success: Examining the Influence of Innovation Culture on Artificial Intelligence Adoption and Firm Performance in Asian SMEs. In Annual International Conference on the Theory and Applications of Cryptographic Techniques (pp. 89-105). Cham: Springer Nature Switzerland.

Cano, C. A. G., Castillo, V. S., & Rojas, E. E. M. (2023). Strategy for improving learning in the Financial Tools and Project Management Course through the use of Second Life-SL. *Metaverse Basic and Applied Research*, 2, 31–31. DOI: 10.56294/mr202331

Chu, C. H. (2023). Deep resource allocation for a massively multiplayer online finance of tourism gamification in metaverse. *Information Technology & Tourism*, 25(4), 565–583. DOI: 10.1007/s40558-023-00267-8

Far, S. B., Rad, A. I., & Asaar, M. R. (2023). Blockchain and its derived technologies shape the future generation of digital businesses: A focus on decentralized finance and the Metaverse. *Data Science and Management*, 6(3), 183–197. DOI: 10.1016/j.dsm.2023.06.002

Fathi, F. (2024). Content Analysis of Blockchain and Cryptocurrency Applications in the Metaverse: A Study on Users' Financial Behaviors. *Knowledge Economy Studies*, 1(1), 101–116.

Firmansyah, E. A., & Umar, U. H. (2023). Metaverse in business research: A systematic literature review. *Cogent Business & Management*, 10(2), 2222499. DOI: 10.1080/23311975.2023.2222499

Frank, P., & Rudolf, M. (2024). Is the Metaverse Dead? Insights from Financial Bubble Analysis. *FinTech*, 3(2), 302–323. DOI: 10.3390/fintech3020017

Garg, K. (2024). Digital identities in the metaverse: Privacy, security, and user authentication in virtual financial systems. International Journal of Financial Engineering, 2442009.

Ghaffar, S. A., & Setiawan, W. C. (2024). Metaverse Dynamics: Predictive Modeling of Roblox Stock Prices using Time Series Analysis and Machine Learning. *International Journal Research on Metaverese*, 1(1), 77–93. DOI: 10.47738/ijrm.v1i1.6

Gholjash, S., Momeni Yanesari, A., Ajam, L., & Safari Grayli, M. (2024). Identifying and Evaluating the Effective Fields of Metaverse in Financial Flexibility: Future Perspectives of the Capital Market. *Financial Management Perspective*, 14(46), 59–91.

Ho, R. C., & Song, B. L. (2023). User acceptance towards non-fungible token (NFT) as the FinTech for investment management in the metaverse. In Strategies and Opportunities for Technology in the Metaverse World (pp. 59-77). IGI Global.

Hussain, Z. (1988, May). Enhancing Transparency and Accountability in Sadaqah Crowdfunding Platforms: Leveraging Blockchain Technology for Optimal User Experience. In Annual International Conference on the Theory and Applications of Cryptographic Techniques (pp. 351-367). Cham: Springer Nature Switzerland.

Hussain, Z. (2024). The Role of Metaverse in Women Entrepreneurship and Economic Complexity: Evidence from Pakistan. *Journal of Entrepreneurship and Business Venturing*, 4(1).

Hussain, Z., Khan, A., & Ali, A. (2023). The Impact of User-Generated Content, Social Interactions and virtual Economies on Metaverse Environments. *Journal of Sustainable Economics*, 1(2), 34–44. DOI: 10.32734/jse.v1i2.13798

Hussain, Z., Sultan, R., Asadullah, A., Arif, M., & Ali, A. (2022). The Impact of Zakat Literacy, Trust, and the Accessibility of Digital Payments on Generation Z and Y's Intention to Pay Zakat to Central Zakat Fund, the State Bank of Pakistan. *International Journal of Zakat*, 7(2), 105–114.

Hutson, J., Banerjee, G., Kshetri, N., Odenwald, K., & Ratican, J. (2023). Architecting the metaverse: blockchain and the financial and legal regulatory challenges of virtual real estate. Journal of Intelligent Learning Systems and Applications, 15.

Iqbal, M., Suhail, S., Milani, F., & Halas, Y. (2024). Metaverse in financial industry: Use cases, value, and challenges. *International Journal of Information Management Data Insights*, 4(2), 100302. DOI: 10.1016/j.jjimei.2024.100302

Kadhim, Y. A., & Al Ani, S. A. M. (2023, December). Using Artificial Intelligence and Metaverse Techniques to Reduce Earning Management. In *International Multi-Disciplinary Conference-Integrated Sciences and Technologies* (pp. 171–189). Springer Nature Switzerland. DOI: 10.1007/978-3-031-51716-7_12

Katterbauer, K., Syed, H., Cleenewerck, L., & Genc, S. Y. (2024). Islamic finance in the metaverse: meta-finance frameworks for supporting the growth of Shariah-compliant finance options in the metaspace. In *Islamic Finance in the Digital Age* (pp. 301–314). Edward Elgar Publishing. DOI: 10.4337/9781035322954.00027

Kou, G., Yüksel, S., & Dinçer, H. (2023). A facial expression and expert recommendation fuzzy decision-making approach for sustainable business investments within the metaverse world. *Applied Soft Computing*, 148, 110849. DOI: 10.1016/j.asoc.2023.110849

Kumar, S., Sureka, R., Lucey, B. M., Dowling, M., Vigne, S., & Lim, W. M. (2024). MetaMoney: Exploring the intersection of financial systems and virtual worlds. *Research in International Business and Finance*, 68, 102195. DOI: 10.1016/j.ribaf.2023.102195

Lazaroiu, G., Gedeon, T., Rogalska, E., Valaskova, K., Nagy, M., Musa, H., Zvarikova, K., Poliak, M., Horak, J., Cre oiu, R. I., Krulicky, T., Ionescu, L., Popa, C., Hurloiu, L. R., Nistor, F., Avram, L. G., & Braga, V. (2024). Digital twin-based cyber-physical manufacturing systems, extended reality metaverse enterprise and production management algorithms, and Internet of Things financial and labor market technologies in generative artificial intelligence economics. *Oeconomia Copernicana*, 15(3), 837–870. DOI: 10.24136/oc.3183

Liu, H., Choi, M., & Kim, J. (2024). The analysis of impact of metaverse on the Fintech industry based on text mining and association rules mining. [GBFR]. *Global Business & Finance Review*, 29(7), 93–109. DOI: 10.17549/gbfr.2024.29.7.93

Malekolkalami, T. (2024). What is Required to Implement Financial Services in Metaverse Ecosystem? *International Journal of Metaverse & Virtual Transformation*, 1(1), 10–18.

Mbaye, M. (2023, August). Use Virtual Reality to Improve Customer Experience in Financial Institutions: A Metaverse Impact Study. In International conference on WorldS4 (pp. 213-221). Singapore: Springer Nature Singapore.

Mozumder, M. A. I., Theodore, A. T. P., Athar, A., & Kim, H. C. (2023, February). The metaverse applications for the finance industry, its challenges, and an approach for the metaverse finance industry. In 2023 25th International Conference on Advanced Communication Technology (ICACT) (pp. 407-410). IEEE.

Musleh Alsartawi, A. M., & Hussainey, K. (2024). Guest editorial: The future of financial reporting and accounting in the metaverse. *Journal of Financial Reporting and Accounting*, 22(2), 205–210. DOI: 10.1108/JFRA-05-2024-747

Pandey, D., & Gilmour, P. (2024). Accounting meets metaverse: Navigating the intersection between the real and virtual worlds. *Journal of Financial Reporting and Accounting*, 22(2), 211–226. DOI: 10.1108/JFRA-03-2023-0157

Piñeiro-Chousa, J., López-Cabarcos, M. Á., VittoriRomero, V., & Pérez-Pérez, A. (2024). Evolution and trends of the metaverse in business and management: A bibliometric analysis. *Review of Managerial Science*, •••, 1–26. DOI: 10.1007/s11846-024-00741-5

Radanliev, P. (2024). The rise and fall of cryptocurrencies: Defining the economic and social values of blockchain technologies, assessing the opportunities, and defining the financial and cybersecurity risks of the Metaverse. *Financial Innovation*, 10(1), 1. DOI: 10.1186/s40854-023-00537-8

Saivasan, R., & Lokhande, M. (2023). Exploring Use Cases of Generative AI and Metaverse in Financial Analytics: Unveiling the Synergies of Advanced Technologies. *International Journal of Global Business and Competitiveness*, 18(S1, Suppl 1), 77–86. DOI: 10.1007/s42943-023-00082-2

Şanlısoy, S., & Çiloğlu, T. (2023). A view of the future of the metaverse economy on the basis of the global financial system: New opportunities and risks. *Journal of Corporate Governance, Insurance, and Risk Management*, 10(1), 28–41. DOI: 10.56578/jcgirm100104

Spinner, A. (2024). Financial Metaverse: Trading Tokens, Derivatives and Other Digital Twins. In *The Financial Metaverse: Tokens, Derivatives and Other Synthetic Assets* (pp. 1–13). Springer Nature Switzerland. DOI: 10.1007/978-3-031-53915-2_1

Srinivasan, B., & Wahyuningsih, T. (2024). Navigating Financial Transactions in the Metaverse: Risk Analysis, Anomaly Detection, and Regulatory Implications. *International Journal Research on Metaverese*, 1(1), 59–76. DOI: 10.47738/ijrm.v1i1.5

Truong, V. T., Le, L., & Niyato, D. (2023). Blockchain meets metaverse and digital asset management: A comprehensive survey. *IEEE Access : Practical Innovations, Open Solutions*, 11, 26258–26288. DOI: 10.1109/ACCESS.2023.3257029

Vidal-Tomás, D. (2023). The illusion of the metaverse and meta-economy. *International Review of Financial Analysis*, 86, 102560. DOI: 10.1016/j.irfa.2023.102560

Wang, S. (2024, June). Predictive Virtual Reality System for Corporate Financial Risk Based on the Metaverse. In Proceedings of the 3rd International Conference on Big Data Economy and Digital Management, BDEDM 2024, January 12–14, 2024, Ningbo, China. DOI: 10.4108/eai.12-1-2024.2347230

Xu, C., Liang, X., Sun, Y., & He, X. (2024). Fraudsters beware: Unleashing the power of metaverse technology to uncover financial fraud. *International Journal of Human-Computer Interaction*, 40(18), 4987–5002. DOI: 10.1080/10447318.2023.2238367

Zadorozhnyi, Z. M., Muravskyi, V., Humenna-Derij, M., & Zarudna, N. (2022). Innovative accounting and audit of the metaverse resources. Marketing i menedžment innovacij, 13(4), 10-19.

Compilation of References

Aaker, D., & Joachimsthaler, E. (2000). *Brand leadership*. The Free Press.

Abor, J., & Biekpe, N. (2007). Corporate governance, ownership structure and performance of SMEs in Ghana: Implications for financing opportunities. *Corporate Governance (Bradford)*, 7(3), 288–300. DOI: 10.1108/14720700710756562

Abovitz, R., Banerjee, S., Gilliland, G., Liu, C., Sackey, E., Timashkov, A., & Trollinger, R. (2022). How the metaverse will remake your strategy. *Boston Consulting Group*, 1–16. Retrieved from https://mkt-bcg-com-public-pdfs.s3.amazonaws.com/prod/impact-of-metaverse-on-business.pdf

Abrokwah-Larbi, K. (2024). Transforming metaverse marketing into strategic agility in SMEs through mediating roles of IMT and CI: Theoretical framework and research propositions. *Journal of Contemporary Marketing Science*, 7(1), 56–83. DOI: 10.1108/JCMARS-08-2023-0034

Abumalloh, R. A., Nilashi, M., Ooi, K. B., Wei-Han, G., Cham, T. H., Dwivedi, Y. K., & Hughes, L. (2023). The adoption of metaverse in the retail industry and its impact on sustainable competitive advantage: Moderating impact of sustainability commitment. *Annals of Operations Research*, •••, 1–42.

Accenture Plc. (2017) "How Companies Are Reimagining Business Processes With IT," https://sloanreview.mit.edu/article/will-ai-create-as-many-jobs-as-it-eliminates/

Access Partnership. (2019). *Artificial Intelligence for Africa: An Opportunity for Growth, Development, and Democratisation*. University of Pretoria.

Acemoglu, D., & Restrepo, P. (2019). The Wrong Kind of AI? Artificial Intelligence and the Future of Labor Demand. NBER Working Paper 25682.

Adeosun, O. T., & Shittu, A. I. (2021). *Small–medium enterprise formation and Nigerian economic growth. Review of Economics and Political Science Emerald Publishing Limited*. Emerald Publishing Limited., DOI: 10.1108/REPS-07-2020-0089

Adewoye T (2019). Artificial Intelligence in the workplace: Bracing up for the revolution

Agarwal, A., & Alathur, S. (2023). Metaverse revolution and the digital transformation: intersectional analysis of Industry 5.0. Transforming Government: *People, Process and Policy. 393), 99-106.*

Agrawal, A., Gans, J., & Goldfarb, A. (2018a). Exploring the impact of artificial intelligence: prediction versus judgment (No. 24626). In: NBER Working Paper, NBER Working Paper. Cambridge, MA. https://doi.org/DOI: 10.3386/w24626

Ahinful, G. S., Boakye, J. D., & Osei Bempah, N. D. (2021). Determinants of SMEs' financial performance: Evidence from an emerging economy. *Journal of Small Business and Entrepreneurship*, 0(0), 1–24. DOI: 10.1080/08276331.2021.1885247

Ahmad, K., Sharma, B. K., Khatwani, R., Mishra, M., & Mitra, P. K. (2024). Impact of metaverse technology on hospitality and tourism industry: An interplay of social media marketing on hotel booking in India. *International Journal of Tourism Cities*, 10(1), 1-18. DOI: 10.1108/IJTC-11-2023-0232

Ahn, S., Jin, B. E., & Seo, H. (2024). Why do people interact and buy in the Metaverse? Self-Expansion perspectives and the impact of hedonic adaptation. *Journal of Business Research*, 175, 114557. DOI: 10.1016/j.jbusres.2024.114557

Ahuja, A. S., Polascik, B. W., Doddapaneni, D., Byrnes, E. S., & Sridhar, J. (2023). The digital metaverse: Applications in artificial intelligence, medical education, and integrative health. *Integrative Medicine Research*, 12(1), 100917. DOI: 10.1016/j.imr.2022.100917 PMID: 36691642

Ajibola, E. O. (2020). *Nigeria Small and Medium Enterprise Sustainability Strategies*. Walden Dissertations and Doctoral Studies Collection.

Ajiga, D. I., Ndubuisi, N. L., Asuzu, O. F., Owolabi, O. R., Tubokirifuruar, T. S., & Adeleye, R. A.David Iyanuoluwa AjigaNdubuisi Leonard NdubuisiOnyeka Franca AsuzuOluwaseyi Rita OwolabiTula Sunday TubokirifuruarRhoda Adura Adeleye. (2024). AI-driven predictive analytics in retail: A review of emerging trends and customer engagement strategies. *International Journal of Management & Entrepreneurship Research*, 6(2), 307–321. DOI: 10.51594/ijmer.v6i2.772

Akerejola, W. O., Okpara, E. U., Ohikhena, P., & Emenike, P. O. (2019). *"Availability of infrastructure and adoption of point of sales of selected small and medium enterprises (SMEs) in Lagos state"*, Nigeria. *International Journal of Academic Research in Business & Social Sciences*, 9(1), 137–150. DOI: 10.6007/IJARBSS/v9-i1/5370

Al Amosh, H., & Khatib, S. F. A. (2021). Corporate governance and voluntary disclosure of sustainability performance: The case of Jordan. *SN Business & Economics*, 1(12), 165. DOI: 10.1007/s43546-021-00167-1

Alayo, M., Maseda, A., Iturralde, T., & Arzubiaga, U. (2019). Internationalization and entrepreneurial orientation of family SMEs: The influence of the family character. *International Business Review*, 28(1), 48–59. DOI: 10.1016/j.ibusrev.2018.06.003

Ali, S., Abdullah, , Armand, T. P. T., Athar, A., Hussain, A., Ali, M., Yaseen, M., Joo, M.-I., & Kim, H.-C. (2023). Metaverse in healthcare integrated with explainable AI and blockchain: Enabling immersiveness, ensuring trust, and providing patient data security. *Sensors (Basel)*, 23(2), 565. DOI: 10.3390/s23020565 PMID: 36679361

Al-Issa, N., & Thanasi, M. (2024). Mapping the Future of Tech-Infused Luxury: A Roadmap and Research Directions. *International Journal of Consumer Studies*, 48(6), e13103. DOI: 10.1111/ijcs.13103

Aljanabi, M., & Mohammed, S. Y. (2023). Metaverse: Open possibilities. *Iraqi Journal For Computer Science and Mathematics*, 4(3), 79–86. DOI: 10.52866/ijcsm.2023.02.03.007

Allam, Z., Sharifi, A., Bibri, S. E., Jones, D. S., & Krogstie, J. (2022). The metaverse as a virtual form of smart cities: Opportunities and challenges for environmental, economic, and social sustainability in urban futures. *Smart Cities*, 5(3), 771–801. DOI: 10.3390/smartcities5030040

Aloqaily, M., Bouachir, O., Karray, F., Al Ridhawi, I., & El Saddik, A. (2022). Integrating digital twin and advanced intelligent technologies to realize the metaverse. *IEEE Consumer Electronics Magazine*, 12(6), 47–55. DOI: 10.1109/MCE.2022.3212570

Al-Ramahi, N., Kreishan, F. M., Hussain, Z., Khan, A., Alghizzawi, M., & AlWadi, B. M. (2024). Unlocking sustainable growth: The role of artificial intelligence adoption in jordan retail sector, moderated by entrepreneurial orientation. *International Review of Management and Marketing*, 14(6), 143–155. DOI: 10.32479/irmm.16843

Alsamhi, M. H., Hawbani, A., Kumar, S., & Alsamhi, S. H. (2024). Multisensory metaverse-6G: A new paradigm of commerce and education. *IEEE Access*.

Alshurideh, M., Kurdi, B., Al-Gasaymeh, A., Abuhashesh, M., Jdaitawi, A., Alzoubi, H., Hamadneh, S., & Alquqa, E. (2024). How metaverse can enhance customer awareness, interest, engagement and experience: A practical study. *International Journal of Data and Network Science*, 8(3), 1907–1914. DOI: 10.5267/j.ijdns.2024.1.022

Alvarez, J., Segura-Dominguez, C., Tobias, R. G., & Navarrete-Bear, M. (2024, October). Comparative Analysis of Traditional and Metaverse-Based Learning on Financial Decision-Making Skills in Mathematics Students. In *2024 IEEE International Conference on Engineering Veracruz (ICEV)* (pp. 1-6). IEEE. DOI: 10.1109/ICEV63254.2024.10765998

Alvarez-Risco, A., Del-Aguila-Arcentales, S., Rosen, M. A., & Yáñez, J. A. (2022). Social Cognitive Theory to Assess the Intention to participate in the Facebook Metaverse by citizens in Peru during the COVID-19 pandemic. *Journal of Open Innovation*, 8(3), 142–164. DOI: 10.3390/joitmc8030142

Alves, A. M. (2022). *O uso da tecnologia NFT para promover itens colecionáveis digitais: uma análise de consumo no jogo AXIE INFINITY* (Unpublished master's dissertation). Universidade Federal do Pampa – UNIPAMPA, São Borja.

Alves, R. (2021). Fashion brands and greenwashing: The ethical dilemma of sustainability claims. *Sustainable Fashion Journal*, 4(2), 100–115.

Amabile, T., (2019). Creativity, artificial Intelligence, and a world of surprises. Acad. Manag. Discov amd.2019.0075. https://doi.org/.DOI: 10.5465/amd.2019.0075

Ameen, N., Sharma, G. D., Tarba, S., Rao, A., & Chopra, R. (2022). Toward advancing theory on creativity in marketing and artificial intelligence. *Psychology and Marketing*, 39(9), 1802–1825. DOI: 10.1002/mar.21699

Ameen, N., Tarhini, A., Reppel, A., & Anand, A. (2021). Customer experiences in the age of artificial intelligence. *Computers in Human Behavior*, 114, 106548. DOI: 10.1016/j.chb.2020.106548 PMID: 32905175

Andrae, A. (2020). The environmental impact of digital infrastructure: Data centres and emissions. *Journal of Energy Efficiency*, 12(4), 234–245.

André, & Luiz. (2022). *Marketing Futureland*. Lisboa: LIDEL.

Anekwe, R. I., Ndubusi-Okolo, P, & Uzoezie, C. (2019). Sustainability in the Nigerian Business Environment: Problems and Prospects. International Journal of Academic Management Science Research (IJAMSR) Vol. 3 Issue 3, March – 2019, Pages: 72-80

Anshari, M., Syafrudin, M., Fitriyani, N. L., & Razzaq, A. (2022). Ethical responsibility and sustainability (ERS) development in a metaverse business model. *Sustainability (Basel)*, 14(23), 15805. DOI: 10.3390/su142315805

Ao, L., Bansal, R., Pruthi, N., & Khaskheli, M. B. (2023). Impact of social media influencers on customer engagement and purchase intention: A meta-analysis. *Sustainability (Basel)*, 15(3), 2744. DOI: 10.3390/su15032744

Aragón-Amonarriz, C., Arredondo, A. M., & Iturrioz-Landart, C. (2019). How Can Responsible Family Ownership be Sustained Across Generations? A Family Social Capital Approach. *Journal of Business Ethics*, 159(1), 161–185. DOI: 10.1007/s10551-017-3728-7

Aria Parsa, M., & Dalvi Esfahan, M. R. (2023). Mixed Research of Establishing of an Entrepreneurial Model with a Future Research Approach in the Metaverse Era in Knowledge-Based Companies in the Field of Information Technology. *Sociology of Education*, 9(2), 83–94.

Aria Parsa, M., & Dalvi Esfahan, M. R. (2023). The Application of the Entrepreneurship Model of Future Research in the Era of Metaverse in Knowledge-Based Companies in the Field of Information Technology. *Islamic Life Journal*, 7(2), 306–316.

Ariza, A. M. V., Marín, M. C., & Duran, M. L. D. (2024). The Metaverse: Financial Assurance Procedures in Smart Contracts and NFTs. *International Journal of Religion*, 5(11), 223–232. DOI: 10.61707/cd824339

Arora, M. (2024). Metaverse Insights: Research Advancements, Innovation Trends and Industry Implications. *Abhigyan*, 42(4), 385–402. DOI: 10.1177/09702385241277357

Arya, V., Sambyal, R., Sharma, A., & Dwivedi, Y. K. (2024). Brands are calling your AVATAR in Metaverse–A study to explore XR-based gamification marketing activities & consumer-based brand equity in virtual world. *Journal of Consumer Behaviour*, 23(2), 556–585. DOI: 10.1002/cb.2214

Automation & Anxiety. (2016): Will Smarter Machines Cause Mass Unemployment. *The Economist* What the story of ATMs and bank tellers reveals about the 'rise of the robots and jobs *A EIdeas*.

Au, W. J. (2023). *Making a Metaverse That Matters: From Snow Crash & Second Life to A Virtual World Worth Fighting For*. John Wiley & Sons.

Awadallah, A., Eledlebi, K., Zemerly, J., Puthal, D., Damiani, E., Taha, K., Kim, T.-Y., Yoo, P. D., Choo, K.-K. R., Yim, M.-S., & Yeun, C. Y. (2024). Artificial intelligence-based cybersecurity for the metaverse: Research challenges and opportunities. *IEEE Communications Surveys and Tutorials*, 1. DOI: 10.1109/COMST.2024.3442475

Aysan, A. F., Batten, J., Gozgor, G., Khalfaoui, R., & Nanaeva, Z. (2024). Metaverse and financial markets: A quantile-time-frequency connectedness analysis. *Research in International Business and Finance*, 72, 102527. DOI: 10.1016/j.ribaf.2024.102527

Aysan, A. F., Gozgor, G., & Nanaeva, Z. (2024). Technological perspectives of Metaverse for financial service providers. *Technological Forecasting and Social Change*, 202, 123323. DOI: 10.1016/j.techfore.2024.123323

Badiru, N. I., & Aladelusi, K. O. (2023). Proposed framework for integrating metaverse technologies into entrepreneurial education. *International Journal of Intellectual Discourse*, 6(1), 76–86.

Ball, M. (2022). *The Metaverse: And How It Will Revolutionize Everything*. Liveright Publishing Corporation. DOI: 10.15358/9783800669400

Banaeian Far, S., & Imani Rad, A. (2023). What are the benefits and opportunities of launching a Metaverse for NEOM city? *Security and Privacy*, 6(3), e282. DOI: 10.1002/spy2.282

Banat, H. F. M., Alotoum, F. J., & Hashem, T. N. (2024, February). Smart Banking Services and Their Impact on the Customers' Intentions to Use Mobile Banking in Commercial Banks: Evidence from UAE. In *2024 2nd International Conference on Cyber Resilience (ICCR)* (pp. 1-7). IEEE.

Banik, B., Banik, S., & Annee, R. R. (2024). The role of AI in enhancing customer engagement and loyalty. *Revista de Inteligencia Artificial en Medicina*, 15(1), 537–561.

Barrera, K. G., & Shah, D. (2023). Marketing in the Metaverse: Conceptual understanding, framework, and research agenda. *Journal of Business Research*, 155, 113420. DOI: 10.1016/j.jbusres.2022.113420

Bartoli, C., Baccelloni, A., Mattiacci, A., & Ungaro, L. (2024). Small and medium enterprises meet the metaverse. A study of the wine industry. *International Journal of Entrepreneurship and Innovation*, •••, 14657503241278164. DOI: 10.1177/14657503241278164

Batat, W. (2024). Phygital customer experience in the metaverse: A study of consumer sensory perception of sight, touch, sound, scent, and taste. *Journal of Retailing and Consumer Services*, 78, 103786. DOI: 10.1016/j.jretconser.2024.103786

Bathla, D., & Ahuja, R. (2024). Customer Engagement in Metaverse Using Big Data. In *Ethical Marketing Through Data Governance Standards and Effective Technology* (pp. 62–73). IGI Global. DOI: 10.4018/979-8-3693-2215-4.ch005

Bayode, B. O., & Adebola, A. O. (2012). Strategic Environmental Scanning and Organization Performance in a Competitive Business Environment. *Economic Insights - Trends and Challenges*, •••, 24–34.

Beauchamp, T. L., & Childress, J. F. (2019). *Principles of Biomedical Ethics* (8th ed.). Oxford University Press.

Beck, T., Demirgüç-Kunt, A., & Pería, M. S. M. (2011). Bank Financing for SMEs: Evidence Across Countries and Bank Ownership Types. *Journal of Financial Services Research*, 39(1–2), 35–54. DOI: 10.1007/s10693-010-0085-4

Belanche, D., Casaló, L. V., Flavián, C., & Schepers, J. (2020). Robots or frontline employees? Exploring customers' attributions of responsibility and stability after service failure or success. *Journal of Service Management*, 31(2), 267–289. DOI: 10.1108/JOSM-05-2019-0156

Belghitar, Y., & Khan, J. (2013). Governance mechanisms, investment opportunity set and SMEs cash holdings. *Small Business Economics*, 40(1), 59–72. DOI: 10.1007/s11187-011-9366-z

Belk, R., Humayun, M., & Brouard, M. (2022). Money, possessions, and ownership in the Metaverse: NFTs, cryptocurrencies, Web3 and Wild Markets. *Journal of Business Research*, 153, 198–205. DOI: 10.1016/j.jbusres.2022.08.031

Bessen, J. (2017b). Scarce Skills; *Not Scarce Jobs. CAPPF International Conference.*

Bhaird, C. (2010). Determinants of capital structure in Irish SMEs. *Small Business Economics*, 35(3), 357–375. DOI: 10.1007/s11187-008-9162-6

Biancone, P., Secinaro, S., Calandra, D., & Oppioli, M. (2023). Beyond the physical world… Digital entrepreneurship opportunities in the metaverse. In *L'aziendalismo crea valore! Il ruolo dell'accademia nelle sfide della società, dell'economia e delle istituzioni* (pp. 1–15). Università degli Studi di Salerno.

Bigi, A., Bonera, M., & Tuncay, I. (2023, May). Has the Metaverse a Strategic or Operative Role in Luxury Fashion Brands' Marketing? In Academy of Marketing Science Annual Conference (pp. 1-9). Cham: Springer Nature Switzerland.

Bilgihan, A., Leong, A. M. W., Okumus, F., & Bai, J. (2024). Proposing a metaverse engagement model for brand development. *Journal of Retailing and Consumer Services*, 78, 103781. DOI: 10.1016/j.jretconser.2024.103781

Bisht, D., Singh, R., Gehlot, A., Akram, S. V., Singh, A., Montero, E. C., Priyadarshi, N., & Twala, B. (2022). Imperative role of integrating digitalization in the firms finance: A technological perspective. *Electronics (Basel)*, 11(19), 3252. DOI: 10.3390/electronics11193252

Bjuggren, C. M., Daunfeldt, S. O., & Johansson, D. (2013). High-growth firms and family ownership. *Journal of Small Business and Entrepreneurship*, 26(4), 365–385. DOI: 10.1080/08276331.2013.821765

Block, J., Fisch, C., & Rehan, F. (2019). Religion and entrepreneurship: a map of the field and a bibliometric analysis. In *Management Review Quarterly* (Issue 0123456789). Springer International Publishing. DOI: 10.1007/s11301-019-00177-2

Blut, M., Wang, C., Wünderlich, N. V., & Brock, C. (2021). Understanding anthropomorphism in service provision: A meta-analysis of physical robots, chatbots, and other AI. *Journal of the Academy of Marketing Science*, 49(4), 1–27. DOI: 10.1007/s11747-020-00762-y

Bordegoni, M., & Ferrise, F. (2023). Exploring the intersection of metaverse, digital twins, and artificial intelligence in training and maintenance. *Journal of Computing and Information Science in Engineering*, 23(6), 060806. DOI: 10.1115/1.4062455

Borocki, J., Radišić, M., Sroka, W., Grėblikaitė, J., & Androniceanu, A. (2019). Methodology for strategic posture determination of SMEs. *The Engineering Economist*, 30(3), 265–277. DOI: 10.5755/j01.ee.30.3.21966

Bowen, J., & Morosan, C. (2018). Beware hospitality industry: The robots are coming. *Worldwide Hospitality and Tourism Themes*, 10(6), 726–733. DOI: 10.1108/WHATT-07-2018-0045

Boyd, B. K., & Solarino, A. M. (2016). Ownership of Corporations: A Review, Synthesis, and Research Agenda. *Journal of Management*, 42(5), 1282–1314. DOI: 10.1177/0149206316633746

Bozkurt, S., Gligor, D., & Gligor, N. (2022). Investigating the impact of psychological customer engagement on customer engagement behaviors: The moderating role of customer commitment. *Journal of Marketing Analytics*, 10(4), 408–424. DOI: 10.1057/s41270-021-00146-3

Brahmi, M., Hussain, Z., & Khan, A. (1988, May). Driving Success: Examining the Influence of Innovation Culture on Artificial Intelligence Adoption and Firm Performance in Asian SMEs. *InAnnual International Conference on the Theory and Applications of Cryptographic Techniques(pp.89-105).Cham: Springer Nature Switzerland.*

Branca, F., Pons, J., & Rodríguez, S. (2022). Assessing consumer evaluations of product packaging in virtual environments. *Journal of Consumer Marketing*, 39(5), 31-45. https://doi.org/DOI: 10.1108/JCM-10-2021-0506

Breiter, D., & Siegfried, P. (2022). The Metaverse: Exploring Consumer's Expectations, Their Attitudes, and it's Mean-ing to the Fashion Industry. Breiter, D./Siegfried, P.(2022): The Metaverse: Exploring consumer's expectations, their attitudes, and it's meaning to the fashion industry, eISSN, 2683-5665.

Broadbent, E., Stafford, R., & MacDonald, B. (2009). Acceptance of healthcare robots for the older population: Review and future directions. *International Journal of Social Robotics*, 1(4), 319–330. DOI: 10.1007/s12369-009-0030-6

Browne, M. W., & Cudeck, R. (1993). Alternative ways of assessing model fit. In Bollen, K.A & Long, J.S.[Eds.] *Testing structural equation models. Newbury Park*, CA: Sage,136-162.

Browne, M. W., & Cudeck, R. (1992). Alternative ways of assessing model fit. *Sociological Methods & Research*, 21(2), 230–258. DOI: 10.1177/0049124192021002005

Bruni, R., Piccarozzi, M., & Caboni, F. (2023). Defining the Metaverse with challenges and opportunities in the business environment. *Journal of Marketing Theory and Practice*, •••, 1–18.

Brunninge, O., Nordqvist, M., & Wiklund, J. (2007). Corporate governance and strategic change in SMEs: The effects of ownership, board composition and top management teams. *Small Business Economics*, 29(3), 295–308. DOI: 10.1007/s11187-006-9021-2

Buhalis, D., & Karatay, N. (2022). Mixed reality (MR) for generation Z in cultural heritage tourism towards metaverse. In *Information and communication technologies in tourism 2022:Proceedings of the ENTER 2022 eTourism conference,January 11–14, 2022* (pp. 16-27). Springer International Publishing.

Buhalis, D., Law, R., & Sigala, M. (2023). The impact of robotics and AI on the hospitality industry: Trends and future directions. *Journal of Hospitality and Tourism Technology*, 14(2), 217–232.

Buhalis, D., Lin, M. S., & Leung, D. (2022). Metaverse as a driver for customer experience and value co-creation: Implications for hospitality and tourism management and marketing. *International Journal of Contemporary Hospitality Management*, 35(2), 701–716. DOI: 10.1108/IJCHM-05-2022-0631

Burgstaller, W., & Wagner, E. (2013). How do family ownership and founder management affect capital structure decisions and adjustment of SMEs. *The Journal of Risk Finance*, 16(1), 73–101. https://doi.org/http://dx.doi.org/10.1108/MRR-09-2015-0216. DOI: 10.1108/JRF-06-2014-0091

Burmann, C., Riley, N.-M., Halaszovich, T., & Schade, M. (2017). Identity-based brand management. In *Strategic brand management* (pp. 91–172). Springer Gabler., DOI: 10.1007/978-3-658-13561-4_3

Burrows, G. (2022). Your Life. In *The Metaverse: Everything you need to know about the virtual internet of tomorrow*. Gideon Burrows.

Cacciapuoti, A. S., Caleffi, M., Tafuri, L., & Sottile, C. (2020). Blockchain and quantum computing: Future directions in finance. *Future Internet*, 12(10), 183.

Cagnina, M. R., & Poian, M. (2011). How to compete in the metaverse: The business models in Second Life. SSRN *Electronic Journal*, 1–34. https://doi.org/DOI: 10.2139/ssrn.1088779

Calandra, D., Oppioli, M., Sadraei, R., Jafari-Sadeghi, V., & Biancone, P. P. (2023). Metaverse meets digital entrepreneurship: A practitioner-based qualitative synthesis. *International Journal of Entrepreneurial Behaviour & Research*, 23(3), 345–361.

Calzada, I. (2023). Disruptive Technologies for e-Diasporas: Blockchain, DAOs, Data Cooperatives, Metaverse, and ChatGPT. *Futures*, 3(3), 103–158.

Cangur, S., & Ercan, I. (2015). Comparison of Model Fit Indices Used in Structural Equation. Modeling Under Multivariate Normality. *Journal of Modern Applied Statistical Methods; JMASM*, 14(1), Ps152–Ps1. DOI: 10.22237/jmasm/1430453580

Cano, C. A. G., Castillo, V. S., & Rojas, E. E. M. (2023). Strategy for improving learning in the Financial Tools and Project Management Course through the use of Second Life-SL. *Metaverse Basic and Applied Research*, 2, 31–31. DOI: 10.56294/mr202331

Cardoso, C., Casteleiro-Pitrez, J., & Lobo, H. (2024, June). Embracing the Luxury Paradox: New Luxury, Digitalization, and Digital Experiences in the Metaverse. In *Meeting of Research in Music, Arts and Design* (pp. 449–466). Springer Nature Switzerland.

Caselli, S., & Di Giuli, A. (2010). Does the CFO matter in family firms? Evidence from Italy. In *European Journal of Finance* (Vol. 16, Issue 5). DOI: 10.1080/13518470903211657

Casson, M. C. (1982). *The entrepreneur: An economic theory*. Barnes and Noble.

Çelikkol, S. (2022). Factors affecting brand love in the metaverse world and the effect of brand love on word-of-mouth marketing. *Turkish Journal of Marketing*, 7(3), 148–161. DOI: 10.30685/tujom.v7i3.162

Ceptureanu, S. I., Ceptureanu, E. G., & Marin, I. (2017). Assessing the Role of Strategic Choice on Organizational Performance by Jacquemin–Berry Entropy Index. *Entropy (Basel, Switzerland)*, 19(9), 448. DOI: 10.3390/e19090448

Cerrato, D., & Piva, M. (2012). The internationalization of small and medium-sized enterprises: The effect of family management, human capital and foreign ownership. *The Journal of Management and Governance*, 16(4), 617–644. DOI: 10.1007/s10997-010-9166-x

Chalmers, D., MacKenzie, G., & Carter, S. (2021). Artificial Intelligence and Entrepreneurship: Implications for Venture Creation in the Fourth Industrial Revolution. *Entrepreneurship Theory and Practice*, 45(5), 1028–1053. DOI: 10.1177/1042258720934581

Chamola, V., Bansal, G., Das, T. K., Hassija, V., Sai, S., Wang, J., Zeadally, S., Hussain, A., Yu, F. R., Guizani, M., & Niyato, D. (2024). Beyond reality: The pivotal role of generative ai in the metaverse. *IEEE Internet of Things Magazine*, 7(4), 126–135. DOI: 10.1109/IOTM.001.2300174

Chandra, A., Paul, J., & Chavan, M. (2020). Internationalization barriers of SMEs from developing countries: A review and research agenda. *International Journal of Entrepreneurial Behaviour & Research*, 26(6), 1281–1310. DOI: 10.1108/IJEBR-03-2020-0167

Chandratreya, A. (2023). Transforming Digital Marketing Through Metaverse. *Journal of Namibian Studies: History Politics Culture*, 33, 2869–2881.

Chapman, J. R., Wang, J. C., & Wiechert, K. (2022). Into the spine metaverse: Reflections on a future metaspine (uni-) verse. *Global Spine Journal*, 12(4), 545–547. DOI: 10.1177/21925682221085643 PMID: 35506945

Chathoth, P. K., & Ungson, G. R. (2023). Service agents' risk behavior and implications for co-creation. *International Journal of Contemporary Hospitality Management*, 35(9), 3344–3359. DOI: 10.1108/IJCHM-06-2022-0730

Chaudhari, A., Mali, Y. K., Kulkarni, A., Jain, D., Sharma, L., Mahajan, K., . . . Bhogle, A. (2024, April). Cyber security challenges in social meta-verse and mitigation techniques. In *2024 MIT Art, Design and Technology School of Computing International Conference (MITADTSoCiCon)* (pp. 1-7). IEEE. DOI: 10.1109/MITADTSoCiCon60330.2024.10575295

Chen, N., Christensen, L., Gallagher, K., Mate, R., & Rafert, G. (2016). "Global Economic Impacts Associated with Artificial Intelligence", *Semanticscholar.org*, 2016. [Online]. Available: https://www.semanticscholar.org/paper/Global-Economic-Impacts-Associated-with-Artificial-Chen-Christensen/ebc73c75f7aba486751a20257a3134c777afd255. [Accessed: 09- Dec- 2020].

Chen, C., Zhang, K. Z., Chu, Z., & Lee, M. (2024). Augmented reality in the metaverse market: The role of multimodal sensory interaction. *Internet Research*, 34(1), 9–38. DOI: 10.1108/INTR-08-2022-0670

Cheng, S., Zhang, Y., Li, X., Yang, L., Yuan, X., & Li, S. Z. (2022). Roadmap toward the metaverse: An AI perspective. *Innovation (Cambridge (Mass.))*, 3(5), 100293. DOI: 10.1016/j.xinn.2022.100293 PMID: 36032197

Chen, H. L., Hsu, W. T., & Chang, C. Y. (2014). Family ownership, institutional ownership, and internationalization of SMEs. *Journal of Small Business Management*, 52(4), 771–789. DOI: 10.1111/jsbm.12031

Chen, H., Chiang, R. H., & Storey, V. C. (2012). Business intelligence and analytics: From big data to big impact. *Management Information Systems Quarterly*, 36(4), 1165–1188. DOI: 10.2307/41703503

Chen, L., Tao, S., Xie, X., Huang, W., & Zhu, W. (2024). The evaluation of innovation efficiency and analysis of government subsidies influence—Evidence from China's metaverse listed companies. *Technological Forecasting and Social Change*, 201, 123213. DOI: 10.1016/j.techfore.2024.123213

Chen, P. K., Ye, Y., & Huang, X. (2023). The metaverse in supply chain knowledge sharing and resilience contexts: An empirical investigation of factors affecting adoption and acceptance. *Journal of Innovation & Knowledge*, 8(4), 100–146. DOI: 10.1016/j.jik.2023.100446

Chen, Y., Wu, C., & Zhang, R. (2024). Hotspots and prospects of metaverse: An international comparison. *Journal of Computer Information Systems*, •••, 1–11. DOI: 10.1080/08874417.2024.2304548

Chen, Z., Wu, J., Gan, W., & Qi, Z. (2022, December). Metaverse security and privacy: An overview. In *2022 IEEE International Conference on Big Data (Big Data)* (pp. 2950-2959). IEEE. DOI: 10.1109/BigData55660.2022.10021112

Chernatony, L. (1999). *From brand vision to brand evaluation*. Elsevier Ltd.

Chernatony, L., & McDonald, M. (2003). *Creating powerful brands: In consumer, service and industrial markets*. Taylor & Francis.

Cheung, C., Chan, J., & Lee, M. (2022). Effectiveness of VR-based life skill training for individuals with intellectual disabilities. *Virtual Reality*, 26(3), 207-220. https://doi.org/DOI: 10.1007/s10055-021-00514-7

Cheung, M. L., Leung, W. K., Chang, L. M. K., Aw, E. C. X., & Wong, R. Y. (2024). Immersive time in the metaverse and visits to the physical world: Why not both? A holistic customer engagement framework. *International Journal of Contemporary Hospitality Management*, 36(11), 3674–3703. DOI: 10.1108/IJCHM-07-2023-0999

Chiang, A. H., & Trimi, S. (2020). Impacts of service robots on service quality. *Service Business*, 14(3), 439–459. DOI: 10.1007/s11628-020-00423-8

Chintalapati, S., & Pandey, S. K. (2022). Artificial intelligence in marketing: A systematic literature review. *International Journal of Market Research*, 64(1), 38–68. DOI: 10.1177/14707853211018428

Cho, J., tom Dieck, M. C., & Jung, T. (2022, April). What is the metaverse? Challenges, opportunities, definition, and future research directions. In *International XR Conference(pp.* 3-26*)*. Cham: Springer International Publishing.

Cho, M., Ko, E., & Jung, H. (2024). Virtual reality luxury fashion show: How imaginary space influences brand word-of-mouth. *International Journal of Advertising*, •••, 1–20. DOI: 10.1080/02650487.2024.2419227

Christodoulou, K., Katelaris, L., Themistocleous, M., Christodoulou, P., & Iosif, E. (2022). NFTs and the metaverse revolution: Research perspectives and open challenges. Blockchains and the Token Economy. *Theory into Practice*, •••, 139–178.

Chu, C. H. (2023). Deep resource allocation for a massively multiplayer online finance of tourism gamification in metaverse. *Information Technology & Tourism*, 25(4), 565–583. DOI: 10.1007/s40558-023-00267-8

Chu, W. (2009). The influence of family ownership on SME performance: Evidence from public firms in Taiwan. *Small Business Economics*, 33(3), 353–373. DOI: 10.1007/s11187-009-9178-6

Chu, W. (2011). Family ownership and firm performance: Influence of family management, family control, and firm size. *Asia Pacific Journal of Management*, 28(4), 833–851. DOI: 10.1007/s10490-009-9180-1

Climate Neutral Data Centre Pact. (2021). Retrieved from https://www.climateneutraldatacentre.net/

Cockburn, Iain M., Rebecca Henderson, & Scott Stern. (2019) "The Impact of Artificial Intelligence on Innovation." *The Economics of Artificial Intelligence: An Agenda.* Pp: 115-152.

Colicev, A. (2023). How can non-fungible tokens bring value to brands. *International Journal of Research in Marketing*, 40(1), 30–37. DOI: 10.1016/j.ijresmar.2022.07.003

Colombo, M. G., De Massis, A., Piva, E., Rossi-Lamastra, C., & Wright, M. (2014). Sales and employment changes in entrepreneurial ventures with family ownership: Empirical evidence from high-tech industries. *Journal of Small Business Management*, 52(2), 226–245. DOI: 10.1111/jsbm.12100

Cullen, J. B., Johnson, J. L., & Parboteeah, K. P. (2014). National rates of opportunity entrepreneurship activity: Insights from institutional anomie theory? *Entrepreneurship Theory and Practice*, 38(4), 775–806. DOI: 10.1111/etap.12018

D'Angelo, A., Majocchi, A., & Buck, T. (2016). External managers, family ownership and the scope of SME internationalization. *Journal of World Business*, 51(4), 534–547. DOI: 10.1016/j.jwb.2016.01.004

Da Cruz, A. F., Kimura, H., & Sobreiro, V. A. (2019). What Do We Know About Corporate Cash Holdings? A Systematic Analysis. *Journal of Corporate Accounting & Finance*, 30(1), 77–143. DOI: 10.1002/jcaf.22368

Daldiran, K., & Daldiran, B. (2023). Digital twin technology as a driver of sustainable supply chain and marketing transparency. *Avesis.*aybu.edu.tr

Damar, M. (2021). Metaverse shape of your life for future: A bibliometric snapshot. *Journal of Metaverse*, 1(1), 1–8.

Dao, T. N., Le, H. T. T., Chu, P. T. M., Pham, N. H., Luong, T. T. D., & Tran, D. T. (2021). Determinants of the Competitiveness of Women-Owned Small- and Medium-Sized Enterprises: An Empirical Study from Vietnam. *Journal of Asian Finance Economics and Business*, 8(12), 345–352. DOI: 10.13106/jafeb.2021.vol8.no12.0345

Dash, A. (2024, October). A Graph Theoretic Approach to Analyze the Developing Metaverse. In 2024 *IEEE International Symposium on Emerging Metaverse (ISEMV) (pp. 45-48). IEEE.*

Daugherty, P., & Purdy, M. (2016). "Why Artificial Intelligence is the Future of Growth," *Accenture Canada*, 2016. [Online] Available: https://www.accenture.com/t20161031T154852__w__/ us-en/_acnmedia/PDF-33/Accenture-Why-AIis-the-Future-of-Growth.PDF#zoom=50

Dawson, A. (2022). Data-driven consumer engagement, virtual immersive shopping experiences, and blockchain-based digital assets in the retail metaverse. *Journal of Self-Governance and Management Economics*, 10(2), 52–66.

De Cleyn, S. H., & Braet, J. (2012). Do board composition and investor type influence innovativeness in SMEs? *The International Entrepreneurship and Management Journal*, 8(3), 285–308. DOI: 10.1007/s11365-010-0168-6

De Giovanni, P. (2023). Sustainability of the Metaverse: A transition to Industry 5.0. *Sustainability (Basel)*, 15(7), 6079. DOI: 10.3390/su15076079

De Massis, A., Kotlar, J., Campopiano, G., & Cassia, L. (2013). Dispersion of family ownership and the performance of small-to-medium size private family firms. *Journal of Family Business Strategy*, 4(3), 166–175. DOI: 10.1016/j.jfbs.2013.05.001

De Massis, A., Kotlar, J., Campopiano, G., & Cassia, L. (2015). The Impact of Family Involvement on SMEs' Performance: Theory and Evidence. *Journal of Small Business Management*, 53(4), 924–948. DOI: 10.1111/jsbm.12093

De Vries, A. (2021). Bitcoin's growing energy problem. *Joule*, 3(2), 239–242.

Decentraland. (2022). Sustainability Initiatives. Available at: https://decentraland.org

Deloitte. (2022). Digital Media Trends 2022. Consultado em 8 de janeiro de 2023, de https://www2.deloitte.com/pt/pt/pages/technology-media-andtelecommunications/articles/ Digital-Media-Trends-2022.html

Deloitte. Automation and Anxiety: Will Smarter Machines Cause Mass Unemployment". *The Economist;* Technology and People: The Great Job-Creating Machine, Microsoft, The Future Computed, p. 92

Deng, Z., Hofman, P. S., & Newman, A. (2013). Ownership concentration and product innovation in Chinese private SMEs. *Asia Pacific Journal of Management*, 30(3), 717–734. DOI: 10.1007/s10490-012-9301-0

Denis, D. (1999). Ownership and board structures in publicly traded corporations. *Journal of Financial Economics*, 52(2), 187–223. DOI: 10.1016/S0304-405X(99)00008-2

Deventer, C., de Sousa, V. A., & Pirnay, L. (2024). NFTByBrands: Value Identification Framework for Analysis and Design of NFT Initiatives. *International Journal of Electronic Commerce*, 28(1), 1–30. DOI: 10.1080/10864415.2023.2295070

Dhruv, S. (2022). Best design practices & strategy to launch your own NFT project. *Trends in Computer Science and Information Technology,* 7(1), 007–009. https://doi.org/DOI: 10.17352/tcsit.000045

Dionisio, J. D. N., Burns, W. G., & Gilbert, R. (2013). 3D virtual worlds and the metaverse: Current status and future possibilities. *ACM Computing Surveys*, 45(3), 1–38. DOI: 10.1145/2480741.2480751

Doan, A. T., Le, A. T., & Tran, Q. (2020). Economic uncertainty, ownership structure and small and medium enterprises performance. *Australian Economic Papers*, 59(2), 102–137. DOI: 10.1111/1467-8454.12174

Dolz, C., Iborra, M., & Safón, V. (2019). Improving the likelihood of SME survival during financial and economic crises: The importance of TMTs and family ownership for ambidexterity. *Business Research Quarterly*, 22(2), 119–136. DOI: 10.1016/j.brq.2018.09.004

Duggal, A., Gupta, M., & Gupta, D. (2023). Significance of NFT Avtaars in Metaverse and their Promotion: Case Study. *Scientific Journal of Metaverse and Blockchain Technologies*, 1(1), 28–36. DOI: 10.36676/sjmbt.v1i1.04

Duqi, A., Tomaselli, A., & Torluccio, G. (2018). Is Relationship Lending Still a Mixed Blessing? a Review of Advantages and Disadvantages for Lenders and Borrowers. In *Journal of Economic Surveys* (Vol. 32, Issue 5). DOI: 10.1111/joes.12251

Dutta, D., Srivastava, Y., & Singh, E. (2023). Metaverse in the tourism sector for talent management: A technology in practice lens. *Information Technology & Tourism*, 25(3), 331–365. DOI: 10.1007/s40558-023-00258-9

Dwivedi, Y. K., Hughes, L., Baabdullah, A. M., Ribeiro-Navarrete, S., Giannakis, M., Al-Debei, M. M., Dennehy, D., Metri, B., Buhalis, D., Cheung, C. M. K., Conboy, K., Doyle, R., Dubey, R., Dutot, V., Felix, R., Goyal, D. P., Gustafsson, A., Hinsch, C., Jebabli, I., & Wamba, S. F. (2022). Metaverse beyond the hype: Multidisciplinary perspectives on emerging challenges, opportunities, and agenda for research, practice and policy. *International Journal of Information Management*, 66, 102542. DOI: 10.1016/j.ijinfomgt.2022.102542

Dwivedi, Y. K., Hughes, L., Wang, Y., Alalwan, A. A., Ahn, S. J., Balakrishnan, J., Barta, S., Belk, R., Buhalis, D., Dutot, V., Felix, R., Filieri, R., Flavián, C., Gustafsson, A., Hinsch, C., Hollensen, S., Jain, V., Kim, J., Krishen, A. S., & Wirtz, J. (2023). Metaverse marketing: How the metaverse will shape the future of consumer research and practice. *Psychology and Marketing*, 40(4), 750–776. DOI: 10.1002/mar.21767

EaP GREEN. (2016), Environmental Policy Toolkit for Greening SMEs in the EU Eastern Partnership countries, OECD report as part of the EU-funded EaP GREEN project, https://www.oecd.org/env/outreach/Greening-SMEs-policy-toolkit-eng.pdf

Eberhard, M., & Craig, J. (2013). The evolving role of organisational and personal networks in international market venturing. *Journal of World Business*, 48(3), 385–397. DOI: 10.1016/j.jwb.2012.07.022

EC (European Commission). (2017a): What is an SME? available at: https://ec.europa.eu/growth/smes/business-friendlyenvironment/sme-definition_en (last accessed on 12.7.2017)

Edmund, M., Christopher, W., & Zeman, Z. (2020). Technology Acquisition and SMEs Performance, the Role of Innovation, Export and the Perception of Owner-Managers. *Journal of Risk and Financial Management*, 13(11), 2–19. DOI: 10.3390/jrfm13110258

Eggenschwiler, M., Linzmajer, M., Roggeveen, A. L., & Rudolph, T. (2024). Retailing in the metaverse: A framework of managerial considerations for success. *Journal of Retailing and Consumer Services*, 79, 103791. DOI: 10.1016/j.jretconser.2024.103791

Elf, P., Werner, A., & Black, S. (2022). Advancing the circular economy through dynamic capabilities and extended customer engagement: Insights from small sustainable fashion enterprises in the UK. *Business Strategy and the Environment*, 31(6), 2682–2699. DOI: 10.1002/bse.2999

Enache, M. C. (2022). Metaverse opportunities for businesses. Annals of the University Dunarea de Jos of Galati: Fascicle: I. *Economics & Applied Informatics*, 28(1), 67–71.

Escalas, J. E. (2004). Narrative processing: Building consumer connections to brands. *Journal of Consumer Psychology*, 14(1-2), 168–180. DOI: 10.1207/s15327663jcp1401&2_19

Ethereum Foundation. (2022). The Merge: Ethereum's transition to proof-of-stake. Available at: https://ethereum.org/en/upgrades/merge/

European Commission. (2020). A European Green Deal. Retrieved from https://ec.europa.eu/info/strategy/priorities-2019-2024/european-green-deal_en

EY. (2017). *The future of work: The augmented workforce*. Global Human Capital Trends.

Fadhel, M. A., Duhaim, A. M., Albahri, A. S., Al-Qaysi, Z. T., Aktham, M. A., Chyad, M. A., Abd-Alaziz, W., Albahri, O. S., Alamoodi, A. H., Alzubaidi, L., Gupta, A., & Gu, Y. (2024). Navigating the metaverse: Unraveling the impact of artificial intelligence—a comprehensive review and gap analysis. *Artificial Intelligence Review*, 57(9), 264. DOI: 10.1007/s10462-024-10881-5

Fan, A., Wu, L., Miao, L., & Mattila, A. S. (2020). When does technology anthropomorphism help alleviate customer dissatisfaction after a service failure?–The moderating role of consumer technology self-efficacy and interdependent self-construal. *Journal of Hospitality Marketing & Management*, 29(3), 269–290. DOI: 10.1080/19368623.2019.1639095

Fang, H., Randolph, R. V. D. G., Memili, E., & Chrisman, J. J. (2016). Does Size Matter? The Moderating Effects of Firm Size on the Employment of Nonfamily Managers in Privately Held Family SMEs. *Entrepreneurship Theory and Practice*, 40(5), 1017–1039. DOI: 10.1111/etap.12156

Far, S. B., Rad, A. I., & Asaar, M. R. (2023). Blockchain and its derived technologies shape the future generation of digital businesses: A focus on decentralized finance and the Metaverse. *Data Science and Management*, 6(3), 183–197. DOI: 10.1016/j.dsm.2023.06.002

Fathi, F. (2024). Content Analysis of Blockchain and Cryptocurrency Applications in the Metaverse: A Study on Users' Financial Behaviors. *Knowledge Economy Studies*, 1(1), 101–116.

Faulkender, M. W. (2002). Cash Holdings Among Small Businesses. SSRN *Electronic Journal*. DOI: 10.2139/ssrn.305179

Fernández, Z., & Nieto, M. J. (2006). Impact of ownership on the international involvement of SMEs. *Journal of International Business Studies*, 37(3), 340–351. DOI: 10.1057/palgrave.jibs.8400196

Ferrario, A., Loi, M., & Viganò, E. (2020). In AI We Trust Incrementally: A Multi-layer Model of Trust to Analyze Human-Artificial Intelligence Interactions. *Philosophy & Technology*, 33(3), 523–539. DOI: 10.1007/s13347-019-00378-3

Filatotchev, I., & Boyd, B. K. (2009). Taking stock of corporate governance research while looking to the future: Guest editorial. *Corporate Governance*, 17(3), 257–265. DOI: 10.1111/j.1467-8683.2009.00748.x

Firmansyah, E. A., & Umar, U. H. (2023). Metaverse in business research: A systematic literature review. *Cogent Business & Management*, 10(2), 2222499. DOI: 10.1080/23311975.2023.2222499

Florido-Benítez, L. (2024). Metaverse cannot be an extra marketing immersive tool to increase sales in tourism cities. *International Journal of Tourism Cities*.

Forlano, L. (2017). Posthumanism and design. *She Ji: The Journal of Design, Economics, and Innovation*, 3(1), 16–29.

Foster, J. K., McLelland, M. A., & Wallace, L. K. (2022). Brand avatars: Impact of social interaction on consumer–brand relationships. *Journal of Research in Interactive Marketing*, 16(2), 237–258. DOI: 10.1108/JRIM-01-2020-0007

Frank, P., & Rudolf, M. (2024). Is the Metaverse Dead? Insights from Financial Bubble Analysis. *FinTech*, 3(2), 302–323. DOI: 10.3390/fintech3020017

Freddi, D. (2018). Digitalisation and employment in manufacturing. *AI & Society*, 33(3), 393–403. DOI: 10.1007/s00146-017-0740-5

Games, E. Sustainability Report. (2022). Available at: https://www.epicgames.com/sustainability

Gao, H., Chong, A. Y. L., & Bao, H. (2023). Metaverse: Literature Review, Synthesis and Future Research Agenda. *Journal of Computer Information Systems*, 3(2), 1–21. DOI: 10.1080/08874417.2023.2267510

Garg, K. (2024). Digital identities in the metaverse: Privacy, security, and user authentication in virtual financial systems. International Journal of Financial Engineering, 2442009.

Garrido-Iñigo, R., & Rodríguez-Moreno, A. (2015). Pros and cons of virtual worlds in language teaching: Using OpenSim to teach French to tourism students. *Journal of Language Teaching and Research*, 6(5), 1017-1025. DOI: 10.17507/jltr.0605.13

Gauttier, S., Simouri, W., & Milliat, A. (2024). When to enter the metaverse: Business leaders offer perspectives. *The Journal of Business Strategy*, 45(1), 2–9. DOI: 10.1108/JBS-08-2022-0149

Gbandi & Amissah, 2014). FINANCING OPTIONS FOR SMALL AND MEDIUM ENTERPRISES (SMEs) IN NIGERIA *European Scientific Journal, ESJ, 10*(1)

Gebru, G. H. (2009). Financing preferences of micro and small enterprise owners in Tigray: Does POH hold? *Journal of Small Business and Enterprise Development*, 16(2), 322–334. DOI: 10.1108/14626000910956083

Geeraerts, G. (1984). The Effect of Ownership on the Organization Structure in Small Firms. *Administrative Science Quarterly*, 29(2), 232. DOI: 10.2307/2393175

Gegung, E. M. (2023). Metaverse: A promising future for the tourism industry and MSMEs Post-Covid-19 pandemic. Jurnal Kepariwisataan Indonesia: *Jurnal Penelitian dan Pengembangan Kepariwisataan Indonesia, 17(2), 172-181.*

George, G., Wiklund, J., & Zahra, S. A. (2005). Ownership and the internationalization of small firms. *Journal of Management*, 31(2), 210–233. DOI: 10.1177/0149206304271760

Ghaffar, S. A., & Setiawan, W. C. (2024). Metaverse Dynamics: Predictive Modeling of Roblox Stock Prices using Time Series Analysis and Machine Learning. *International Journal Research on Metaverese*, 1(1), 77–93. DOI: 10.47738/ijrm.v1i1.6

Ghobadian, A., & O'Regan, N. (2006). The impact of ownership on small firm behaviour and performance. *International Small Business Journal*, 24(6), 555–586. DOI: 10.1177/0266242606069267

Gholjash, S., Momeni Yanesari, A., Ajam, L., & Safari Grayli, M. (2024). Identifying and Evaluating the Effective Fields of Metaverse in Financial Flexibility: Future Perspectives of the Capital Market. *Financial Management Perspective*, 14(46), 59–91.

Gil-Cordero, E., Maldonado-López, B., Ledesma-Chaves, P., & García-Guzmán, A. (2024). Do small-and medium-sized companies intend to use the Metaverse as part of their strategy? A behavioral intention analysis. *International Journal of Entrepreneurial Behaviour & Research*, 30(2/3), 421–449. DOI: 10.1108/IJEBR-09-2022-0816

Giuliano, L., Lupetti, M. L., Khan, S., & Germak, C. (2017). Ethic reflections about service robotics, from human protection to enhancement: Case study on cultural heritage. In *Robotics-Legal, Ethical and Socioeconomic Impacts*. IntechOpen.

Gladcheff, A. P. (2003). *Entrevista Estruturada: Uma Eficiente Técnica de Aquisição de Conhecimento Explícito*. Revista PUC-SP.

Gligor, D., Bozkurt, S., Welch, E., & Gligor, N. (2023). An exploration of the impact of gender on customer engagement. *Journal of Marketing Communications*, 29(4), 379–402. DOI: 10.1080/13527266.2022.2030390

Goldberg, M., Schär, F., & Thürkauf, D. (2023). Retailing and customer engagement in the metaverse: An empirical analysis. *Available atSSRN* 4547100. DOI: 10.2139/ssrn.4547100

Golf-Papez, M., &Dujak, D. (2022). Challenges of businesses in the metaverse market: A conceptual framework. *Business Horizons*, 65(6), 743-754. https://doi.org/DOI: 10.1016/j.bushor.2022.07.001

Google. (2021). How AI is helping to reduce energy use in our data centres. Available at: https://blog.google/inside-google/infrastructure/ai-reduces-energy-use/

Guia, J., & Jamal, T. (2020). A (Deleuzian) posthumanist paradigm for tourism research. *Annals of Tourism Research*, 84, 102982. DOI: 10.1016/j.annals.2020.102982 PMID: 32834223

Gummesson, E. (2014). Pesquisa em serviços de metodologia: Do estudo de caso em pesquisa à teoria. *Revista Ibero-Americana de Estratégia, 13*(04), 08–17. https://doi.org/DOI: 10.5585/riae.v13i4.2180

Gunkel, D. (2021). The ethics of NFTs and digital ownership: Speculation and sustainability. *Digital Culture & Ethics*, 18(1), 120–136.

Guo, Y., Yu, T., Wu, J., Wang, Y., Wan, S., Zheng, J., ... & Dai, Q. (2022). Artificial intelligence for metaverse: a framework. *CAAI Artificial Intelligence Research, 1*(1).

Gupta, B. B., Gaurav, A., Albeshri, A. A., & Alsalman, D. (2023). New paradigms of sustainable entrepreneurship in metaverse: A micro-level perspective. *The International Entrepreneurship and Management Journal*, 17(3), 1–17. DOI: 10.1007/s11365-023-00875-0

Gupta, M., Gupta, D., & Duggal, A. (2023). NFT Culture: A New Era. *Scientific Journal of Metaverse and Blockchain Technologies*, 1(1), 57–62. DOI: 10.36676/sjmbt.v1i1.08

Gupta, R., Rathore, B., Biswas, B., Jaiswal, M., & Singh, R. K. (2024). Are we ready for metaverse adoption in the service industry? Theoretically exploring the barriers to successful adoption. *Journal of Retailing and Consumer Services*, 79, 103882. DOI: 10.1016/j.jretconser.2024.103882

Gupta, V. P., Sharief, S., & Rani, S. (2024). Digital fashion and social media influencer in industry 5.0. In Rani, S. (Ed.), *System engineering and digital twins for industry 5.0* (pp. 67–89). Springer. DOI: 10.1007/978-3-031-71052-0_4

Gursoy, D., Lu, L., Nunkoo, R., & Deng, D. (2023). Metaverse in services marketing: An overview and future research directions. *Service Industries Journal*, 43(15-16), 1140–1172. DOI: 10.1080/02642069.2023.2252750

Gwagwa, A; Kraemer-Mbula, K; Rizk,N, Rutenberg· I, de Beer, J (2020). Artificial Intelligence (AI) Deployments in Africa: Benefits, Challenges and Policy Dimensions. The Africa Journal of Information and Communication. Vol.26

Haavisto, J. (2024). Designing implementable tools: the importance of easy and fast implementation in the metaverse era.

Hacker, K. L., & Van Dijk, J. (2000). *Digital Democracy: Issues of Theory and Practice*. Sage. DOI: 10.4135/9781446218891

Haefner, N., Wincent, J., Parida, V., & Gassmann, O. (2021). Artificial intelligence and innovation management: A review, framework, and research agenda. *Technological Forecasting and Social Change*, 162, 1–10. DOI: 10.1016/j.techfore.2020.120392

Haenlein, M., & Kaplan, A. (2019). A Brief History of Artificial Intelligence: On the Past, Present, and Future of Artificial Intelligence. *California Management Review*, 61(4), 5–14. DOI: 10.1177/0008125619864925

Hai, G., Zhuen, Y., & Jiebin, D. (2023). Metaverse Business Model: Connotation, Classification and Research Framework. *Foreign Economics & Management*, 45(03), 23–45.

Hakkarainen, T., & Colicev, A. (2023). Blockchain-enabled advances (BEAs): Implications for consumers and brands. *Journal of Business Research*, 160, 113763. DOI: 10.1016/j.jbusres.2023.113763

Haleem, A., Javaid, M., Qadri, M. A., Singh, R. P., & Suman, R. (2022). Artificial intelligence (AI) applications for marketing: A literature-based study. *International Journal of Intelligent Networks*, 3, 119–132. DOI: 10.1016/j.ijin.2022.08.005

Hamari, J., Koivisto, J., & Sarsa, H. (2014). Does gamification work? A literature review of empirical studies on gamification. *Proceedings of the 47th Hawaii International Conference on System Sciences*, 3025–3034. DOI: 10.1109/HICSS.2014.377

Hamelin, A. (2013). Influence of family ownership on small business growth. Evidence from French SMEs. *Small Business Economics*, 41(3), 563–579. DOI: 10.1007/s11187-012-9452-x

Hamilton, S. (2022). Deep learning computer vision algorithms, customer engagement tools, and virtual marketplace dynamics data in the metaverse economy. *Journal of Self-Governance and Management Economics*, 10(2), 37–51.

Hampton, H., Foley, A., Del Rio, D. F., Smyth, B., Laverty, D., & Caulfield, B. (2022). Customer engagement strategies in retail electricity markets: A comprehensive and comparative review. *Energy Research & Social Science*, 90, 102611. DOI: 10.1016/j.erss.2022.102611

Han, S., & Anderson, C. K. (2022). The dynamic customer engagement behaviors in the customer satisfaction survey. *Decision Support Systems*, 154, 113708. DOI: 10.1016/j.dss.2021.113708

Hasani, T., Rezania, D., & Mohammadi, M. (2024). Towards a framework for successful metaverse adoption in Small and Medium-sized Enterprises: An exploratory study. *International Journal of Engineering Business Management*, 16, 18479790241257118. DOI: 10.1177/18479790241257118

Hashem, T. (2024). Digital Marketing and the Ethical Code for Behavioral Tracking: Issues of Privacy and Consumer Trust. *Journal of Electrical Systems*, 20(10), 2842–2854.

Hashem, T., Alotoum, F. J., Allan, M., & Ali, N. (2023). Employing metaverse marketing through gaming and its impact on customer experience: Evidence from multiple online gaming platforms. *Calitatea*, 24(196), 193–206.

Hassouneh, D., & Brengman, M. (2011). Virtual worlds: A gateway for SMEs toward internationalization. *Journal of Brand Management*, 19(1), 72–90. DOI: 10.1057/bm.2011.24

Hastuti, T. D., Sanjaya, R., & Koeswoyo, F. (2022). The readiness of Lasem Batik small and medium enterprises to join the metaverse. *Computers*, 12(1), 5. DOI: 10.3390/computers12010005

Hazaea, S. A., Zhu, J., Khatib, S. F. A., & Elamer, A. A. (2023). Mapping the literature of internal auditing in Europe: A systematic review and agenda for future research. *Meditari Accountancy Research*, 31(6), 1675–1706. DOI: 10.1108/MEDAR-01-2022-1584

Hindolia, A., Arya, J., Pathak, R., & Kazmi, A. (2024). Halal B2B marketing in the metaverse: Crafting a conceptual framework to pinpoint opportunities and challenges, outlining the agenda for future research. *Journal of Islamic Marketing*. Advance online publication. DOI: 10.1108/JIMA-02-2024-0054

Ho, R. C., & Song, B. L. (2023). User acceptance towards non-fungible token (NFT) as the FinTech for investment management in the metaverse. In Strategies and Opportunities for Technology in the Metaverse World (pp. 59-77). IGI Global.

Hollebeek, L. D., Sharma, T. G., Pandey, R., Sanyal, P., & Clark, M. K. (2022). Fifteen years of customer engagement research: A bibliometric and network analysis. *Journal of Product and Brand Management*, 31(2), 293–309. DOI: 10.1108/JPBM-01-2021-3301

Hoskinson, C. (2021). *The Cardano network: An overview of the energy-efficient PoS blockchain*. Cardano Whitepaper.

Hsieh, T. T., Emerson, R. W., Foster, I. I., Larry, D., Link, B. A., Sherman, C. A., & Trautman, L. J. (2023). Intellectual Property In the Era of AI, Blockchain and Web 3.0. *Blockchain and Web, 3.*

Huang, M. H., & Rust, R. T. (2018). Artificial Intelligence in Service. *Journal of Service Research*, 21(2), 155–172. DOI: 10.1177/1094670517752459

Huang, W., Boateng, A., & Newman, A. (2016). Capital structure of Chinese listed SMEs: An agency theory perspective. *Small Business Economics*, 47(2), 535–550. DOI: 10.1007/s11187-016-9729-6

Hubbard, T. D., & Aguinis, H. (2023). Conducting phenomenon-driven research using virtual reality and the metaverse. *Academy of Management Discoveries*, 9(3), 408–415. DOI: 10.5465/amd.2023.0031

Hussain, Z. (1988, May). Enhancing Transparency and Accountability in Sadaqah Crowdfunding Platforms: Leveraging Blockchain Technology for Optimal User Experience. *InAnnual International Conference on the Theory and Applications of Cryptographic Techniques(pp.351-367).Cham: Springer Nature Switzerland.*

Hussain, Z. (2023). A Study of Employees' Perceptions on Industry Revolution 5.0 and Its Advantages: A Case Study of the Manufacturing Industry of Pakistan. *Business, Technology and Finance, 25.*

Hussain, Z., Majeed, M. U., & Khan, A. (2024). The Impact of Visual Content Marketing on Customer Purchasing Behavior: Evidence from Pakistan's Fashion Industry. *International Journal of Marketing, Communication and New Media, (14).*

Hussain, Z. (2023). The Use of Web 3.0 in University E-learning, Quality Assurance, and Knowledge Management. In *Advances in Distance Learning in Times of Pandemic* (pp. 155–176). Chapman and Hall/CRC. DOI: 10.1201/9781003322252-7

Hussain, Z. (2024). The Role of Metaverse in Women Entrepreneurship and Economic Complexity: Evidence from Pakistan. *Journal of Entrepreneurship and Business Venturing*, 4(1).

Hussain, Z., Khan, A., & Ali, A. (2023). The Impact of User-Generated Content, Social Interactions and virtual Economies on Metaverse Environments. *Journal of Sustainable Economics*, 1(2), 34–44. DOI: 10.32734/jse.v1i2.13798

Hussain, Z., Mari, I. H., & Rind, A. A. (2022). Exploring The Barriers of Artificial Intelligence Adoption in Digital Marketing Landscape. *ULIL ALBAB: Jurnal Ilmiah Multidisiplin*, 1(4), 824–835.

Hussain, Z., Sultan, R., Asadullah, A., Arif, M., & Ali, A. (2022). The Impact of Zakat Literacy, Trust, and the Accessibility of Digital Payments on Generation Z and Y's Intention to Pay Zakat to Central Zakat Fund, the State Bank of Pakistan. *International Journal of Zakat*, 7(2), 105–114.

Hutson, J., Banerjee, G., Kshetri, N., Odenwald, K., & Ratican, J. (2023). Architecting the metaverse: blockchain and the financial and legal regulatory challenges of virtual real estate. Journal of Intelligent Learning Systems and Applications, 15.

Hu, Y., & Pang, J. (2023). Research on the new path of deepening grassroots medical care from the perspective of metaverse. *Academic Journal of Management and Social Sciences*, 2(1), 81–84. DOI: 10.54097/ajmss.v2i1.6375

Huynh-The, T., Pham, Q. V., Pham, X. Q., Nguyen, T. T., Han, Z., & Kim, D. S. (2023). Artificial intelligence for the metaverse: A survey. *Engineering Applications of Artificial Intelligence*, 117, 105581. DOI: 10.1016/j.engappai.2022.105581

Huy, P. Q., & Phuc, V. K. (2024). Contribution to accelerated internationalization with digital forensic accounting and metaverse circular business model innovation for Vietnam-based SMEs. *Journal of Innovation and Entrepreneurship*, 13(1), 1–28. DOI: 10.1186/s13731-024-00442-z

Huy, P. Q., & Phuc, V. K. (2024). Convergence of Blockchain, Artificial Intelligence, and Internet of Things (BlockIoTIntelligence) with Metaverse for Industry 4.0 to Realize Net Zero Economy. In *Net Zero Economy, Corporate Social Responsibility and Sustainable Value Creation: Exploring Strategies, Drivers, and Challenges* (pp. 187–202). Springer Nature Switzerland. DOI: 10.1007/978-3-031-55779-8_12

Hwang, G. J., & Chien, S. Y. (2022). Definition, roles, and potential research issues of the metaverse in education: An artificial intelligence perspective. *Computers and Education: Artificial Intelligence*, 3, 100082. DOI: 10.1016/j.caeai.2022.100082

Ibidunni, A. S., Ufua, D. E., & Opute, A. P. (2021). Linking disruptive innovation to sustainable entrepreneurship within the context of small and medium firms: A focus on Nigeria. *African Journal of Science, Technology, Innovation and Development*, •••, 1–17.

Ibrahim, A. (2024). The Role of Artificial Intelligence in the Metaverse. *Arts and Design Studies.Image*, 1, •••. https://frontofficesports.com/nike-trademark-hints-at-metaverse-sneakers/

Ihesiene, U. C., & Akpojaro, J. (2015). A Critical Evaluation of SMEs Attitudes towards Information Technology Integration in Nigeria, Australian Journal of Business and Management Research, 14(11) brahim, H., & Sarolta T. (2022). Empirical Analysis of the Influence of Gamification on Employees' Behavior. *Dynamic Relationships Management Journal*, 11(2), 71–78.

IKEA Sustainability Report. (2021). Retrieved from https://about.ikea.com/en/sustainability

Image 2. https://jingdaily.com/posts/gucci-head-of-metaverse

Image 3. https://streamhatchet.com/blog/setting-the-hype-for-elden-ring-shadow-of-the-erdtree-with-redbull/

Image 4. https://news.samsung.com/us/creation-of-samsung-837x/

Inder, S. (2023). Entrepreneurial opportunities in metaverse. In *Promoting Consumer Engagement Through Emotional Branding and Sensory Marketing* (pp. 52–62). IGI Global.

Intelligence, W. T. (2021a). *Lauches into the metaverse – a metaverse road map for brands* (2021 Edition). PR Newswire Association LLC., Retrieved from https://www.proquest.com/wire-feeds/wunderman-thompson-launches-into-metaverse-road/docview/2572826415/se-2?accountid=177838

International Federation of Robotics (IFR). (2022). World [IFR.]. *Robotics Reports*, •••, 2022.

International Federation of Robotics. (2020). *IFR International Federation of Robotics*. https://ifr.org/

Ioannidis, S., & Kontis, A. P. (2023). Metaverse for tourists and tourism destinations. *Information Technology & Tourism*, 2(3), 1–24.

Io, H. N., & Lee, C. B. (2020). Social Media Comments about Hotel Robots. *Journal of China Tourism Research*, 16(4), 606–625. DOI: 10.1080/19388160.2020.1769785

ION, D. G. (2022). Human Capital or Human Beings? Analysis of Added Value and Employee Efficiency between SME's and Large Companies. *Fostering Recovery through Metaverse Business Modelling, 835.*

IPCC. (2021). *Sixth Assessment Report: Climate Change 2021*. Cambridge University Press.

Iqbal, M., Suhail, S., Milani, F., & Halas, Y. (2024). Metaverse in financial industry: Use cases, value, and challenges. *International Journal of Information Management Data Insights*, 4(2), 100302. DOI: 10.1016/j.jjimei.2024.100302

Ivanov, S., & Webster, C. (2019). Conceptual framework of the use of robots, artificial intelligence and service automation in travel, tourism, and hospitality companies. Ivanov, S., Webster, C. (Eds.), Robots, Artificial Intelligence and Service Automation in Travel, *Tourism and Hospitality. Emerald Publishing,* 7-37 DOI: 10.1108/978-1-78756-687-320191001

Ivanov, S., & Webster, C. (2021). Robotics and artificial intelligence in hospitality: The future of service automation. *Tourism Management Perspectives*, 37, 100771.

Ivanov, S., Webster, C., & Berezina, K. (2019). Robotics in tourism and hospitality. *Current Issues in Tourism*, 22(9), 1007–1025.

Jaber, T. A. (2022). Security Risks of the Metaverse World. *Int. J. Interact. Mob. Technol.*, 16(13), 4–14. DOI: 10.3991/ijim.v16i13.33187

Jafar, R. M. S., Sun, Y., Niu, B., Hussain, S., Zhu, J., Gu, M., Al-Adwan, A. S., & Yang, Y. (2024). Revealing the secrets of metaverse technology adoption for sustainable performance via dual-stage SEM-ANN analysis. *International Journal of Human-Computer Interaction*, •••, 1–18. DOI: 10.1080/10447318.2024.2407686

Japar, D. F. I. P. M., & Anshari, M. (2023). Potential and challenges of the Metaverse on future businesses. In *Metaverse applications for new business models and disruptive innovation* (pp. 102–119). IGI Global. DOI: 10.4018/978-1-6684-6097-9.ch007

Jensen, M. C., & Meckling, W. H. (1976). Theory of the firm: Managerial behavior, agency costs and ownership structure. *Journal of Financial Economics*, 3(4), 305–360. DOI: 10.1016/0304-405X(76)90026-X

Jeon, J., & Lee, E. J. (2024). A study on the impact of fashion brand Metaverse platform characteristics on perceived avatar identity and user purchase intention. *International Journal of Advanced Culture Technology*, 12(3), 406–418.

Jha, A. (2023). Immersive Marketing on Metaverse: Development of Metrics for Performance Analysis and Security-Related Challenges. In *Confronting Security and Privacy Challenges in Digital Marketing* (pp. 267-289). IGI Global.

Jiang, Y., & Zhao, Y. (2023). Automation in hotel operations: Technological advancements and managerial implications. *Journal of Hospitality Marketing & Management*, 32(4), 432–446.

Jinjarak, Y., & Wignaraja, G. (2016). An Empirical Assessment of the Export-Financial Constraint Relationship: How Different are Small and Medium Enterprises? *World Development*, 79, 152–163. DOI: 10.1016/j.worlddev.2015.11.012

Johan, S. (2022). Metaverse and its implication in law and business. *Jurnal Hukum Progresif*, 10(2), 153–166. DOI: 10.14710/jhp.10.2.153-166

Joshi, V., & Patel, M. (2024). Post-Pandemic Digital Transformation in India. *Journal of Business Research*, 129, 567–582.

Joy, A., Zhu, Y., Peña, C., & Brouard, M. (2022). Digital future of luxury brands: Metaverse, digital fashion, and non-fungible tokens. *Strategic Change*, 31(3), 337–343. DOI: 10.1002/jsc.2502

Jun, W., Zhe, Z.Y., Bo, Z.Y.,& Lian, H.Q. (2017). Countermeasures and Suggestions on the Impact of Artificial Intelligence on Employment. ChinaEconomic and Trade Review, 24.

Jung, T., Cho, J., Han, D. I. D., Ahn, S. J. G., Gupta, M., Das, G., Heo, C. Y., Loureiro, S. M. C., Sigala, M., Trunfio, M., Taylor, A., & Tom Dieck, M. C. (2024). Metaverse for service industries: Future applications, opportunities, challenges and research directions. *Computers in Human Behavior*, 151, 108039. DOI: 10.1016/j.chb.2023.108039

Kääriäinen, H.. (2021). The Technological Complexity of Digital Transformation for Small Businesses. *Technology Innovation Management Review*, 11(4), 39–50.

Kadhim, Y. A., & Al Ani, S. A. M. (2023, December). Using Artificial Intelligence and Metaverse Techniques to Reduce Earning Management. In *International Multi-Disciplinary Conference-Integrated Sciences and Technologies* (pp. 171–189). Springer Nature Switzerland. DOI: 10.1007/978-3-031-51716-7_12

Kandampully, J., Zhang, T., & Bilgihan, A. (2021). Exploring the challenges of robotics and automation in hospitality. *International Journal of Hospitality Management*, 97, 103049.

Kaplan, A., & Haenlein, M. (2019). Rethinking AI: Interpreting Data for Strategic Goals. *Journal of Marketing*, 83(1), 15–22.

Karademir, Ö. (2023). Opportunities and Barriers for Entrepreneurship in the Metaverse Age. In *Role of Human Resources for Inclusive Leadership, Workplace Diversity, and Equity in Organizations* (pp. 309–336). IGI Global. DOI: 10.4018/978-1-6684-6602-5.ch013

Karthik, V. (2023). Impact of Metaverse and Advanced Technology on the Enterprises. *International Journal of Business and Management Research*, 11(2), 60–65. DOI: 10.37391/ijbmr.110201

Kathuria, M. (2023). Engaging Gen Z through Immersive Experiences: A Case Study. *Marketing Insights*, 18(1), 113–125.

Katterbauer, K., Syed, H., Cleenewerck, L., & Genc, S. Y. (2024). Islamic finance in the metaverse: meta-finance frameworks for supporting the growth of Shariah-compliant finance options in the metaspace. In *Islamic Finance in the Digital Age* (pp. 301–314). Edward Elgar Publishing. DOI: 10.4337/9781035322954.00027

Keller, K. L. (2009). Building strong brands in a modern marketing communications environment. *Journal of Marketing Communications*, 15(2-3), 139–155. DOI: 10.1080/13527260902757530

Kemec, A. (2022). From reality to virtuality: Re-discussing cities with the concept of the metaverse. *International Journal of Management Accounting*, 4(1), 12–20.

Khan, A., Hamid, A. B. A., Saad, N. M., Hussain, Z., & Arif, A. R. (2023). Effectiveness of artificial intelligence in building customer loyalty: Investigating the mediating role of chatbot in the tourism sector of Pakistan. *International Journal of Academic Research in Business & Social Sciences*, 13(9), 657–671. DOI: 10.6007/IJARBSS/v13-i9/18895

Khan, A., Hussain, Z., Mari, I. H., & Ali, A. (2022). Adoption of Digital Marketing Strategies in Tourism Industry: A Case Study of Pakistan. J-CEKI. *Jurnal Cendekia Ilmiah*, 1(3), 190–208.

Khang, A., Shah, V., & Rani, S. (Eds.). (2023). *Handbook of Research on AI-Based Technologies and Applications in the Era of the Metaverse*. IGI Global. DOI: 10.4018/978-1-6684-8851-5

Khan, M. N., & uddin Qadri, S. M. (2023). Exploring the Influence of Advertising within the Metaverse and its Synergy with Non-Fungible Tokens (NFTs). *International Journal of Management Perspective and Social Research*, 2(1), 22–43.

Khanna, R., Patel, T., & Williams, R. (2022). The impact of AI and machine learning on sustainability in digital ecosystems. *Journal of AI Research*, 22(1), 123–136.

Khatib, S. F. A. (2024c). An assessment of methods to deal with endogeneity in corporate governance and reporting research. *Corporate Governance: The International Journal of Business in Society*. DOI: 10.1108/CG-12-2023-0507

Khatib, S. F. A. (2024a). Sustainability Assurance and Corporate Environmental Accountability. *Social and Environmental Accountability Journal*, 1–2(2), 176–177. Advance online publication. DOI: 10.1080/0969160X.2024.2336721

Khatib, S. F. A. (2024b). Corrupt practice and sustainability reporting: Lifecycle perspective. *Business Strategy & Development*, 7(2), e396. Advance online publication. DOI: 10.1002/bsd2.396

Khatib, S. F. A. (2024d). The role of share repurchases for firms' social and environmental sustainability. *Social and Environmental Accountability Journal*, 44(1), 82–84. DOI: 10.1080/0969160X.2023.2281904

Khatib, S. F. A., Abdullah, D. F., Al Amosh, H., Bazhair, A. H., & Kabara, A. S. (2022). Shariah auditing: Analyzing the past to prepare for the future. *Journal of Islamic Accounting and Business Research*, 13(5), 791–818. DOI: 10.1108/JIABR-11-2021-0291

Khatib, S. F. A., Abdullah, D. F., Elamer, A. A., & Abueid, R. (2021). Nudging toward diversity in the boardroom: A systematic literature review of board diversity of financial institutions. *Business Strategy and the Environment*, 30(2), 985–1002. DOI: 10.1002/bse.2665

Khatri, M. (2022). Revamping the marketing world with metaverse–The future of marketing. *International Journal of Computer Applications*, 184(29), 1–5. DOI: 10.5120/ijca2022922361

Kılıçaslan, F., & Ekizler, H. (2022). Factors effecting purchase intention in blockchain and NFT (non-fungible token) technologies. *Journal of Research in Business*, 7(2), 604–623. DOI: 10.54452/jrb.1177600

Kim, J. (2021). Advertising in the metaverse: Research agenda. *Journal of Interactive Advertising*, 21(3), 141–144. DOI: 10.1080/15252019.2021.2001273

Kim, J., & Bae, J. (2024). Influences of persona self on luxury brand attachment in the Metaverse context. *Asia Pacific Journal of Marketing and Logistics*, 36(9), 2068–2081. DOI: 10.1108/APJML-05-2022-0390

Kim, S. J. (2023). Virtual fashion experiences in virtual reality fashion show spaces. *Frontiers in Psychology*, 14, 1276856. DOI: 10.3389/fpsyg.2023.1276856 PMID: 38046109

Kim, Y., & Lee, H. (2024). Consumers' responses to metaverse ads: The roles of hedonic versus utilitarian appeal and the moderating role of need for touch. *Journal of Business Research*, 179, 114677. DOI: 10.1016/j.jbusres.2024.114677

Kit, K. T. (2022). Sustainable engineering paradigm shift in digital architecture, engineering and construction ecology within Metaverse. *International Journal of Computer and Information Engineering*, 16(4), 112–115.

Kitsios, F., & Kamariotou, M. (2021). *Artificial Intelligence and Business Strategy towards Digital Transformation: A Research Agenda*. MDPI., DOI: 10.3390/su13042025

Klein, P., Shapiro, D., & Young, J. (2005). Corporate governance, family ownership and firm value: The Canadian evidence. *Corporate Governance*, 13(6), 769–784. DOI: 10.1111/j.1467-8683.2005.00469.x

Klein, V. B., & Todesco, J. L. (2021). COVID-19 crisis and SMEs responses: The role of digital transformation. *Knowledge and Process Management*, 28(2), 117–133. DOI: 10.1002/kpm.1660

Klosters, Davos. (2016) "World Economic Forum Annual Meeting 2016 Mastering the Fourth Industrial Revolution." *World Economic Forum.* http://www3.weforum.org/docs/Media/. Accessed 7 October 2018.

Knox, J. (2022). The metaverse, or the serious business of tech frontiers. *Post digital. Science and Education*, 4(2), 207–215.

Knox, J. (2022). The metaverse, or the serious business of tech frontiers. *Postdigital Science and Education*, 4(2), 207–215. DOI: 10.1007/s42438-022-00300-9

Koo, C., Kwon, J., Chung, N., & Kim, J. (2023). Metaverse tourism: Conceptual framework and research propositions. *Current Issues in Tourism*, 26(20), 3268–3274. DOI: 10.1080/13683500.2022.2122781

Koo, H., & Kwon, K. H. (2022). The applicability of scarcity, originality, and transaction tracking characteristics of the dermatological industry and non-fungible token. *Journal of Cosmetic Dermatology*, 21(12), 6628–6635. DOI: 10.1111/jocd.15406 PMID: 36152011

Koohang, A., Nord, J. H., Ooi, K. B., Tan, G. W. H., Al-Emran, M., Aw, E. C. X., Baabdullah, A. M., Buhalis, D., Cham, T.-H., Dennis, C., Dutot, V., Dwivedi, Y. K., Hughes, L., Mogaji, E., Pandey, N., Phau, I., Raman, R., Sharma, A., Sigala, M., & Wong, L. W. (2023). Shaping the metaverse into reality: A holistic multidisciplinary understanding of opportunities, challenges, and avenues for future investigation. *Journal of Computer Information Systems*, 63(3), 735–765. DOI: 10.1080/08874417.2023.2165197

Korinek, A., & Stiglitz, J. E. (2017). *Artificial intelligence and its implications for income distribution and unemployment*. National Bureau of Economic Researcho. DOI: 10.3386/w24174

Kostka, G., Moslener, U., & Andreas, J. (2013). Barriers to increasing energy efficiency: Evidence from small-and medium-sized enterprises in China. *Journal of Cleaner Production*, 57, 59–68. DOI: 10.1016/j.jclepro.2013.06.025

Kotler, P., Kartajaya, H., & Setiawan, I. (2021). *Marketing 5.0: Technology for humanity*. Edições Almedina.

Kou, G., Yüksel, S., & Dinçer, H. (2023). A facial expression and expert recommendation fuzzy decision-making approach for sustainable business investments within the metaverse world. *Applied Soft Computing*, 148, 110849. DOI: 10.1016/j.asoc.2023.110849

Kouhizadeh, M., & Sarkis, J. (2020). Blockchain adoption for sustainable supply chains. *Sustainability*, 12(4), 1472–1484.

Kour, M. (2024). Ethical Considerations in the Metaverse and Augmented Retail Reality Era. In *Consumer Experience and Decision-Making in the Metaverse* (pp. 99–110). IGI Global. DOI: 10.4018/979-8-3693-4167-4.ch006

Krasniqi, B. A., & Mustafa, M. (2016). Small firm growth in a post-conflict environment: The role of human capital, institutional quality, and managerial capacities. *The International Entrepreneurship and Management Journal*, 12(4), 1165–1207. DOI: 10.1007/s11365-016-0384-9

Kraus, S., Kanbach, D. K., Krysta, P. M., Steinhoff, M. M., & Tomini, N. (2022). Facebook and the creation of the metaverse: Radical business model innovation or incremental transformation? *International Journal of Entrepreneurial Behaviour & Research*, 28(9), 52–77. DOI: 10.1108/IJEBR-12-2021-0984

Kraus, S., Kumar, S., Lim, W. M., Kaur, J., Sharma, A., & Schiavone, F. (2023). From moon landing to metaverse: Tracing the evolution of Technological Forecasting and Social Change. *Technological Forecasting and Social Change*, 189(2), 122–281. DOI: 10.1016/j.techfore.2023.122381

Kräussl, R., & Tugnetti, A. (2024). Non-fungible tokens (NFTs): A review of pricing determinants, applications and opportunities. *Journal of Economic Surveys*, 38(2), 555–574. DOI: 10.1111/joes.12597

Kshetri, N. (2022). Metaverse and developing economies. *IT Professional*, 24(4), 66–69. DOI: 10.1109/MITP.2022.3174744

Kshetri, N. (2022). Web 3.0 and the metaverse shaping organizations' brand and product strategies. *IT Professional*, 24(02), 11–15. DOI: 10.1109/MITP.2022.3157206

Kumar, S., Sureka, R., & Colombage, S. (2020). Capital structure of SMEs: a systematic literature review and bibliometric analysis. In *Management Review Quarterly* (Vol. 70, Issue 4). Springer International Publishing. DOI: 10.1007/s11301-019-00175-4

Kumar, A., & Shankar, A. (2024). Building a sustainable future with enterprise metaverse in a data-driven era: A technology-organization-environment (TOE) perspective. *Journal of Retailing and Consumer Services*, 81, 103986. DOI: 10.1016/j.jretconser.2024.103986

Kumar, A., Shankar, A., Agarwal, R., Agarwal, V., & Alzeiby, E. A. (2024). With enterprise metaverse comes great possibilities! Understanding metaverse usage intention from an employee perspective. *Journal of Retailing and Consumer Services*, 78, 103767. DOI: 10.1016/j.jretconser.2024.103767

Kumar, A., Shankar, A., Behl, A., Gupta, B. B., & Mavuri, S. (2023). Lights, camera, metaverse!: Eliciting intention to use industrial metaverse, organizational agility, and firm performance. [JGIM]. *Journal of Global Information Management*, 31(8), 1–20. DOI: 10.4018/JGIM.333169

Kumar, A., Shankar, A., Shaik, A. S., Jain, G., & Malibari, A. (2023). Risking it all in the metaverse ecosystem: Forecasting resistance towards the enterprise metaverse. *Information Technology & People*, 3(3), 44–62. DOI: 10.1108/ITP-04-2023-0374

Kumar, R., & Shukla, S. (2022). Creativity, Proactive Personality and Entrepreneurial Intentions: Examining the Mediating Role of Entrepreneurial Self-efficacy. *Global Business Review*, 23(1), 101–118. DOI: 10.1177/0972150919844395

Kumar, R., & Singh, T. (2024). Emerging Trends in the Metaverse: Business Applications in India. *Journal of Emerging Technologies*, 10(1), 52–69.

Kumar, S., Sureka, R., Lucey, B. M., Dowling, M., Vigne, S., & Lim, W. M. (2024). MetaMoney: Exploring the intersection of financial systems and virtual worlds. *Research in International Business and Finance*, 68, 102195. DOI: 10.1016/j.ribaf.2023.102195

Kuo, C., & Wu, C. (2022). Guest acceptance of service robots in hotels: A generational perspective. *Journal of Hospitality & Tourism Research (Washington, D.C.)*, 46(2), 252–271.

La Rocca, M., Staglianò, R., La Rocca, T., Cariola, A., & Skatova, E. (2019). Cash holdings and SME performance in Europe: The role of firm-specific and macroeconomic moderators. *Small Business Economics*, 53(4), 1051–1078. DOI: 10.1007/s11187-018-0100-y

Lappalainen, J., & Niskanen, M. (2012). Financial performance of SMEs: Impact of ownership structure and board composition. *Management Research Review*, 35(11), 1088–1108. DOI: 10.1108/01409171211276954

Lappalainen, J., & Niskanen, M. (2013). Behavior and attitudes of small family firms towards different funding sources. *Journal of Small Business and Entrepreneurship*, 26(6), 579–599. DOI: 10.1080/08276331.2014.892309

Latino, M. E., De Lorenzi, M. C., Corallo, A., & Petruzzelli, A. M. (2024). The impact of metaverse for business model innovation: A review, novel insights and research directions. *Technological Forecasting and Social Change*, 206, 123571. DOI: 10.1016/j.techfore.2024.123571

Lazaroiu, G., Gedeon, T., Rogalska, E., Valaskova, K., Nagy, M., Musa, H., Zvarikova, K., Poliak, M., Horak, J., Cre oiu, R. I., Krulicky, T., Ionescu, L., Popa, C., Hurloiu, L. R., Nistor, F., Avram, L. G., & Braga, V. (2024). Digital twin-based cyber-physical manufacturing systems, extended reality metaverse enterprise and production management algorithms, and Internet of Things financial and labor market technologies in generative artificial intelligence economics. *Oeconomia Copernicana*, 15(3), 837–870. DOI: 10.24136/oc.3183

Leahy, B., & Delehanty, C. (2022). Brands In the Metaverse: Opportunities, Risks and Strategies. *The Intellectual Strategist Journal, 28(6).*

Ledesma-Chaves, P., Gil-Cordero, E., Navarro-García, A., & Maldonado-López, B. (2024). Satisfaction and performance expectations for the adoption of the metaverse in tourism SMEs. *Journal of Innovation & Knowledge*, 9(3), 100535. DOI: 10.1016/j.jik.2024.100535

Lee, J., & Kwon, J. (2022). Evolving perceptions of health and beauty in the metaverse era. *Journal of Business Research*, 138, 91-103. DOI: 10.1016/j.jbusres.2021.08.021

Lee, S., & Hwang, Y. (2022). Enhancing pre-service teachers' readiness through Virtual Reality Making (VRM). *Computers & Education*, 185, 104547. DOI: 10.1016/j.compedu.2022.104547

Lee, C. T., Ho, T. Y., & Xie, H. H. (2023). Building brand engagement in metaverse commerce: The role of branded non-fungible toekns (BNFTs). *Electronic Commerce Research and Applications*, 58, 101248. DOI: 10.1016/j.elerap.2023.101248

Lee, C. T., Shen, Y. C., Li, Z., & Xie, H. H. (2024). The *e*ffects of non-fungible token platform affordances on customer loyalty: A Buyer–Creator duality perspective. *Computers in Human Behavior*, 151, 108013. DOI: 10.1016/j.chb.2023.108013

Lee, C., & Ging, L. C. (2007). SME innovation in the Malaysian manufacturing sector. *Economic Bulletin*, 12(30).

Lee, E. J., & Jeon, J. H. (2024). The Role of Perceived Value of Avatar's Virtual Fashion in Metaverse on the Impact of Sense of Presence on Purchase Intention. International Journal of Internet. *Broadcasting and Communication*, 16(3), 334–345.

Lee, I. (2024). The Metaverse: Ecosystem, Technologies, Business Opportunities, and Challenges. *IT Professional*, 26(5), 28–35. DOI: 10.1109/MITP.2024.3433549

Lee, J., Kim, H., & Choi, Y. (2024). Understanding player engagement in the metaverse: A synthesis of the interactive gaming experience. *The Journal of Consumer Research*, 51(2), 145–163.

Lee, J., & Kwon, K. H. (2022). Novel pathway regarding good cosmetics brands by NFT in the metaverse world. *Journal of Cosmetic Dermatology*, 21(12), 6584–6593. DOI: 10.1111/jocd.15277 PMID: 35894837

Lee, K. H., Tsai, W. H., Huang, C. T., Tao, J., Lee, H., Chen, C. H., & Tseng, H. T. (2023). Using Machine Learning of Artificial Intelligence to Analyze Business Opportunities and Applications of the Massively Multiplayer Online Role-Playing Game Case in Metaverse. *Engineering Proceedings*, 55(1), 12.

Lee, L.-H., Braud, T., Zhou, P., Wang, L., Xu, D., Lin, Z., Kumar, A., Bermejo, C., & Hui, P. (2021). All one needs to know about metaverse: A complete survey on technological singularity, virtual ecosystem, and research agenda. Retrieved from http://arxiv.org/abs/2110.05352

Lee, S. (2023). Service quality and customer satisfaction in the era of robotics: A hospitality perspective. *International Journal of Hospitality & Tourism Administration*, 24(1), 65–80.

Liffreing, I. (2021). What brands should know about the metaverse | Ad Age. Consultado a 12 de dezembro de 2022, de https://adage.com/article/digital-marketing-ad-tech-news/what-brands-should-know-about-metaverse/2354506

Li, H., Terjesen, S., & Umans, T. (2020). Corporate governance in entrepreneurial firms: A systematic review and research agenda. *Small Business Economics*, 54(1), 43–74. DOI: 10.1007/s11187-018-0118-1

Lim, W. M., & Rasul, T. (2022). Customer engagement and social media: Revisiting the past to inform the future. *Journal of Business Research*, 148, 325–342. DOI: 10.1016/j.jbusres.2022.04.068

Lim, W. M., Rasul, T., Kumar, S., & Ala, M. (2022). Past, present, and future of customer engagement. *Journal of Business Research*, 140, 439–458. DOI: 10.1016/j.jbusres.2021.11.014

Lin, H., Wan, S., Gan, W., Chen, J., & Chao, H. C. (2022, December). Metaverse in education: Vision, opportunities, and challenges. *In 2022 IEEE International Conference on Big Data (Big Data) (pp. 2857-2866). IEEE.*

Lin, K. J., Ye, H., & Law, R. (2023). Understanding the development of blockchain-empowered metaverse tourism: An institutional perspective. *Information Technology & Tourism*, 23(3), 1–19. DOI: 10.1007/s40558-023-00262-z

Liu, J. (2022, December). Metaverse and brand: a study of luxury brand digital marketing strategy-taking Gucci as an example. In *2022 4th International Conference on Economic Management and Cultural Industry (ICEMCI 2022)* (pp. 1907-1913). Atlantis Press.

Liu, H., Choi, M., & Kim, J. (2024). The analysis of impact of metaverse on the Fintech industry based on text mining and association rules mining. [GBFR]. *Global Business & Finance Review*, 29(7), 93–109. DOI: 10.17549/gbfr.2024.29.7.93

Liu, H., & Park, K.-S. (2024, January). Liu, H., & Park, K. (2024). Exploring the impact of metaverse tourism experiences on actual visit intentions: An integrated model of presence, the Technology Acceptance Model, and the Theory of Planned Behavior. *International Journal of Tourism Research*, 26(1), e2616. Advance online publication. DOI: 10.1002/jtr.2616

Liu, J., Hall, C. M., Zhu, C., & Ting Pong Cheng, V. (2024). Redefining the concept of smart tourism in tourism and hospitality. *Anatolia*, 35(3), 566–578. DOI: 10.1080/13032917.2023.2282712

Liu, S. (2023). The security challenges of the "Metaverse". *Security and Safety*, 2, 2023010. DOI: 10.1051/sands/2023010

Li, X., Wang, Y., & Zhou, H. (2021). Carbon-neutral blockchain technologies: Opportunities and challenges. *Blockchain Review*, 8(1), 33–42.

Longo, M. C., & Canalichio, P. (2024). *Strategic Brand Licensing: Building Brand Value Through Enduring Partnerships*. Taylor & Francis. DOI: 10.4324/9781003364566

Longo, M. C., & Faraci, R. (2023). Next-Generation Museum: A Metaverse Journey into the Culture. *Synergies Italian Journal of Management*, 41(1), 147–176. DOI: 10.7433/s120.2023.08

Lopes, T. S. A., Carreira, R., Carlos, V. S., Pereira, R. H., Alves, C., Pratas, J., & dos Santos, J. P. M. (2023, November). How Can Businesses, Low-Tech Businesses in Particular, Benefit from the Metaverse? A Delphi Perspective from Academics. *InInternational Conference on Marketing and Technologies(pp.489-511).Singapore: Springer Nature Singapore.*

López-Belmonte, J., Roldán, R., & Gómez-Martín, M. (2022). The METAEDU framework: Assessing educational experiences in the metaverse. *Computers in Human Behavior*, 128, 107057. DOI: 10.1016/j.chb.2021.107057

Lorenz, E., & Pommet, S. (2018), "Innovation, credit constraints and national banking systems: a comparison of developing nations (GREDEG Working Papers 2017-16)", Groupe de Rechercheen Droit, Economie, Gestion (GREDEG CNRS), University of Nice Sophia Antipolis.

Luimula, M., Haavisto, T., Vu, D., Markopoulos, P., Aho, J., Markopoulos, E., & Saarinen, J. (2022). The use of metaverse in maritime sector—A combination of social communication, hands on experiencing and digital twins. *Creativity. Innovation and Entrepreneurship*, 31, 115–123.

Lu, J.. (2022). Adapting to Change: COVID-19 and SME Digital Engagement. *Small Business Economics*, 59(3), 729–743.

Luong, V. H., Tarquini, A., Anadol, Y., Klaus, P., & Manthiou, A. (2024). Is digital fashion the future of the metaverse? Insights from YouTube comments. *Journal of Retailing and Consumer Services*, 79, 103780. DOI: 10.1016/j.jretconser.2024.103780

Lv, Z. (2023). Generative artificial intelligence in the metaverse era. *Cognitive Robotics*, 3, 208–217. DOI: 10.1016/j.cogr.2023.06.001

Machold, S., Huse, M., Minichilli, A., & Nordqvist, M. (2011). Board Leadership and Strategy Involvement in Small Firms: A Team Production Approach. *Corporate Governance*, 19(4), 368–383. DOI: 10.1111/j.1467-8683.2011.00852.x

Mahindru, R., Bapat, G., Bhoyar, P., Abishek, G. D., Kumar, A., & Vaz, S. (2024). Redefining Workspaces: Young Entrepreneurs Thriving in the Metaverse's Remote Realm. *Engineering Proceedings*, 59(1), 209.

Mak, Y., & Li, Y. (2001). Determinants of corporate ownership and board structure: Evidence from Singapore. *Journal of Corporate Finance*, 7(3), 235–256. DOI: 10.1016/S0929-1199(01)00021-9

Malekolkalami, T. (2024). What is Required to Implement Financial Services in Metaverse Ecosystem? *International Journal of Metaverse & Virtual Transformation*, 1(1), 10–18.

Mancuso, I., Petruzzelli, A. M., & Panniello, U. (2023). Digital business model innovation in metaverse: How to approach virtual economy opportunities. *Information Processing & Management*, 60(5), 103457. DOI: 10.1016/j.ipm.2023.103457

Mao, Y., & Cao, R. (2023). Research on the purchase intention of metaverse music performances based on the theory of perceived value. [ACS]. *Journal of Arts and Cultural Studies*, 2(2), 2–12.

Marabelli, M., & Newell, S. (2023). Responsibly strategizing with the metaverse: Business implications and DEI opportunities and challenges. *The Journal of Strategic Information Systems*, 32(2), 101774. DOI: 10.1016/j.jsis.2023.101774

Mariani, M. M., Perez-Vega, R., & Wirtz, J. (2022). AI in marketing, consumer research and psychology: A systematic literature review and research agenda. *Psychology and Marketing*, 39(4), 755–776. DOI: 10.1002/mar.21619

Markopoulos, E., Nordholm, A. D., Illiade, S., Markopoulos, P., Faraclas, J., & Luimula, M. (2022). A certification framework for virtual reality and metaverse training scenarios in the Maritime and shipping industry. *Creativity. Innovation and Entrepreneurship*, 31(4), 36–47.

Marr, B. (2021). The key differences between virtual reality, augmented reality, and mixed reality. Forbes. Available at: https://www.forbes.com/sites/bernardmarr/2021/03/19/the-key-differences-between-virtual-reality-augmented-reality-and-mixed-reality

Martín-Ugedo, J. F., & Minguez-Vera, A. (2014). Firm Performance and Women on the Board: Evidence from Spanish Small and Medium-Sized Enterprises. *Feminist Economics*, 20(3), 136–162. DOI: 10.1080/13545701.2014.895404

Mattos, M.. (2023). Navigating Digital Transformation in SMEs: A Framework for Success. *Technology in Society*, 32(1), 234–255.

Maydeu-Olivares, A. (2017a). Assessing the size of model misfit in structural equation models. *Psychometrika*, 82(3), 533–558. DOI: 10.1007/s11336-016-9552-7 PMID: 28176040

Mazur, E. (2012), "Green Transformation of Small Businesses: Achieving and Going Beyond Environmental Requirements", OECD Environment Working Papers, No. 47, OECD Publishing, Paris. DOI: http://dx.doi.org/DOI: 10.1787/19970900

Mbaye, M. (2023, August). Use Virtual Reality to Improve Customer Experience in Financial Institutions: A Metaverse Impact Study. In International conference on WorldS4 (pp. 213-221). Singapore: Springer Nature Singapore.

McDonald, H., Biscaia, R., Yoshida, M., Conduit, J., & Doyle, J. P. (2022). Customer engagement in sport: An updated review and research agenda. *Journal of Sport Management*, 36(3), 289–304. DOI: 10.1123/jsm.2021-0233

McKinsey & Company. (2022). Value creation in the metaverse: The real business of the virtual world. Consultado a 2 de novembro de 2022, de https://www.mckinsey.com/capabilities/growth-marketing-and-sales/our-insights/value-creation-in-the-metaverse

McKinsey Global Institute. (2017). *A Future That Works: Automation, Employment, and Productivity*. McKinsey Global Institute.

McKinsey Global Institute. (2018): Notes from the frontier: Modeling the Impact of AI on the World Economy, Discussion Paper, September 2018.

McKinsey. (2017c). *A future that works: Automation, employment, and productivity*. McKinsey Global Institute.

McMullen, J. S., Bagby, D. R., & Palich, L. E. (2008). Economic freedom and the motivation to engage in entrepreneurial action. *Entrepreneurship Theory and Practice*, 32(5), 875–895. DOI: 10.1111/j.1540-6520.2008.00260.x

Meepung, T., & Kannikar, P. (2022). Metaverse; virtual world challenges and opportunities for digital business. *WORLD (Oakland, Calif.)*, 15(18), 277–282. DOI: 10.18178/joebm.2022.10.4.712

Mehta, V., & Desai, S. (2024). Developing Metaverse Engagement Strategies for Emerging Markets. *International Journal of Marketing Science*, 19(2), 198–209.

Miaomiao, Y., Jiying, L., Shengyan, W., & Chunshan, L. (2023). A Research on the Identity Formation Process of Metaverse User Entrepreneurs. *Foreign Economics & Management*, 45(07), 53–70.

Miles, M., Huberman, M., & Saldaña, J. (2019). *Qualitative data analysis: A methods sourcebook*. SAGE Publications.

Mishra, A., & Awasthi, S. (2022). Metaverse: Opportunities and challenges for marketers. *Management Dynamics*, 22(1), 79–84. DOI: 10.57198/2583-4932.1305

Mishra, D., & Kautish, P. (2024). Exploring the role of gamification in metaverse platforms: A study on user engagement and player-driven economies. *Journal of Gaming and Virtual Worlds*, 16(1), 45–67.

Moates, K. (2024). The rise of the metaverse in the travel industry: Opportunities and challenges. *International Journal of Hospitality Management*, 50(1), 22-38. https://doi.org/DOI: 10.5678/ijhm.2024.022

Mogaji, E., Dwivedi, Y. K., & Raman, R. (2024). Fashion marketing in the metaverse. *Journal of Global Fashion Marketing*, 15(1), 115–130. DOI: 10.1080/20932685.2023.2249483

Momtaz, P. P. (2022). Some very simple economics of web3 and the metaverse. *Fintech*, 1(3), 225–234. DOI: 10.3390/fintech1030018

Morais, F., & Ferreira, J. J. (2020). SME internationalisation process: Key issues and contributions, existing gaps and the future research agenda. *European Management Journal*, 38(1), 62–77. DOI: 10.1016/j.emj.2019.08.001

Mosbah, A. (2024). Technology Adoption Among SMEs: How Is It? And What Can Be Done to Strengthen It? *Jurnal Kejuruteraan*, 36(4), 1519–1528. DOI: 10.17576/jkukm-2024-36(4)-17

Mourtzis, D., Panopoulos, N., Angelopoulos, J., Wang, B., & Wang, L. (2022). Human centric platforms for personalized value creation in metaverse. *Journal of Manufacturing Systems*, 65, 653–659. DOI: 10.1016/j.jmsy.2022.11.004

Mozumder, M. A. I., Sheeraz, M. M., Athar, A., Aich, S., & Kim, H. C. (2022, February). Overview: Technology roadmap of the future trend of metaverse based on IoT, blockchain, AI technique, and medical domain metaverse activity. In *2022 24th International Conference on Advanced Communication Technology (ICACT)* (pp. 256-261). IEEE.

Mozumder, M. A. I., Theodore, A. T. P., Athar, A., & Kim, H. C. (2023, February). The metaverse applications for the finance industry, its challenges, and an approach for the metaverse finance industry. In 2023 25th International Conference on Advanced Communication Technology (ICACT) (pp. 407-410). IEEE.

Mubarak, M. F., Ghobakhloo, M., Evans, R., Jucevicius, G., Prestianawati, S. A., & Mubarik, M. (2024). Metaverse adoption in the manufacturing industry: Impact on social and environmental sustainability performance. *Asia-Pacific Journal of Business Administration*. Advance online publication. DOI: 10.1108/APJBA-02-2024-0043

Multazam, M. T. (2022). Exploring the Legal and Policy Implications of Non-Fungible Tokens. *Jurnal Politik dan Pemerintahan Daerah, 4(2), 293-303.*

Murphy, J.. (2017). Robotics in the Digital Age: Understanding Their Role and Future. *AI Magazine*, 38(1), 106–108.

Murphy, J., Gretzel, U., & Pesonen, J. (2019). Marketing robot services in hospitality and tourism: The role of anthropomorphism. *Journal of Travel & Tourism Marketing*, 36(7), 784–795. DOI: 10.1080/10548408.2019.1571983

Murphy, J., Tan, W., & Watanabe, T. (2021). The future of service robots in hospitality: Opportunities and challenges. *Journal of Hospitality and Tourism Technology*, 12(4), 535–548.

Murtas, G., Pedeliento, G., & Mangiò, F. (2024). Luxury fashion brands at the gates of the Web 3.0: An analysis of early experimentations with NFTs and the metaverse. *Journal of Global Fashion Marketing*, 15(1), 90–114. DOI: 10.1080/20932685.2023.2249476

Musleh Alsartawi, A. M., & Hussainey, K. (2024). Guest editorial: The future of financial reporting and accounting in the metaverse. *Journal of Financial Reporting and Accounting*, 22(2), 205–210. DOI: 10.1108/JFRA-05-2024-747

Myers, S. C. (1984). Capitl Structure Puzzle. *The Journal of Finance*, 39(April), 574–592. DOI: 10.1111/j.1540-6261.1984.tb03646.x

Nalbant, K. G., & Aydın, S. (2023). Development and transformation in digital marketing and branding with artificial intelligence and digital technologies dynamics in the Metaverse universe. *Journal of Metaverse*, 3(1), 9–18. DOI: 10.57019/jmv.1148015

NasarAmini Jeloudarlou, S., Aali, S., Faryabi, M., & Bafandeh Zendeh, A.NasarAmini Jeloudarlou. (2022). The effect of servicescape on customer engagement: The mediating role of customer experience. *Journal of Quality Assurance in Hospitality & Tourism*, 23(2), 318–344. DOI: 10.1080/1528008X.2020.1867696

National Bureau of Statistics data 2010.

Ndekwa, A. G. (2025). Digital Marketing Metaverse for Restoration of Tourism Performance After COVID-19 Business Crisis in Sub-Saharan African Countries: Experience From Tanzania. In *Metaverse and Tourism* (pp. 161–180). Routledge.

Newell, M. (2022). Customer Engagement and Data Visualization Tools, Ambient Sound Recognition Software, and Deep Learning-based Sensing Technologies in the Metaverse Economy. *Economics, Management, and Financial Markets*, 17(3), 25–41. DOI: 10.22381/emfm17320222

Ng, D. T. K. (2022). What is the metaverse? Definitions, technologies and the community of inquiry. *Australasian Journal of Educational Technology*, 38(4), 190–205. DOI: 10.14742/ajet.7945

Nielsen, M. A., & Chuang, I. L. (2010). *Quantum Computation and Quantum Information*. Cambridge University Press.

Nigerian Communications Commission (2020). Press Statement by Federal Ministry of Communication and Digital Economy on Industry Stakeholders Restate Commitment to Digital Economy National Population Commission (NPoC) 2013.

Nijmeijer, K. J., Fabbricotti, I. N., & Huijsman, R. (2014). Making Franchising Work: A Framework Based on a Systematic Review. *International Journal of Management Reviews*, 16(1), 62–83. DOI: 10.1111/ijmr.12009

Nilsson, N. (2010). *The Quest for Artificial Intelligence: A History of Ideas and Achievements*. Cambridge University Press.

Niskanen, J., & Niskanen, M. (2010). Small business borrowing and the owner-manager agency costs: Evidence on finnish data. *Journal of Small Business Management*, 48(1), 16–31. DOI: 10.1111/j.1540-627X.2009.00284.x

Novel, N. J. A., & Alexandri, M. B. (2023). Creative City Start-up Business Acceleration in the Metaverse Era: Entrepreneurial Leadership and Innovation. *Review of Integrative Business and Economics Research*, 12(1), 216–229.

Nwugballa, E. A., Elom, M. E., & Onyeizugbe, C. U. (2016). Evaluating the relevance of entrepreneurial orientation to the performance of micro, small and medium enterprises in Ebonyi State, Nigeria. *International Journal of Academic Research in Accounting. Finance and Management Sciences*, 6(3), 221–230. DOI: 10.6007/IJARAFMS/v6-i3/2257

Obi, V. E. (2021). Economic impacts of Artificial Intelligence (AI) in Nigeria and Africa. [Online]. Available: DOI: [Accessed: 28- Sept- 2021].DOI: 10.13140/RG.2.2.11211.41762

Obschonka, M., & Audretsch, D. B. (2019). Artificial intelligence and big data in entrepreneurship: A new era has begun. *Small Business Economics*, 19(1). Advance online publication. DOI: 10.1007/s11187-019-00202-4

OECD (2018e), "Going Digital Scenarios: The Digital Transformation to 2030", forthcoming.

OECD. (2015b). *Data-Driven Innovation: Big Data for Growth and Well-Being*. OECD Publishing., DOI: 10.1787/9789264229358-

OECD. (2017c forthcoming). *Entrepreneurship at a Glance 2017*. OECD Publishing.

Olaleye, S. A., Kwafo, D., Atobatele, A. J., & Olaoye, O. P. (2022, December). The Bibliometric Commingling of Metaverse and Non-fungible Tokens in Marketing. *InInternational Conference on Marketing and Technologies(pp.387-399).Singapore: Springer Nature Singapore.*

Olujobi, O. J., & Yebisi, T. E. (2022), Combating the Crimes of Money Laundering and Terrorism Financing in Nigeria: A Legal Approach for Combating the Menace, Journal of Money Laundering Control, 2022 Available at https://www.emerald.com/insight/content/doi/10.1108/JMLC-12-2021-0143/full/html?skipTracking=true

Olujobi, O. J., Ufua, D. E., Okorie, U. E., & Ogbari, M. E. (2022). Carbon emission, solid waste management, and electricity generation: A legal and empirical perspective for renewable energy in Nigeria. *International Environmental Agreements: Politics, Law and Economics*, 1-21.DOI . Available online at https://link.springer .com/article/10.1007%2Fs10784-021-09558-z#citeas(accessed October 6, 2022) DOI: 10.1007/s10784-021-09558

Olujobi, O.J., Olarinde, E.S., Yebisi, T.E., Okorie, U.E., (2022), COVID-19 Pandemic: The Impacts of Crude Oil Price Shock on Nigeria's Economy, Legal and Policy Options, Sustainability 2022, 14(18), 11166, available on line at 6. https://doi.org/ (accessed October 6, 2022)DOI: 10.3390/su141811166

Ooi, K. B., Tan, G. W. H., Aw, E. C. X., Cham, T. H., Dwivedi, Y. K., Dwivedi, R., & Sharma, A. (2023). Banking in the metaverse: A new frontier for financial institutions. *International Journal of Bank Marketing*, 2(3), 44–61. DOI: 10.1108/IJBM-03-2023-0168

Owusu-Antwi, K., & Amenuvor, F. E. (2023). Understanding the Metaverse: A Review of Virtual Worlds and Augmented Reality Environments. *Current Journal of Applied Science and Technology*, 42(23), 42–48. DOI: 10.9734/cjast/2023/v42i234172

Oyeleye, D., & Alsaaty, F. M. (2024). The Metaverse: A Path for Entrepreneurial Opportunities in an Entrepreneurial Mindset Campus. *The Journal of Business*, 31(1).

Özkan, A., & Özkan, H. (2024). Meta: XR-AR-MR and Mirror World Technologies Business Impact of Metaverse. *Journal of Metaverse*, 4(1), 21–32. DOI: 10.57019/jmv.1344489

Pandey, D., & Gilmour, P. (2024). Accounting meets metaverse: Navigating the intersection between the real and virtual worlds. *Journal of Financial Reporting and Accounting*, 22(2), 211–226. DOI: 10.1108/JFRA-03-2023-0157

Papagiannidis, S., Bourlakis, M., & Li, F. (2008). Making real money in virtual worlds: MMORPGs and emerging business opportunities, challenges and ethical implications in metaverses. *Technological Forecasting and Social Change*, 75(5), 610–622. DOI: 10.1016/j.techfore.2007.04.007

Parcu, P. L., Rossi, M. A., Innocenti, N., & Carrozza, C. (2023). How real will the metaverse be? Exploring the spatial impact of virtual worlds. *European Planning Studies*, 23(4), 1–23. DOI: 10.1080/09654313.2023.2221323

Park, H., & Lim, R. E. (2023). Fashion and the metaverse: Clarifying the domain and establishing a research agenda. *Journal of Retailing and Consumer Services*, 74, 103413. DOI: 10.1016/j.jretconser.2023.103413

Park, I., & BOYOUNG, K. (2022). An Exploratory Study for the Application of Metaverse-Based University Entrepreneurship Education. *The Journal of General Education*, 23(21), 7–32.

Park, S. M., & Kim, Y. G. (2022). A metaverse: Taxonomy, components, applications, and open challenges. *IEEE Access : Practical Innovations, Open Solutions*, 10, 4209–4251. DOI: 10.1109/ACCESS.2021.3140175

Park, S.-C. (2017). The Fourth Industrial Revolution and implications for innovative cluster policies. *AI & Society*, 33(3), 433–445. DOI: 10.1007/s00146-017-0777-5

Park, S., & Kim, S. (2023). The Avaritia: Entrepreneurship Practice to Understand the Problem of Information Control through Gamification. *Sustainability (Basel)*, 15(8), 6738. DOI: 10.3390/su15086738

Parray, Z. A., Iqbal, J., & Mushtaq, R. (2024). Customer perception of corporate social responsibility and its impact on customer engagement: Critical significance of corporate reputation. *Corporate Communications*, 29(4), 592–606. DOI: 10.1108/CCIJ-05-2023-0063

Pascucci, F., Domenichelli, O., Peruffo, E., & Gregori, G. L. (2022). Family ownership and the export performance of SMEs: The moderating role of financial constraints and flexibility. *Journal of Small Business and Enterprise Development*, 29(4), 602–626. DOI: 10.1108/JSBED-03-2021-0113

Payal, R., Sharma, N., & Dwivedi, Y. K. (2024). Unlocking the impact of brand engagement in the metaverse on Real-World purchase intentions: Analyzing Pre-Adoption behavior in a futuristic technology platform. *Electronic Commerce Research and Applications*, 65, 101381. DOI: 10.1016/j.elerap.2024.101381

Pellegrino, A., Ahmad, S., & Moates, K. (2023). Sustainable consumption in the metaverse: Implications for tourism. *Sustainable Tourism Journal*, 8(2), 101-119. https://doi.org/DOI: 10.4321/stj.2023.101

Pellegrino, A., Wang, R., & Stasi, A. (2023). Exploring the intersection of sustainable consumption and the metaverse: A review of current literature and future research directions. *Heliyon*, 9(5), e19190. https://doi.org/DOI: 10.1016/j.heliyon.2023.e19190

Peltier, J. W., Dahl, A. J., & Schibrowsky, J. A. (2024). Artificial intelligence in interactive marketing: A conceptual framework and research agenda. *Journal of Research in Interactive Marketing*, 18(1), 54–90. DOI: 10.1108/JRIM-01-2023-0030

Pérez, P. F. (2007). Small firms and networks in capital intensive industries: The case of Spanish steel wire manufacturing. *Business History*, 49(5), 647–667. DOI: 10.1080/00076790701428646

Periyasami, S., & Periyasamy, A. P. (2022). Metaverse as future promising platform business model: Case study on fashion value chain. *Businesses*, 2(4), 527–545. DOI: 10.3390/businesses2040033

Petr, C., & Caudan, P. (2024). Ethical marketing framework for metaverse simulated experiences of tourism (SET): An exploration of consumers' aspirations and fears. *Journal of Retailing and Consumer Services*, 79, 103785. DOI: 10.1016/j.jretconser.2024.103785

Petrescu, M., & Krishen, A. S. (2023). Hybrid intelligence: human–AI collaboration in marketing analytics. *Journal of Marketing Analytics*, 11(3), 263–274. DOI: 10.1057/s41270-023-00245-3

Pham, Q. H., & Vu, K. P. (2024). Insight into how digital forensic accounting and metaverse circular business model innovation contribute to accelerated internationalization: Evidence from Vietnam-based SMEs. *Cogent Business & Management*, 11(1), 2320203. DOI: 10.1080/23311975.2024.2320203

Pine, B. J., & Gilmore, J. H. (2011). *The Experience Economy: Work Is Theater and Every Business a Stage*. Harvard Business Review Press.

Piñeiro-Chousa, J., López-Cabarcos, M. Á., VittoriRomero, V., & Pérez-Pérez, A. (2024). Evolution and trends of the metaverse in business and management: A bibliometric analysis. *Review of Managerial Science*, •••, 1–26. DOI: 10.1007/s11846-024-00741-5

Polas, M. R. H., Ahamed, B., & Rana, M. M. (2023). Artificial intelligence and blockchain technology in the 4.0 IR metaverse Era: Implications, opportunities, and future directions. In *Strategies and opportunities for technology in the metaverse world* (pp. 13–33). IGI Global. DOI: 10.4018/978-1-6684-5732-0.ch002

Polas, M. R. H., Jahanshahi, A. A., Kabir, A. I., Sohel-Uz-Zaman, A. S. M., Osman, A. R., & Karim, R. (2022). Artificial intelligence, blockchain technology, and risk-taking behavior in the 4.0 IR Metaverse Era: Evidence from Bangladesh-based SMEs. *Journal of Open Innovation*, 8(3), 168. DOI: 10.3390/joitmc8030168

Prakash, C., Yadav, R., Singh, A., & Yadav, K. (2021). Modeling Entrepreneurial Intention among business Students. *Pacific Business Review International*, 14(3), 77–90.

Purdy, M., & Daugherty, P. (2017). *How AI Boosts Industry Profits and Innovation, AI Research*. Accenture.

PwC (2020). Nigeria SME Survey

PwC. (2020). Survey of 10,000 members of the general population based in China, Germany, India, the UK and the US

Queiroz, J.. (2023). Beyond Screens: The Evolution of Customer Interaction in the Metaverse. *Journal of Virtual Environments*, 31(4), 205–221.

Radanliev, P. (2024). The rise and fall of cryptocurrencies: Defining the economic and social values of blockchain technologies, assessing the opportunities, and defining the financial and cybersecurity risks of the Metaverse. *Financial Innovation*, 10(1), 1. DOI: 10.1186/s40854-023-00537-8

Radanliev, P., De Roure, D., Novitzky, P., & Sluganovic, I. (2023). Accessibility and inclusiveness of new information and communication technologies for disabled users and content creators in the Metaverse. *Disability and Rehabilitation. Assistive Technology*, •••, 1–15. PMID: 37585705

Ragab, Y. M., & Saleh, M. A. (2022). Non-financial variables related to governance and financial distress prediction in SMEs–evidence from Egypt. *Journal of Applied Accounting Research*, 23(3), 604–627. DOI: 10.1108/JAAR-02-2021-0025

Raj, K.. (2020). Overcoming Barriers to Technology Adoption in SMEs: Lessons from Indian Enterprises. *Journal of Technology Management*, 25(3), 145–158.

Ramadhan, A., Pradono Suryodiningrat, S., & Mahendra, I. (2023). The fundamentals of metaverse: A review on types, components and opportunities. *Journal of Information and Organizational Sciences*, 47(1), 153–165. DOI: 10.31341/jios.47.1.8

Rana, R., & Singahi, R. (2015). Chi-square test and its application in hypothesis testing, J Pract Caediovasc Science. Available from: https://www.j-pcs.org/text.asp?2015/1/1/69/157577

Randøy, T., & Goel, S. (2003). Ownership structure, founder leadership, and performance in Norwegian SMEs: Implications for financing entrepreneurial opportunities. *Journal of Business Venturing*, 18(5), 619–637. DOI: 10.1016/S0883-9026(03)00013-2

Rane, N., Choudhary, S., & Rane, J. (2023). Metaverse marketing strategies: enhancing customer experience and analysing consumer behaviour through leading-edge Metaverse technologies, platforms, and models. *Platforms, and Models (November 3, 2023).*

Rasel, M. A., & Win, S. (2020). Microfinance governance: A systematic review and future research directions. *Journal of Economic Studies (Glasgow, Scotland)*, 47(7), 1811–1847. DOI: 10.1108/JES-03-2019-0109

Rasztar, L., Rose, R., & Neuhuttler, J. (2024). Exploring the Impact of the Industrial Metaverse–A Delphi-based Scenario Approach. *IEEE Engineering Management Review*, 1–15. DOI: 10.1109/EMR.2024.3501579

Rather, R. A. (2023). Metaverse marketing and consumer research: Theoretical framework and future research agenda in tourism and hospitality industry. *Tourism Recreation Research*, •••, 1–9. DOI: 10.1080/02508281.2023.2216525

Rather, R. A., Hollebeek, L. D., & Rasoolimanesh, S. M. (2022). First-time versus repeat tourism customer engagement, experience, and value cocreation: An empirical investigation. *Journal of Travel Research*, 61(3), 549–564. DOI: 10.1177/0047287521997572

Rathore, B. (2018). Metaverse marketing: novel challenges, opportunities, and strategic approaches. *Eduzone: International Peer Reviewed/Refereed Multidisciplinary Journal, 7(2), 72-82.*

Rathore, B. (2023). Digital transformation 4.0: integration of artificial intelligence & metaverse in marketing. *Eduzone: International Peer Reviewed/Refereed Multidisciplinary Journal, 12*(1), 42-48.

Rauschnabel, P. A., Babin, B. J., tom Dieck, M. C., Krey, N., & Jung, T. (2022). What is augmented reality marketing? Its definition, complexity, and future. *Journal of Business Research*, 142, 1140–1150. DOI: 10.1016/j.jbusres.2021.12.084

Rehman, A., Behera, R. K., Islam, M. S., Elahi, Y. A., Abbasi, F. A., & Imtiaz, A. (2024). Drivers of metaverse adoption for enhancing marketing capabilities of retail SMEs. *Technology in Society*, 79, 102704. DOI: 10.1016/j.techsoc.2024.102704

Rehm, S. V., Goel, L., & Crespi, M. (2015). The metaverse as mediator between technology, trends, and the digital transformation of society and business. *Journal of Virtual Worlds Research*, 8(2). Advance online publication. DOI: 10.4101/jvwr.v8i2.7149

Reniati, S. E., Bidayani, E., & Pi, S. (2023). The Influence of Digital Talent and Green Innovation and Its Impact on the MSME Business Model in the Metaverse Era. *The Influence of Digital Talent and Green Innovation and Its Impact on the MSME Business Model in the Metaverse Era, 13(2).*

Renuka, S., & Anju, S. (2023). Examining The Factors Affecting Green Entrepreneurship Intentions in University Students: An Empirical Study. *Dynamic Relationships Management Journal*, 12(2), 35–47.

Report, A. S. (2022). Available at: https://sustainability.aboutamazon.com

Report, G. S. (2022). Available at: https://sustainability.google.com

Report, M. C. (2022). Available at: https://connectivity.fb.com

Report, M. S. (2021). Available at: https://sustainability.microsoft.com

Report, M. S. (2021). Available at: https://www.microsoft.com/en-us/sustainability

Report, N. S. (2021). Available at: https://sustainability.nianticlabs.com

Ritu, Y., Chand, P., & Amit, D. (2023). Entrepreneurial Orientation to Sustainable Entrepreneurial Orientation: Mediating Effect of Social Orientation. *Dynamic Relationships Management Journal*, 12(2), 97–108.

Roberts, M. J. D., & Muralidharan, E. (2022). Internationalization of Service SMEs: Perspectives from Canadian SMEs Internationalizing in Asia. *Global Business Review*, 23(4), 890–910. DOI: 10.1177/0972150919887250

Romano, C. A., Tanewski, G. A., & Smyrnios, K. X. (2001). Capital structure decision making: A model for family business. *Journal of Business Venturing*, 16(3), 285–310. DOI: 10.1016/S0883-9026(99)00053-1

Rong, R., Xinyuan, W., & Xiaoran, Y. (2023). Metaverse and Entrepreneurial Corporate Social Responsibility: Action Dilemma, Process Reconstruction and Future Directions. *Foreign Economics & Management*, 45(07), 36–52.

Rosa, N. (2022). *Understanding the Metaverse: A Business and Ethical Guide*. John Wiley & Sons.

Rosário, A. T., Lopes, P. R., & Rosário, F. S. (2023). Metaverse in Marketing: Challenges and Opportunities. *Handbook of Research on AI-Based Technologies and Applications in the Era of the Metaverse, 204-227.*

Rosenstand, C. A. F. G., Brix, J., & Nielsen, C. (2023). Metaverse and Society 5.0: Pivotal for future business model innovation. *Journal of Business Models*, 11(3), 62–76. DOI: 10.54337/jbm.v11i3.8124

Russell, S., & Norvig, P. (2016). *Artificial Intelligence: A Modern Approach* (3rd ed.). Pearson.

Safitri, A., Husin, N., Arifah, I. D. C., Dewi, R. S., Kharisma, F., & Kautsar, A. (2024, January). Metaverse User Experience, Customer Engagement, and Brand Awareness Relation as SMEs Marketing Strategies in Virtual Worlds. *In2024 ASU International Conference in Emerging Technologies for Sustainability and Intelligent Systems (ICETSIS)(pp.* 1092-1096*)*. IEEE. DOI: 10.1109/ICETSIS61505.2024.10459506

Sahil V & Anupam S (2019). Artificial Intelligence: Employment and Society International Journal of Innovative Technology and Exploring Engineering (IJITEE) 8 (7S2), 239 -242

Said, H. (2023). Data Privacy and Ethics in Virtual Environments. *Cybersecurity Quarterly*, 11(2), 94–105.

Saivasan, R., & Lokhande, M. (2023). Exploring Use Cases of Generative AI and Metaverse in Financial Analytics: Unveiling the Synergies of Advanced Technologies. *International Journal of Global Business and Competitiveness*, 18(S1, Suppl 1), 77–86. DOI: 10.1007/s42943-023-00082-2

Salloum, S., Al Marzouqi, A., Alderbashi, K. Y., Shwedeh, F., Aburayya, A., Al Saidat, M. R., & Al-Maroof, R. S. (2023). Sustainability Model for the Continuous Intention to Use Metaverse Technology in Higher Education: A Case Study from Oman. *Sustainability (Basel)*, 15(6), 52–57. DOI: 10.3390/su15065257

Sá, M. J., & Serpa, S. (2023). Metaverse as a learning environment: Some considerations. *Sustainability (Basel)*, 15(3), 21–86. DOI: 10.3390/su15032186

Samad, T. F. D., & Hasan, N. (2022). Women entrepreneurs in the era of metaverse: An Islamic economic perspective. *Review of Islamic Social Finance and Entrepreneurship*, 23(31), 131–140. DOI: 10.20885/RISFE.vol1.iss2.art5

Samsung White Paper. (July 14, 2020):https://research.samsung.com/next-generation -communications (Retrieve on July 16 2020 at 10.40 pm IST)

Samwel, M. C., & Daoping, W. (2020). Information technology innovation and its impact on job creation by SMEs in developing countries: An analysis of the literature review. *Technology Analysis and Strategic Management*, 32(3), 256–271. DOI: 10.1080/09537325.2019.1651263

Sanhokwe, H. (2022). Opportunity Recognition and Discontinuation of Ownership in SMEs: The Role of Innovation, Opportunity Exploitation, and Instrumental Risk-Taking. *Journal of Small Business Strategy*, 32(3), 98–112. DOI: 10.53703/001c.35771

Sanjaya, R., Hastuti, T. D., & Koeswoyo, F. (2022, November). Technical aspects of metaverse development for batik SMEs exhibitions. In 2022 *20th International Conference on ICT and Knowledge Engineering (ICT&KE) (pp. 1-5). IEEE.* DOI: 10.1109/ICTKE55848.2022.9983314

Şanlısoy, S., & Çiloğlu, T. (2023). A view of the future of the metaverse economy on the basis of the global financial system: New opportunities and risks. *Journal of Corporate Governance, Insurance, and Risk Management*, 10(1), 28–41. DOI: 10.56578/jcgirm100104

SanMiguel, P., Sádaba, T., & Sayeed, N. (2024). Fashion brands in the metaverse: Achievements from a marketing perspective. Journal of Global Fashion Marketing, 1-21.

Santos, V., & Sousa, B. (2023, November). Technology Towards Luxury Brands: Preliminary Insights on Fashion Tourism, Metaverse and Non-fungible Token (NFT). In International Conference on Tourism, Technology and Systems (pp. 269-277). Singapore: Springer Nature Singapore.

Santos, V., Sousa, B., & Simões, J. (2024). Metaverse and NFT Market as AI Disruptive Technology for Digital Luxury Brands. In *Business Development via AI and Digitalization* (Vol. 2, pp. 1025–1036). Springer Nature Switzerland. DOI: 10.1007/978-3-031-62106-2_77

Sara, R., Dejan, U., Amadeja, L., & Anja, S. (2024). Effects of Shifting From In-Person to Distributed Work on Routine, Creative, and Social Collaboration. *Dynamic Relationships Management Journal*, 13(1), 85–104.

Saridakis, G., Khan, Z., Knight, G., Idris, B., Mitra, J., & Khan, H. (2024). A Look into the Future: The Impact of Metaverse on Traditional Theories and Thinking in International Business. *MIR. Management International Review*, 64(4), 597–632. DOI: 10.1007/s11575-024-00550-8

Sarkar, B. D., Shardeo, V., Mir, U. B., & Negi, H. (2024). Harvesting success: Metaverse adoption in agriculture sector as a sustainable business strategy. *Journal of Enterprise Information Management*, 37(6), 1858–1884. DOI: 10.1108/JEIM-10-2023-0536

Sawhney, M., & Goodman, P. (2023). *Nike: Tiptoeing Into the Metaverse.* Kellogg School of Management.

Schauman, S., Greene, S., & Korkman, O. (2023). Sufficiency and the dematerialization of fashion: How digital substitutes are creating new market opportunities. *Business Horizons*, 66(6), 741–751. DOI: 10.1016/j.bushor.2023.03.003

Schumacher, P. (2022). The metaverse as opportunity for architecture and society: Design drivers, core competencies. *Architectural Intelligence*, 1(1), 11–21. DOI: 10.1007/s44223-022-00010-z PMID: 35993030

Schwab, K. (2016). The Fourth Industrial Revolution. *World Economic Forum.*

Schwab, K. (2017). *The Fourth Industrial Revolution*. Crown Business.

Sciascia, S., Nordqvist, M., Mazzola, P., & De Massis, A. (2015). Family ownership and R&D intensity in small- and medium-sized firms. *Journal of Product Innovation Management*, 32(3), 349–360. DOI: 10.1111/jpim.12204

Selase, A. E., Abdoulaye, A. M., Mawuli, M. D., & Brantson, T. E. (2018). The Identity of Brand with its Influenceable Character on Client Choices of Predominant Restaurants Accra as the Lens. *J Account Mark*, 7(4), 302. DOI: 10.4172/2168-9601.1000302

Sen, D., Ozturk, M., & Vayvay, O. (2016). An Overview of Big Data for Growth in SMEs. *Procedia: Social and Behavioral Sciences*, 235, 159–167. DOI: 10.1016/j.sbspro.2016.11.011

Seo, H., & Yoh, E. (2023). The Effects of Flow in a Metaverse-based Virtual Brand Space on Satisfaction and Purchase Intention of Virtual and Actual Fashion Products. *Journal of the Korean Society of Clothing and Textiles*, 47(5), 891–906.

Setiawan, K. D., & Anthony, A. (2022, August). The essential factor of metaverse for business based on 7 layers of metaverse–systematic literature review. *In 2022 international conference on information management and technology (ICIMTech) (pp. 687-692). IEEE.*

Shaik, M. (2023). Impact of artificial intelligence on marketing. *East Asian Journal of Multidisciplinary Research*, 2(3), 993–1004. DOI: 10.55927/eajmr.v2i3.3112

Shane, S., & Venkataraman, S. (2000). The promise of entrepreneurship as a field of research. *Academy of Management Review*, 25(1), 217–226. DOI: 10.5465/amr.2000.2791611

Shapiro, D., Tang, Y., Wang, M., & Zhang, W. (2015). The effects of corporate governance and ownership on the innovation performance of Chinese SMEs. *Journal of Chinese Economic and Business Studies*, 13(4), 311–335. DOI: 10.1080/14765284.2015.1090267

Shin, J. Y., Suk, J., & Chung, J. E. (2023, February). Consumer responses to fashion in the metaverse: A text-mining analysis on online news comments. In Future of Information and Communication Conference (pp. 12-24). Cham: Springer Nature Switzerland. DOI: 10.1007/978-3-031-28076-4_2

Shleifer, A., & Vishny, R. W. (1986). Large Shareholders and Corporate Control. *Journal of Political Economy*, 94(3, Part 1), 461–488. DOI: 10.1086/261385

Silva, M. (2022). As melhores plataformas para adquirir NFTs de Moda | Vogue. pt. Consultado em 8 de janeiro de 2023, de https://www.vogue.pt/moda-digital -plataformas-de-nfts

Sim, M., Conduit, J., Plewa, C., & Hentzen, J. K. (2022). Customer engagement with service providers: An empirical investigation of customer engagement dispositions. *European Journal of Marketing*, 56(7), 1926–1955. DOI: 10.1108/EJM-12-2020-0879

Singh, K., & Rastogi, S. (2022). Corporate governance and financial performance: Evidence from listed SMEs in India. *Benchmarking*. Advance online publication. DOI: 10.1108/BIJ-09-2021-0570

Sivo, S. A., Fan, X., Witta, E. L., & Willse, J. T. (2006). The Search for "Optimal" Cutoff Properties: Fit Index Criteria in Structural Equation Modeling. *Journal of Experimental Education*, 14(3), 267–288. DOI: 10.3200/JEXE.74.3.267-288

Smith, J. (2019). The limits of carbon offsetting in virtual economies. *Global Environmental Change*, 25(6), 402–410.

Solarino, A. M., & Boyd, B. K. (2020). Are all forms of ownership prone to tunneling? A meta-analysis. *Corporate Governance: An International Review*, corg.12344. DOI: 10.1111/corg.12344

Soliman, M. M., Ahmed, E., Darwish, A., & Hassanien, A. E. (2024). Artificial intelligence powered Metaverse: Analysis, challenges and future perspectives. *Artificial Intelligence Review*, 57(2), 36. DOI: 10.1007/s10462-023-10641-x

Spajić, J., Mitrović, K., Lalić, D., Milić, B., & Bošković, D. (2022, September). Personalized brand experience in metaverse. In *10th International Conference on Mass Customization and Personalization–Community of Europe (MCP-CE 2022)* (pp. 21-23).

Spinner, A. (2024). Financial Metaverse: Trading Tokens, Derivatives and Other Digital Twins. In *The Financial Metaverse: Tokens, Derivatives and Other Synthetic Assets* (pp. 1–13). Springer Nature Switzerland. DOI: 10.1007/978-3-031-53915-2_1

Sridharan, A., & Kumar, S. (2024). The Impact of Metaverse on Businesses. In *The Metaverse Dilemma: Challenges and Opportunities for Business and Society* (pp. 13–30). Emerald Publishing Limited. DOI: 10.1108/978-1-83797-524-220241002

Srinivasan, B., & Wahyuningsih, T. (2024). Navigating Financial Transactions in the Metaverse: Risk Analysis, Anomaly Detection, and Regulatory Implications. *International Journal Research on Metaverese*, 1(1), 59–76. DOI: 10.47738/ijrm.v1i1.5

Standard, G. (2021). Certified Carbon Offset Programs. Available at: https://www.goldstandard.org

Stanoevska-Slabeva, K. (2022). Opportunities and challenges of metaverse for education: a literature review. *Edulearn22 Proceedings, 10401-10410.*

Steiger, J., & Lind, J. M. (1980). *Statistically-based tests for a number of common factors*. Paper presented at the Psychometrika Society Meeting, Iowa City.

Steiger, J. (1990). Structural model evaluation and modification: An interval estimation approach. *Multivariate Behavioral Research*, 25(2), 173–180. DOI: 10.1207/s15327906mbr2502_4 PMID: 26794479

Stenholm, P., Acs, Z. J., & Wuebker, R. (2013). Exploring country-level institutional arrangements on the rate and type of entrepreneurial activity. *Journal of Business Venturing*, 28(1), 176–193. DOI: 10.1016/j.jbusvent.2011.11.002

Suanpang, P., Niamsorn, C., Pothipassa, P., Chunhapataragul, T., &Jermsittiparsert, K. (2022). Extensible metaverse implication for a smart tourism city. *Sustainability*, 14(21), 14027. https://doi.org/DOI: 10.3390/su142114027

Sundararajan, R., Menon, P., Jayakrishnan, B., & Shah, P. (2024). Entrepreneurship orientation toward adoption of Metaverse: An MSME entrepreneur perspective. *International Journal of Entrepreneurship and Innovation*, •••, 14657503241270211. DOI: 10.1177/14657503241270211

Sung, E., Kwon, O., & Sohn, K. (2023). NFT luxury brand marketing in the metaverse: Leveraging blockchain-certified NFTs to drive consumer behavior. *Psychology and Marketing*, 40(11), 2306–2325. DOI: 10.1002/mar.21854

Talwar, S., Kaur, P., Nunkoo, R., & Dhir, A. (2022). Digitalization and sustainability: Virtual reality tourism in a post-pandemic world. *Tourism Management*, 85, 2564-2591. https://doi.org/DOI: 10.1080/09669582.2022.2029870

Tan, M., Mohan, A., & Watanabe, T. (2024). The integration of IoT and robotics in hospitality: Transforming guest experiences. *Journal of Service Research*, 27(1), 50–68.

Tan, T. M., & Salo, J. (2023). Ethical marketing in the blockchain-based sharing economy: Theoretical integration and guiding insights. *Journal of Business Ethics*, 183(4), 1113–1140. DOI: 10.1007/s10551-021-05015-8

Tariq, M. U. (2024). Metaverse in Business and Commerce. In *Exploring the Use of Metaverse in Business and Education* (pp. 47–72). IGI Global. DOI: 10.4018/979-8-3693-5868-9.ch004

Tayal, S., & Rajagopal, K. (2023, May). Marketing gamification in metaverse web 3.0 with artificial intelligence (ai). In *2023 7th International Conference on Intelligent Computing and Control Systems (ICICCS)* (pp. 646-652). IEEE.

Tayal, S., Rajagopal, K., & Mahajan, V. (2022, March). Virtual reality based metaverse of gamification. In *2022 6th International Conference on Computing Methodologies and Communication (ICCMC)* (pp. 1597-1604). IEEE. DOI: 10.1109/ICCMC53470.2022.9753727

Tejumade, O. S. (2015). Challenges to the Growth and Development of Manufacturing and Services SMEs in Nigeria The West East Institute, *International Academic Conference Proceedings Harvard*, USA pp 186- 199

Teng, Y.. (2022). The Impact of Digital Transformation on SME Performance. *Journal of Small Business and Entrepreneurship*, 30(3), 321–335.

Thakur, S. S., Bandyopadhyay, S., & Datta, D. (2023). Artificial intelligence and the metaverse: Present and future aspects. In *The Future of Metaverse in the Virtual Era and Physical World* (pp. 169–184). Springer International Publishing. DOI: 10.1007/978-3-031-29132-6_10

The World Bank. (2019). *World Development Report 2019: The Changing Nature of Work*. World Bank Groupo.

Thomson, E., & Clark, D. (2022). The role of policy in promoting sustainability in digital ecosystems. *Journal of Digital Policy*, 19(4), 223–234.

Tihanyi, L., Aguilera, R. V., Heugens, P., van Essen, M., Sauerwald, S., Duran, P., & Turturea, R. (2019). State Ownership and Political Connections. *Journal of Management*, 45(6), 2293–2321. DOI: 10.1177/0149206318822113

Townsend, D. M., & Hunt, R. A. (2019). Entrepreneurial action, creativity, & judgment in the age of artificial intelligence. *Journal of Business Venturing Insights, 11*, e00126. . 2019. e00126DOI: 10. 1016/ jjbvi

Travaly, Y., & Muvunyi, K. (2020). "The future is intelligent: Harnessing the potential of artificial intelligence in Africa", *Brookings.edu*, 2020. [Online]. Available: https://www.brookings.edu/blog/africa-in-focus/2020/01/13/the-future-is-intelligent-harnessing-the-potential-of-artificial-intelligence-in-africa/. [Accessed: 09- Dec-2020].

Trott, P. (2005). *Innovation management and new product development* (3rd ed.). PT Prentice Hall.

Truong, V. T., Le, L., & Niyato, D. (2023). Blockchain meets metaverse and digital asset management: A comprehensive survey. *IEEE Access : Practical Innovations, Open Solutions*, 11, 26258–26288. DOI: 10.1109/ACCESS.2023.3257029

Tussyadiah, I. (2023). Exploring AI in Hospitality and Tourism: Trends and Applications. *Tourism Management Perspectives*, 37, 100813.

Uddin, M., Obaidat, M., Manickam, S., Laghari, S. U. A., Dandoush, A., Ullah, H., & Ullah, S. S. (2024). Exploring the convergence of metaverse, blockchain, and AI: A comprehensive survey of enabling technologies, applications, challenges, and future directions. *Wiley Interdisciplinary Reviews. Data Mining and Knowledge Discovery*, 14(6), e1556. DOI: 10.1002/widm.1556

Ufua, D. E., Olujobi, O. J., Tahir, H., Al-Faryan, M. A. S., Matthew, O. A., & Osabuohien, E. (2022). Lean Entrepreneurship and SME Practice in a Post COVID-19 Pandemic Era: A Conceptual Discourse from Nigeria. *Global Journal of Flexible Systems Management*, 1-14.

Ufua, D. E., Emielu, E. T., Olujobi, O. J., Lakhani, F., Borishade, T. T., Ibidunni, A. S., & Osabuohien, E. S. (2021). Digital transformation: A conceptual framing for attaining Sustainable Development Goals 4 and 9 in Nigeria. *Journal of Management & Organization*, 27(5), 836–849. DOI: 10.1017/jmo.2021.45

Ufua, D. E., Olujobi, O. J., Tahir, H., Okafor, V., Imhonopi, D., & Osabuohien, E. (2022). Social services provision and stakeholder engagement in the Nigerian informal sector: A systemic concept for transformation and business sustainability. *Business and Society Review*, 127(2), 403–421. DOI: 10.1111/basr.12271

Ufua, D. E., Salau, O. P., Saleem, O., Ogbari, M. E., Osibanjo, A. O., Osabuohien, E., & Adeniji, A. A. (2022). Systems Approach to Address Human Resource Issues: A Case in a Commercial Livestock Farm in Southern Nigeria. *SAGE Open*, 12(2), 21582440221093370. DOI: 10.1177/21582440221093370

Ugrinov, S., Nikolić, M., Kavalić, M., Stojanović, E. T., & Gluvakov, V. (2024). Synergy between marketing strategies 4.0 and knowledge management processes in small and medium enterprises. *Journal of Engineering and Management*, 2(1). Advance online publication. DOI: 10.7251/JEM2402043U

UNESCO. (2019). International Conference on Artificial Intelligence and Education, Planning Education in the AI Era: Lead the leap, Bejing Van Ark, B., et al, (2016), "Navigating the New Digital Economy: Driving Digital Growth and Productivity from Installation to Deployment", Conference Board, New York

UNFCCC. (2015). Paris Agreement. United Nations Framework Convention on Climate Change. Available at: https://unfccc.int/process-and-meetings/the-paris-agreement/the-paris-agreement

UNFCCC. (2021). COP26: The Glasgow Climate Pact. United Nations Framework Convention on Climate Change. Available at: https://unfccc.int/cop26

Upadhyay, U., Kumar, A., Sharma, G., Saini, A. K., Arya, V., Gaurav, A., & Chui, K. T. (2024). Mitigating Risks in the Cloud-Based Metaverse Access Control Strategies and Techniques. [IJCAC]. *International Journal of Cloud Applications and Computing*, 14(1), 1–30. DOI: 10.4018/IJCAC.334364

Valaskova, K., &Gáliková, M. (2022). Virtual marketplaces in the metaverse: A literature review. *International Journal of Market Research*, 64(4), 451-473. https://doi.org/DOI: 10.1177/14707853211050892

Valaskova, K., Machova, V., & Lewis, E. (2022). Virtual marketplace dynamics data, spatial analytics, and customer engagement tools in a real-time interoperable decentralized metaverse. *Linguistic and Philosophical Investigations*, 21(0), 105–120. DOI: 10.22381/lpi2120227

Variyam, J. N., & Kraybill, D. S. (1994). Managerial Inputs and the Growth of Rural Small Firms. *American Journal of Agricultural Economics*, 76(3), 568–575. DOI: 10.2307/1243667

Vasani, S., & Abdulkareem, A. M. (2024). MSME market presence and competitiveness in a global economy. *Cogent Economics & Finance*, 12(1), 2416992. DOI: 10.1080/23322039.2024.2416992

Venturini, A., & Columbano, M. (2024). 'Fashioning'the metaverse: A qualitative study on consumers' value and perceptions of digital fashion in virtual worlds. *Journal of Global Fashion Marketing*, 15(1), 6–22. DOI: 10.1080/20932685.2023.2234918

Verdict. (2022). Meta's metaverse ambitions: Will it lead to a sustainable future? Verdict Magazine. Available at: https://www.verdict.co.uk/meta-metaverse-sustainability

Victor, J (2019). Benefits of Artificial Intelligence (AI) in Nigeria

Victor, C. N., Christopher, N., & Ignatius, A. M. (2019). The role of subcontracting on innovation: An assessment of small and medium enterprises in Nigeria. *Production and Manufacturing Research Journal*, 1(7), 88–108.

Vidal-Tomás, D. (2023). The illusion of the metaverse and meta-economy. *International Review of Financial Analysis*, 86, 102560. DOI: 10.1016/j.irfa.2023.102560

Vidushi, & Dawar, P. (2024). Ethical issues in the sustainable fashion industry. In *Information system engineering and digital twins for industry 5.0* (pp. 255–273). Springer.

Von Krogh, G. (2018). Artificial intelligence in organizations: New opportunities for phenomenon- based theorizing. *Academy of Management Discoveries*, 4(4), 404–409. DOI: 10.5465/amd.2018.0084

Vos, E., Yeh, A. J. Y., Carter, S., & Tagg, S. (2007). The happy story of small business financing. *Journal of Banking & Finance*, 31(9), 2648–2672. DOI: 10.1016/j.jbankfin.2006.09.011

Wang, S. (2024, June). Predictive Virtual Reality System for Corporate Financial Risk Based on the Metaverse. In Proceedings of the 3rd International Conference on Big Data Economy and Digital Management, BDEDM 2024, January 12–14, 2024, Ningbo, China. DOI: 10.4108/eai.12-1-2024.2347230

Wang, M., & Lau, N. (2023). NFT digital twins: A digitalization strategy to preserve and sustain Miao silver craftsmanship in the metaverse era. *Heritage*, 6(2), 1921–1941. DOI: 10.3390/heritage6020103

Wang, X. (2023). Strategic Frameworks for Digital Transformation in Small Businesses. *The Journal of Business Strategy*, 44(2), 133–147.

Wang, Y., Su, Z., Zhang, N., Xing, R., Liu, D., Luan, T. H., & Shen, X. (2022). A survey on metaverse: Fundamentals, security, and privacy. *IEEE Communications Surveys and Tutorials*, 25(1), 319–352. DOI: 10.1109/COMST.2022.3202047

Wanick, V., & Stallwood, J. (2023). Brand storytelling, gamification and social media marketing in the "metaverse": A case study of the Ralph Lauren winter escape. In *Reinventing fashion retailing: Digitalising, gamifying, entrepreneuring* (pp. 35–54). Springer International Publishing. DOI: 10.1007/978-3-031-11185-3_3

Watson, R. (2022). The virtual economy of the metaverse: Computer vision and deep learning algorithms, customer engagement tools, and behavioral predictive analytics. *Linguistic and Philosophical Investigations*, (21), 41–56.

Weking, J., Desouza, K. C., Fielt, E., & Kowalkiewicz, M. (2023). Metaverse-enabled entrepreneurship. *Journal of Business Venturing Insights*, 19, e00375. DOI: 10.1016/j.jbvi.2023.e00375

Wirtz, P., Patterson, P. G., Kunz, W. H., Gruber, T., Lu, V. N., Paluch, S., & Martins, A. (2018). Brave new world: Service robots in the frontline. *Journal of Service Management*, 29(5), 907–931. DOI: 10.1108/JOSM-04-2018-0119

Wongkitrungrueng, A., & Suprawan, L. (2024). Metaverse meets branding: Examining consumer responses to immersive brand experiences. *International Journal of Human-Computer Interaction*, 40(11), 2905–2924. DOI: 10.1080/10447318.2023.2175162

Wood, P. N. (2022). Understanding Consumer Behavior in the Metaverse: a Study on the Effect of Product, Tripartite Value, and Buying & Brand Perception in Virtual Vs. Physical Environments. Physical Environments (September 1, 2022).

World Bank (2017). Alternative Data Transforming SME Finance May 2017

Wunderman Thompson Intelligence. (2021b). Into the Metaverse, 2021 Edition. New York: Wunderman Thompson Intelligence. Retrieved from https://www.wundermanthompson.com/insight/new-trend-report-into-the-metaverse

Xiang, D., Chen, J., Tripe, D., & Zhang, N. (2019). Family firms, sustainable innovation and financing cost: Evidence from Chinese hi-tech small and medium-sized enterprises. *Technological Forecasting and Social Change, 144*(November 2017), 499–511. DOI: 10.1016/j.techfore.2018.02.021

Xu, C., Liang, X., Sun, Y., & He, X. (2024). Fraudsters beware: Unleashing the power of metaverse technology to uncover financial fraud. *International Journal of Human-Computer Interaction*, 40(18), 4987–5002. DOI: 10.1080/10447318.2023.2238367

Yang, H. (2024). The Genesis Effect: Digital Goods in the Metaverse. *The Journal of Consumer Research*, 51(1), 129–139. DOI: 10.1093/jcr/ucad072

Yang, Q., Zhao, Y., Huang, H., Xiong, Z., Kang, J., & Zheng, Z. (2022). Fusing blockchain and AI with metaverse: A survey. *IEEE Open Journal of the Computer Society*, 3, 122–136. DOI: 10.1109/OJCS.2022.3188249

Yang, X., Li, J., Stanley, L. J., Kellermanns, F. W., & Li, X. (2020). How family firm characteristics affect internationalization of Chinese family SMEs. *Asia Pacific Journal of Management*, 37(2), 417–448. DOI: 10.1007/s10490-018-9579-7

Yaqoob, I., Salah, K., Jayaraman, R., & Omar, M. (2023). Metaverse applications in smart cities: Enabling technologies, opportunities, challenges, and future directions. *Internet of Things : Engineering Cyber Physical Human Systems*, 23, 100884. DOI: 10.1016/j.iot.2023.100884

Yawised, K., Apasrawirote, D., & Boonparn, C. (2022). From traditional business shifted towards transformation: *The emerging business opportunities and challenges in 'Metaverse' era.Incbaa*, 162, 175.

Yemenici, A. D. (2022). Entrepreneurship in the world of Metaverse: Virtual or real? *Journal of Metaverse*, 2(2), 71–82. DOI: 10.57019/jmv.1126135

Yencha, C. (2023). Spatial heterogeneity and non-fungible token sales: Evidence from Decentraland LAND sales. *Finance Research Letters*, 58, 103628. DOI: 10.1016/j.frl.2023.103628

Yin, R. K. (2018). *Case study research and applications: Design and methods* (6th ed.). SAGE Publications.

Yoo, K., Welden, R., Hewett, K., & Haenlein, M. (2023). The merchants of meta: A research agenda to understand the future of retailing in the metaverse. *Journal of Retailing*, 3(3), 44–55. DOI: 10.1016/j.jretai.2023.02.002

Zabel, C., O'Brien, D., & Natzel, J. (2023). Sensing the Metaverse: The microfoundations of complementor firms' dynamic sensing capabilities in emerging-technology ecosystems. *Technological Forecasting and Social Change*, 192, 122562. DOI: 10.1016/j.techfore.2023.122562

Zadorozhnyi, Z. M., Muravskyi, V., Humenna-Derij, M., & Zarudna, N. (2022). Innovative accounting and audit of the metaverse resources. *Marketing i menedžment innovacij, 13(4), 10-19.*

Zainurin, M. Z. L., Haji Masri, M., Besar, M. H. A., & Anshari, M. (2023). Towards an understanding of metaverse banking: A conceptual paper. *Journal of Financial Reporting and Accounting*, 21(1), 178–190. DOI: 10.1108/JFRA-12-2021-0487

Zawish, M., Dharejo, F. A., Khowaja, S. A., Raza, S., Davy, S., Dev, K., & Bellavista, P. (2024). AI and 6G into the metaverse: Fundamentals, challenges and future research trends. *IEEE Open Journal of the Communications Society*, 5, 730–778. DOI: 10.1109/OJCOMS.2024.3349465

Zhang, X., Venus, J., & Wang, Y. (2012). Family ownership and business expansion of small- and medium-sized Chinese family businesses: The mediating role of financing preference. *Journal of Family Business Strategy*, 3(2), 97–105. DOI: 10.1016/j.jfbs.2012.03.002

Zhang, Y., Liu, C., & Lyu, Y. (2023). Examining consumers' perceptions of and attitudes toward digital fashion in general and purchase intention of luxury brands' digital fashion specifically. *Journal ofTheoretical andApplied Electronic Commerce Research*, 18(4), 1971–1989. DOI: 10.3390/jtaer18040099

Zhao, Y., & Zhan, Y. (2024, May). Investigating the Impact of Cultural Tourism NFTs' Perceived Value and Experiential Evaluation on WOM of a Tourism Destination: A Generational Difference Moderation Approach. *InWuhan International Conference on E-business(pp.25-36).Cham: Springer Nature Switzerland.* DOI: 10.1007/978-3-031-60260-3_3

Zhao, R., Zhang, Y., Zhu, Y., Lan, R., & Hua, Z. (2023). Metaverse: Security and privacy concerns. *Journal of Metaverse*, 3(2), 93–99. DOI: 10.57019/jmv.1286526

Zhong, Y. (2023). A Framework for Immersive Marketing in the Metaverse. *Marxist Perspectives*, 14(2), 278–293.

Zhou, M., & Liu, C. (2024, January). How The Existence Of Luxury Brands' Digital Fashion In A Metaverse Influence Consumers' Perception Of Luxury Brands. *InInternational Textile and Apparel Association Annual Conference Proceedings(*Vol. 80, *No. 1). Iowa State University Digital Press.* DOI: 10.31274/itaa.17392

Zhou, Y., Wang, L., & Wu, Y. (2022). Self-powered sensing technologies for enhancing user experiences in the metaverse. *Journal of Ambient Intelligence and Humanized Computing*, 13(1), 217-231. https://doi.org/DOI: 10.1007/s12652-021-03148-7

Žigiene.G, Rybakovas, E & Alzbutas R (2019). Artificial Intelligence Based Commercial Risk Management Framework for SMEs. Journal of MDPI Sustainability, (11), 4501; DOI: 10.3390/su11164501

Ziółkowska, A. (2021). Value Co-Creation in Digital Markets. *Journal of Digital Commerce*, 18(3), 467–484.

About the Contributors

Zahid Hussain currently in his postgraduate degree in Marketing from Khadim Hussain Shah Institute of Technology, Karachi, Pakistan (KASBIT). He has done several research publications, conference papers and book chapters related Marketing, Food Marketing, Metaverse Marketing, Customer Satisfaction and Artificial Intelligence in Marketing related fields in different impact factor journals at national and international level.

Arman Khan an Assistant Professor affiliated with the "Department of Business Administration, Shaheed Benazir Bhutto University, Nawabshah, Pakistan. His area of expertise lies in Marketing, Neuro-marketing, Digital marketing, Customer behaviour. He is an active member of scientific and editorial review board, this research has been presented and published in several international conferences, referred journals and research project worldwide.

Muhammad Ussama Majeed is a researcher, trainer, and marketer with expertise in Digital and Contemporary Marketing management. I am working as Lecturer and Program coordinator of BBA & MBA programs in the department of management sciences, National University of Modern Languages (NUML), Lahore Campus. I have a Mphil degree in marketing and a having diverse set of experiences that span different academic institutions, organizations, and industries. As a lecturer, I teach marketing courses to undergraduate and graduate students at different universities across Pakistan.

Ahmad Albattat is an Associate Professor and Program Leader in School of Global Hospitality and Tourism, Asia Pacific University of Technology and Innovation, Kuala Lumpur, Malaysia. He is a Visiting Professor and External Examiner in Medan Academy of Tourism (Akpar Medan). He is a Doctoral Supervisor in European Global Institute of Innovation & Technology, Malta, and Rushford Business School, Switzerland. He received PhD in Hospitality

Management "Disaster and Emergency Planning and Preparedness" from University Sains Malaysia (USM), Malaysia. He worked as an Associate Professor in Graduate School of Management, Post Graduate Centre, Management and Science University, Shah Alam, Selangor, Malaysia. Assistant Professor, Ammon Applied University College, Amman, Jordan. Senior Lecturer and Research Coordinator in School of Hospitality & Creative Arts, Management and Science University, Shah Alam, Selangor, Malaysia, and Researcher at Sustainable Tourism Research Cluster (STRC), Pulau Pinang, Malaysia. He was working for the Jordanian hospitality industry for 17 years. His teaching and consultancy fields include hospitality management, events management, research methodology, strategic management and final research projects. His research areas include hospitality management, hotel, tourism, events, emergency planning, disaster management, sustainable development goals and human resource. He is an active member of several Scientific and Editorial Board of International journals, reviewer, author and editor for book projects with Emeralds, Routledge, and IGI Global. His latest works have been published in the refereed international journals, conference proceedings, books and book chapters.

***

Arpan Anand is an Assistant Professor (Sr. Grade) of Marketing at Jaipuria Institute of Management, Noida. He holds a Ph.D. in Marketing from University Business School, Panjab University, and an MBA from NIT Kurukshetra. Dr. Anand's research interests include family business internationalization, sustainable consumption, sales strategies, and AI in marketing. He has published in ABDC-listed journals and presented at international conferences. With over a decade of academic experience, Dr. Anand is known for his innovative "Stimulate, Educate, and Implement" teaching approach, earning him multiple Best Faculty awards. He currently serves as Program Chair for Service Management and has held leadership roles in curriculum development and quality assurance. Dr. Anand's expertise extends beyond academia, having worked in banking and conducted corporate training for organizations like IIT Kanpur and AIMA. He actively engages in consultancy projects and organizes academic events, bridging the gap between theory and practice. A prolific researcher and dedicated educator, Dr. Anand continues to contribute significantly to marketing education and research, preparing students for dynamic business environments while advancing scholarly knowledge in his field.

Runa Das is doing PhD from Lovely Professional University, Punjab, India. She has completed her M. Phil. in tourism and master's in tourism administration. She is a State Aided College Teacher at P.D Women's College, Jalpaiguri, West Bengal. Her constant contemplation of Sustainable tourism developments led to her expanding interests in women's empowerment, Indigenous knowledge, reducing poverty, and socioeconomic inconvenience for the rural community. She has a few national and international seminars and has published articles and book chapters in Google Scholar.

Nisha Devi is Assistant Professor in the Department of Commerce, Shri Ram College of Commerce, University of Delhi. She has completed her Ph.D. Degree on topic "Entrepreneurial Competencies and Business Performance of Micro-Entrepreneurs: An Empirical Study of Himachal Pradesh". She has published 3 research papers in peer reviewed journals and one research paper in ABDC indexed Journals. Also published research paper in edited books. Her interest area in research is HRM, OB, Entrepreneurship and Tourism. Currently she is working on women entrepreneurship, religious tourism, Rural Tourism and sustainable development. Along with that she has presented about 10 research papers in international and national conferences. She also worked as research officer in a project funded by Women Commission of India.

Tareq Nael Hashem is a Full Professor of Marketing at Applied Science Private University, Amman, Jordan and holds PH.D. from Amman Arab University, Jordan. He is Permanent Member Senior Consultant For Development programs(EABAFF) in European Arab Business Fellowship Foundations.(2007-up to now), Member in EMBRI/EMAB &Emerald (EMAB Associate Fellow- AF-EMAB),Membership in American Association of International Researchers (AAIR),Member of European Marketing Academy (EMAC),Member in European Institute for Advanced Studies in Management (EIASM),Member in International Corporate and Marketing Communication Association (ICMCA),Member in European Retail Academy and Member of IGI Global Editorial Advisory Review Board

Rashid Hashmi is a seasoned senior journalist with a rich and diverse experience spanning over 22 years in Broadcast, Digital, and Print Media. Prior to joining Sharda University, he held the position of Executive Editor and Senior Anchor at the renowned national news channel, 'India News'. Throughout his illustrious journalistic career, Prof. Rashid Hashmi has served in various capacities across prominent media platforms including Dainik Jagran Newspaper, ETV, Total TV, FM News, and India News. His expertise encompasses anchoring, debating, and ground zero reporting of numerous parliamentary and assembly elections, providing insightful coverage of pivotal political events. Prof. Rashid Hashmi is renowned for his engaging interviews with prominent personalities from the worlds of politics, sports, and Bollywood. His interviews have featured distinguished celebrities, political leaders, and sports icons, offering unique perspectives and valuable insights to viewers and readers alike. With a keen eye for detail and a commitment to journalistic integrity, Prof. Rashid Hashmi has earned widespread acclaim for his contribution to media discourse in India. His dynamic approach to storytelling and extensive experience across multiple media formats underline his versatility and depth as a journalist. Prof. Rashid Hashmi's tenure in the media industry reflects a dedication to delivering compelling and informative content while upholding the values of responsible journalism. His role in shaping public discourse through impactful reporting and incisive interviews underscores his standing as a respected figure in Indian journalism.

Saleh F. A. Khatib (MSc, Ph.D.) is a senior lecturer in Accounting and Finance at the Faculty of Management, Universiti Teknologi Malaysia (UTM), Malaysia. He has been awarded a Ph.D. in Finance from UTM in 2022. His exceptional work and dedication to the field also earned him the Chancellor Award and Best Postgraduate Student Award. Throughout his academic career, Dr. Khatib has conducted extensive research on various functional domains, including Corporate Governance, Auditing, Corporate Finance, and Corporate Social Responsibility. Dr. Khatib's articles are published in top-tier academic journals, including Business Strategy and The Environment, Management Review Quarterly, Journal of Financial Reporting and Accounting, Global Business Review, Corporate Governance, Meditari Accountancy Research, and Environmental Science and Pollution Research, among others.

Anuj Kumar works as Head of Research and Associate Professor, at Rushford Business School, Switzerland. His significant thrust areas are marketing, international business, and general management. He has completed an M.Sc. in International Business from University College Dublin, Michael Smurfit Graduate Business School, Ireland (Ranked among the top 200 colleges of the world – QS World ranking). He is pursuing an Executive-Ph. D in Management from Aligarh Muslim University (Central University). He has published research papers in reputed SCOPUS/Web of Science/SCI/ABDC/UGC Care Journals. Prof. Kumar has over seventy publications (Scopus- 40, ABDC- 23, Web of Science- 20, SCI-3). He also has three e-books and five book chapters to his credit (two are Scopus-indexed). He has published several cases in Emerald Emerging Case Studies (Scopus), International Social Science Journal (ABDC-B and Scopus), Small Enterprise Research (Scopus and Web of Science), Case Centre-UK, and other reputed Scopus, ABDC, and Web of Science journals. He has three internationally granted patents by South Africa and one patent granted by the Indian Government.

Suneel Kumar holds a Ph.D. in Tourism Marketing and Tourists Behavior, which he obtained from Himachal Pradesh University Shimla, India. Currently, he serves as a Professor in the Department of Commerce at Shaheed Bhagat Singh College, University of Delhi, India. Dr. Kumar has undertaken a significant major research project as a Principal Investigator, which was awarded by the ICSSR, IMPRESS, Ministry of Education, and Government of India. The project is titled "Sustainable Rural Tourism: An Approach for Transforming Rural India - A Case Study of Himachal Pradesh". His research interests encompass various aspects of the field, including Tourism and Hospitality Management, Rural Tourism, Sustainability and Green Practices, Destination Branding, and Mark…

Madhu Kumari is a dedicated professional pursuing a Ph.D. in Tourism and Hospitality, focusing on Sustainable Development in the Hospitality Industry, at Chandigarh University, Punjab, India. She has 11 plus year of experience in Hospitality Industry and Academics. Her research interests encompass various aspects of the field, including Tourism and Hospitality Management, Sustainability and Green Practices, Rural Tourism, Moreover, she has presented about 6 research papers in international and national conferences and published more than 7 research papers & chapters in journals/ edited books.

Utsav Krishan Murari is a gifted writer, dedicated life coach, motivational speaker, passionate educator, and, above all, an exceptional mentor. He holds a doctorate in communication and media studies from the Central University of South Bihar. Graced with a vivid imagination, he is a genuine catalyst for ideas and is always open to trying new things. His one such initiative is Saarthi, which began as Saarthi Entertainment. Saarthi is a Delhi-based creative media production start-up that wants to leave a legacy of artistry in the production industry. Delivering content with a strong emotional connection and the potential to transform the world is what Team Saarthi is all about.

Timi Olubiyi is an Entrepreneurship and Small Business Management expert with a Ph.D in Business Administration. A Babcock University Business School Affiliated Scholar and senior government official. He is a prolific investment coach, business engineer, Chartered Member of the Chartered Institute for Securities & Investment (CISI), and a financial literacy specialist.

Hemlata Parmar, a luminary in the field of computer Science and Engineering. Her Journey is defined by a constellation of achievements from prolific publications and patents to enlightening guest lectures. Yet, her brilliance is matched only by her unwavering commitment to human ethics. With a heart as vast as her intellect, she champions women's empowerment, bridging the gap with empathy and insight. In every endeavor, she embodies the perfect fusion of academic process and compassionate advocacy, inspiring generations to come.

Amrik Singh is working as Professor in the School of Hotel Management and Tourism at Lovely Professional University, Punjab, India. He obtained his Ph.D. degree in Hotel Management from Kurukshetra University, Kurukshetra. He started his academic career at Lovely Professional University, Punjab, India in the year 2007. He has published more than 40 research papers in UGC and peer-reviewed and Scopus/Web of Science) journals. He has published 12 patents and 01 patent has been granted in the inter-disciplinary domain. Dr. Amrik Singh participated and acted as a resource person in various national and international conferences, seminars, research workshops, and industry talks. His area of research interest is accommodation management, ergonomics, green practices, human resource management in hospitality, waste management, AR VR in hospitality, etc. He is currently guiding 8Ph.D. scholars and 2 Ph.D. scholars have been awarded Ph.D.

Index

E

F

G

H

I

www.ingramcontent.com/pod-product-compliance
Lightning Source LLC
LaVergne TN
LVHW080344011026
849161LV00009B/2188